The Jamaican Stage, 1655–1900

THE JAMAICAN STAGE

1655–1900

Profile of a
Colonial Theatre

ERROL HILL

THE UNIVERSITY OF MASSACHUSETTS PRESS ■ AMHERST

LC 91–33344
ISBN 0-87023-779-9
Designed by Susan Bishop
Set in Trump Medieval Type
Printed and bound by Thomson-Shore, Inc.

Library of Congress Cataloging-in-Publication Data
Hill, Errol.
The Jamaican stage, 1655–1900 : profile of a colonial theatre / Errol Hill.
p.   cm.
Includes bibliographical references (p.   ) and index.
ISBN 0-87023-779-9 (alk. paper)
1. Theater—Jamaica—History.   2. Jamaica—Social life and customs.   I. Title.
PN2421.H55   1992
792'.097292—dc20   91–33344
British Library Cataloguing in Publication data are available.

Parts of chapter 11 appeared in "The Emergence of a National Drama in the West
Indies," *Caribbean Quarterly* 18, no. 4 (December 1972), © Errol Hill and the
University of the West Indies. A shortened version of chapter 7 appeared as "The
First Playwrights of Jamaica," in *Carib No. 4* (1986), Journal of the West Indian
Association for Commonwealth Literature and Language Studies, © Errol Hill. A
section of chapter 6 appeared as "Morton Tavares: Jamaican and International
Actor," in *Theatre Research International* 15, no. 3 (Autumn 1990), © Errol Hill
and Oxford University Press.

To the ancestral spirits

Indisputably, the love of drama abounds to an extent
which we venture to assert is unequalled
in this quarter of the globe.
Colonial Standard, Jamaica, April 17, 1889

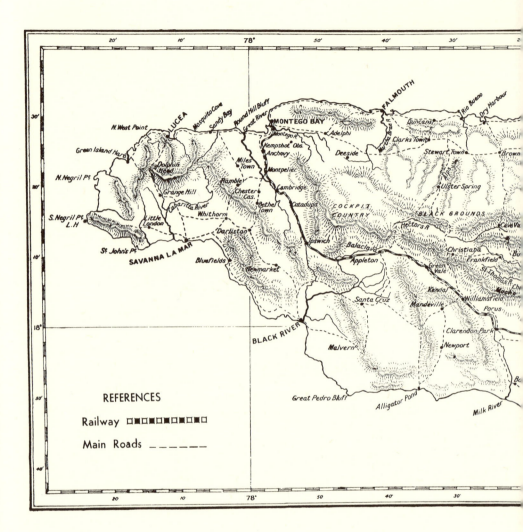

REFERENCES

Railway ☐■☐■☐■☐■☐■☐

Main Roads ⎯ ⎯ ⎯ ⎯ ⎯

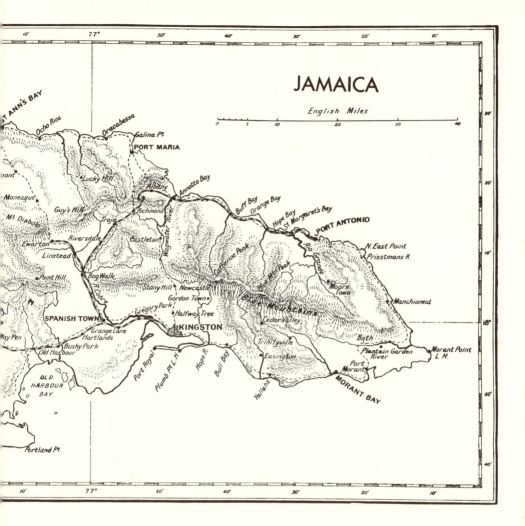

Contents

Illustrations

Acknowledgments

I wish to acknowledge with sincere gratitude the help and encouragement of many people in the writing of this book. Lack of space will preclude mention of the names of all those to whom I am indebted, but special thanks are due the following: Ursula Raymond, Trinidad librarian, for my first copy of Richardson Wright's *Revels in Jamaica* and for the transcript of George Bernard Shaw's comments on his 1911 visit to Jamaica; the Rockefeller Foundation for a five-week residency at the scholars' center at Bellagio on Lake Como, Italy, where I began to sift through voluminous research notes and organize my material; and to the Council for the International Exchange of Scholars for a six-month research and writing Fulbright Fellowship to Jamaica for completion of the first draft of this study.

For their solicitous attention to my requests and inquiries, I wish to thank librarians at the National Library of Jamaica; the Jamaica Archives; the New York Public Library; the Library of Congress in Washington, District of Columbia; the Baker Library of Dartmouth College in Hanover, New Hampshire; the Newspaper Library of the British Museum at Colindale, London; the Public Records Office at Kew Gardens, London; the National Library in Canberra, and the John Oxley Library in Queensland, Australia.

To D. Schauffer of the University of Durban-Westville, P. J. Scholtz of the University of Natal, and Temple Hauptfleisch of the University of Stellinbosch, South Africa; and to Robert Jordan and Susan Ross at the University of New South Wales, Australia, I am indebted for material on Morton Tavares not otherwise available.

I am also very grateful to those Jamaican colleagues who read parts of the manuscript and gave useful suggestions, including Wycliffe Bennett, Clifford Lashley, Mervyn Morris, and especially Hazel Bennett, who perused an entire first draft and made detailed comments; and to Rex Nettleford, not only for reading sections of the manuscript but also, in conjunction with Noel Vaz, for providing occasions for me to visit the University of the West Indies, Jamaica, to lecture on the topic while research was in progress. As well, Professor Nettleford graciously provided office space during the tenure of my Fulbright Fellowship. Grateful thanks are due also to Caldwell Titcomb, professor emeritus of Brandeis University in Waltham, Massachusetts, who read the manuscript thoroughly and made many suggestions for its improvement.

Finally, I give credit to my wife, Grace, for the many hours spent by my side leafing through dusty archives and poring over decaying newsprint. I can only hope that the present volume merits in some small way the selfless and unstinting support I have received over the years in its preparation.

The Jamaican Stage, 1655–1900

1

Prologue: Charting the Course

In 1911 George Bernard Shaw paid his only visit to Jamaica. The Irish-born, internationally famous playwright, critic, author, lecturer, and social reformer had come out from England to visit his old friend and fellow Fabian Sir Sydney Olivier, then governor of Jamaica. Asked by an eager journalist for his first impressions of the island, Shaw replied with characteristic candor that he had none worth recording but he could say what was wrong with Jamaica if his questioner was willing to concede there was anything wrong with it. Shaw then launched into an audacious criticism of the inadequacies of Jamaica's cultural life.

"If," he said, "a Jamaican wishes his son to be a fully civilized man of the world in the best sense—to belong to a great intellectual and artistic culture—he has to send him to Europe. Now that's not a necessary state of things. On the contrary, it ought to be far easier to build up a Jamaican culture." To do so, Shaw continued, three things were needed: a first-rate orchestra, a theatre, and good architecture in well-planned towns. Pressed by the reporter to acknowledge that the Institute of Jamaica was already sponsoring certain cultural activities, Shaw added to his list of requirements a public library, good writers, and painters. On the need for a theatre Shaw declared: "The next thing you want is a theatre, with all the ordinary travelling companies from England and America sternly kept out of it, for unless you do your own acting and write your own plays, your theatre will be of no use; it will, in fact, vulgarise and degrade you." With culture thus repaired, Shaw concluded: "Your Kingston man need be no longer a colonial. People will begin to send their sons from England to old Jamaica to get culture."[1]

When in 1957 I first read the report of that interview, I was engaged in teaching drama for the Extramural Department of the then University College of the West Indies based in Jamaica. As part of that assignment, we had encouraged the writing and staging of West Indian plays and had begun to publish the most promising playscripts under university auspices. Since there were those who questioned the desirability of our program, Shaw's comments came as an authoritative endorsement from the grave of our mission. Stripped of their piquancy, his words seemed to be a reproach of the colonial mentality that revered the metropolitan culture while it disdained whatever was native to the home colony. Yet I could not but wonder whether Shaw was aware, when he spoke, of the task involved in creating an indigenous theatre against the background of an English theatrical tradition that had enjoyed centuries-long dominance in Jamaica. That tradition was well entrenched. It had established forms and standards for writing and playing not easily challenged by a new set of perspectives.

Part of its history had been leisurely recounted in Richardson Wright's book *Revels in Jamaica* (1937),[2] which dealt with the period 1682 to 1838—or the Jamaican theatre during the years of slavery. In his labor of love, Wright had made a complete survey of the island's public records and newspapers and had followed the fortunes of visiting professional players on their return to North America. The thought occurred to me that the record should some day be carried further in order that one might judge whether freedom for the vast majority of Jamaican workers had altered the perception of the few involved in the making of theatre. Once launched on an enquiry, however, I was obliged to review the period covered by Wright. For not only was his record incomplete in parts but also his point of view was different from mine, which focused on the development of an indigenous theatre and on the contributions of different elements toward that end.

Tracking the history of the Jamaican theatre from the English conquest in 1655 to the end of the nineteenth century involved three separate pursuits. The first dealt with the touring professionals from England and North America who visited the island recurrently to perform their repertoire of plays. The second concerned the resident amateurs who strove to maintain active theatre in the absence of the professionals. The third pursuit, markedly different from the previous two, led to an examination of performance elements inherent in traditional expressions of the Jamaican peasantry and working class. What each of these groups produced, how and where they have intersected, and their individual and joint contributions to the growth of an indigenous theatre form the story of this book.

Jamaica, an English-speaking island situated in the northwestern Caribbean Sea, lies some ninety miles south of Cuba and a similar distance west of Haiti, previously Saint Domingue. It is the largest island of the anglophone Caribbean, being 144 miles long and some 50 miles across at its widest part. Seized by Columbus from the aboriginal Arawak Indians in 1494, the island remained in Spanish hands until 1655, when it was captured by the English. That no record exists of a theatre under Spanish rule is not surprising since at the time of its conquest there were only fifteen hundred Spaniards on the island, most of them settled in the southern town of St. Jago de la Vega, now known as Spanish Town.

Three towns are of importance in this study. Spanish Town was the administrative capital until 1872. Thirteen miles due east lies Kingston, the present capital and chief port. Away on the northwestern coast is Montego Bay, reached by traveling directly across the mountainous Cockpit Country or by taking the much longer coast road around the island. Of lesser interest than these three towns is Port Royal. Resting at the tip of the peninsula that protects Kingston Harbor, Port Royal was the island's first major seaport and trading center until it was destroyed in the great earthquake of 1692.

The economy of Jamaica, like that of other New World countries, was based on plantation slavery, its staple crop being sugarcane. English vessels began bringing African slaves to the island in 1666 for work on the estates and for transshipment to North America. Upward of one million Africans were off-loaded in Jamaica before the traffic officially ceased in 1807 when the British government abolished the slave trade. Slavery itself ended in 1834, followed by four years of required apprenticeship on the estates for the ex-slaves. At the time full freedom was achieved in 1838, the blacks in Jamaica numbered around 250,000, compared with 15,000 whites and 40,000 coloreds or mulattoes. By the end of the century the population had increased substantially to 672,000 in round numbers. The number of blacks had doubled to 500,000, coloreds and others had quadrupled to 160,000, while whites had dropped to 12,000. Free Jamaica in the nineteenth century showed a growing preponderance of blacks over whites, with a significant increase in the colored population, not least in the urban townships.

From its earliest days as an English colony, Jamaica attracted touring professional actors and acting companies from England, most coming via North America. In England these troupes played in provincial towns rather than in London. They lived a frugal existence and were drawn across the Atlantic by stories of affluent New World settlements in need of cultured entertainment. Jamaica had the added inducement of storied buccaneers in their haven at Port Royal tossing around pieces of eight as if they were penny-farthings. Players coming over to Charleston (South Carolina) or Williamsburg (Virginia) would be tempted to make the journey farther south to the largest and most prized English colony in the Caribbean. It was also fairly secure in those days of colony grabbing by voracious European powers. With Spanish Cuba to the north and French Saint Domingue to the west, Jamaica was constantly on the watch for attack from enemy forces and was protected by army and naval stations in addition to an island militia.

Lamentably sparse records from this early period suggest the existence of a theatre in Jamaica in the 1680s with occasional activity through the mid-1700s. Thereafter the situation brightens considerably with the arrival in Jamaica of the Company of Comedians under Lewis Hallam, Sr. This Hallam, David Douglass who succeeded him, and his son Lewis Hallam, Jr., are renowned in American theatre annals for leading some of the earliest and most highly regarded theatrical companies in mainland towns during the eighteenth and early nineteenth centuries. The senior Hallam's company had originally come to Virginia from England in 1752. Between 1755 and 1758 and again from 1775 to 1785 the company and its successor, the American Company of Comedians, spent two sojourns in Jamaica for a total of thirteen years.

No records exist of the company's productions on its first visit but there are considerable data regarding the second tour. These productions in Jamaica, biographical data on the players, and relevant social conditions have been documented in Wright's previously mentioned book. Wright, it seems, was primarily interested in the work of the American Company, for which he industriously prepared a playbook year by year. Repetition of details of these productions has been avoided except for the year 1783, which was omitted from Wright's record, newspapers for that year being unavailable to him at the time he wrote. They have since been acquired by the New York Public Library and reveal continued weekly productions in Kingston from January 8 through early November, with the company preparing to leave for Spanish Town and Montego Bay later that month. In Appendix A are listed the performances for 1783 in order to complete the playbook and because productions of this important company, no less than its members and the parts they played, may be of interest to a wide circle of scholars. Wright's record also overlooked a number of locally organized productions in the early nineteenth century and provided dates for the building of several Kingston theatres that in my view are incorrect. These omissions and inaccuracies have been rectified in the present volume.

This book begins with an attempt to identify theatre buildings that were in use in Jamaica from 1682 to 1912. The existence of a playhouse presupposes theatrical activity of some constancy since the investment in real estate would hardly be made were it not likely to produce a reasonable financial return. As Henry Fowler, longtime leader of the Little Theatre Movement of Jamaica has written: "Theatre buildings provide an unmistakable index and clearly visible statistic of dramatic development in a community; their quantity, their size, their location and their design bear silent and unimpeachable witness."[3] I have, however, been cautious to distinguish between a playhouse, or a building constructed primarily for the purpose of staging plays, and a so-called theatre which could be any suitable long room that was temporarily adapted into an auditorium and stage where plays would be performed for public viewing. It is my opinion that a number of theatres mentioned in the records really belong in the second category. Because confusion remains regarding the number and date of construction of playhouses, pains have been taken to review scrupulously all available data before coming to conclusions.

Another reason for carefully pursuing the question of theatre buildings is that their existence demonstrated the persistence of a sector of the community in having a proper playhouse available for use by touring players and local amateurs. Throughout the vicissitudes of civic life in the late eighteenth and the nineteenth centuries, one determination by certain Kingston townsfolk was unwavering: the principal town and future capital city would have a proper theatre of which its citizens could be proud. In their view the live theatre was indicative of a civilized community and was historically an indispensable part of the cultural life of Jamaica.

Following the discussion of playhouses, attention turns to the acting companies, professional and amateur, that inhabited them and to the plays performed in them. The Hallam companies' visits had confirmed the reputation of Jamaica as a theatre-conscious community. Itinerant players seemed eager to include the island in their tours. They first came from England via North America or via Barbados in the Eastern Caribbean. Then American troupes followed. Operatic troupes from Spain stopped over on their visits to Cuba and other Latin American cities. In addition there was in Jamaica a small cadre of professional actors who had taken up residence on the island. Members from this group were often invited to join the tourists and sometimes they formed a company among themselves to present a season of plays in Kingston and Spanish Town. Finally there were regular amateur groups that had bursts of activity between periods of quiescence. Other forms of entertainment, such as concerts, variety shows, circuses, gymnastics, and the like, frequently vied with the dramatic theatre for public support. These popular shows are beyond the focus of this volume and will be mentioned only when pertinent to the ensuing discussion.

Nor is it proposed to prepare a day-by-day log of every production of which there is a record. Such a task would require a book of its own. Rather, I am interested in indicating the general choice of repertoire of a company, the quality of performance, the impact on audiences, the success or failure of the enterprise, and the reasons therefor. I rely on critiques in the Jamaican press for an assessment of the work of players. Eighteenth-century newspapers that have survived occasionally carried press reviews of productions, but regular and thoughtful critiques were begun early in the nineteenth century and continued through 1900, oftentimes with generous space allotted to reviewing of performances. This was done partly as a quid pro quo for paid advertisements of each day's bill in the paper, but also, one suspects, because the public expected it. Theatre columnists took pains to remind actors and readers alike that the players were servants of the public. It was therefore important that the public's opinion of their work, as expressed in a critic's report or in letters to the press, should be made known to them as well as to all who supported them. The reviews tended to be informed and encouraging but not sycophantic; a good performance was applauded, a poor one denounced, and a bad one invariably brought forth the critic's wrath.

Acting companies came to Jamaica with fair regularity in normal times, two or three troupes a year. But travel was often inhibited by war, natural disaster, or other calamitous events. The risks involved in making these tours were serious and should not be overlooked. Ship travel was still primitive in the eighteenth and for a good part of the nineteenth century. The steam engine was not introduced in oceangoing ships until the mid-1800s. Crossing the Atlantic had taken the Hallam troupe six weeks in 1752; a century later the voyage would still take up to three weeks. Ocean travel in Caribbean waters at certain times of the year was subject to encounters with storms and hurricanes. Once a troupe arrived on the island, it would likely have to contend with new hazards such as harsh living conditions, tropical fevers, and the much-feared eventuality that the tour might be a financial failure.

Most troupes were kept to a moderate number of players, ten or twelve, including a manager and scenic artist. A play with a large cast meant doubling the parts or inviting resident actors to join the company as needed. Musicians were always recruited locally; for special occasions the military band would be asked to perform. Only a few companies visited the island more than once, although certain actors would return under different auspices. A successful company could expect a warm welcome for a second or third visit, its leading players having won a devoted following among local theatregoers.

Resident amateurs also played an important role in maintaining an active theatre scene in Jamaica. As early as 1763 Gentlemen Amateurs presented a play in the Kingston theatre, and throughout the period covered by this study, professional troupes drew constantly from the ranks of amateurs to fill out their casts. In addition, the amateurs could be relied on to stage their own productions, the proceeds going to local charities, or for the benefit of touring companies, or in relief of company members and their families who had been left stranded on the island. There were occasions when amateur groups competed with career players for space in the theatre; on other occasions they bickered fiercely among themselves. The best of these groups recruited their members from young adults who had been trained in secondary schools and, as may be expected, clubs were formed along social and racial lines. Thus in 1849, after a new theatre had been built in Kingston and amateurs were vying to use it regularly, among those presenting plays were two all-black groups called the Ethiopian Amateur Society and the Numidian Amateur Association.

From time to time amateurs would opt for a career in the theatre and become professionals, traveling out of Jamaica to play on foreign boards. Some of them achieved notable success, and difficult as it has been to trace their careers, I thought it fitting to devote a chapter to their attainments and failures. In one instance a Jamaican actor carried his talent to four continents, surely a unique record for any colonial histrion in the nineteenth century. No less important, in my view, were the first recorded attempts to produce plays pertaining to Jamaican life. The earliest of these efforts, written by expatriates, followed the convention of making fun of island-born Creoles; later scripts dealt with life on the plantation. Some scripts questioned political decisions following Emancipation, while others depicted well-known historical figures. Not all of these scripts were intended to be performed, yet all showed a knowledge of the theatre and could be staged. Professional companies as well as enterprising amateur and school groups were among the producers of these first original plays of Jamaica. They are discussed in some detail, and for ease of reference, a list of them is provided as Appendix B.

In his book Wright emphasized that the theatre public he wrote

9

about consisted of "only the upper crust, the very thin upper crust of the Jamaican social scale—white Europeans, white Creoles, and those who were so near white that their fraction of color didn't make any difference."[4] Wright is correct if his reference is to that class of drama enthusiast prior to Emancipation who sponsored professional activity and pressed for the maintenance of a suitable playhouse in Kingston. This was no mean challenge, given the steady decline in the island's economy as the nineteenth century progressed. But concerning play-goers in general, Wright's label of "the upper crust" is inadequate. It omits a significant number of other classes of patrons who attended the theatre before and after Emancipation.

By 1802 the Kingston theatre was advertising separate seats for people of color, suggesting that their number in the auditorium was on the increase and a special section had to be set aside for them.[5] There were, at the time and later, colored men who had advanced to positions of importance in Kingston and other towns. They attended the theatre out of their love for literature and the art of public speaking. Some had qualified for professions in England; some were teachers who passed their love of elocution on to their students. In Wolmer's Free School in Kingston, for example, colored students were in the majority by 1822,[6] while the Jamaican Union School, established in 1832, was open to youths and adults of both sexes and of every religious denomination and complexion.[7]

It is unlikely that the respectable colored middle class accepted meekly this overt form of racial segregation in the theatre. Some probably stayed away altogether. When protest demonstrations did occur they were said to be led by rabble-rousers who were arrested, taken to court, and given jail sentences or fines.[8] Another class of theatregoers were the black and colored servants of the white upper class. They attended their masters and mistresses at the theatre and might be allowed to watch the play from the gallery. It is fair to say that by the beginning of the nineteenth century the Jamaican theatre catered to a broad cross section of the public, if indeed it had been exclusive before that time.

All of this work, be it noted, represented an attempt to transfer the Western European theatre tradition to an English-owned colony in the West Indies. The theatres built, the plays acted in them, the style of performance, even the original dramas written for production were all strongly influenced by that tradition. To a large degree the work produced was of acceptable quality, based on standards created over the years by acknowledged leaders of the European and Euro-American theatre. The singular problem was that the overwhelming majority of

Jamaicans were neither European nor American. For them the theatre in Jamaica was a medium of expression to be observed, one in which few of their kind might participate but which had little significant bearing on their own experience. Their theatre culture, derived from African traditions of performance, had been adapted to the New World environment in which they and their progeny were forced to shape their lives. Only when the leaders of the Jamaican theatre began to turn their attention to the experiences and performance culture of this majority could it be said that the theatre in Jamaica truly belonged to Jamaica and had become representative of the main body of the Jamaican people.

This change in perspective could not occur while black Jamaicans were enslaved, for the stigma attached to victims of the peculiar institution would not allow that they had anything of value to contribute to the island's culture, save only their labor in the fields or as house servants. Nor could a change in perspective take place in the years immediately following Emancipation. For, as we shall see, prominent among the abolitionists in Jamaica were those who equated slavery with pagan African ways that had to be eradicated once freedom was achieved. With the best intentions, they sought to blot out the African past while urging adoption of European culture in its place. It would be decades before enlightened leaders of opinion saw the necessity of investigating and understanding the folkways of the Jamaican people. Ivy Baxter in her study entitled *The Arts of an Island* (1970) contends that not until the 1870s, with the establishment of the Institute of Jamaica, did the cultural orientation of Jamaicans change "to one in which the center, while still reflecting British cultural influences, was firmly based in Jamaica."[9]

Because this study involves a plurality of cultures, it has seemed important to introduce into the discussion the question of origins. Recalling briefly the origins of Western theatre might enable us to find points of synergy between European and Afro-Jamaican performance traditions leading toward the creation of an indigenous Jamaican theatre. One particular area of contact is storytelling, a form of theatre that is both ancient and universal. Readers and storytellers have been among the career actors who came to Jamaica from England and North America beginning in the late eighteenth century, but there have also been professional Jamaican storytellers at home and abroad. They performed original texts in standard English while others, using the creole tongue, became popular entertainers across the country beginning in the third quarter of the nineteenth century. A chapter is devoted to this form of theatre that represents the beginnings of fusion

11

between the dominant minority and the subordinate majority cultures of the island.

The next two chapters deal with the performance culture of the black underclass, first as slaves then as free men and women. In their limited free time, the slaves indulged in various performance-oriented activities. They played music on percussion instruments devised by themselves or on fiddles and flutes provided by their masters. They improvised songs of praise and derision as they had done in their African homeland and they danced an infinite variety of steps, their pantomimed movements conveying actions in the service of their gods or as part of other inherited customs. At festival time they played masquerades and enacted scenes based on plays seen in the regular theatres. They told stories, which were acted out in the recital of them. Theirs was an open-air theatre, sometimes taking place in daylight on the public street, at other times held at night in the privacy of the compound near the slave quarters on the estate. Contemporary commentary on these exhibitions was sparse until the late eighteenth century when the debate was joined in England and the colonies over freeing the slaves. Then writers took sides for or against abolition and their reports were colored by their persuasion on this issue. A useful summary of slave traditions is given in the booklet entitled *Folk Culture of the Slaves in Jamaica* (1981) by Edward Kamau Brathwaite.[10]

Slave performance traditions were continued after Emancipation regardless of attempts by civic authorities to stamp them out. In some areas Freedom Day street celebrations were turned into dignified occasions of thanksgiving by church leaders, while in other areas the Christmas masquerades became formal pageants of great pomp and ceremony. But while official celebrations were respectfully attended by the black working class, often this class would also hold their own more lively version of the celebration, as in the case of the church Tea Meeting or the Freedom Day Bruckin's Party. With the coming of Emancipation the African-derived religions also found a new lease on life and perpetuated the songs, chants, drumming, and dances associated with these cults. Thus as the century developed the creolizing of African folkways into an identifiable Jamaican product was a constant phenomenon, enriching the culture and exhibiting many performance-oriented elements.

I cannot pretend that the present volume, charting its course through 1900, has completed the survey of the Jamaican theatre. It has but delineated the background history against which enormous strides have been and continue to be made throughout the twentieth

century. Details of that further journey, stimulated by the establishment of a regional university in 1947 and by the attainment of national
independence in 1962, await renewed research and writing. The concluding chapter or epilogue takes the liberty of looking ahead and
pointing to some of the signal accomplishments in the theatre arts
coming as a result of honest evaluation of indigenous materials coupled with what has been learned from a long association with Western
theatre. In doing so I have dared to broaden my perspective, viewing
the anglophone Caribbean as a contiguous cultural region in which
the problems of one are the problems of all, and the achievements of
one give promise of similar achievements by all units. The dominant
minority culture that reigned for three hundred years is no more;
Caribbean theatre artists can march forward with confidence to seize
and proclaim what is rightfully their own.

2

Theatres of the Slave Era

Theatre buildings or playhouses were first erected in response to the need for a physical facility where the performed event could be heard and seen to advantage by spectators and where they could be conveniently housed and controlled. The earliest forms of theatre, however, had no physical structure of any kind because they needed none. The theatre of precolonial Africa, for instance, particularly those countries on the midwestern coast that are ancestral to black Jamaicans, was primarily one of ritual and festival observance where an entire village or township would attend a performance. Procession through the streets by the chief participants, with images of gods or effigies of ancestors borne aloft, and accompanied by a chorus of singers chanting appropriate songs, was an important preliminary feature of the event. Shrines were visited en route. Eventually actors and audience would assemble in the forecourt of the king's palace or in a public square where, under the open sky without even a raised platform to serve as a stage, various episodes of the performance would be presented to the accompaniment of female singers and an orchestra of drums and other indigenous instruments.

The public theatre of Europe was for centuries a festival-oriented theatre. Beginning in the pre-Christian era, dramatic and other kinds of performances were arranged at specific times of the year to celebrate some religious or historic event of significance to the community. Such were the public theatres of Greece and Rome; so, too, the folk theatre and the religious drama of Europe in the Middle Ages. Even when, in Roman times, a theatrical production was privately commissioned by a bereaved family to mark the death of an important public figure, the intention was that all the citizens of Rome should be free to participate, by attendance at the play or other funeral games, in honoring the memory of a great soldier or civic administrator who had rendered distinguished service to his country.

Theatre, in these circumstances, was for all the people.[1] This prin-

14

ciple determined the mode of presentation and the kinds of physical structures that were eventually erected as seeing places for performances. One essential characteristic of the festival theatre is that it was held in the open air, allowing as many people as possible to witness and participate in the event. The Greeks carved their hillsides into acoustically flawless amphitheatres seating thousands of spectators. The Romans at first used temporary platform stages, erected in open piazzas before temples, and later also built amphitheatres adapted from the Greek ones. The religious dramas of the Middle Ages, once disengaged from divine service, likewise took place out-of-doors. Performances were arranged in extensive arenas or in town squares where dispersed scenic units would be installed to represent acting locales. Sometimes, too, ambulatory carts turned into acting platforms would move from one station to another on a prearranged route, the audience gathering from early morning to watch the cyclical drama unfold in a series of episodes as cart succeeded cart throughout the day until nightfall.

Also in the Middle Ages pagan folk plays were acted on the village green or in the public square. When these rustic amateurs paid a courtesy visit to the Great House in order that their liege lord might share in the revels, their manner of presentation was just as informal inside as out, drawing the noble host and his guests into respected, if amused, involvement in their performance. The rude mechanicals presenting their play of *Pyramus and Thisbe* before King Theseus to honor his wedding to the Amazon queen, Hippolyta, as depicted in Shakespeare's *A Midsummer Night's Dream*, is a clear example of this type of folk performance taking place in the monarch's palace.

Performance under these conditions was designed to recognize the presence of an audience. It sought to turn mere spectators into active participants through the means of enactment. One way of achieving the desired collaboration between actor and audience was to invoke the presence of guardian or ancestral spirits of the community to witness the performance. The audience would understand that the performance was being done for its welfare and would consequently be more attentive. Hence Shakespeare, well steeped in folk theatre practice, brings on his fairies at the end of *A Midsummer Night's Dream* to bless the house in which the performance has just taken place. Another method adopted to reinforce the actor-audience relationship was to choose material with which the audience was familiar. Instant recognition of story, characters, and forms of expression would keep the audience involved in the flow of dramatic action and give it a stake in the final resolution of the conflict.

15

A third method to gain audience involvement was the use of chorus as character. Employing song or choral chant, it represented the community's viewpoint concerning issues raised in the play. A fourth method was by direct appeal to the audience in certain parts of the dialogue, and a fifth method would be for some adventurous actors to come down among the audience and engage them physically in the action of the piece, as did medieval devils in biblical pageant plays when they sought souls for hellfire among the spectators.

Whatever the means employed, the festival theatre made it abundantly clear that performance was an act of commemoration, of celebration, and that actors were simply carrying out their tasks on behalf of the audience whose approbation was eagerly sought as public testimony of a job well done.

In many essentials, the festival theatre was close to ritual drama, from which it most probably derived. But there are important differences between them. In the former, playing a given scenario, be it dialogue, dance, song, pantomime, or a combination of these elements, is addressed to the audience and is done as an act of remembrance and celebration. Incidentally, the performance helps to unite the community by reminding it of ancestral beliefs and shared history, and by calling upon all members of the group to join in common thanksgiving.

In the case of the older ritual drama, however, the enactment is addressed not to the audience but to the god or ancestor whose favor is sought. Parts of the ritual may be considered too sacred for public viewing and may be performed in secret by priests only. Finally, ritual drama is not simply commemorative but also aimed at persuading the deity addressed to grant some need that is crucial to the community's welfare. The community knows that the god's favor will not be withheld provided the ritual is performed in an acceptable way. In ritual drama there is no question of community involvement; the very survival of the group is at stake and demands it.

Neither in Africa nor in Europe did the public festival theatre require a playhouse in the modern sense of an enclosed auditorium. The origin of our contemporary indoor theatre with its proscenium stage framing a high degree of scenic, lighting, and mechanical devices is to be found in the permanent theatres built for learned academies and ducal courts of Italy beginning in the sixteenth century. It was at this time that theatre became divorced from the people it was originally intended to serve and began to cater to the tastes of an elite aristocracy. Under the impetus of the European Renaissance with its awakened interest in the classical heritage of Greece and Rome, Italian architects and designers strove to reconstruct the theatres of ancient times. But they were working with a private rather than a public audience in mind; their aim was to please princely patrons and enhance the reputations of their courts. They had newly discovered techniques of geometric perspective at their command to help in creating a sense of illusion in scenic representations. As a result, the architects designed attractive indoor auditoriums with a stage at one end of a hall and with tiered seating at the other end, the tiers wrapping around the sides of the room in a horseshoe shape. In front of the stage at floor level was a spacious area reserved for elaborate theatrical processions that entered the hall through side doors. The level floor area was also used for courtly dances that provided a joyous climax to the stage presentation.

In this theatre the stage area was by degrees converted to present a picture of a lived-in environment. The stage floor was sloped to enhance the illusion of distance on the painted scenery, which consisted of side wings, overhead borders or sky-cloths, and backdrops or backshutters. Below the stage floor mechanical contrivances were developed that changed the scenery in what seemed a miraculous transformation before the amazed eyes of beholders. For indoor performances artificial lighting became a necessity. Candelabras and oil lamps were used in great measure, and ingenious devices were developed to achieve tinted lighting effects on the sets, which were beginning to acquire an importance equal to or surpassing that of the play itself.

In some theatres, for instance, so skillfully were the settings designed to deceive the eye as to scale and distance that the actor was not allowed to perform within the scenery for fear of ruining the illusion. He was forced to play downstage of the painted scenes, which stood behind him as silent witness to the marvels of the painter's craft and his mastery of perspective representation. Within a short period of time the entire scenic area of the stage was enclosed behind a proscenium frame. When later a front curtain was added and the auditorium was darkened, the stage area was effectively shut off from the rest of the hall leading to the final separation of the actor from his audience.

The Italian court theatres soon spread to France and Germany, to England and Spain. In England, they were the inspiration for the staging of the highly exclusive masques of the Jacobean court while, at the same time, the public open-air theatres of Shakespeare and his contemporaries continued to cater to a broad cross section of the English public from rustic groundling to noble lord. But the days of both these types of theatre were numbered. The puritans of Lord Protector Cromwell, long nursing a hatred of the stage and particularly incensed at the extravagance of the royal entertainments, closed all playhouses in England during the Commonwealth period. Many of them were destroyed. When the theatres reopened with the restoration of the monarchy in 1660, the new king Charles II, returning from exile in France, brought back with him the indoor theatre of Europe, which then crossed the Atlantic to American and Caribbean shores. With periodic modifications, this indoor theatre has remained the most prevalent style of playhouse in the Western world, although much of the paraphernalia of production is often discarded in the interest of economy. There has also been a growing realization of the need to focus once more on the actor and his relationship to the audience, a concern that has led to various experiments in novel forms of staging.

Admittedly, the indoor theatre has advantages over the outdoor amphitheatre, especially in the modern world. For one thing, performances are less subject to interruption from inclement weather or from extraneous noise. For another, patrons can be made more comfortable indoors than out. The indoor theatre provides more control over scenery and lighting, now considered integral to production. Of greater consequence than these benefits, however, for a colonial settlement eager to establish the theatrical tradition of the ruling metropolitan country, the indoor theatre could be created quickly and at relatively little cost. It could also rank the audience more easily according to caste. Any suitably large, rectangular room could be converted into a temporary theatre, simply by erecting a platform at one end for a stage, by placing wing pieces or curtain legs at the sides to permit entrances and exits, and by dropping a back curtain with a painting on it to represent a locale. A curtain hung at the front of the stage would hide changes of scenery and permit discovery scenes.

In the rest of the hall, several rows of benches could be placed in front of the stage on the floor area, extending back into the hall until viewing of the performance became too restricted. Then it would be necessary to raise the back benches by constructing a low platform or series of stepped platforms. Private boxes could be installed by partitioning sections of the raised seating, the favored positions for these being along the side walls of the hall adjoining the stage. Elevated side boxes were sought after by those patrons who could afford them not only because they allowed a view of the stage and the auditorium, but also because their occupants could be seen and admired by others in the house.

A theatre such as that described would not, of course, have the comforts and conveniences of a permanent playhouse specifically designed and built for the purpose of stage productions. It would, nevertheless, be suitable as a viewing place for the limited number of patrons among the expatriates and upper-class residents in the colonial territory who were devotees of the drama and who wished to preserve symbols of the metropolitan culture in their colonial home. Besides, the temporary theatre had one distinct advantage over the permanent one. With a level floor, seats could always be cleared away and seating platforms dismantled to provide a spacious and unimpeded flat floor area upon which other social functions, such as receptions and dances, could be held.

This is doubtless the kind of makeshift theatre facility that is signified in the earliest accounts of playhouses in Jamaica. Unless it can be proven otherwise, reference to a theatre building should be assumed to mean no more than a large room in an existing building that has been temporarily fitted up to serve as a theatre. So far as we now know, throughout the long history of Jamaican theatre up to the twentieth century, there was only one site where a formal, architecturally designed theatre existed. This site was northeast of the old Parade Ground in Kingston (later known as Victoria Park, now as Sir William Grant Park) where the present Ward Theatre stands.

There may have been another theatre building in Spanish Town that was intended to be permanent, but its history is so short that questions remain concerning its original design and construction. The dozen or so other theatres to which reference is made over the years in Kingston, Spanish Town, Montego Bay, and elsewhere on the island were all converted halls in which plays were presented for a period of time but which served a multitude of other purposes. They were frequently restored to their original state when they were no longer used for stage performances.

THE SEVENTEENTH AND EIGHTEENTH CENTURIES

When in 1655 Jamaica became an English colony, public theatricals were officially banned by the imperial government. After seizing power in England, Oliver Cromwell had closed the theatres in 1642, and it is unlikely that stage productions would have been allowed in any of his overseas possessions. By 1655 his stern regime had only five more years to run before the English people brought back their king. Some two decades after the restoration of the monarchy, there is the first mention of theatre activity in Jamaica. Francis Hanson, writing an account of the island "in or about the year 1682," speaks of its

19

flourishing condition as exemplified by horse races, bowls, dancing, music, and plays at a public theatre.[2]

No one knows for sure where this public theatre was located but a reasonable assumption can be made. In 1682 there were but two populated towns on the island: Port Royal and Spanish Town. Kingston, the present capital, was then merely a small cluster of houses. Port Royal was the more populous of the two, a bustling center of trading, commercial, and even piratical activity with a reputation for fast living. Yet it contained many merchants' houses and a vacation home for the island's governor. Spanish Town, on the other hand, was the administrative capital where the governor and public officials resided, and where the land-owning gentry either retained town homes or visited from their country estates at regular intervals in order to attend meetings of the legislative assembly and quarterly sessions of the Grand Court.

While it is very probable that some sort of makeshift showplace existed in Port Royal, whose reputation for extravagant living would have attracted performers of all types, I incline to the view that Hanson was referring to Spanish Town when he spoke of "plays at a public theatre." Following English practice, the theatre of this period was indoors and catered primarily to the elite and educated segment of society, rather than the disorderly populace of a rowdy seaport.[3] There were in fact in the capital town seasons of social activity that were associated with the February Court and with race meetings when theatrical productions would have provided an appropriate form of rational entertainment. Hanson was most likely describing Spanish Town when, in mentioning the theatre, he wrote also of gentlemen's coaches with six horses apiece, and the gallantry, good housekeeping, and recreations that typified the manner of living there. The actors in this first public theatre were probably not hardy professionals but resident expatriates or noncommissioned officers of British troops stationed on the island, or both. The audience was made up primarily of European settlers in Jamaica and visitors from overseas.

The next reference to a theatre in Jamaica locates it unquestionably in Spanish Town. Charles Leslie's *New History of Jamaica* (1740) took the form of thirteen letters to a friend. Of Spanish Town residents he reports: "They have frequent Balls, and lately got a Play-House, where they retain a Set of Extraordinary Good Actors. In short, they live as happily as if they were within the Verge of the British Court. And to do them justice, they seem perfectly polite, and have a delicacy of Behaviour, which is exceedingly taking."[4] John Oldmixon corroborates this report in the second edition of his book on *The British Empire in*

America (1741). He says that Spanish Town has "frequent Balls and Assemblies, a Play-House, and a Company of Players."[5]

At first glance Leslie's statement that the town *lately* got a playhouse might suggest that the first theatre was in fact located in Port Royal, was destroyed in the earthquake of 1692, and that the next theatre was built in Spanish Town just prior to 1740. Apart from the fact that this scenario would leave the flourishing country without a theatre for almost fifty years, it also ignores a report that in 1733 a company of players from England came to Jamaica and performed there.[6] This company either found a suitable theatre space in the capital town or had one fitted up for its use. Seven years later in 1740 the space need only be refurbished for the next set of extraordinarily good actors to arrive in Jamaica.

By the year 1776 Spanish Town had outgrown its makeshift theatre. New public buildings had been started in 1758 and an attractive new governor's mansion or King's House was erected in 1762 at a cost of over £21,000 sterling.[7] Patrons of the theatre felt that they too deserved a building of their own. They raised a subscription and in 1776 a new theatre was opened, built at private expense, the stated cost being £2,471 16s. 1¼d.[8] On a plan of the town prepared by John Pitcairne for Governor Dalling (1772–74 and 1777–81) this building is indicated as item no. 15, positioned east of the Church Parade on White Church Street [fig. 1]. The new playhouse may still have retained a level-floor auditorium to enable dances and other social events to be held there. For a period of seven years, from 1792 to 1799, it was appropriated by the government and used as a barracks for soldiers. Without major reconstruction, it would have been most uncomfortable living quarters for military residents had the floor been sloped throughout as it is in regular playhouses to give spectators a clear view of the stage over the heads of those seated in front.

Just prior to the mid-eighteenth century, Kingston was ready to receive its first public theatre. Amateurs of the town had been staging plays in a ballroom when in 1745 there arrived on the scene an enterprising Irish actor named John Moody (1727?–1812). He soon organized a number of Shakespearean productions, playing all the leading roles himself as was the custom of actor-managers of his time. Sensing a fertile field in Jamaica for a professional stage career, Moody proposed to erect a theatre in Kingston by public subscription and returned to England a year later in order to recruit a company of resident actors.

That a theatre was established in Kingston at this time is beyond doubt. There are several references to its existence. First, mention is

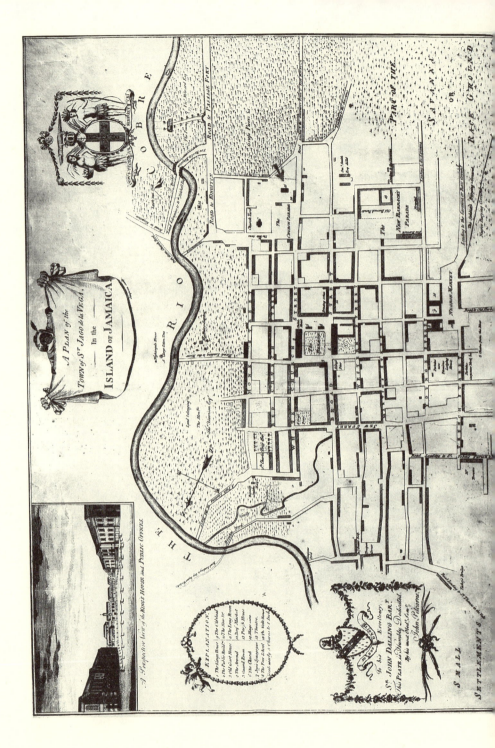

A PLAN of the TOWN of St. JAGO de la VEGA, In the ISLAND of JAMAICA

22

made of an indenture dated May 4, 1753, in which William Jenkyns and his wife, Hannah, sold some property "except the old messuage formerly called the Old Play-House in Harbour Street." Second, the tax rolls of Kingston for the year 1754 list Comedians as tenants of the King's Store in Harbour Street for which they paid £120 a year in rent.[9] Finally, the single theatrical notice that appears in the few surviving newspapers of this period advertises a production to be held on July 1, 1754, "at the New Theatre in Harbour Street."[10] These references lead to the following conclusions.

Some time in 1746, when John Moody returned to Jamaica with his newly recruited troupe of English actors, among whom was David Douglass, he established a theatre in Harbour Street by converting a suitable long room to the purpose. Moody remained in Jamaica about three more years until 1749, when he left permanently for England. His company, reinforced by new arrivals, continued to perform under the management of Douglass. At some time prior to 1753 Douglass abandoned the theatre Moody had set up, which, in the indenture of that year, was referred to as "the Old Play-House," and got himself a new facility. Where exactly along Harbour Street the first Kingston theatre was located is unknown, but based on the tax rolls for 1754 we can conjecture that the second Kingston theatre, established by the Douglass Company, was in the building known as the King's Store on Harbour Street. The company paid rent for it and in the same year mounted a production billed to take place at "the New Theatre in Harbour Street." From a plan of Kingston by Michael Hay dated 1702, the King's Store appears to be a group of buildings, presumably warehouses owned by the Crown, that stood on three adjoining lots in Harbour Street at the northeast intersection with Low West Street.

In the year 1755 a Company of Comedians led by Lewis Hallam, Sr., paid the first of two extended visits to Jamaica. This was a professional English troupe that had come to America in 1752 and had played in cities along the eastern seaboard. Among those arriving in Jamaica was Lewis Hallam, Jr., then fifteen years old. The troupe stayed on the island for three years during which time they joined forces with the Douglass company and presumably presented several seasons of plays in the new theatre on Harbour Street—presumably, because no records have been found of their performances. What is known is that the elder Hallam died within a year of his arrival in Jamaica and Doug-

1. *(facing page)* Pitcairne's Plan of St. Jago de la Vega, showing the site of Spanish Town Theatre, No. 15, in upper right segment near the Church Parade, 1786

lass married his widow. Douglass then became manager, with the young Lewis Hallam as principal actor, when the company returned to America in 1758. Another reason to presume an enlivened theatrical scene in Kingston during these years was the establishment by the lieutenant governor in 1757–58 of the office of Master of the Revels. In England this was a court official, first appointed in the reign of Henry VIII, for the purpose of superintending royal entertainments. In Jamaica the duties included authority over public theatricals as well as supervision of entertainments given by the governor. The first holder of the post in Jamaica was the notorious adventuress Teresa Constantia Phillips.[11]

The second Kingston theatre, situated in a converted warehouse on Harbour Street, served the needs of players and playgoers of the burgeoning town for many years. It was last heard of in 1785, but details of its appearance inside or out remain sketchy. An account by Edward Long, published in 1774, states: "In the lower part of the town is a very pretty theatre, exceedingly well contrived and neatly furnished. Dramatical performances were exhibited here during the last war, at which time there was a considerable quantity of prize money in circulation, but in time of peace, the town is not able or not disposed, to support so costly an amusement."[12] Long locates the theatre in lower Kingston (i.e., on Harbour Street) and confirms the view that the Douglass company was in residence there for at least part of the period covered by the Seven Years' War of 1755 to 1763. A lull in dramatic activity apparently occurred some years after the comedians left for America in 1758, for Long deplored the absence of an active theatre in Kingston in the mid-1760s. The final mention of this Harbour Street theatre is given by Eola Willis in her book on the Charleston stage. She cites a reprint from the *Jamaica Gazette* appearing in "another of Charleston's weekly papers" in which reference is made to a performance at the theatre, presumably in 1785.[13] On this basis we may conclude that the second Harbour Street theatre was in use, periodically, for some thirty-two years from about 1753 to 1785.

With ominous signs of approaching war between Britain and the American colonies, the Continental Congress in 1774 outlawed what it called frivolous entertainments including plays. Douglass's company, now called the American Comedians, thought it prudent to return to Jamaica in 1774–75 for their second visit to the island. Many of the players would remain there for up to a decade, waiting for the end of the revolutionary war; others would take up permanent residence on the island. In theory Douglass was still in charge of the company, but he had become interested in setting up a printing establishment in Kingston, leaving Lewis Hallam and John Henry as co-managers of the troupe. A decision was taken not to occupy the existing Harbour Street playhouse, and a third Kingston theatre was established in time for the commencement of the comedians' season in July 1775. Because of the importance of this theatre, the first on the historic site on the Parade, it is best to proceed with caution to examine the evidence relating to its construction.

The first reference is a contemporary account to be found in the memoirs of William Hickey for the year 1775. Hickey is invited by a friend to join him on a trip to Kingston, "for there is a famous play performed in the evening at the theatre, being the first of the season." Later, reporting on their trip, Hickey writes: "We adjourned to the theatre, which was commodious, neatly fitted up, and had a more than tolerable set of actors then recently arrived from New York in America, which city they had quitted in consequence of the popular commotion and probability of hostilities commencing with the Mother Country. The manager was Mr. Hallam."[14]

Hickey thus confirms the arrival of the American Company to open a season of productions at the Kingston theatre in 1775. However, from his report we cannot say with assurance that the theatre is newly built, nor can we tell its precise location. The famous play selected for the season's opening on July 1 was Shakespeare's *Romeo and Juliet*. The *Jamaica Gazette* for that day carried the Prologue, specially composed by Benjamin Moseley, surgeon general of the island, and containing the following extract:

> This PILE [sic.] a lively lasting sense imparts
> Of highest gratitude to feeling hearts;
> For which, exerting all our strength, we'll shew
> How much we wish to pay—how much we owe!
> Indulgent take the thanks your aid demands.
> 'Tis all you can expect at Players' hands.[15]

In plain English this may be translated as follows: "This building instills in our hearts a sense of deep gratitude which we'll do our utmost to deserve by our efforts. For your aid, accept all that poor Players can give, our thanks." Clearly, the prologue draws attention to the playhouse and thanks members of the audience for their help in its construction.

The next reference to this theatre appears more than a decade later, in 1788, when Peter Marsden published his *Account of the Island of Jamaica* with the following passage: "In the north part of the town is a neat church with a low spire; and nearly adjoining is a spacious parade with barracks for soldiers. There is also a theatre, assembly rooms, and other places of amusement."[16] This is the first indication that the theatre is no longer in lower (i.e., south) Kingston but in the northern part of town. Confirmation of the new theatre's location comes from two sources. From the few surviving newspapers for 1788, Wright quotes a curious advertisement for a performance of the comic opera titled *The Agreeable Surprize* scheduled to take place in Kingston on July 19. The notice begins, "Never performed in this Town," followed by the line "Assembly Room in the Parade," and then "By permission of the Master of Revels." The advertisement proceeds to print the complete evening's bill with full cast, ending with the subscription: "No person will be admitted behind the scenes, either at Rehearsals or the Performance. Places to be taken on the days of performance from nine till five at the Theatre."[17] Here the theatre is not only on the Parade but also is identified with the so-called Assembly Room where assemblies of the upper classes held their quarterly dinner dances.

The third source is J. B. Moreton, who spent five years in Jamaica in the 1780s and published his *Manners and Customs in the West India Islands* in 1790 with the following observation: "The church, barrack and theatre stand on a large airy plain, on that end of the town called the Parade, leading to Spanish Town. . . . The theatre is a little, mean, narrow, close fabrick."[18] Moreton's description of the new playhouse as little, mean, narrow, and close has caused some confusion, contradicting as it does Hickey's finding of a commodious auditorium. One writer has even suggested that Moreton may have visited another theatre in Kingston, first mentioned about this time.[19] An advertisement in 1790 announced tightrope performances and a pantomime by Mr. Curtis and Troop at Dallas's Long Room in Church Street. Then in February 1799 another tightrope walker was billed to perform "at the New Theatre in Church Street, near the Parade, a house formerly known by the name of Dallas's Lodging House."[20]

From the minutes of the Kingston Town Council dated October 18, 1803, we learn that the Kingston theatre at this time occupied lots 818 and 819, which were situated on the north side of the Parade at the corner where it joined Love Lane. This is the identical site where a public theatre has stood from the late eighteenth century up to the present day. The so-called theatre in Dallas's Long Room, on the other hand, was situated not *on* but *near* the Parade. It was part of a rooming house that stood on Church Street, which begins at the southeastern extremity of the Parade and runs south into lower Kingston. There is no reason, therefore, to confuse it with the Kingston theatre.

Additional references to the new theatre occur in the closing decade of the century. In April 1791 a concert is advertised "at the Theatre on the Parade" to be followed by a Ball; in July 1796 the theatre on the Parade is used for divine service; and in July 1799 it is billed to open next month for dramatic performances. But the most crucial reference of all occurs in a report of a meeting held on August 8, 1814, by the Kingston Common Council to consider allowing a subscription fund to be opened to improve the Kingston theatre by extending it into the Parade. In the course of discussion by the council the following statement was made: "The moment the building was finished [it was] given in possession of the American company of comedians . . . who performed therein for ten or eleven years thereafter, nor has any rent ever been exacted from persons exhibiting therein for the amusement of the public since it was erected."[21] On its return visit the American Company spent ten years in Jamaica and apparently commenced its first season in a new theatre on the Parade. We may therefore conclude that the date of its first performance—July 1, 1775—represents the opening of the first Kingston theatre on the Parade.

On November 21, 1814, the council resolved to extend the theatre into the Parade "to run in a line with the other buildings to the East and West thereof."[22] The new building was placed under the supervision of the Master of the Revels, but from the first it was designated as a civic center for varied activities of which the live theatre was the most prominent. As early as July 1786 we learn that the Kingston Assembly took over the building "for the first time when about sixty Ladies were present and an hundred gentlemen, among whom was his Honour the Lieutenant Governor. . . . The company did not separate till about three o'clock yesterday morning."[23]

What were the interior features of this playhouse that would serve Kingston for well over half a century? From the published prices of admission, we learn that the seating arrangements contained a pit on the ground floor and a second level stepped and divided into boxes, behind which was a raised section for an open gallery. The customary backless benches were provided throughout the house, although patrons holding season tickets for boxes were permitted to supply their own chairs if they wished. The floor of the auditorium was flat rather than sloped in order that other amusements such as dancing could be accommodated. In the hall immediately in front of the stage a space was reserved for a small orchestra that might comprise no more than a few fiddles and a pianoforte. These musicians provided overture and interlude music between the two or more plays on the bill. They accompanied songs and dances in the plays and during act breaks. For musical plays and pantomimes, the orchestra would be strengthened by hiring additional musicians.

As was often the case in theatres of the period, the backstage area was cramped. Stock scenery was the common practice at the time in England as well as in Jamaica. Each playhouse was supplied with a number of painted flats representing the most regularly used settings such as a library, living room, garden, park, or city street, that would be employed repeatedly for different plays. Very occasionally the scene painter, who might also double as actor when necessary, would produce a new set of scenery for an unusually spectacular plot. Once the scenery was placed in position at the Kingston theatre, working space backstage was at a premium, and in 1782 the American Company was forced to announce that gentlemen of the audience would in future be denied admission backstage, since "the scenes for some time past have been so crowded as in great measure to impede the performances."[24] A front curtain was drawn up in festoon fashion at the start of the play and lowered between acts to facilitate scene changes. The stage floor, also level, was thrust forward beyond the curtain line so that entr'acte performances of a song, a sailor's hornpipe, or a ballet excerpt could be given. Lighting was supplied by candelabra hung from the auditorium ceiling, by candles in brackets on the side walls and in front of boxes, and by suspended candelabra on stage as required. These would be lit throughout the performance in accordance with the practice at that time. There were also footlights or "floats," so called because they were lighted wicks floating in small containers of oil, the containers being sunken in a groove at the front end of the stage floor. They did not carry glass shades, and a report in 1785 stated that during a performance "lamps in the front of the orchestra, being overcharged with oil, set fire to the wooden channel in which they were enclosed."[25]

This theatre catered primarily to the elite of society, with ticket prices ranging from 13s.4d. for a box seat to 7s.6d. for the pit and 6s.8d. for the gallery. Even so Hallam found it difficult at times to balance the books and in January 1780 he offered a subscription scheme to the public under which his company would present twenty-four plays for a season ticket costing £8. At 6s.8d. for the best seats this was a considerable bargain. In a season of three months between February and May the company would perform twice a week. Hallam computed that the production of each play would cost on average £75 for a total expense of £1,800. He hoped to attract two hundred subscribers who would guarantee him a box-office income of £1,600, leaving a shortfall of £200 to be covered by receipts from ticket sales to the pit and to nonsubscribers in boxes who would pay regular prices. He presented this plan, he said, for the future support of the theatre and to enable the manager and actors to carry on their profession with the assurance of a reasonable income for their labors.[26] With a potential Kingston audience of five thousand whites and twelve hundred coloreds, Hallam's scheme was probably well subscribed. His seasons of 1781 and 1782 reached the twenty-four-play mark, although, interrupted by martial law and other emergencies, they extended beyond the prescribed three months.

A final question concerns ownership of the new Kingston theatre. In his 1943 memorandum to the deputy keeper of records, Spanish Town, Langston Robertson argued, not very convincingly, that the theatre on the Parade was from its earliest erection a municipal building owned by the public. In the same document he retreated from that position and asserted that "from 1803 onwards, the theatre is definitely 'public' property."[27] It is not possible to support either statement. According to Wright, a Kingston playhouse, referred to as the Royalty Theatre, was sold in 1790 for £1,600, but the location of this theatre and the parties involved in the transaction remain unknown.[28] If this were the theatre on the Parade, it would indicate that the playhouse was purchased by an unknown party or parties in order that the original subscribers could be repaid.

Let us now try to reconstruct a possible scenario for the establishment of the Kingston theatre on the Parade. Toward the end of 1774 and early in 1775 Douglass, Hallam, and members of their troupe arrive in Jamaica. They find the Harbour Street theatre in the King's warehouse to be unsuitable for their planned season. In the twenty years since their last visit, the city has grown and expanded uptown. They approach a group of influential citizens who subscribe toward the building of a modest theatre on the Parade situated on land donated by the town, or it may be that there was already on the desired site an old building that was purchased and converted into a theatre in time for the season's opening on July 1. If the latter were the case it might explain why Moreton saw the building as a little, mean, narrow, close fabrick, and why some years later the Kingston Town Council agreed to extend the building into the Parade. Since no rent was charged for the theatre, it lacked a ready source of income from which money could be appropriated to keep it in good repair. In 1790 the building might have been sold to new owners and the money used to repay the original subscribers. However, the building continued to be used as a theatre and, as will be shown later, the Kingston theatre was still privately owned in 1814, after which time it gradually became public property.

Discussion, so far, having focused on the theatres of Spanish Town and Kingston up to the close of the eighteenth century, a brief look must now be given at Montego Bay. By the second half of that century Montego Bay had become a major port for the slave traffic, second only to Kingston. Wright reports that in a single year close to ten thousand slaves were landed there.[29] During their second stay on the island the American Company paid regular visits to the north-shore town and was responsible for setting up several theatres there. According to admittedly incomplete records, the company was first resident in Montego Bay in 1777, when it performed in a theatre that had been fitted up in Mr. John Lugg's Great Room. The interior arrangements included a pit and boxes but no gallery. Performances took place four times a week on Monday, Wednesday, Thursday, and Saturday. A contemporary account extols "the commodious and neat construction of the house."[30]

When the players are next reported in Montego Bay in 1783, the theatre they occupy is not identified but is probably in a different location from the first. It now contains side boxes, front and side seats, and a gallery. In January 1784 the company's stock scenery arrived by schooner from Kingston but could not be accommodated on the stage then in use. Faced with the problem of altering their scenery or fitting up another stage, the company chose the latter alternative. A month later we find them announcing their performances in a new theatre in Montego Bay that contained a pit and boxes but no gallery, and playing weekly on Wednesday, Thursday, and Saturday.

The three theatres that the American Company supposedly built in Montego Bay at this time were no more than large halls in lodging houses, stores, or other suitable buildings that had been converted into theatrical facilities in the manner earlier described.[31] If lumber was available from a previously "fitted up" room it would be neither so costly nor so formidable a task to dismantle, transport, and reinstall in a new building, making the interior arrangements conform to the dimensions of the hall, the whole exercise being completed in less than a month. Due to the circumstances of construction and the impermanence of the visiting professionals, these converted theatres were apt to be temporary arrangements, allowing for rapid reconversion into their original or some other useful space.

THE EARLY NINETEENTH CENTURY

Interest in theatre buildings in nineteenth-century Jamaica focuses primarily on Kingston and to a lesser degree on Spanish Town. As the century progressed stage performances became fairly widespread across the island, but only in Kingston was there a consistent demand for a proper theatre building, in appearance worthy of the country's principal city, and equipped with facilities necessary to accommodate productions of the highest quality. These demands occasionally spurred neighboring Spanish Town to similar action. In some districts town halls were built or refurbished to provide minimally adequate space for theatrical productions, but Kingston alone throughout the century enjoyed the distinction of having a theatre building devoted primarily to the staging of plays.

As we have seen, the Spanish Town theatre that was built by private subscription in 1776 had been commandeered for a regimental barracks from 1792 to 1799. When the soldiers left, this building probably did not immediately revert to its former use, for in November 1812 a subscription was raised for fitting up the Long Room, so that the comedians lately arrived might perform there after playing in Kingston.[32] John Pitcairne's plan [see above, fig. 1] shows a Long Room on Broad Street east of King's House; thus the earlier theatre on White Church Street must have fallen into disuse. In 1813 the Theatrical Amateur Society of Spanish Town gave its third production in aid of funds to establish a regular theatre, and a year later the *St. Jago de la Vega Gazette* formally opened a subscription for "erecting or fitting up a theatre in Spanish Town," the old playhouse allegedly being too decayed for restoration.[33]

Eventually, however, it was decided to restore the old theatre. The outside walls were repaired, strengthened, and painted, jalousies were installed around the upper part to ensure coolness at all times, and the interior decorations, undertaken at the expense of the incoming company manager, W. F. Adamson, included a promenade around the boxes and padded box seats covered with green cloth. The report of these improvements concluded that the restored building "will be as cool, as airy, and as pleasant a theatre as any in the West Indies."[34] When this house was visited by Matthew Gregory "Monk" Lewis in 1816 he found it "neat enough but, I am told, very inferior to that in Kingston . . . the orchestra consisting of nothing more than a couple of fiddles."[35] This Spanish Town theatre would be in use in the capital city for another quarter of a century, after which it disappeared from the records.

Emphasis on maintaining a proper Kingston theatre is due primarily to a coterie of influential and literate businessmen who were passionate devotees of the stage. For them, their families, and friends, the theatre provided one of the approved means of intellectual refreshment. A good number of these stagestruck entrepreneurs came from the Jewish community. The Jews had first come to Jamaica in the seventeenth century and, after the Spaniards, could be considered in

Wright's phrase "the aristocrats of the island—if aristocracy is based merely on who got there first."[36] Yet they were denied voting rights, were barred from holding public office, and were subject to special taxation. It was as important for them, in British-controlled Jamaica, to demonstrate their admiration for English culture as it was to be free to practice their Jewish faith. They established two synagogues in Kingston and two separate burial places: one for English and German (Ashkenazic) Jews and the other for Spanish and Portuguese (Sephardic) Jews. They were fully enfranchised in 1826, long before they enjoyed a similar liberty in Great Britain.

The major papers in the island also played a significant role in mounting campaigns to renovate or rebuild the Kingston theatre when its improvement or replacement became imperative. Among these papers were the *Morning Journal* (1838–c.1875), the *Colonial Standard* (1849–95), and the *Gleaner and De Cordova's Advertising Sheet* (later the *Daily Gleaner*) first published in 1833 and still the country's principal newspaper. It was owned by the de Cordova family. For four generations members of this Jewish family were among the leading lights of the Jamaican stage either as performers, directors, managers, or agents for visiting professional troupes.

Kingston officially became a city in 1802.[37] In place of vestrymen, the town was now administered by a mayor, aldermen, and members of a common council. That the Town Council had inherited proprietary control of the public theatre is evident from contemporary records in the early part of the century. In 1803, for instance, the council voted to erect a watch house on the space at the back of the theatre.[38] In 1812 it appointed an ad hoc committee to inspect the theatre for much-needed repairs and agreed to pay for the work out of the magistrates' chest. Theatrical companies had previously advertised their productions "by permission of the Master of Revels" or "with permission of His Excellency the Governor," but now in the new city performances were given "under the patronage of the Corporate Body." In 1814 the council took several actions relating to the theatre. It resolved to close down the theatre when a quarrel arose between competing companies, then it appointed a manager to engage performers and superintend the stage requirements (the office of Master of the Revels being then in abeyance). The new manager was W. F. Adamson, leader of a professional troupe that had recently arrived from Barbados. Further, as we have seen, the council passed a resolution to extend the front of the theatre into the Parade; and finally, it appointed a standing committee from among its members to inspect and control the management of the theatre.[39] In 1815 when the restored theatre in Spanish Town spurred Kingstonians into completing the renovation of their own playhouse on the Parade, the Court of Common Council voted £500 to increase the subscribed fund, which was inadequate for the job. The theatre reopened on April 5, with new decorations and enlargements that were generally applauded, although colored patrons protested a new side entrance that led up to segregated seating.[40] From that time on, all major decisions affecting the occupancy, leasing, maintenance, and renovation or rebuilding of the theatre were the responsibility of the Kingston City Council. The text accompanying a collection of drawings that were made on the island in 1820–21 and printed in 1825 stated that the theatre belonged to the people and that performers were required to pay £10 into the public treasury for each night of performance.[41]

Two additional references help to explain how and when the city came to acquire the theatre. When in 1893 the *Daily Gleaner* was again leading a campaign to rebuild the Kingston theatre that had fallen into disrepair, it published several articles on the origin of the theatre. Among them was a letter from a contributor whose name was not given but whose family connections were obvious. He was a scion of the de Cordova family and was then resident in the United States. His letter gave a number of details about theatrical activities in Jamaica, all of which have been corroborated, except part of the information conveyed in this passage: "Father told me that the old building was erected in 1808 on the tontine plan—the last survivor to own it—and at the time he believed he was the last survivor of all the subscribers. I suppose the way the City got control of the building at first was because it was necessary, before any performance could be had, to get permission of the Mayor." This passage provides confirmation that the theatre was privately owned and then acquired by the city, but it gives the unacceptable date of 1808 for the building of a new theatre on the Parade. That the building was, in fact, already in existence and simply purchased at that time by a group of Kingston citizens is explained in another of the newspaper articles. Here is the relevant extract:

> The old Theatre . . . was purchased by several gentlemen and was their joint property. This possession was, however, qualified by the understanding that the building was to be used for the public benefit. The possession was somewhat of the nature of a tontine. The Theatre was always considered the property of the parish, and could be conveyed for the use of the parish. This old building was a wretched structure, small and cramped, rickety, badly ventilated, and more in the nature of a barn than a theatre.[42]

The first Kingston theatre on the Parade was therefore built in 1775 by private subscription. It may have been sold in 1790 to an unknown purchaser. Once Kingston became a city in 1802 it was necessary to secure the mayor's permission to hold a public performance, and this requirement gave the council certain prerogatives over the theatre. In 1808 the building was purchased by a group of Kingston businessmen who may have had it repaired and who handed it back to the council to be managed on behalf of the Kingston public. For almost two hundred years the public theatre on the Parade has belonged to the people of Kingston.

The early decades of the nineteenth century were perilous times for Jamaica and other Caribbean lands. Two significant events in France and England affected the stability of the island, kept the Kingston public preoccupied with serious and urgent affairs, and caused a decline in theatrical production. The outbreak of the French Revolution in 1789 had sent shock waves through the West Indies, especially so in Jamaica when the eruption reached neighboring Saint Domingue, where black slaves rose up against their masters. The Jamaican government had maintained a company of black Maroons to track down runaway slaves and, in a national emergency, to serve as an added security force.[43] But the Maroons themselves had rioted in 1795 and were at war with government troops, until the rebels were subdued and hundreds of them deported to Nova Scotia in 1796. The question of forming companies of mulatto and black troops to fight the Maroons had been considered, but in the general uncertainty of the times the assembly was opposed to supporting a regular corps of black soldiers. Now, faced with the successful slave insurrection on its doorstep, the defeat of the British expeditionary force sent against Saint Domingue, and a revolt of Jamaican slaves in the parish of Saint James, the assembly quickly reversed its decision. Martial law was declared, and troops were recruited from the free black population to help defend the island from the threat of invasion.

In Britain Parliament had begun debate on a motion to end the slave trade, which was merely preliminary to the abolition of slavery itself. This action provoked a stiffening of attitude among the Jamaican ruling class and as the news spread across the island caused unrest among the slave population. The planters were enjoying a temporary economic boom from rising prices for sugar and coffee during the war years as a result of the drop in exports from Saint Domingue, their chief competitor. They could see nothing ahead save economic disaster if their slaves were freed. Many feared for their lives. In this atmosphere of uncertainty and anxiety, there was little enthusiasm for the thespian art. John Stewart, who had lived in Jamaica for twenty-one years, could write in 1808:

> There are no theatrical exhibitions in this island. About twenty-five years ago a company of the sons and daughters of Thespis came here. They had some years before migrated from North America, terrified and proscribed as they must have been by the fierceness of civil discord. But on peace being restored to that country, they returned to it; and have not since, nor have any others, visited the shores of the island. . . . In Kingston, there are occasionally tolerable concerts, the principal performers in which are French emigrants from St. Domingo.[44]

The French newcomers were forced to exploit what histrionic and musical talents they possessed in order to make a living in their country of refuge. As the Jamaican government, in 1792–93, had forbidden entrance to free persons of color from Saint Domingue, these refugees were all white. With the specter of racial conflict lurking in many minds, it is not surprising to learn that theatre audiences were at this time strictly divided along racial lines.

Back in 1790 a Mr. Ullman, bird and dog trainer lately arrived from Germany, had advertised exhibitions by his feathered flock to be given separately to white and colored persons at the house of Mr. Caroso on High Holbourne Street in Kingston. This separation of the races, the first explicitly recorded in the Jamaican theatre, may be taken as an error of judgment on the part of Mr. Ullman and his host that did not reflect common theatre practice on the island. It was, however, prophetic of a new trend in catering for public entertainments. In 1802 a newspaper advertisement advised that Mr. Augustus Tessier, manager of a company of artistes from Saint Domingue who were installed in the Kingston theatre, "has erected a vast and commodious amphitheatre for the accommodation of people of colour, to which he has added a row of the second boxes adjoining the circus, by which means the people of colour will have a very spacious, airy and distinct place to which they ascend by a separate passage."[45] Tessier, lately driven from Saint Domingue by "people of colour," was at pains to segregate them more strictly in his country of refuge. Not only would there be separate seating but also access into the theatre would be by different routes for whites and nonwhites. It is an index of the times that no public outcry followed this announcement. The deference in tone of his notice leads one to believe that Tessier suspected Jamaican society was more tolerant of racial difference than his experiences in Saint Domingue allowed. That same year Lady Nugent, wife of the governor, attended a performance by a solo artist in Montego Bay and recorded that the audience "were of all colours and descriptions: blacks, browns, Jews, and whites."[46] The good lady did not say whether seating was in fact segregated; if so, we might have expected her to mention it.

By 1813 segregation had become commonplace in the Kingston theatre. Two separate prices were quoted for box seats at the theatre: 13s.4d. and 10s., the latter price representing boxes for people of color.[47] An advertisement for a performance in Spanish Town a year later informed prospective patrons: "No white person to be admitted into the Upper Boxes or Gallery."[48] One of the few extant reviews of performances at the Kingston theatre in this period noted that the upper boxes were "inhabited by coloureds."[49] Racial separation in the theatre reflected the rise of a segregationist attitude in the society at large. In May 1813, for instance, the Kingston Common Council required special reserved-seating sections for whites in the Anglican church in Kingston, and in December of that year a public meeting was held in the city, under the chairmanship of the mayor, to protest against a bill, passed by the assembly, that enabled free people of color to be judges, justices of the peace, jurors, officers of the militia, or electors of assembly members. The petitioners resolved that such rights were highly injurious to the welfare of Jamaica and a direct attack upon the constitution of the island.[50]

Not all colored folk accepted the new restrictions submissively. During Sunday service, a young man named Martin Halhead refused to leave a pew reserved for whites, and when he was forcibly ejected he warned the white officials: "Your power is over or at an end; take care how you act!"[51] In 1815 the same Halhead in company with nine other colored men was involved in a riot outside the Kingston theatre. They had signed a statement objecting to the separate entrance stairway erected on a side lane for colored people entering the upper boxes and they vowed to prevent others from using it. They were also incensed by certain disparaging racial remarks attributed to the manager of the theatre. In the course of the disturbance the steps were pulled down, and a white magistrate who intervened was severely beaten. Taken to court, the protesters were fined and given jail terms, but after a few months' incarceration the governor ordered their release and remitted the fines.[52]

The most graphic picture of the separation of races in the Kingston theatre is given by Michael Scott in his book *The Cruise of the Midge* (1836). It is worth quoting at length not only because it provides valuable information but also because it unwittingly reveals the attitude of a certain type of Englishman of the colonial era. Scott, who first arrived in Jamaica in 1806 at age seventeen and left in 1822, attended an amateur performance during the festive week of horse racing and provided this report:

> I was admiring the neatness of the house, which was great for a provincial theatre anywhere, and the comical appearance of the division of castes produced, as thus: The pit seemed to be almost exclusively filled with the children of Israel, as peculiar in their natural features here as everywhere else; the dress boxes contained the other white inhabitants and their families; the second tier the brown *ladies,* who seemed more intent on catching the eyes of the young buccras *below,* than attending to the civil things the males of their own shades were pouring into their ears *above;* the gallery was tended by Bungo himself, in all his glory of black face, blubber lips, white eyes, and ivory teeth. This black parterre being powdered here and there with a sprinkling of white sailors, like snow-drops in a bed of purple anemones; Jack being, as usual on such occasions, pretty well drunk.[53]

The caste system evidently overrode racial lines. White sailors, probably transients in port for a few days, could claim no better accommodation than blacks. They were admitted to the open gallery reserved for patrons of the lowest caste.

One might speculate who these blacks were that attended the theatre. In 1824 the population of Kingston consisted of 18,000 slaves, 2,500 free negroes, 2,500 free coloreds, and 10,000 whites for a total of 33,000. It is unlikely that free blacks of the working class could afford to go to the theatre at 6s. 3d. a seat when the average pay for a laborer was 10s. to 12s. a week and 15s. to 20s. if skilled. The educated coloreds would surely not sit in the gallery but in the upper boxes. That leaves the black slave population, many of whom were attached as domestic servants to city folk.

In England and America it was the custom for gentlemen and ladies attending the theatre to send their servants ahead of them to secure their seats until they arrived just before the play began. This was a needful precaution because there were no reserved seats, and the front chairs in boxes or the front benches in the pit would be filled by patrons who came early. When the gentry arrived in their coaches before curtain time, the house slaves would surrender the seats they had been holding and would repair to the gallery if they were permitted to watch the play. Coachmen and attendants might also be allowed to sit through the play in the gallery so as to be on hand at the end of the performance to drive the gentry home. In this way black slaves or household servants in and around the city might have had their first taste of Western theatre and have become acquainted with the works of Shakespeare and other leading English dramatists. Then in their own form of theatre, such as the Jonkonnu masquerade that they were allowed to perform during the Christmas holidays, they would parody the plays they saw in the public theatre, a ferocious Richard III in full Actor-boy regalia waving his wooden sword and crying: "A horse, a horse, my kingdom for a horse" on the streets of Kingston.[54] How long the policy of segregated seating persisted in the Jamaican theatre can only be surmised. Further reference to the practice does not appear in the records searched beyond 1816.

The earliest picture on record of the Kingston Theatre comes from this period [fig. 2]. It was reproduced in the *Jamaica Almanac* of 1831 in a lithograph by Adolphe Duperly. It shows the theatre as a rectangular structure, presumably wooden, with three high-pitched gabled roofs running the length of the building from east to west. It has two stories. The lower, at street level, is surrounded by a wall that contains narrow slits for light and air instead of regular windows. That part of the building must have been used for storage. The upper story stands on pillars some seven or eight feet above ground, and in the fashion of those days, it has a double flight of steps leading to a front portal that is framed by four columns, upon which rests an imposing pediment. This is the enlarged building that was extended into the Parade in 1815 so that the playhouse used by the American Company was even smaller. To the west adjoining the theatre and jutting slightly in front of it is a much smaller structure used as a bar and called Shakespeare's Tavern. This playhouse appears in a panoramic view of the Parade drawn by J. B. Kidd sometime prior to 1839 [fig. 3]. In the foreground of the picture is the graveyard to the church that stands south of the Parade ground; the barracks are at upper left and the theatre to the far right of the barracks with the Saint Andrew hills in the distant background.

The capacity of this house was given in 1821 as seven hundred. From Scott's acid portrait of the audience we learn that the theatre at this time had a pit, a tier of dress boxes (sometimes called the dress circle), a second tier of upper boxes, and a gallery. Prices advertised in 1816 were 13s.4d. for box seats, 10s. each for the pit and upper boxes, and 6s.3d. for the gallery. A performance of John Home's *Douglas* in 1812 reported gate receipts of £438, which represented a full house for the opening night of a new visiting company from Barbados.[55] When Monk Lewis attended this theatre in 1818 to witness a performance of

2. Kingston Theatre on the Parade, by A. Duperly, 1831. Photograph ©
reserved, National Library of Jamaica.

3. Panoramic view of the Parade, by J. B. Kidd, showing barracks to the
left and theatre to the right. The church cemetery is in the foreground,
ca. 1838. Photograph © reserved, National Library of Jamaica.

his tragedy *Adelgitha,* he found the exterior of the building to be picturesque but felt that the scenery and dresses were shabby and the stage poorly lit. He was clearly disappointed in the performance and may have viewed the interior surroundings with a somewhat jaundiced eye.

A disturbing aspect of Kingston audiences of this time was their unseemly behavior. Richardson Wright refers to their proverbial rowdiness, citing the case of one manager of a visiting and popular vaudeville team who in 1812 threatened to leave the island after one of his clowns had been assaulted on stage by rowdies, who as well demolished some scenery and fixtures.[56] Michael Scott also reported that his evening at the theatre eventually degenerated into a free-for-all battle between patrons in different parts of the house. The Kingston magistrates were determined to stamp out this incivility, and in 1812 they passed an ordinance setting out rules of conduct in the theatre and imposing fines from £10 to £50 or imprisonment from ten days to two months upon those found guilty of infringement. Nevertheless, disturbances continued and in 1828 another ordinance was passed with stiffer penalties. A white or colored delinquent could be fined £20 to £50 or sentenced from ten days to three months in jail. A slave found guilty of a similar offense could receive thirty-nine lashes and thirty days of hard labor. When, some weeks later, two Kingstonians were brought before the magistrate for smoking "seegars" and acting riotously in a box at the theatre, the offenders were sentenced to thirty days' imprisonment in the common jail.[57] Despite these severe penalties, rowdyism in the theatre prevailed, as shall be seen.

Emancipation took place on August 1, 1834, and a quarter of a million black slaves were set free, subject to a transitional period of six years (later reduced to four) during which they were supposed to remain in service as paid apprentices. Apart from local amateur productions, interest in the Kingston theatre had waned during the years of uncertainty preceding abolition. Now it began to revive. The playhouse itself was in a sorry state of repair. The *Jamaica Almanac* of 1838 reported that the theatre had deteriorated so badly as to render it unfit for use, and sometime earlier a balustrade in the gallery section had collapsed causing an unfortunate young man to plunge to his death in the pit below.[58] Something had to be done and quickly.

3

Post-Emancipation Theatres

 In May 1838, a few months before all slaves were officially freed on August 1, a petition "to which two-thirds of the community affixed their names" was sent to the Kingston Town Council urging that a new theatre should be built. A public subscription was raised with some enthusiastic employers causing a furor when they arbitrarily deducted a portion of their workers' wages in order to help swell the fund. The petition to rebuild was laboriously debated in council. Eventually the building was put out to tender and a Mr. Robert Hancock won the contract. What happened next is best reported verbatim from the *Gleaner*'s retrospective article:

> During 1839 the building was in progress, and a most peculiar progress it made. The contractor had had no experience of theatre building and had never seen a theatre save the old Kingston one. His ideas on the subject were consequently somewhat vague, and several ludicrous events occurred. When first completed, the floors of the upper part of the house were put all on the same level and the result as might be expected was that those at the back could not see the stage at all. Next the balustrade in front of the gallery [this was the one that caused the tragedy] was made too high and the unfortunate "gods" had to stand on tiptoe and crick their necks to ascertain what was going on on the stage. It had been intended to construct the building so that it could on necessity be converted into a circus, but the architectural skill of the contractor was not equal to the occasion and the project had to be abandoned.[1]

To entrust the design and construction of a theatre facility to a builder who knew little or nothing of theatre practice could only invite disaster. Yet government authorities in the West Indies and elsewhere have been known to repeat the error at great cost to the public treasury. Moreover, the idea of constructing an all-purpose civic auditorium to accommodate the theatre, receptions and dances, circuses, boxing matches, and such other forms of indoor public entertainment is one that often appeals to authorities who are hard-pressed to justify spending public funds on a building that is meant primarily for theatrical performance. Invariably, however, the resultant compromises lead to dissatisfaction by all concerned parties with the facilities provided; there are conflicting claims on the use of the building, and a lack of appreciation of the physical environment necessary to maintain a theatrical enterprise of quality often results in shoddy and unimaginative productions.

In Kingston, after the Hancock debacle, an entirely new plan was drawn up and the building was completed at a cost of £5,750. The original contracted cost was £5,000, in addition to which the charge for interior decoration was £400, chandeliers were priced at £200, and there was an additional sum of £150 spent on correcting the flat gallery floor.[2] Hancock had again been retained as builder. A Mr. Prieur, citizen artist, executed the interior designs. But the man who eventually rescued the project from total calamity by serving as building consultant and supervising both the construction and the interior arrangements was J. T. Dias.

Dias, a dentist by profession, was a well-known amateur performer and theatre enthusiast. He managed the Kingston Amateur Association and was familiarly referred to as "John Kemble Macready Dias" after the leading actor-managers of the contemporary English stage. It was he who had presented the petition to the City Council and had headed the subscription list. He had also raised monies to pay for the decorations in the new theatre and had sacrificed both time and his private practice to oversee its construction. In recognition of his services the council appointed him agent for the theatre, and a complimentary benefit performance in his honor was arranged by Kingston amateurs for the theatre's opening "as a small remuneration for his indefatigable exertions towards the erection of the present building."[3]

Kingston proudly opened its "beautiful new theatre" on Wednesday, September 2, 1840.[4] The daguerreotype picture made by Adolphe Duperly and published in Kingston about 1844 shows it to be a handsome brick edifice [fig. 4]. The facade, simple in conception yet well proportioned and strikingly effective, had an imposing flight of steps leading up to a Doric colonnade that gave entry to a recessed portico. Above the columns was an attractive low stone balustrade that added a touch of lightness to an otherwise austere and majestic building. It was built of brick and "best lime mortar" with a shingled roof. The outside walls had a thickness of two-and-a-half bricks and stood

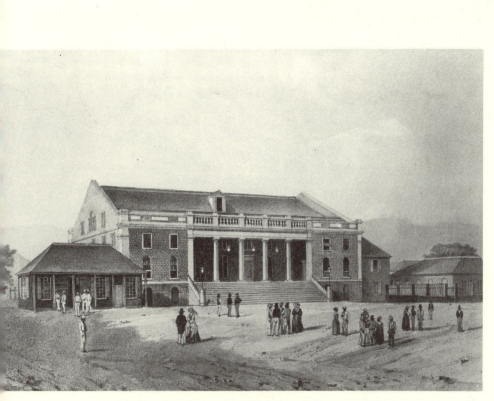

4. Theatre Royal, ca. 1844. Photograph © reserved,
National Library of Jamaica.

twenty-five feet high from the ground. The front doors contained six
panels each. Still called the Kingston Theatre when it opened, its
name was first changed in 1842 to the Theatre Royal (after the historic
Drury Lane Theatre in London) when it housed a company managed
jointly by Mrs. Monier, a resident player, and a touring professional
actor, J. H. Oxley. Thereafter the building was advertised under either
name, according to the taste of the company occupying it, until the
more impressive-sounding Theatre Royal eventually supplanted the
earlier name. The building served the city for half a century.

Combining bits of information from reports of performances over
the next several decades, it is possible to reconstruct some of the
theatre's interior features. If the facade was impressive, the internal
arrangements, despite Dias's supervision, were distinctly less than
satisfactory. The auditorium had a seating capacity of about six hundred, which in later years was considered too small. It contained a pit,
dressing rooms, and a greenroom. The stage held traps, but in hind-

43

sight it was also too small, and the "resound" (or acoustics) was execrable. There were insufficient doors for entrance and egress. The pit area, for instance, had only one door, which, at the time criticism was voiced in 1865, had been kept locked because the key was lost. As a result ladies attending the opera had to "go up a most uncomfortable ladder" to exit from the dress circle. As the complainant remarked, in case of fire the audience could not possibly escape without serious injury. Benches were still being used for seating in the pit, upper boxes, and gallery, with chairs in the dress circle.

New lighting fixtures ordered from abroad had not arrived in time for the grand opening of the building. They were installed some weeks later when it was announced that "the Theatre will be for the first time brilliantly illuminated by the elegant chandeliers and lamps imported by the Corporation."[5] These consisted of a large central chandelier suspended from the ceiling and ten smaller ones dispersed about the auditorium and stage. Oil lamps were also used for additional general lighting. Many years later, in 1868, during a performance by Japanese gymnasts, a kerosene lamp burst causing a considerable alarm among the audience who thought that the theatre was on fire.[6] Oil-burning footlights were still being used and they sometimes exuded a pungent smoke, which affected the actors who had to perform in the downstage area for any length of time. Occasionally the floats were replaced by candlesticks with tin reflectors, but these dazzled the eyes of the audience and provoked complaints from those affected.[7]

The new theatre needed a supply of new scenery. This was secured through negotiation with professional companies who occupied the building for extended seasons. On March 24, 1841, for instance, it was announced that Mr. Rogers, scene painter to Oxley's Company of Comedians then playing in Kingston, would bring forward "a splendid picturesque landscape scene . . . as No. 1 of a series to be painted and attached to the stock of the Kingston Theatre in pursuance of an arrangement entered into by Mr. Oxley and the Committee."[8] That evening's performance was *King Lear*, and Rogers received repeated applause for his landscape setting. Four years later Mr. Solomon de Cordova brought out a company from New York. His venture failed financially, and in the course of applying to the council for abatement of his lease he argued that the theatre had been considerably improved under his tenancy, "the amount of scenery being nearly double and of a far better and more elegant description than the old stock. The amount of labour alone expended on these scenes has amounted to fully One Hundred Pounds."[9]

A new theatre committee was appointed and regulations were drawn up governing the use of the new playhouse. For each performance rent was fixed at £5 (later reduced to £3) and £1 10s. for each of the three concession bars serving different parts of the house. No spirits, wines, malts, or meats were to be sold in the theatre. The agent's salary was 20 percent of the amount collected in rent; he was required to keep an inventory of the theatre's equipment and furnishings and to report promptly any injury to the building. The rules fixed the bottom prices for theatre tickets at 6s. for the dress circle and pit, 4s. for upper boxes, and 3s. for the gallery. Smoking was forbidden in the house, and gentlemen in round coats were disallowed entry into the dress circle.

The most exacting of all the rules and the one calculated to cause great hardship to theatre groups, professional and particularly amateur, was the requirement that a bond of £120 or $600 be posted to cover possible damages before use of the building was allowed. This rule was still in force in 1872 when, following a protest by one of the newspaper editors acting as agent for a visiting company, the bond was reduced to £20. Apparently lower rates were applicable when the theatre was used for other kinds of activities. For a lecture the rental was £1, and sometimes the theatre might be granted free of charge if occasion warranted. This occurred in 1864 when Signora Garbato was having difficulty attracting an audience for her concert and applied for the use of the theatre free of charge. The editor of a Kingston paper urged the corporation to agree to extend to the lady the same favor it had already shown to others.[10]

Another source of irritation was the policy of renting the building on a first-come, first-served basis for as long as the tenant paid the rental fee. This meant, in effect, that a visiting professional company could occupy the theatre for a year or more, so long as it was performing regularly to good business and able to pay its bills. Any other company that happened to be visiting Jamaica, on its way to or from South America or the other West Indian islands, would be precluded from playing in the theatre unless the current occupants were willing to suspend business for a time or to make some amicable arrangement with the new group for a share of the box office.

On one occasion W. M. Holland, an enterprising and not too scrupulous manager who had been in Jamaica for some months, tried to capitalize on this situation. First he persuaded the Municipal Board to lease him the theatre for two months at a reduced rate of £6 a week, payable in advance. Then he sought and got the board's permission to sublet the building to another company whose arrival was imminently expected, at a rate of £3 a night, an arrangement that one outraged newspaper editor called "an abominable piece of jobbery."[11] Sensibly, the board later rescinded the agreement as being in violation of the rules since the custos or chief magistrate of the parish, as chairman of the board, was the only one empowered to rent the theatre and he happened to be absent from the meeting that had approved the lease. Holland was then required to pay £3 a night for each performance like everyone else.

If professionals were upset by the rules under which the theatre could be held by one company for an extended period, local amateurs were furious. They had, after all, subscribed to building the theatre. They were principally responsible for getting it constructed. They sensed instinctively that the future of drama in Jamaica would depend ultimately on their efforts. While it was always inspiring to watch a company of outstanding professionals on the local boards, the amateurs were expected to present tolerable productions between the visits of professionals, and quite often they were called upon to assist the career actors by filling out large casts. If anyone deserved precedence in the use of the theatre, the amateurs did. Instead, a formal application to the council each time they wished the theatre was an onerous burden and put them in unfair competition with touring troupes whose visits were planned weeks ahead. In order to resolve these concerns and after waiting out two long seasons by visiting companies, H. S. Henry, secretary of the Amateur Theatrical Association in Kingston, addressed a petition to the council in 1846. He requested the use of the theatre "at all and at any time when not in the occupation of a professional company."[12] This request was granted, and the years immediately following proved to be the most active in amateur theatricals during the nineteenth century. No less than eight amateur groups performed in Kingston and Spanish Town, not including military and naval amateurs who must be counted as birds of passage. It was a period that witnessed the formation for the first time in Jamaica of groups of black and colored actors, who played briefly in the Kingston theatre and then disappeared from the records.[13]

The increased level of theatrical activity that had been stimulated by the new theatre in Kingston led to the opening of several other places of public amusement. Most of these premises were no more than spacious meeting and lecture halls in public buildings, hotels, and the like, where rudimentary stage facilities would be set up if necessary and speedily dismantled at the end of a performance. From time to time a more permanent amusement center might be established when an attraction was offered for an extended run. The new

46

theatre on the Parade might claim to be the temple of histrionic art but Harbour Street, on which the first public theatre in Kingston was located, continued to be a busy thoroughfare and offered a variety of attractions. The view along Harbour Street looking eastward from King Street drawn by James Hakewill in 1820–21 shows a flag prominently displayed over a building to indicate that a public entertainment was being offered there [fig. 5].

In September 1839 Señor Juan Dal-Ponte advertised mechanically devised performances at the "Theatre at 121 Harbour Street," which in July and August had housed an optical exhibition of panoramic views, portraits, and fireworks. Mechanical puppet theatre had become quite popular at this time. In December the "New Italian Theatre at 36 Harbour Street, opposite that lately occupied by Madame Nief" also advertised a number of newly invented entertainments including a comedy, interlude, and a pantomime dance by puppets.[14] In 1841, when a small troupe of Italian opera artistes failed to obtain the Kingston Theatre, then occupied by Oxley's comedians, they decided to perform in a "Room formerly the *Despatch Office* in Harbour Street." The arrangement could not have been successful since only two concerts were given at this venue. Also on Harbour Street, at no. 27, were the Philharmonic Society's Rooms where a concert was advertised in October 1849 as a first step in reactivating the society that had become dormant.[15] It was reconstituted later that year.

The most active of all Harbour Street premises offering public entertainment was Freemason's Hall. The Masons previously owned a hall on Port Royal Street, and in July 1839 it had housed a series of vocal and instrumental concerts by visiting artistes. This was during the building of the Kingston Theatre when there was no other public room in the city to accommodate such performances. The next year the Masons moved to new premises at 46–47 Harbour Street, corner of Hanover Street, where their spacious hall became the venue for all sorts of entertainments. The Kingston Bazaar was held there in April 1840, the organizers announcing that it would be a quarterly affair to coincide with the sitting of the Assize Court. An exhibition of wax statuary opened at the hall in 1864 and a marionette show the year after.

In May 1867 a comic monologuist and showman called Walter Hope Wallack, who was not above exploiting his famous theatrical name in promoting his shows, arrived in Jamaica to seek his fortune. After performing for some years around the country he opened the Gallery of Illustration at Freemason's Hall, naming it after the much-admired gallery run by Mr. and Mrs. German Reed in London. Wallack, how-

5. View along Harbour Street, Kingston, by James Hakewill. The flag indicates a show to be held in the building beneath it, ca. 1820–21.

ever, had neither the taste nor the circumspection of his English models. His kind of entertainment was denounced in the press as unsuited to the upper circle of society, and Wallack's disclaimer that he was not responsible for shows that were offered when his gallery was rented out only made matters worse. To answer his critics Wallack engaged a couple of popular and inoffensive comic reciters, then offered his gallery for a series of lectures by well-respected speakers. In December 1874 he brought back the Italian marionettes that had a ready audience among the city's children. He may have relinquished his lease of the Freemason's Hall a year later when Le Théâtre Petit, an amateur group, presented two plays to a private audience "at the spacious room in Harbour Street above Freemason's Hall,"[16] and he was definitely out when the prestidigitator Jules Bosco worked his magic at "Freemason's Hall, late Wallack's Gallery, on Harbour Street" in September 1879.[17]

There were several other places in Kingston where performances of one kind or another were advertised in the decades following Emancipation. The city was expanding steadily as the population moved into the northern suburbs of Saint Andrew, which itself increased in number of residents from 18,960 in 1844 to 23,451 in 1861. The white urban population was also growing. It doubled in the two decades between 1846 and 1865 from 2,474 to 4,909, while the colored or "brown" residents as designated by the census and reported only in the latter year were numbered at a substantial 13,772.

Concerts for select but paying patrons were held in residential premises. In 1839 Miss Green's Room on North Street and Miss Davis's on East Street, and, in 1849, Mrs. Edwarde's on King Street, all presumably privately run boardinghouses, were used for vocal and instrumental concerts. At Mrs. Edwarde's a performance by Cuban amateurs, including the two highly favored and youthful Señoritas Ramos, was attended by a "moderately numerous but highly respectable audience composed chiefly of our Jewish gentry and their families."[18] The grand salons of several hotels, such as the Wellington and the Commercial, also held concerts but more often feats of legerdemain and ventriloquism that, after dinner, could be relied on to titillate the senses of well-fed guests. Increasingly, too, church and school halls housed concerts, readings, debates, and other appropriate cultural and intellectual events, usually arranged to raise funds for the hosting institution.

By 1848 Kingston had a new or, more probably, newly refurbished courthouse that was provided with a suitable hall for public assemblies. A choral concert was held there in December that year and thereafter the courthouse became the most important locale, after the Theatre Royal, for public readings and musical events of high quality. Charles Kean, the admired actor-manager of the English stage in the mid-nineteenth century, performed there with his wife when they visited the island in 1865. There was also another courthouse at Halfway Tree, Saint Andrew, where concerts were given as early as 1848, and yet another concert auditorium was available from that year at "the large and elegant saloon of Date Tree Hall" on East Street. This hall was later acquired by the government to hold the libraries of the House of Assembly and the Legislative Council when Kingston became the official capital in 1872, and the two libraries were amalgamated to form the library of the Institute of Jamaica in 1879.

As if these several places where the public could be variously entertained were not enough, Kingston opened two more theatres in the 1840s, both of which existed for only a brief period of time. The first, called the Theatre of Varieties, was managed by Mme C. Villalave, who announced in an advertisement on August 4, 1840, that "she has erected near and comfortable boxes for the reception of those who may favor her with their presence."[19] The show offered was yet another mechanical contrivance of exotic changing scenes with figures moving to music. Admission prices were one dollar for box seats and five shillings for the pit, with children admitted at half-price. In September 1841 the diligent Madame announced her return to the city to open her theatre or rather, as stated in the notice, her amphitheatre located at the back of the Kingston barracks. This time live acrobats and a live clown were added attractions to the mechanical metamorphoses and maritime views promised in the bill. After these two announcements the Theatre of Varieties is heard from no more.

The other theatre of the period remains something of a mystery. In 1842 the Theatre Royal was enjoying a busy season. Oxley's professional troupe had disbanded, but he and some members of his company had regrouped under the management of Mrs. Monier, who ran an acting school and had herself been a career actor. The new combination offered to Theatre Royal patrons a respectable repertoire of English drama, including Shakespeare, with farcical afterpieces. Suddenly, without prior notice of preparations for the event, an advertisement appeared in the daily press to the effect that the Royal Victoria Theatre would open a season of plays, commencing on Saturday, October 8.[20] No manager was named, nor was the new company identified, although some of the names of the performers seemed to be erstwhile professional troupers who had settled on the island, at least one actor coming from Oxley's former troupe.

It is not possible to determine where this new theatre was located. It was apparently a small house containing only a pit and box seats. Its prices were competitive—3s. and 2s.—and it no doubt gave the company at the larger house a run for its money. The new company offered popular fare, farces, and melodramas twice and sometimes three times a week in October and November, then a gap occurs in available newspapers. Unless further information is found, the Royal Victoria Theatre must remain shrouded in its misty past with the intriguing comment of the *Morning Journal:* "Kingston need not now complain of the want of theatricals. We have now two theatres opened—the Theatre Royal and the Royal Victoria. A performance at the Royal Victoria will take place this evening and one also at the Theatre Royal."[21]

Of all the Kingston theatres so far discussed only one, Mme Villalave's Theatre of Varieties, was open-air. This is surprising seeing that the evenings in Kingston are often cool and salubrious, with rain seldom falling after dark. In the recent past a number of open-air

50

cinemas and some theatres have attested to the attractiveness (and small risk of cancellation because of inclement weather) of theatre under the sky. It can offer sizable seating capacity at minimum maintenance expense, production costs are cheaper since scenery becomes less important outdoors than in an enclosed space, and there are opportunities for inventive staging with an emphasis on acting.

Circuses, popular then as now, provided the only regular form of amphitheatre staging, with audiences numbering thousands under the big tent and with most programs ending in an amusing pantomime played in the round by the whole company. These tents were at first set up on a corner of the Parade grounds where they must have caused some noisy interference with productions at the theatre in the immediate vicinity or with church meetings and services. In 1864 a new circus site was found on East Street, and by 1875 the favorite and most proper location for the circus was the Kingston Race Course. Ticket prices were not cheap for select seats, but they could drop as low as two shillings for the gallery, which would be within reach of the ordinary citizen.

The circuses were all visiting companies that performed for a few weeks in the city, then moved on to country towns before shipping out to other lands. Some excitement must therefore have greeted the announcement in 1874 that Kingston would have its own circus permanently located in the city, for which a light but substantial arena would be built.[22] The structure was eighty feet across and sixty feet high at the center. It had wooden walls, a canvas roof, and a ring of orthodox diameter measuring forty-two feet. There were nine tiers of permanent wooden seating, and 450 chairs constituting a dress circle were installed in a section of the arena. Retiring and dressing rooms were provided, and strategically placed lamps supplied the lighting. The manager of this enterprise was Achile S. Philion. Prices, originally posted at 4s. and 2s., were reduced after a month for lack of patronage to 3s. and 1s. Performances were given daily except for Friday night and Sunday, the holy days for Jews and Christians. After playing about six weeks in the city the permanent Kingston circus left for a tour of the Jamaican countryside, after which it dropped from the records. With its exciting physical action and pantomime offerings at bargain prices, it may well have been the circus rather than the more select dramatic stage that brought a flavor of live theatre to the broad mass of the Jamaican public in the decades following Emancipation.

The legendary noisiness of Kingston audiences continued to be a problem in the theatre. Nor were the offenders limited to patrons in the cheaper gallery seats or "gods," who were often the target of criticism for their lively behavior. At one of the earliest productions in the new playhouse in 1840, the performance was rendered inaudible to the dress circle owing to the noise of conversation emanating from the pit. This incident should have served as an early warning of troublesome acoustics about which complaints were aired later in the century. Theatre regulations had little success in curbing the boisterous audience. Most gentlemen carried walking sticks, which they used to pound the floor and slap against benches in a demonstration of either praise or disapproval. Benches were frequently damaged as a result of constant battering. On one occasion when a visiting company could raise only a feeble group of musicians for its orchestra, the audience, its patience exhausted, exploded in anger each time the orchestra attempted to play. At another time an actor who failed to appear in an advertised role was vehemently heckled on his next appearance, having omitted to offer a public apology for his absence.

Police were posted in the theatre and were repeatedly urged to make an arrest so as to set an example for unruly patrons. In 1873 a magistrate, levying fines from 5s. to 10s. each on five persons for creating a noise inside and outside the theatre, took the time to lecture them on the need for proper behavior in places of public amusement. The next year a show by a visiting pantomime company had to be terminated when a fight at the box office threatened to wreck the performance. It probably deserved no better reception, the orchestra being "execrable." A year later the fine imposed on one young delinquent caught noisemaking in front of the theatre was raised to 40s., the magistrate cautioning that, since disturbances of this kind were becoming so frequent, he intended to inflict heavy punishment in an effort to stop them altogether. In 1879 the fine had given way to imprisonment for disorderly conduct at the circus.

Kingston was not singular in having to cope with volatile audiences. The whole country was undergoing drastic social change, and tumult in the body politic was reflected in behavior at public gatherings. A review of an 1838 amateur performance in Spanish Town disclosed that a fight erupted at the theatre when a troublesome apprentice named Thomas was denied admission.[23] This incident is of greater interest than news of yet another theatre disturbance might suggest. It indicates that ex-slaves serving out their apprenticeship prior to full freedom were voluntarily seeking to visit the live theatre and were prepared to insist on their right of admission. Another report, coming from the town of Falmouth in 1868, tells of an amateur performance at the courthouse having been stopped by the custos in order to protect public property that was being greatly injured.[24]

Outside of Kingston no theatres of consequence were built or fitted up in the post-Emancipation period. Spanish Town received new public buildings in 1825 that were erected around the main plaza known as King's House Square. Among the buildings was a courthouse with a large hall, which became the center for cultural activity: concerts, readings, variety acts, amateur and professional theatricals were held there in succession, as if indeed no other suitable auditorium existed for such presentations. Those who chose not to use the courthouse had no other alternative but to move into private homes. A concert was advertised at Miss Marshall's House near the cathedral in March 1848, and the previous year a group of enterprising young men calling themselves the Spanish Town Dramatic Society "fitted up a small but very neat theatre at the house in King Street, lately occupied by Messrs. Aikman and Myers as their office."[25] The society mounted two productions at their neat little playhouse but then moved to the public buildings for future shows.

Across the country courthouses were the most readily available halls for public cultural events. These buildings were usually two stories high. Government offices occupied the lower floor. The upper story comprised a large hall with a platform at one end. It was used for court hearings during the day and at night became the only public meeting room in the district, barring the school that was owned by a religious body and was not always open to public shows. In towns outside of Kingston where regular theatre performances were given—in Spanish Town, Mandeville, Falmouth, Port Royal, Montego Bay, and elsewhere—the courthouse was the principal if not the only venue for these events. It is a sobering thought that people who entered the building by day to have their problems settled in the legal drama of the courtroom returned to the same building at night to watch fictional characters settle their problems, often in a more violent fashion.

The last quarter of the nineteenth century was a perilous time for the established Kingston theatre. A combination of events conspired to put the future of the Theatre Royal in jeopardy. For quite some years past the island had been experiencing a serious economic slump owing mainly to the decline of sugar cultivation, which was in competition with the slave-produced crops of Cuba and Brazil. Sugar production had fallen from an average yield of around sixty-eight thousand tons in 1833 to twenty-five thousand tons in 1866. The increase in population after the end of slavery and the concomitant lack of gainful employment had brought great hardship to the working class, finally erupting in the Morant Bay rebellion of 1865. That rebellion had been suppressed with cruel severity, the supposed leaders (including a member of the legislature) had been hanged without fair trial, and the island's representative government was replaced by colonial rule in which the British governor held full power under the queen. Nevertheless the island's financial position did not improve. Evidence of the decline could be plainly seen in the numbers of unemployed workers, the poor condition of the city's roads, and the lack of proper means of transport from one town to the next.

In the past, decisions concerning the Kingston theatre had been made by an elected municipal council on the advice of members who composed the Theatre Committee. Now, however, the council had been replaced by a board wholly appointed by the governor and serving at his pleasure. The old council had tried with its limited funds to keep the Theatre Royal in good repair. Each time a new professional company was due to arrive from abroad an effort would be made to spruce up the building. The interior had been painted and the benches repaired, for instance, in time for the visit of the de Cordova company in 1846; minor repairs were undertaken in 1858; and the inside of the house was again "improved under the artistic pen of Hite Waldron" for the return visit of Holland's company in 1874. These cosmetic applications, however welcome, could not arrest the ravages of termites, high wind, floods, and earth tremors in subtropical Jamaica, and the building stood in need of structural repair.

As the year 1879 began, it was clear that the Theatre Royal, which had served Kingston so well for almost forty years, was in desperate need of renovation. A meeting of the Theatre Committee in February of that year resolved that the building "is in a very dilapidated state and urgently demands attention, requiring as it does instant renovation, if not complete reconstruction."[26] That conclusion, dutifully reported in the columns of the press, sparked a fiery debate between supporters and opponents of the theatre on the question of whether public funds should be spent to restore or replace the building. In the middle of the controversy stood not the Municipal Board, which had little money and less power, but the lieutenant governor of the island, acting for the governor who was on furlough overseas.

A troublesome source of opposition to the theatre were the so-called dissenting religions, the Baptists, Methodists, and Presbyterians.[27] They had led the fight in Jamaica for the abolition of slavery and they were loath to see their emancipated flock corrupted by the unseemly traffic of stage plays and the highly suspect lives of professional actors. Individual clerics were not always united in their views on the evil influence of the stage, and truth to say, one of the leading Presbyterian ministers on the island was himself for many years a poet and play-wright who often spoke in support of the drama. But others were strongly antagonistic and viewed the ensuing debate as an opportunity to deprive theatre worshipers of their principal temple, without which play production activities would substantially diminish. The Theatre Committee had estimated that it would cost between £4,000 and £5,000 to reconstruct the theatre and install new seats. It was hoped that government would provide a loan of this sum to the Municipal Board rather than having the board resort to issuing debentures on the open market at a time when money was in short supply.

In letters to the *Gleaner* newspaper, Alexander Robb, a spokesman for the opposition, denounced the prospect of a treasury loan and urged instead that the money should be spent to build a bridge over the Yallahs River or a mile or two of railway. He argued that "not more than 2,000 of our 20,000 inhabitants ever visit the theatre," the large majority being deterred on account of religious or moral scruple. He insisted that the minority view should not override the wishes of the majority and continued: "A section of this Jamaican community, as of all communities in Christendom . . . are as of settled principle and conscience opposed to the theatre."28 Backers of the theatre countered by pointing to its intellectual character, the high excellence attained by amateur players, and the unedifying alternative of billiard saloons and the like as leisuretime activity for young men.

The situation was further aggravated when Spanish Town opened what some enthusiastic thespians of the town hailed as the Bijou Theatre, a "new and elegant place of amusement, lately handed over to the public by the Government." The Bijou, prematurely christened with a name that didn't stick, turned out to be the main room in the renovated Town Hall, which had been tastefully decorated and equipped with scenery, stage devices, and a new drop curtain of green baize. Kingston, long the unchallenged ruler in the realm of his-trionics, had suddenly been eclipsed by its rival city. The *Gleaner* wrote dejectedly that Kingstonians had

a rotten old shed dignified by the appellation [of theatre] and they have a draft on futurity in the shape of a promise of £4,000 to be devoted to renovation. Meanwhile, thanks to the vigorous policy pursued by the Custos of St. Catherine, the Hon. Isaac Levy, the inhabitants of Spanish Town . . . have come into possession of a fine hall, and with a united liberality they have equipped it with all necessary stage furniture, decorations and machinery, spe-cially imported.

The writer went on to describe the attractive decor of the room, which held about four hundred people. The Prologue for the opening night's performance, from which the following lines have been extracted, emphasized that the new hall was intended to be multifunctional:

> Not consecrate alone to Thespian art,
> This Hall's designed to play a varied part
> When Patriots true with public questions deal
> And take wise measures for the common weal.
>
> . . . .
>
> In this brave Hall to Music's tuneful rhyme
> Light foot and laughing eye will keep the time.

Modest as it turned out to be, the achievement of Spanish Town served to redouble efforts in the city for a new theatre. The *Gleaner* editorialized regularly on the intolerable condition of the Theatre Royal, pointing out that inquiries from theatre managers abroad had to be turned down for lack of a proper performance hall, thereby losing revenue for the city and recreation for its citizens. When the treasury loan was finally denied and it transpired that government had plans to acquire the site on which the theatre stood for new public buildings, the paper urged the Municipal Board to stand firm, though it acknowledged that since Jamaica had lost its constitution, the board's power was "no better than *obeah* on behalf of the citizens against the obnoxious schemes of the Government."[29]

It happened that in 1870, during the administration of Governor John Peter Grant, government had appropriated the surplus funds of the Kingston Savings Bank, about £3,200, promising in return to provide a town hall for the city of Kingston. That promise had never materialized. The present courthouse, too, had been taken over years ago by government from the city, with no rent paid. Citing this history, the *Gleaner* contended that government was greatly in debt to the city. It felt that citizens would be willing to settle, as a last resort, for the building of a proper town hall that would double as a theatre, concert room, or lecture hall. The editor wrote: "Provided with such a hall of audience, there is no reason why Kingston should not boast of a Philharmonic Society and a Dramatic Society, and be able to indulge in the intellectual dissipation of a series of lectures on themes sacred and profane during the cool months."[30] A public meeting attended by an estimated six hundred to nine hundred people called on government to clarify its intentions with respect to a new town hall, and a petition to the Municipal Board asking for the repair of the Theatre Royal collected four hundred signatures in two days. As if in response to the *Gleaner's* prediction, the formation of a new philharmonic society and a dramatic association brought more pressure on the board to provide a suitable auditorium for stage performances.

The demand for a new theatre had been voiced first in February 1879. In April 1880, Lieutenant Governor Edward Newton, acting for absent governor Anthony Musgrave, agreed that government would fit up as a city hall the room above the Post Office, which the Municipal Board used for its meetings. This was to be a temporary measure until government built a proper town hall for the city. This palliative proved to be unsatisfactory. Newton Hall, as the *Gleaner* sarcastically dubbed the new facility, was closed to dramatic performances pending a report from the Public Works Department on its suitability. When that report came, the hall was found to require extensive renovations before theatrical productions could be accommodated. Moreover it was more susceptible to street noises than the old Theatre Royal had been. Streetcars rolling outside created such a racket during a band concert that straw had to be placed along the metal lines in front of the hall to muffle the rattle of the cars. "We consider it a most regrettable thing," moaned the *Gleaner*, when a variety circus opened at the race course that April, "that circuses should be opened and theatres closed. . . . Shall the people be encouraged to feast their eyes on the feats and frolics of the ring, and debarred from hearing the plays of Shakespeare, of Lytton and of Sheridan?"[31] To add fuel to fire it was revealed that the sum of £35 had been appropriated from the theatre fund to install gas lights in Newton Hall, which was closed to theatre groups.

Upon intercession by the lieutenant governor, permission was granted for amateurs to use Newton Hall, but no stage scenery was allowed in. A further disadvantage was that, while the hall was nominally free to all legitimate applicants, the cost of hiring and transporting chairs was prohibitive. Then there was the problem of acoustics and the rattle of streetcar bells and iron wheels outside. The situation was clearly intolerable and, realizing that it would probably be years before a new theatre could be built, the *Gleaner* renewed its plea for the old Theatre Royal to be restored. The Public Works Department had said that it could make the building structurally sound by fastening the loose beams and repairing the roof for the modest sum of £50. There was enough money in the theatre fund to carry out these minimal repairs, and the work was put in hand. In June 1880 the paper that had vigorously led the fight to maintain the public Kingston theatre editorialized as follows: "After the vexatious delay and discussion of the last twelve months, the citizens have actually won back for their use the Theatre. . . . We modestly flatter ourselves that the efforts of this journal have contributed to the result."[32]

The struggle to preserve Kingston's theatre against the government's veiled intention to close it down should be seen in the broader context of the political situation then existing in Jamaica. Already the clamor was mounting for political reform. Citizens wanted back their own government that they had lost in 1865 following the Morant Bay uprising. While this had been a government dominated by the plantocracy, the voice of the people could be heard through their elected representatives. In any event home rule was to be preferred to colonial rule. The Kingston theatre, an institution built and supported by the citizenry, came to be viewed as an autogenous symbol whose fate should not be determined by the imperial power.

The Theatre Royal on the Parade was reopened to public performances on June 3, 1880. The bill was a magic show by Professor Philion, "French Illusionist and Wonder Worker" who was already known in Kingston, but negotiations were under way for a professional acting company to take up residency during the racing and festive seasons in November/December. The island had not seen good drama by first-class professionals for seven or more years, and playgoing Kingstonians deplored this hiatus in their cultural life. Though the theatre had been made structurally sound in the short term, it was obvious that a long-range solution warranted more extensive renovations or, preferably, total replacement of the building. Nor was its present appearance inviting to a new company of visiting artistes. The building was in a shabby state, to say the least, hardly emblematic of the pride Kingston took in its distinguished record as a nursery of high-quality theatrical production. To make matters worse, the *New York Dramatic Magazine* at this time published a report that could only add salt to the wound already borne by theatre lovers. It gave a dismal portrait of the aging Theatre Royal:

> Musty, mouldy, and dusty; full of lizards, bats, fleas and creeping creatures of all kinds—a lot of half-fed natives find a shelter in its nooks and corners, who are generally useful by being in the way during the use of the theatre; they are indeed the attachés of this Royal temple of Thespis, but they have not life enough in them to break up a mouse nest or brush down the massive cobwebs.[33]

The report was harsh but not entirely undeserved. The fact is that as the years passed the Theatre Royal lacked proper management. It was the business of the agent and the Theatre Committee to maintain the building in a respectable condition, but the former was not salaried and the latter were now the governor's lackeys with little money to spend on maintenance. As to the backstage attendants, they must have been a motley crew of ill-paid novices. During an 1878 performance of the tower scene in the opera *Il Trovatore,* the stage crew suddenly pulled up the tower flat leaving the tenor singer standing on a ladder in his shirtsleeves, in full view of an audience convulsed with laughter.[34]

In 1870 "the energetic old Agent of the Theatre" was D. M. de Cordova, who that year directed the Kingston Amateurs in a handsomely dressed production of Mary Braddon's *Lady Audley's Secret,* the proceeds from one performance being donated to him in appreciation of his work. De Cordova died in 1876 and was succeeded by the aging Sidney Levien when the *Gleaner,* complaining of the high fees for renting the theatre, suggested that the agent had done nothing to keep the house tidy and should be replaced by a common janitor. Under the terms of his appointment, the agent received no salary but was paid £1 by the producing company for each performance. Since there had been no productions for several months the agent remained unpaid and therefore had little incentive to keep the building clean and tidy. On assuming his job Levien had attempted to charge Kingston amateurs £1 for each rehearsal in the theatre, contending that, as he was responsible for the safety of the building when in use, he had to be present at rehearsals as well as performances. The amateurs promptly disputed the charge, claiming that it violated their contract; they appealed to the board, which upheld their claim.

A further irritant was the cost of lighting. By this time gas had replaced oil and candles for interior illumination. An additional charge of £2 a night for gas was levied and considered preposterously high. Stung by the wave of criticism at home and abroad the Theatre Committee decided to have the auditorium scoured and to tidy up the seats. It had no funds to replace broken benches and suggested that owners of boxes might put in their own chairs temporarily if they wished. With regard to other facilities such as a visiting company might expect to find in place, the Theatre Committee announced that it would be the responsibility of the incoming troupe, which went by the cumbersome name of E. A. McDowell's Vaudeville Company and Canadian Artists, to make the theatre habitable and congenial for themselves and their audiences.

At the height of controversy over the future of the Theatre Royal and sensing an opportunity to provide profitable public entertainment, James Gall opened an auditorium on the lawn of his Myrtle Bank Hotel in lower Kingston. It was open-air and, with a great deal of fanfare, christened the "Politheama." Gall was a feisty Scotsman, born in 1834, and grandson of James Gall of Myrtle Bank, Edinburgh, the founder of literature for the blind. The younger Gall had come to Jamaica to restore his health and decided to settle there. He became a Kingston proprietor, was manager of the *Gleaner* newspaper at the time of the Morant Bay disturbances, after which he published and edited *Gall's Newsletter*, an irregular news sheet of independent views. He advised readers that his amphitheatre was designed "after the style and model of the Politheama of Florence where outdoor amusements are frequent and the climate, like that of Jamaica, suitable."[35] Numbered front seats were provided for ladies and children, beyond which was a promenade and, close by, a restaurant. The arrangement appears to have been nothing more elaborate than a large platform with adjacent retiring rooms facing rows of chairs arranged on the lawn, the whole complex being covered with an awning or tent. Capacity was over five hundred.

In his address at the opening of the Politheama on February 26, 1880, Gall promised a varied program of entertainment including lectures, concerts, panorama, dramatic readings, ventriloquism, performing animals, perhaps a dramatic performance or oratorio by children. Ticket prices for the opening were 2s. for front seats and 1s. for back seats, with children paying half-price. A six-penny ticket gave entrance to the promenade. The featured attraction at the opening performance was Bosco the Magician, whose feats included: (1) the decapitation of a young man; (2) the struggle for life; (3) the bleeding head held up to view; (4) it is magnetized and speaks; (5) it laughs and sings a solo. Gall, a vigorous and contentious Scottish journalist frequently in conflict with the establishment, was not without a sense of mordant humor. He offered himself as the professor's first victim and advertised that he would be beheaded for sedition and libel and would make a last dying speech confessing his shortcomings as an editor.[36]

The Politheama attracted attention for a while as a novel form of entertainment but, judging from the records, it never fulfilled its promise to offer dramatic productions. Variety concerts were billed periodically and a military band played afternoon concerts on the lawn, but mostly it was a theatre of curiosities. Wild beasts were fenced off in one section. During the festive Christmas season of its first year, when the McDowell Company was at the Theatre Royal, the best the Politheama could offer was a bazaar and lottery with dancing on the lawn. The next April, a midget was advertised as weighing only eleven pounds: "a lady perfect in form possessing very handsome features, twelve years old and speaking two languages."[37] Gall's much-touted Politheama turned out to be closer to a Roman circus than an al fresco Florentine theatre.

If the troubles surrounding the dilapidated Theatre Royal curtailed visits by professional players and hindered productions by Kingston's leading amateurs, the situation was not without its brighter side. Many years of active theatregoing by adults and young people no less than the extensive play reviews that appeared with regularity in the Kingston press had created a widespread interest in drama among the educated classes. This interest was reflected in the secondary schools, where dramatic recitation and play scenes were featured at graduation exercises. Eventually senior students and recent graduates began presenting plays and *tableaux vivants* for public consumption on rudimentary platform stages in schoolrooms around the city. Various institutions supported these productions, which were usually done for charitable purposes and from which the school or its affiliated church might be the beneficiary. Between the years 1875 and 1880, for instance, plays were offered in halls at the Collegiate School, the Catholic School, the Convent School, and the Church of England East Branch School in Kingston. Spanish Town also had its college theatre. For the rest of the century these school venues, including the Kingston Academy and the Halfway Tree Boys' School, hosted amateur productions and helped to keep the theatre alive even as they spread its influence away from the centralized Theatre Royal to different parts of the city.

British officers in the army and navy also got into the act. The presence of these forces was far more prominent since the rebellion of 1865. They had played a major and not altogether honorable role in quelling the uprising, and their image needed to be restored. Knowing Jamaica's love of theatre, the officers probably surmised that they could reestablish cordial relations with civilian leaders by putting on plays to which the local gentry would be invited. Whether this presumption was valid or not, it is true that theatre productions at military and naval quarters increased markedly in the last quarter of the century. Shows were announced with fair regularity at stations in Port Royal, Newcastle, Stony Hill, and Up Park Camp, all within easy commuting distance of Kingston. At Up Park Camp the Garrison Theatre was established, which survived into the mid-twentieth century.

In May 1888 the Kingston Parish Church under Archdeacon George Downer opened a new large hall on lower Church Street, Kingston, within one block of the Parade. Known as the Conversorium, the building was intended to provide a spacious meeting room for educational and cultural events as well as a modest performing space for local talent. Its opening presentation was a concert by the visiting Tennessee Jubilee Singers from the United States. This was followed by an exhibition of the Magic Lantern novelty. Because of its central location and unpretentious ambience (the Theatre Royal still required its dress-circle patrons to wear formal evening clothes), the Conversorium was quickly pressed into service for musical concerts and amateur theatricals.

At this time the Theatre Royal was again out of commission owing to its terminally ailing condition. Those who argued strenuously for its reconstruction feared that in a time of economic stringency, the Conversorium might be put forward as a reasonable substitute for the theatre. For this reason critics of productions staged at the new hall were careful to point out its inadequacies. In one instance a presentation of *tableaux* was found to be insufficiently illuminated, the writer declaring that, whether or not limelight was used, the *tableaux* required very strong eyesight to distinguish the forms let alone the features of those taking part. In another case, commenting on a concert given to raise funds toward payment of the cost due on the new hall, the reviewer complained carpingly that the Conversorium "has been the means of cheapening public amusement in this city."[38] Clearly nothing but a restored Theatre Royal would suffice to calm the aroused passions of Kingston's devotees of Thespis.

The impoverished Municipal Board had decided that tenants would have to make the building habitable as a condition of their lease, the Board thus abdicating its role as trustee-proprietor on behalf of Kingston citizens. Before the McDowell Company opened its season of two months in 1880–81, several alterations to the theatre were carried out by the company's designer and stage carpenter. The stage, which had jutted out beyond the proscenium, was thrown back five feet and the old steps "on which actors and audience fraternized" were removed. The space created immediately in front of the stage was put to various uses. The musical director's podium occupied one part and in another a large flower-set water fountain was installed, whose spray was intended to cool the atmosphere between the acts. Additional chairs were arranged in this area to take advantage of the excellent view of the stage from front rows, and 120 comfortable seats were put in the second gallery. On the stage itself borders, "a device unknown here before," were hung overhead and an immense quantity of new scenery was brought in representing drawing rooms, primeval forests, gardens, a baronial hall, and so forth. Commenting on the appearance of the theatre on opening night the *Gleaner's* critic approved of the changes, including the red curtains draped in front of the stage and around the dress circle. He found the lowering of house lights during periods of performance extremely pleasing as it cooled the air and enhanced the artistic effect. However, in his view nothing could be done "to relieve the hideousness of the clumsy, barbaric old benches in the Parquette and Circle."[39] The cost of all these improvements totaled £120, of which the Municipal Board allowed the company £40 in rebate.

Two years later the theatre was again extensively renovated by Burroughs New York Ideal Combination Company, prior to its season opening. On this occasion an entirely new stage was constructed with modern appliances, chairs replaced benches in parts of the house, and the steep staircase by which ladies gained access to the parquette was removed. In its place a broad, newly carpeted stairway was built from the dress circle, thus making the parquette a more desirable section. The extent and cost of these changes prompted one commentator to wonder, seeing that the theatre was aptly dubbed "a barn," whether the outlay had been prudent on the part of Mr. Burroughs.[40]

Despite these sporadic improvements intended to freshen up the appearance of the house each time a major dramatic company arrived on the island, the condition of the Theatre Royal was fundamentally beyond repair. The building leaked profusely in spots, joists had decayed, floorboards were sunken, exits inadequate, gas used for lighting escaped and nauseated players and patrons alike, while the gasoliers on the side walls made the atmosphere unpleasantly oppressive. During one performance by a visiting troupe the scenery, suspended by ropes and pulleys, collapsed as the overhead beams were too rotten to support the weight. In 1888 Agent Levien addressed a letter to the mayor of the reconstituted Kingston City Council pointing out the danger to the public in continued use of the theatre: "When the house is filling it shakes very much as does, also, the East front part. A panic ensuing, even by dirt falling through the sarking which requires repairs, might be fatal to many of our best citizens."[41]

By this time both the *Colonial Standard* and the *Gleaner* newspapers had had enough. They mounted a systematic campaign to save the theatre. The *Standard* began by appealing to the governor to make the present condition of the theatre one of his concerns. It advised the Municipal Council to approach His Excellency for a loan to erect a theatre worthy of the chief city of the West Indies. When government denied the loan because of a lack of security, the *Standard* castigated the governor for refusing a loan of £2,000 to rebuild the theatre when the Legislative Council had recently granted £4,000 for a ballroom and billiard rooms at King's House, amusements that were destined for use by the privileged few. It was, declared the paper, the taxpayers' money and the theatre belonged to the people. It was a question of the many versus the few:

What is more elevating than the legitimate drama? It numbers among its patrons the crowned heads and princes of the world. Why then, in the face of all that has transpired, does the Government not show its sense of right and good taste by initiating also a grant of the requisite amount from General Revenue for building a new Theatre in Kingston, which in its broad interpretation means a new Theatre for Jamaica. One of the chief duties of every well regulated Government is to cater for the amusement of the people. To disregard this, whilst extravagant grants are voted towards the enjoyment of the upper classes, can only be viewed as a most unjust and dangerous administration of affairs.[42]

Government had planned to hold an international trade exhibition in Jamaica in 1891 to boost Jamaican products, and the legislature had voted a sum of £3,000 to the governor for entertainment during the exhibition. This His Excellency had declined in favor of remission of duties on imports for himself and staff. The *Standard* argued that the coming exhibition only increased the need for a proper theatre since an undertaking of this kind without amusements—among which a theatre ever ranked first—was like a dance without music. When government finally consented to a loan of £3,000 toward the theatre, the *Standard* reminded the City Council that alterations or repairs to the existing building would be wasteful and that nothing short of the erection of a new theatre would be acceptable.[43]

The response of the City Council to this hullabaloo was typically bureaucratic. First, in obvious pique, its Theatre Committee recommended that, in view of the constantly recurring calls for repairs, the building and premises should be advertised and sold at public auction and the money realized should be applied for the benefit of the city and parish of Kingston. That the city fathers could so cavalierly dispose of the theatre and its historic site was an indication of the frustration felt on all sides. Nevertheless, the council adopted the recommendation in principle but reserved action on the sale. Then the council reversed itself and instructed the city surveyor to prepare plans and estimates for a theatre to accommodate one thousand people. However, the director of public works withheld approval of the plans, pending further consultation, with the observation that since the theatre was being totally rebuilt, additional funding would be needed. The city surveyor had estimated the cost of reconstruction at £6,000 but the council had only half that sum, which was provided by government.

Meanwhile Jamaica opened its first international exhibition on January 27, 1891. With Prince George of Wales in attendance to do the honors, the pageantry was said years later to be the most brilliant and spectacular ever witnessed in Jamaica. In addition to most Caribbean islands, foreign nations participating in the event included Canada, England, India, Russia, and several European countries. The exhibition grounds, covering an area of twenty-three acres, were located in a park to the north of the Kingston Race Course, and a number of impressive pavilions were constructed, all necessarily of a temporary nature, including "an Exhibition Hall or theatre, a large and commodious building with all conveniences for the purpose for which it is intended, although not architecturally prepossessing."[44]

For most of the three-month-long event, this hall was occupied by the London Dramatic Company, which presented a season of light comedies and farces aimed at attracting some of the 300,000 visitors who passed through the exhibition gates. At the same time, the McDowell Dramatic Company paid its third visit to the island to play in the aging Theatre Royal. Thus for the first time in fifty years Kingston was host simultaneously to two professional theatre troupes offering a lively theatrical scene in keeping with the city's well-earned reputation for dramatic art while it was on show to an international gathering. The exhibition closed on May 2 and the hall, with its performing stage, was subsequently dismantled along with other buildings on the fairgrounds.

The trade exhibition came and went, the visiting companies departed, and Kingston was still left with its old decaying Theatre Royal. It was now the *Gleaner*'s turn once more to take up the cudgel. In a January 1893 editorial captioned "Our Shabby Theatre," the paper summarized the negotiations that had taken place and proposed that a more modest renovation be undertaken with the available funds. Then it began to publish a series of long historical articles, under the general title "Kingston's Disgrace," in which it attempted to survey the entire record of theatre activities in Jamaica from earliest times. Its purpose was clear; it would justify the claim that the Kingston theatre was a venerable institution, that it belonged to the people, that the council held it in trust, and that the building should now be promptly remodeled for the sum of money in hand. The paper ended its series of essays with a hard-hitting editorial that charged:

6. New Theatre Royal, 1897. Photograph © reserved,
National Library of Jamaica.

A moral obligation rests upon the existing municipal body to put
the building into such a state as will bring it into harmony with
the times. . . . The City Council are taking an unconscionable
long period to come to the point, which is the complete re-
habilitation of the building . . . their duty is plain, nothing should
now hinder them from placing the building in a satisfactory state
before many months pass away.[45]

Nearly three more years would indeed pass before the *Gleaner*
would be able to publish a drawing by the city surveyor of the proposed new Kingston theatre. The heavy hand of bureaucracy had had
its way. Plans had been drawn and revised, estimates made and hag-
gled over. Recommendations had gone from the Theatre Committee
to the council, to a special committee, to the governor, and back to the
council for referral to the Theatre Committee and then to the council.

7. Interior of New Theatre Royal, 1897. Photograph © reserved,
National Library of Jamaica.

The *Gleaner* sighed wearily: "In the absence of a proper theatre and a play, the antics of the municipal authorities provide some compensating amusement for the tired community."[46] Finally, early in 1896 extensive reconstruction was begun on the Kingston playhouse.

By this time council members considered themselves experts on theatre architecture. The mayor suggested that an opening be left in the roof of the new theatre so that fireworks could be fired from it, but Councillor Alexander countered that the roof should be used as a promenade. Then a contretemps developed over who should open the new theatre. Two parties had applied for opening night: one representing "the Jewish element" was expected to draw a bigger house, but the other was a city councillor with clout. Morton Tavares, a distinguished Jamaican professional actor in failing health, felt that he should have priority by virtue of his past dramatic achievements, which were indeed impressive, but he offered to waive that right if the

8. Colonel Charles James Ward

Kingston Dramatic Association would cast him in the lead of Boucicault's *London Assurance* (a part he had always wanted to play) and
advance him the cash to defray the expenses of his wardrobe. The
association, not wanting to affront Mr. Tavares, explained that it had
already chosen and cast its next play.

In spite of endless bickering the new theatre opened on January 28,
1897 [fig. 6]. Mayor Stern, acting unilaterally, had invited the Dramatic Club of St. George's College to revive the drama *The Hidden
Gem*, written by Cardinal Nicholas Patrick Wiseman, and previously
staged at school closing exercises in June. This was a play whose
probity could hardly be challenged and, moreover, the performance
was designed as a benefit for the theatre itself. A formal opening
ceremony preceded the drama with the governor, Sir Henry Blake, the
mayor and council, prominent citizens, and the regimental band in

68

full attendance. The mayor's action was meant to emphasize the principle that the playhouse was intended to serve Jamaican theatre groups first, with reasonable seasons reserved for touring professionals of high quality.

The new theatre, designed by the Jamaican architect Victor Abrahams, was a magnificent structure very different from its predecessor. The imposing flight of steps leading to the front of the old building had been removed and the frontage brought forward to create more interior space. The steps were seen as a potential hazard in case patrons had to make speedy egress from the building, so the main entrance was now on a level with the pavement. The style of the facade was reminiscent of the Italian Renaissance with columns, pilasters, Ionic mouldings, cornices, and tasteful decorations topped by a balustrade. Within the building a spacious lobby fifty feet by twenty feet gave admittance to the pit and provided a double stairway leading to the dress-circle foyer. There was a special entrance to the gallery from a side lane where tickets could be purchased.

Considerable care had been taken with the interior arrangements [fig. 7]. Chairs replaced benches throughout the house and could be tipped up to admit easy passage between the rows of seats. They were provided with attachments for hats and sticks. Electric light replaced

9. Ward Theatre, built 1912.

gas. A dress circle replaced boxes except for two proscenium boxes intended for the governor and the mayor respectively. There were numerous exits: four from the pit, five from the dress circle, and six from the gallery. Backstage were comfortable dressingrooms for actors and a commodious greenroom. The stage area was considerably enlarged and measured sixty feet by thirty feet, with a height of thirty-five feet from floor to gridiron and a nine-foot substage clearance. Fly galleries were fitted on either side. The proscenium allowed an opening thirty-three feet wide and twenty-six feet high. Four border strip lights overhead and footlights to the front of the stage floor were all electric, governed by an electric switchboard installed on the prompt side of the stage. A splendid set of new scenery had been imported consisting of twelve complete scenes, and there were two stage curtains, an asbestos fire curtain painted to represent drapery, and a second, or act drop curtain representing a Japanese landscape that had been supplied by a Chicago studio. The capacity of the house was nine hundred. The reconstruction cost was £5,500, the entire sum being a loan from the government.[47]

Sidney Levien, the old agent, had fortuitously died in 1895 and a much younger man, a printer and amateur baritone singer named A. M. Sollas, was appointed manager of the new facility. Offering congratulations to all those responsible for the new theatre, the souvenir program for the opening ceremonies crowed: "His Worship the Mayor will have in the Theatre at least one enduring monument of his fruitful labours on behalf of the citizens of Kingston."[48] It was not to be. Just ten years after its grand opening, this attractive and well-appointed building was destroyed in the great earthquake of 1907. Its foundations were so badly shaken that it had to be completely demolished. This was a tragedy of enormous proportions for theatre devotees. No one could realistically expect government, at a time of national calamity, to provide funds once again to rebuild the theatre.

For five years Kingston was without its beloved Theatre Royal. Other available buildings, notably the Conversorium on Church Street, were pressed into service, the latter hosting visiting Italian opera companies in 1910 and 1912. The demand for a proper theatre, however, never ceased and persuaded the custos of Kingston, Colonel Charles James Ward [fig. 8], the "nephew" in the well-known firm of J. Wray and Nephew, to make a most magnanimous gift. At a cost of £12,000, and on the same spot where Kingston theatres have stood since 1775, Colonel Ward had the theatre rebuilt and presented to the mayor and council on December 16, 1912. Called the Ward Theatre, it was constructed by the Henriques Brothers and described at the time as "unquestionably the best theatre anywhere in the West Indies, including Cuba" [fig. 9].[49] The Ward Theatre, recently restored, has rendered yeoman service to the city of Kingston and all Jamaica for over three-quarters of a century.

4

Plays and Players

 Actors are inveterate nomads. They are forever seeking greener pastures. This habit has pervaded the profession from its earliest days in the Western world. The ancient Greeks revered their actors as servants of the god Dionysus, exempted them from military service, and gave them diplomatic passports to travel freely through the Hellenic states in order to perform. The Romans were too busy administering their newly conquered territories to pay much attention to actors, most of whom were of low estate, even slaves. But the Romans did build theatres in their far-flung cities, or at least they restored and adapted the amphitheatres left by the Greeks. Bound to their company manager, the *dominus gregis*, Roman actors traveled throughout the empire performing their comedies, farces, and occasional Greco-Roman tragedies. Even the emperor Nero, we are told, went to Athens to compete in a theatrical contest in which he was judiciously allowed to win the first prize.

In Renaissance Italy, professional acting troupes in improvised farces embroidered the magnificent spectacles that were produced at ducal courts. When Catherine de Medici married Henry II, King of France, one of her first diplomatic acts was to host a visit by the Italian Commedia players from Florence. They were so popular that Italian comedy became a permanent part of the French theatrical scene and had a profound influence on the young Molière when he began writing his plays. A similar cross-fertilization had occurred two thousand years earlier when traveling companies from Athens, performing at the Greek colony of Syracuse and elsewhere in southern Italy, stimulated the writing of the first plays by Roman authors.

Strolling players in England had a much harder time initially. Because they were always on the move, their way of life was deemed wayward and dissolute and a bad influence on God-fearing parishioners. They were dubbed rogues and vagabonds by Puritan authorities and driven out of town, the content of their plays being suspect by civic rulers. Their performances were seen as disruptive of the orderly daily routine, drawing honest people away from work to indulge in frivolous if not licentious pleasures. Actors were forced to perform beyond city limits until noblemen took them under their protection as chamber grooms. Then, wearing their sponsor's livery as a shield, these English troupers could travel safely from one township to another seeking out new audiences. Even Shakespeare's company, based at the Globe Theatre in London, took to the road at times.

In the eighteenth century small groups of English professionals brought Shakespeare's plays to France and Germany, where they were much admired by a young Goethe, who saw them as the true model on which to build an emerging German drama. In the nineteenth century the great black American actor, Ira Aldridge, unable to perform in his own country because of his race, went to England, developed his skill in performance around the British provinces, then took Shakespeare across Europe and Russia playing a range of heroic characters to universal acclaim. Performing his roles in English with local companies speaking their native tongue, he visited several cities that had never before seen Shakespeare on stage.

In West Africa the Yoruba people also had their professional traveling theatre, originally known as the "Alarinjo." The earliest account of a performance by one of these companies before the Alaafin (king) of Oyo and his guests in 1826 is given in the journals of Hugh Clapperton and Richard Lander.[1] In tracing the history of this theatre, J. A. Adedeji found that it descended, about 1590, from the *egungun* (masquerade) cult, which was a form of ancestor worship. Troupes were at first attached to the king's household and performed as a recognized part of court entertainment, but eventually they became fully professional and took to the road, playing before the masses. As Adedeji reports, "the troupes were exposed to all kinds of dire situations and, sometimes, awful experiences when they travelled from place to place."[2] They used charms for protection, sang praise songs to a town before entering the gates, and began each performance with a salute to earth.

The Western theatrical tradition, as we have seen, came to Jamaica around 1682 when a public theatre was reported to be on the island. The fabled wealth of Jamaica coupled with the romance of pirates and buccaneers must have seemed an irresistible lure to English actors venturing across miles of ocean to seek their fortune. One report of the time speaks of Port Royal, before its destruction by an earthquake in 1692, as the storehouse or treasury of the West Indies, with its "bars and cakes of gold, wedges and piggs of silver, pistoles, pieces of eight . . . wrought plate, jewels and rich pearl necklaces,"[3] a regular pirate's dream of plundered treasure. There is, however, no record of a touring theatrical troupe's arrival on the island in the late seventeenth century. If professionals did in fact come at this time they were probably intrepid individuals from England or America on exploratory visits.[4] They could have recruited a company from among the early colonists and played for a season or two before moving on.

Lacking evidence to the contrary, we must assume that actors in the theatre of this period were mostly nonprofessional, that is, gentlemen and military amateurs residing in Jamaica. The gentlemen amateurs would have been well-to-do settlers with a yen for the stage who came together periodically to present a play on a special occasion. The army and navy players had a tradition of theatrical entertainment that British officers organized at overseas stations to while away the long hours of tedium in military life. Their plays provided a healthy diversion for themselves and their citizen friends. Sometimes they would stage performances to raise funds for a deserving local charity or for the relief of distressed persons, thus winning friends among the populace they had been sent to protect and control.

The earliest named professional troupe in the American colonies is the Company of Comedians led by Walter Murray and Thomas Kean who performed Shakespeare and other English plays in various eastern towns from 1749 to 1751. It is unclear whether this troupe came from England as an established company or more probably recruited its members from settlers already in the colonies. There had been earlier attempts by groups of actors to produce a season of plays in America, notably at Charleston, South Carolina, where the Dock Street Theatre was built in 1736. These companies were either composed of amateurs or, if professional, seem to have been short-lived. The Charleston season, for instance, lasted but six weeks, after which the company apparently disbanded and the theatre was advertised for sale.[5]

If we can trust the information supplied in a theatrical anecdote published over a hundred years later, one of the earliest recorded English professional companies to come to the New World landed in Jamaica in 1733.[6] Company members reportedly made a good deal of money and on their opening night of John Gay's *The Beggar's Opera* took in 370 pistoles, a pistole at this time being a Spanish coin worth about $3.80 or slightly more than £1. The company, however, was dogged by misfortune. The Jamaican fever and rum punch took a savage toll of their numbers, and within two months the actors playing Polly, Mrs. Slammekin, Filch, and two other members of Macheath's gang were buried. Some local amateurs filled in and tried to keep the enterprise going, but this did not last long. In a short time other members succumbed until only three of the original corps were left: an old man, a woman, and a boy. This shattered remnant embarked with their earnings of 2,000 pistoles to join another company then playing in Charleston (this may have been the 1736 troupe), but their ship was lost at sea and they too perished.

It is not possible to identify the members of this ill-fated company, and only the one play with which they opened their season is known. Gay's musical drama, *The Beggar's Opera,* thus becomes the first recorded production in Jamaica. It was played there only five years after its premiere in London, where it was a decided hit. The play presented many unique features that accounted for its popularity, and its success is pertinent to efforts to establish a Jamaican national drama and theatre. At a time when Italian opera was enjoying a considerable vogue in London, *The Beggar's Opera* was unabashedly a homegrown product. It satirized the artificiality of the foreign form and it rejected the highfalutin musical composition associated with grand opera, using instead its own musical arrangements based on popular English folk songs. Its characters were not legendary heroes, noblemen, or solid bourgeoisie but common English folk who scuffled for a living—highwaymen, cutpurses, pickpockets, streetwise women, and receivers of stolen goods. They were shown to have a stronger sense of morality and loyalty than people in high places. The play was also political. By analogy it criticized the corrupt government of Prime Minister Sir Robert Walpole, who, seated prominently in a VIP box on opening night at the Lincoln Inn's Fields Theatre in London, applauded louder than anyone else. The reception accorded the play was so overwhelming that Sir Robert, who was privately incensed at the veiled attack on his administration, could do little about it. However, he had his revenge later when Gay's next play, *Polly,* was denied a production permit for close on fifty years.

No one in eighteenth-century Jamaica was able to apply the moral of *The Beggar's Opera* to the local theatrical scene. The common folk of that society were black slaves or working-class freemen whose experiences and amusements were thought to be irrelevant to the cultural ethos of the island. The cross-fertilization that took place in other countries as a result of visits from foreign professionals could not flourish in this setting. Despite a population in 1740 of 10,000 whites to 100,000 blacks,[7] Jamaica was an English colony in name and nature; visiting companies performed primarily for an English or European clientele. More than a century later conscious attempts would be made to rediscover and reassert black culture in order to redress the imbalance caused by decades of suppression and neglect.

The disaster that befell that first touring company of 1733 did not deter others from trying. Sugar was in its heyday and the Jamaican economy prospered. According to contemporary chroniclers, another English professional troupe of "extraordinary good actors" was installed in the Spanish Town theatre in 1740 and 1741, but we are told nothing of their names or their repertoire.[8] They must have moved out after a few years, most likely to America, for when the jaunty Scottish actor, John Moody, arrived in Jamaica in 1745 he found only an amateur company performing in a ballroom in Kingston, then rapidly expanding as the chief port and commercial center of the island. In the mid-eighteenth century, with twelve hundred houses and storehouses, it contained more than twice the number of dwelling houses as Spanish Town.[9]

Moody promptly got himself elected star actor, and working with the amateur players, he staged a number of Shakespearean plays including *Hamlet, King Lear, Macbeth,* and *Romeo and Juliet.* Shakespeare's invasion of the Jamaican theatre had begun in earnest. Moody was so enthralled with the financial prospects of managing a professional troupe in Kingston that within a year he returned to England to recruit his own company. We know precious little of this company or of the plays it performed, though we can be certain that more Shakespeare was done and that, as usual, the Jamaican fever took its fateful toll of the players.[10] By one account Moody left for England a second time to muster reinforcements for his depleted troupe, but he was persuaded to remain there, leaving two of his acting colleagues in charge of the Kingston company.[11] These were David Douglass and Owen Morris.

The next series of events is of utmost significance to the future of the Jamaican theatre. It began in London in 1750 when William Hallam, who belonged to a theatrical family, having accumulated a sizable debt as a theatre manager, decided to try and recoup his fortunes by sending a company out to America with his brother, Lewis, in charge. They sailed in the *Charming Sally* and after a six-week crossing this professional troupe, later to become known as the American Company of Comedians, arrived at Yorktown, Virginia, in May 1752. The company consisted of eight men, four women, and three of Lewis Hallam's children, two of whom were juvenile actors. With a repertoire of twenty-four plays, including four of Shakespeare's, eight farces or afterpieces, and a pantomime, the company opened at Williamsburg, Virginia, in *The Merchant of Venice.* Lewis Hallam, Jr., then only twelve years old, appeared as a servant to Portia and was dreadful. He was destined to become the leading actor-manager in America after the Revolutionary War.

Core members of this company paid their first visit to Jamaica from 1755 to 1758 to extend their circuit and possibly to recruit new talent. Lewis Hallam, who had then been ailing, died within a year and the Hallam company merged with the remnants of Moody's troupe then being managed by David Douglass. Although the few scattered issues of Jamaican papers shed no light on the productions of this company during its three-year sojourn in Jamaica, there is reason to believe, as shown in chapter 2, that it was active in its new theatre on Harbour Street. In any event Douglass married the widow Hallam after two years and in 1758 led the company back north to the American colonies, where it toured the eastern seaboard, opening a number of theatres in various cities.

According to the American theatre historian William Dunlap, the theatrical empire of this touring group stretched from Newport, Rhode Island, in the east to Williamsburg, Virginia, in the south, with occasional performances in Annapolis, Philadelphia, and New York, and in smaller places where a courthouse could be transformed into a theatre.[12] With the advent of the American Revolutionary War, the company in 1775 repaired once more to Jamaica, where it played for ten years, finally leaving the island in 1785.

The American company spent a total of thirteen years in Jamaica performing seasons chiefly in Kingston and Montego Bay, with occasional visits to Spanish Town. Apart from periods of wartime emergency, when theatres were closed or commandeered to quarter troops, the company played either three times a week on Tuesday, Thursday, and Saturday or four times on Monday, Wednesday, Thursday, and Saturday, with a change of bill weekly or biweekly. As a rule an evening's entertainment would comprise a full-length comedy, tragedy, comic opera, or drama followed by a farcical afterpiece. Between the acts or to round off the evening there might also be a comic song or dance, an instrumental solo, or a monologue recitation. For instance, between February 6 and December 8, 1781, the company presented twenty-five major plays and an equal number of farces or pantomimes, among which were two original pieces written by members of the troupe. The offerings that year included Shakespeare's *Hamlet, Measure for Measure, Romeo and Juliet,* and *Richard III,* all no doubt suitably edited to suit the taste of the period and the size of the company. (*The Tempest, Hamlet, The Merchant of Venice,* and *Macbeth* had been given the previous season.) Additional plays staged in

1781 were by Dryden, Sheridan, Isaac Bickerstaffe, David Garrick, Mrs. Centlivre, George Farquhar, Samuel Foote, and other contemporary writers. Overall, Shakespeare, Cumberland, Mrs. Centlivre, Garrick, and Sheridan were most frequently produced. Bickerstaffe's *The Padlock* proved to be the most popular farce; the relations between the comic slave and his doltish master obviously delighted audiences as a burlesque on the social conditions prevalent on the island.

Richardson Wright details the activities of this company and their changing membership. He overlooks the fact that the younger Hallam, who joined the company sometime after their opening season in 1775, assumed management in 1779, thereby displacing both Douglass, who later became a prosperous printer in Jamaica, and John Henry, who had managed the company in a successful 1777 run in Montego Bay and perhaps on its return to Spanish Town and Kingston. This move probably led to a rupture in the ranks, for Henry fails to appear with the company in 1779–80, an absence that did not go unnoticed by the public. By June 1781 the breach was healed and Henry was named comanager with Hallam, prompting the *Jamaica Magazine* to remark: "The late Union of Managers gives us room to hope for considerable improvements in the conduct of our theatre."[13]

In summary, the American company made several contributions to the Jamaican theatre. First, the company was directly responsible for the building or fitting up of theatre facilities in the three principal towns of the island: Kingston, Spanish Town, and Montego Bay. The availability of these theatres stimulated increased production by resident amateurs and army players. Next, the professional company recruited Jamaican residents into its ranks and helped spread the theatrical reputation of the island so that when these actors later played in New York, they were billed as "fresh from the theatre in Jamaica." Third, the company from time to time allowed talented amateurs to appear in its plays, thus improving the skills of the nonprofessionals who lived on the island and were responsible for maintaining live theatre between visits of the touring companies. Fourth, members of the company composed and staged the first plays about Jamaica that were written from firsthand experience on the island. Fifth, the American company demonstrated a capacity for managing a commercial theatre enterprise when in 1780 Lewis Hallam offered his subscription plan to the public. Finally, two of the company's managers served as Master of the Revels: David Douglass in 1779–80 and Hallam in 1781–83. This position made them the principal authorities over theatrical affairs on the island. Unquestionably, the American Company of Comedians, in collaboration with its

Jamaican supporters, provided a level of theatrical experience that Jamaican audiences would be loath to forgo in the difficult days ahead. The single area in which this record can be faulted is theatrical criticism. At no time in the local press was there a serious critical review of performances by the company such as might have helped to build a discriminating public for the theatre. That would come later.

It would be unreasonable to expect that the plays presented in a theatre so strongly reflective of contemporary stage practice in England and America would have much to say about Jamaican life. As shall presently be seen, there were in fact first attempts at composing plays for the Kingston stage as well as a number of commentaries on local affairs, couched in dramatic form, that were published in local papers to be read rather than performed. Those plays by established playwrights that purported to speak of the Jamaican or West Indian experience were inspired mostly by the antislavery campaign in England, their authors being unfamiliar with the reality of life in the Caribbean. Some of these plays found their way to the Jamaican boards.

In the repertoire of the Hallam company, two plays were regularly presented that had some relevance to the local scene. One was the previously mentioned comic opera, *The Padlock* (1768), in which Mungo, slave to old Don Diego, is set to guard a young woman whom his master hopes to force into marriage. Although the part of Mungo is undeniably clownish, his impudent retorts to the pantalonic Don Diego suggest a smouldering resentment of his condition, which finally erupts in the epilogue, reputedly added to the script by a worthy clergyman:

> Thank you, my massas. Have you laugh your fill?
> Then let me speak, nor take that freedom ill . . .
> I am a slave, when all things else are free,
> Yet I was born, as you are, no man's slave.
> An heir to all that lib'ral Nature gave.
> My thoughts can reason, and my limbs can love . . .
> Comes freedom then from colour? Blush with shame
> And let strong nature's crimson mask your blame.[14]

It is safe to assume that the play, as presented in Jamaica in no less than ten recorded productions between 1777 and 1813, did not conclude with Mungo's epilogue. With slavery ended in 1834, the play vanished from the Jamaican theatre and has never been revived.

The second play in the repertoire of the American company that bore reference to Jamaica is Richard Cumberland's *The West Indian* (1771). A wealthy young Jamaican Creole, accustomed to ordering slaves around, arrives in England, where his honest but impetuous nature leads temporarily to complications. All is put right in the end and he wins the lady of his choice. In the comedy the West Indian character is portrayed as hot-blooded and generous with an engaging frankness and levity. Yet another play of the period was the operetta *Inkle and Yarico* (1787), written by George Colman the Younger and based on a legend of earlier vintage. It was produced in Jamaica by Mr. Mahon's troupe in 1788, a year after its premiere in England. Yarico is the beautiful African (or, in some versions, Indian) girl who, in return for saving the life of the English adventurer, Inkle, with whom she falls in love, is taken by him and sold into slavery. The theme, according to one editor of the play, was intended "to stimulate the already awakening sympathy of the British public, in behalf of the untutored, fettered, friendless blacks."[15]

As previously noted, Kingston Jews were most active in promoting professional and amateur productions and in maintaining a proper functioning playhouse in the city. Plays about Jews were therefore of particular interest to this sector of the theatregoing public. Shakespeare's *The Merchant of Venice* was a favored piece with the American company and was, in fact, its inaugural production this side of the Atlantic. The younger Hallam played Shylock in the company's 1780 production in Kingston. Two farces produced in Jamaica in this period were Cumberland's *The Jew Outwitted* by the American company in 1783 and Charles Dibdin's *The Jew and the Doctor*, produced by the company of Messrs. Manning and Read and Mrs. Shaw at the Kingston theatre in 1813. The same year witnessed two performances of Cumberland's comedy *The Jew; or, The Benevolent Hebrew*, which was repeated in 1815. There was also a pantomime titled *Jerusalem Delivered* presented by the French Theatre in 1809. Like the black ones, Jewish characters were stock figures of fun in the English-speaking theatre of this period, but we have no report on how these plays were received by the Jewish community. As the century unfolded and freed blacks became a force to be reckoned with in society, the light skin of Jamaican Jews transcended the prejudice directed at their religion and ethnic origin, thus enabling them to be assimilated socially into white Jamaican society. Touring professionals quickly sensed that they could be guaranteed reasonably strong support if they presented plays sympathetic toward Jewry. Hence the following pathetic dramas appeared on the Kingston stage in the years ahead: *The Jewess of Notre Dame*, *The Jewish Mother*, and two adaptations of H. S. Mosenthal's *Deborah*, namely, Augustin Daly's *Leah, the Forsaken* and Charles Cheltnam's *Deborah; or, The Jewish Maiden's Wrong*.

The American company left the island in July 1785. One might have expected a healthy surge of amateur activity in the wake of the company's departure. Unfortunately, there are no Kingston papers extant for 1786 or 1787, and only a few copies survive for 1788. These reveal that one or two members of Hallam's troupe who had fallen in love with the island had remained behind. They did attempt to keep theatre alive with amateur talent under the direction of Mr. Mahon, a lyric theatre actor lately arrived from England. They presented several comic operas and farces in Kingston to half-filled houses. After the Hallam professionals, these players must have seemed quite raw. Mahon also started a theatrical club in Spanish Town in 1788 and was able to present two short seasons late that year and during the February Court in 1789, but events beyond his control undermined all efforts.

Hurricanes and earthquakes, economic troubles caused by absentee ownership of estates, the slave revolt in neighboring Saint Domingue, slave uprisings, and Maroon wars at home preoccupied the island in the last decade of the eighteenth and the early years of the nineteenth century. Above all, talk of slave emancipation was in the air, given credence by the abolition of the slave trade in British possessions in 1807. Apart from a few short runs of light opera at the Kingston theatre by French actors fleeing the upheaval in Saint Domingue, there is no record of sustained dramatic activity until October 1812, when a company recently arrived from Barbados and managed by Charles Manning, Jesse Read, and Mrs. Elizabeth Shaw took up residence at the theatre in Kingston.

For the past twenty-five years the public had been fed mostly circus acts and spectacles where noisy crowds were tolerated. As a result their behavior in the theatre, never exemplary, had deteriorated. The opening performance of the Manning/Shaw company on October 12 contained a prologue in rhymed verse, written by a Kingston gentleman. Twenty-seven of its fifty-five lines appealed for proper audience conduct. The house was crowded, the audience attentive, and the season was off to a fine start except that receipts for the first night totaled only £438 because "several persons had false tickets and a considerable part of the monies taken at the doors was unaccounted for."[16] This news could not have cheered poor Manning whose constitution could not have been very resilient. After a farewell performance as Hamlet in the middle of the season, he left for England with his family and died there in December 1813.

With Manning gone, Mrs. Shaw and Read kept the season going until September 1813, when the Kingston theatre was closed owing to

Mrs. Shaw's indisposition. Actually, the company was running out of steam, playing no more than once a week and reviving old pieces. Thus it was with a measure of relief that it greeted the arrival, in March 1814, of William Adamson and some members of his company, who had left Barbados "because of lack of support in that colony."[17] The combined companies mounted seasons of plays in Kingston and Spanish Town over the next three or four years (records are spotty at this time), but not without encountering serious difficulties, both internal and external.

Adamson had earlier worked with Read and Mrs. Shaw in Barbados, where the lady trouper had a reputation for being troublesome. The new combination did not always work smoothly. Monk Lewis, the English writer on a visit to his Jamaican estates, reports that although the professional troupe had no more than twenty members, squabbles between Adamson and Mrs. Shaw caused a rift and half of the company left to begin performing at Falmouth. Lewis also gives a rather scathing review of the company's production of his tragedy *Adelgitha* at the Kingston theatre in a benefit for Mrs. Shaw. Adamson was not in the cast but Mrs. Shaw played the title role. Lewis considered his outing at the theatre to be "an ill-starred expedition . . . the scenery and dresses were shabby, the actors wretched, and the stage ill-lighted." The author, he wrote, had meant Adelgitha to be killed in the last act, not murdered in all five. Only the heroine, a professional player for whose benefit the drama was presented, was tolerable, "but she was old enough and fat enough for the Widow Cheshire." There was also a young Jamaican Jew in the cast, merely fifteen years old, but dignified locally with the name of "The Creole Roscius."[18] Of this young actor whose name was John Castello, more will be told later.

As company manager Adamson was a tough, strong-willed individual and a good match for the redoubtable Mrs. Shaw. It was he who had built the stairway in a side lane for colored patrons, causing a riot at the Kingston theatre; and one of his own players once publicly accused him of "tyranny and oppression."[19] Yet he was talented and energetic. He helped to restore the Spanish Town theatre in 1814 and refurbished Kingston's playhouse the following year, winning approval of the City Council for his efforts as manager. He produced seasons of plays at Kingston, Spanish Town, and Montego Bay for three years and had recruited additional players, including the lyric stage performers, Mr. and Mrs. Hill, from England. One newspaper columnist was moved to call him "a man possessed of genius, talent and experience [who has] made the theatre of Kingston an ornament and an honour to the city."[20] Even Adamson's constitution, however, was not proof against the virulent Jamaican fever that had claimed his infant son and several of his players including Jesse Read and Miss Montfort. When he succumbed on June 6, 1818, his loss was gravely felt by the comedians.

The mantle of company manager fell to Mr. Burnett, who struggled to keep the players active for several more seasons. The time was unpropitious, and it was becoming increasingly difficult to support a quality professional troupe in Kingston. Admitting that his efforts had met with ill success "owing to late calamitious sickness and other unforeseen accidents," in 1819 Burnett introduced a trained dog "Dragon" in the production of William Barrymore's *The Dog of Montargis, or The Forest of Bondy*, which had three performances in Kingston and two in Spanish Town. He brought in local amateurs to strengthen the company with their talent and the box office with their supporters. These strategies helped temporarily, but by 1821 the agent of the Kingston theatre, Mr. Lyon, whose stipend was derived from a percentage of ticket sales, announced that "in consequence of the decrease of the Theatrical Company" arrangements had been made for gymnasts and animal shows to be exhibited at the theatre. This development so outraged one patron that he wrote in protest: "It is impossible that the Theatre can be more disgraced than it is at present, by the frequent exhibition of 'Cups and Balls', 'Learned Pigs', etc. . . . Oh! shame, that a Theatre erected for the legitimate Drama should have so far dwindled from its original intent as to permit such exhibitions within its walls."[21] Officers of the Kingston Garrison came to the rescue with three performances of Thomas Morton's *Speed the Plough* and an appropriate farce, half the net proceeds from the first show being given to Mr. Lyon. Other income went to keep the building in good repair and to the fund for widows and orphans of deceased soldiers who belonged to regiments stationed on the island. The resident comedians rallied for one more season in 1822 before dispersing.

There was at this time a sizable French-speaking community in Jamaica, mostly urbanites. Some thousands had been brought to the island as prisoners of the Anglo-French wars in the Caribbean in the late eighteenth century. Refugees from the revolution in France had come to the island via America. More recently, numerous others had fled the slave revolt in nearby Saint Domingue. Among these aliens were people of culture, musicians especially, who gave concerts and had found employment in theatre orchestras. Now with a dearth of English-speaking companies for the Kingston theatre, French residents were eager to lend support to a francophone stage. Many regular

Jamaican theatregoers could also be counted on to show support, intrigued as they would be by the French style of acting, by the singing, music, and pantomime. In 1824 a French operatic company under Mr. and Mrs. Armand inhabited the Kingston theatre for five months playing Saturdays only. Its fare, a welcome antidote to times of foreboding, consisted of comic operettas, vaudevilles, and melodramas. Then in April 1827 Mr. and Mrs. Castel, with a lean company of six more men, began a season that must have proved so successful that, apart from an infrequent interruption to make way for an amateur production, the company held the theatre until they were displaced by the English Company in April 1829. They performed twice weekly, sprinkling their light fare with the occasional drama or tragedy.

The English Company that succeeded the Castels was recruited from players resident in Jamaica. Chief among them were Mrs. Monier, a New York actress in equestrian shows and melodrama "who was admired for her beauty and was not without some merit as an actress,"[22] and her daughter Virginia, then a child of eleven years. She played bit parts and sang and danced in interludes. John Castello was the leading male actor, and Mr. Jones was the company manager. Altogether there were six men and four women in the company, which was filled out, when necessary, by amateurs. The English troupe inhabited the Kingston theatre for five months, playing twice weekly. Its repertoire was made up of slight comedies and farces, with August Kotzebue's The Stranger, John Home's Douglas, and Richard Sheil's Evadne the only serious works undertaken. For her benefit night Miss Virginia played the youth Norval in Douglas, a performance that brought enthusiastic applause from the audience as well as the critic. This young woman went on to become a leading actress on the New York stage, playing opposite the famous Edwin Forrest at the National Theatre a decade later.

It was left to the Kingston amateurs to bring a tinge of respectability back to the theatre, in ambition if not actual accomplishment. According to incomplete records, they staged Macbeth, Venice Preserv'd, and She Stoops to Conquer in the early 1830s. The review of Macbeth, tongue-in-cheek though it was, is one of the earliest available for nonprofessionals. Macbeth was played by Bailey, Barrett took the part of Malcolm, and Lady Macbeth was played by a man. Macduff, "one of the best performances of the night," had nevertheless a squeaky voice, and Banquo was overly made up as the Ghost, displaying "a tremendous thump in the eye." Scenery and dresses were remarkably good. The highlight of the performance came when Macbeth's nose "was well nigh shorn off its tip by the gigantic efforts of the frisky Siward who, in his attempts to vanquish the illustrious tyrant, gave his *pas-de-deux* with such goodwill, that it took effect on the proboscis of Mr. B." Bailey, however, bore it with nonchalance and finished his part in gallant style.[23] Notwithstanding these brave efforts the Jamaican theatre lacked the vitality of past times. An extensive slave insurrection in 1831–32 and the impending freedom of a quarter of a million black slaves in 1834 were enough cause for anxiety in the minds of theatre folk.

That touring companies from abroad did not wholly shun Jamaica during these uncertain times can be seen in the report of Mrs. John Drew, well-known actor and manager of the American stage. As a child of eleven, she was taken to Jamaica with a company managed by her father, the English actor Thomas Lane. They left New York in November 1830, and were ten days out when their ship hit a rock off Saint Domingue, stranding them in that country for six weeks. Eventually they arrived in Kingston, where the company, according to report, performed quite successfully. Then the yellow fever struck. It killed her father, her ten-month-old sibling, and almost carried off her mother. On the doctor's advice, the company went north to Falmouth to recuperate, but rumors of a slave revolt in those parts forced them to return to Kingston, "my mother and myself [being] driven by the leader of the orchestra, Mr. Myers, across the country." Finally they embarked again for New York, then to Philadelphia where they arrived during the first cholera season.[24] The actor's life was no less eventful offstage than on.

With Emancipation won and the new governor, Sir Charles Metcalfe, installed in King's House, work soon began on a new theatre to replace the ramshackle one on the Parade. Meanwhile there was no lack of popular amusements to fill the leisure hours of the Kingstonians who could afford the price of a ticket. For 6s.8d., with half-price for children, they could attend "the Theatre at 21 Harbour Street, formerly the Optical Exhibition Theatre," where during the months of September and October 1839, Don Juan Dal Ponte presented "the famous tragical performance entitled *Assassination of a Family by Three of Its Principals in Salemo*. The whole to conclude with a *Grand Dance* in four acts of a new mechanical invention and complete illusion entitled *Feats of Pekin; or, The Grand Chinese Matrimony*." At a subsequent showing, this mechanical extravaganza changed from tragedy to high drama with *The Strength of Samson; or, The Battle of the Philistines* and the *Fall of the Temple*. Yet another performance featured a series of transformations from a Looking Glass to a Magician, a Stone to a Dining Table fully served, to a

Prodigious Dwarf who will grow to the height of a ceiling, and so on; all transformations taking place in the presence of the public.[25] During the nineteenth century scenic transformations were very popular in the theatre of spectacle. Methods were devised of changing scenic units swiftly and simultaneously to reveal new settings. Especially effective was the use of gauze painted with transparent dyes, which, lit from behind, would fade to reveal a more distant scene.

For Christmastime entertainment, the Mathir Circus was in town and set up a large tent near the Parade. For 5s. in the pit or 6s.8d. in a box, the excitement seeker could watch equestrian and gymnastic exhibitions such as rope walking, Indian hunting, and clowning. Most circus performances ended with a pantomime harlequinade. While it is not intended to record these popular forms of entertainment as they occur, it is well to remember that touring troupes were not limited to dramatic performances but offered a wide range of mechanical contrivances, gymnastics, exhibitions of magic, ventriloquism, panoramas, animal shows, and other curious devices and oddities. Such troupes visited Jamaica regularly throughout the century, and mention is made of them here although they do not form an integral part of this study.

In September 1840 the new Theatre Royal opened under the watchful eye of its appointed agent, J. T. Dias, who was also manager of the Kingston Amateur Association. The city geared itself to host a bevy of touring companies that had been, as it were, waiting in the wings. First on the scene were the three Davenports, recently seen at the Park and National Theatres in New York. They arrived before the theatre was quite ready and had to open their unusual season in Spanish Town, transferring to Kingston some months later. Mr. Davenport advertised himself as an ex-stage manager of the Strand Theatre in London. Mrs. Davenport, an actress, was appropriately silent about her credentials, for the star of the trio was their thirteen-year-old daughter, Jean, who played all the leading roles: Richard III, Romeo, Sir Peter Teazle, and sometimes even a female lead like Jane Shore, presumably in shortened versions of these plays. Her parents shared the supporting parts between them, and when they had sufficiently inveigled the Jamaican public into admiration or pity for the juvenile thespian, they invited amateurs to appear on stage with her in full-scale productions. If Miss Davenport intrigued as tragic or comic hero, she overwhelmed audiences as a *farceur*. In one piece, *Old and Young*, this extraordinary child sustained five characters, sang three songs, danced a national dance, performed the British Manual Exercise, and fired a rifle!

This peculiar exercise in juvenile exploitation came to an end in December 1840. In appreciation of their efforts, the Kingston amateurs earlier gave the Davenports a benefit performance of Goldsmith's *She Stoops to Conquer.* Mrs. and Miss Davenport took the roles of Mrs. and Miss Hardcastle respectively, while gentlemen amateurs played the rest of the parts including that of Miss Neville. The gentleman cast in this role elicited the critical comment: "Let nothing in heaven above or earth beneath tempt him to make a second appearance."[26]

After these titillating exhibitions, it was time for a solid dramatic company to take the stage of the new theatre. In December 1840 a full and proper troupe of professionals arrived from the United States of America led by John H. Oxley, the Philadelphian, who had been a supporting actor to Edwin Forrest. His Company of Comedians, comprising eleven men and four women, opened on January 2, 1841 with Sheridan Knowles's *The Hunchback*, followed by a fancy dance by Miss Larrer, and the farce *A Day After the Wedding.* A "brilliantly attended" house gave the comedians a rousing reception. Oxley followed this opening success with his Hamlet, which was deemed by the local reviewer to be "the best ever presented to a Kingston audience . . . his conception and reading of the part were faultless." In fact, although Oxley possessed a combination of talent, energy, and feeling seldom seen on the Kingston boards, his voice lacked range and power. He was, however, a skillful director, especially of picturesque crowd scenes that kept the audience in breathless excitement.[27]

The company continued to perform thrice weekly on Tuesdays, Thursdays, and Saturdays, with a different bill each day for an extended season of six months. Altogether over 100 performances were given of seventy-five plays, often to such small audiences that on one occasion a performance had to be canceled owing to the paucity of the house. It may be questioned whether Oxley's season was too ambitious for the size of his clientele. By 1840 the population of Kingston consisted of about four thousand whites (down from 8,000 in 1790 and 10,000 in 1824) and twenty-four thousand nonwhites, the majority being of the working class. Since the lowest-priced theatre ticket was 3s., roughly equal to a day's wages for the skilled worker and two days' wages for the domestic, it is unlikely that many nonwhites could afford to attend plays with any degree of regularity. At a rough estimate, therefore, the theatregoing public could hardly amount to more than fifteen hundred to two thousand. With three performances a week and a seating capacity of six hundred in the new theatre, a Kingston playgoer would have had to attend performances at least once a week through the run to ensure Oxley a reasonably full house. A gory *Macbeth* with singing witches and a three-minute sword fight, or a visually spectacular *King Lear* with freshly painted scenery that won spontaneous applause would pack the theatre, but generally public support was disappointing.

Oxley's most successful production was a pageant drama, *The Jewess* by William Moncrieff, which, along with Sheridan Knowles's *The Wife*, was twice revived. Summing up the tour, the *Morning Journal* praised Oxley for his courage and contribution to the cultural life of the city. He had arrived after Miss Davenport had reaped a bountiful harvest and when the community was economically depressed. He had persisted despite mediocre support and at a considerable loss, which was somewhat defrayed by the terms he had made with an incoming Italian opera company that wanted the use of the theatre.[28] Oxley had also provided the Kingston theatre with a fresh stock of handsome scenery painted by his stage manager, Mr. Rogers.

The economic distress mentioned above was caused by a serious decline in the plantation economy of Jamaica resulting from actions of the British government. Preferential tariffs previously accorded West Indian cane sugar had been removed while sugar produced more cheaply in slave-holding countries like Cuba and Brazil, as well as sugar from beets, was admitted to the British market. Competition between slave-grown sugar and that produced by wage-earning workers was considered unfair. The planters, already disaffected at being forced by the home government to free their slaves, felt betrayed. Moreover, they now found themselves in the compromising position of having to agitate for the abolition of slavery in all sugar-producing countries. The economic situation in Jamaica would continue to deteriorate, and in 1848 imports exceeded exports to the tune of £400,000. This downturn in the island's prosperity was bound to have an adverse effect on the fortunes of acting companies in the years ahead. For the present, however, Jamaica could rest on its laurels as a theatre-conscious community that provided reasonably comfortable facilities for dramatic production and a warm welcome to visiting troupes.

The Italian Opera Company managed by Senor Gastaldi was a fairly elaborate operation that did not have a very profitable season on its visit in July–August 1841. It was allegedly the first time that Jamaicans hosted grand opera. Company members consisted of four female and six male principals, a four-man chorus and chorus master, a conductor, and five instrumentalists with three additional musicians recruited locally for a company total of twenty-four. Details of the repertoire are not known, but on their return to the island the following year with a more modest troupe, works by Bellini, Rossini, and Donizetti were presented.

At this juncture, in January 1842, a new combination of actors came to the fore. Lately arrived back in Jamaica was the Monier family consisting of Mrs. Monier, her daughter Virginia fresh from the New York stage, and her youngest child, Eliza, another of the juvenile prodigies that infested the theatre of those days. Virginia Monier had acted with John Oxley in one of her New York engagements. Now, teaming up with him and some remnants of his troupe like Mr. and Mrs. Madison and adding a few experienced resident actors like Mrs. Shaw, the new company mounted a series of dramatic productions in Kingston over a ten-month period.

Mrs. Monier managed the enterprise and seldom appeared on stage. (She was busy conducting a school of deportment for young ladies.) Her company occupied the Kingston Theatre, promptly renamed it the Theatre Royal, and surrendered it periodically to make room for others. Their repertoire comprised many of the plays previously performed by Mrs. Monier or Miss Virginia in America, including the first-ever production in Jamaica of *Othello*, "old prejudices and old feelings having up to a very recent period indeed operated to prevent it." The spectacle of an interracial married couple on stage, to say nothing of the murder of a white woman by her black husband, would have been repugnant to a slaveholding society or one recently emerged from that condition. The performance was nevertheless greeted by a full attendance of the beauty and fashion of the island. When patronage lagged, Mrs. Monier reached for her trump card, little Eliza Monier, who appeared in a farce along with another of her mother's youthful pupils, Miss Slater. Coming so soon after the versatile Miss Davenport, the children's efforts seemed unremarkable and made little impression. Sad to report, this experiment in local theatrical management was a financial flop. Ticket prices, set by the Theatre Committee at 6s., 4s., and 3s., had to be reduced to 4s., 3s., and 2s., respectively. On one occasion Mrs. Monier appealed to the public "as the Manager who has suffered deeply by a bad season—as the woman who has been injured by evil reports." The gallant J. T. Dias, theatre agent, was so moved by her distress that he undertook a production himself to relieve the financial embarrassments of the present management.[29]

The failure of the Monier/Oxley combination was in part due to serious local competition. A circus had come to town early in the year and drew two thousand patrons at its first two showings. Later in March the Italian Opera Company returned for an eight-week stay, performing two or three times weekly. Then a rival dramatic company, also locally recruited, seduced some members away from the Monier troupe and opened its season in a new auditorium called the Royal Victoria Theatre. Beginning in early October, this company offered popular-type entertainment consisting of melodramas, short farces, olios, Negro songs, and dances at bargain prices. Its production of Edward Fitzball's nautical melodrama *Tom Cringle's Log,* based on the novel by the long-term Jamaican resident Michael Scott, was probably the only play of the period to contain scenes of island life.

The 1840s witnessed the precursors of blackface minstrelsy in the Jamaican theatre. The origin of this theatrical caricature of the black race has been attributed to Thomas D. Rice, an itinerant American comedian, whose song and dance act labeled "Jim Crow" was first performed in the United States in 1830. But acts portraying whites in blackface had occurred at least a decade earlier. At the Kingston theatre in Jamaica, gentlemen amateurs in 1840 staged the burlesque *Jim Crow in London; or, The Creole Ball* as an afterpiece to Sheridan Knowles's *The Hunchback.* The next year a visiting trouper received several encores for his entr'acte speciality when he sang and jumped "Jim Crow" in imitation of Rice. In 1842 another local company offering a season of light entertainment at the Royal Victoria Theatre in Kingston presented a bill that included two short plays, a comic duet, musical olio, and Negro songs. One of the plays, a farce called *The Virginny Mammy; or, The Liquor of Life* was popular enough to stand repetition the following week and revival in the years ahead. Later in the century professional blackface minstrels visited Jamaica and left behind the burnt-cork tradition that was adopted by black native comedians.

The absence of newspapers for the next several years causes a hiatus in the chronology of the Jamaican theatre, but from City Council minutes it appears that Solomon de Cordova, then resident in the United States, had obtained a year's lease of the Theatre Royal beginning in July 1845. A scion of the venerable Jamaican family, de Cordova undertook to prepare a season of plays beginning that September with a professional company recruited in America and performing at least one night a week. He was granted exclusive use of the theatre at a rental of £150 a year, in addition to the standard fee of £5 for each public performance. By May the following year, with three months still to go, council minutes show that de Cordova had applied for permission to break his lease without penalty, owing to the heavy loss he had sustained in running the repertory company. He argued that his tenancy had doubled the amount of theatrical scenery by providing a better and more elegant stock that had cost him fully £100 for labor alone. The council approved his application.[30] Unfortunately there are no details of the company's composition or the plays it produced.

Kingston amateurs were growing restless. They had pressed to get the new Theatre Royal built and now it was seldom available to them. They viewed with distinct displeasure any arrangement that pre-empted the building from their use for an entire year. Their secretary, H. S. Henry, petitioned the council for use of the theatre at the end of de Cordova's lease, and at any time when it was not occupied by a professional company, thus seeking priority over nondramatic kinds of entertainment. The petition was accepted, and the amateurs prepared for their first uninterrupted tenancy in the new playhouse. The time was propitious for them but, for those metropolitan centers abroad whence came the touring companies, it was catastrophic. In 1847 a severe famine experienced in Scotland and Ireland was followed the next year by an outbreak of Asiatic cholera in England. Within months, the dread disease had spread to North America, affecting population centers in New York, New Orleans, Toronto, and Montreal. The plague effectively shut off visits from foreign companies for about three years, affording local amateurs a clear field for their productions.

Between April 1847 and September 1850 the records, spotty as they are, reveal no fewer than eight different groups of amateur actors performing at the Theatre Royal. The most prestigious was the Kingston Amateur Theatre Association, which offered a monthly representation of a major play, but there were productions also by the Philo-Dramatic Association, the Amateur Thespian Association, an amateur French troupe, two black groups calling themselves the Ethiopian Amateur Society and the Numidian Amateur Association respectively, the Friendly Amateur Society, and the just plain Amateurs. Not to be outdone, Spanish Town in the same period contributed the Spanish Town Dramatic Society and the Juvenile Theatrical Society, while the officers of the Kingston Garrison brought up the rear with three productions presented for charitable purposes.

This flurry of local theatricals created an atmosphere of keen competition. Partiality among critics was rife. Philo-Dramatic was knocked out of contention early by unduly severe notices. Their first play, a comedy titled *The School of Reform* by Thomas Morton, was adjudged to be beyond the powers of the young gentlemen who converted it into a melodrama. They were advised to fire their manager. The selection of their next effort, Sheridan Knowles's *William Tell*, was deemed "extremely unwise and reprehensible." In the critic's view, the play had been mutilated by the group and the performance was "nothing more than an indecent mockery of the commonsense of a playgoing community." On the other hand, this same critic showed his colors when he wrote, ignoring previous professional productions, that "the grandeur and splendor with which Kotzebue's *Pizarro* was produced by the Kingston Amateur Theatrical Association have never been equalled either here or in America. The scenery was beautiful and imposing; the dresses were extremely costly and magnificent; and we could write as favorably of its performance."[31] Incidentally when George Frederick Agustus, the black king of the Mosquito Indian Territory of Central America, visited Jamaica in November 1847, *Pizarro* was revived, followed by the operetta burlesque of *Othello Travestie*. This was in the nature of a command performance with the island's governor and his royal guest in attendance. Not recorded are the king's views on witnessing a representation of the massacre of American Indians by invading Spanish soldiers and the burlesquing of a noble black general driven to self-destruction by a villainous white subordinate.

The Amateur Thespians did tolerably well with *Richard III*, and the Kingston Amateurs attempted *Othello*. Despite its previous airing by Oxley's group, this latter play was now, in the hands of local players, considered by the partial critic "ill-suited to our present times and to gentlemen amateurs to represent." Actually the term *gentlemen amateurs* was almost by this time anachronistic. Women amateurs were slowly being cast in female roles, and the part of Desdemona was on this occasion ably sustained by Mrs. Charles, whose performance elicited much applause. The most devastating criticism leveled at any group was reserved for The Amateurs, who entered what must have been a bruising political squabble by presenting Thomas Otway's *Venice Preserv'd* to celebrate the re-election of a very controversial mayor, Hector Mitchell. The scathing review began by stating that the play was given "by some half-dozen of illiterate individuals of this city." Jaffeir (hero of the drama) might pass, but "the grunting of Pierre, the monstrous strides of Belamar combined with his snorting, represented forcibly to us the disposition of asses to bray and gambol before MARES, and show their grotesque selves in pantomimic contortions."[32] The reviewer left in the third of five acts, mercifully perhaps, for had he stayed the rest of his critique would surely have been unprintable.

Nothing daunted, The Amateurs were back on the boards of the Theatre Royal two weeks later with the musical drama *Rob Roy*, got up as a benefit for an aging Kingston actor, N. Maroney, who played the lead:

Forget not the toils of the youthful Maroney,
He often performed in your presence before,
Then haste to support our favorite crony,
And show that you value an old Amateur.[33]

It was a welcome practice of amateurs of those days to honor in some tangible way those individuals in the society who had given years of devoted service to the Jamaican theatre, and to do so while the beneficiaries were still alive. John Dias, already mentioned, Maroney, Mrs. Gray, James Charles, who directed many of the shows at this period, Morton Tavares, and D. M. de Cordova, who in 1864 was referred to as "the veteran father of amateurs," all received benefit performances and were publicly honored by the local companies with whom they had labored.

No review graced the efforts of the two groups of black amateurs or, as they were called in the press, "the descendants of Africa." The newspaper commended their desire for improvement and noted that their members were synonymous with industrious habits and honest principles, but said nothing about the quality of their performance. The plays they chose were of the same type as those of their fellow histrions: George Lillo's *George Barnwell*, Home's *Douglas*, Hall Hartson's *The Countess of Salisbury*, parts of *Richard II*, and four laughable afterpieces about a Nabob, an Apprentice, a Cobbler, and a Brigand. There was even a *pas de deux*, to quote from a press announcement, danced by three [sic] young ladies from one of the groups.[34]

As the drama of amateur rivalry intensified, the church became involved. A sermon preached by the Reverend Henry Bleby in Coke Chapel, Kingston, on August 1, 1847, denounced the evils of the theatre. He lamented the absence from the service of many young devotees of stage plays, which, the reverend gentleman declared, were "opposed to the word of God since they send us for moral instruction to teachers of loose principles and depraved lives, bring us into hurtful contact with the most profligate and abandoned, and ridicule the sublime verities of our holy religion." The homily was ill-timed. A battery was opened up on the poor preacher, who was assailed with abuse.[35] This lively theatrical scene was brought to a calamitous end in October 1850 when cholera struck. Its deadly march across continents had brought it inexorably to the island. Before it abated, the epidemic would wipe out between twelve thousand and thirteen thousand people, most of whom, as reported in the governor's despatch to the secretary of state for the colonies in London, were blacks and poor coloreds.[36]

5

Travail and Triumph

Conditions in Jamaica worsened steadily. Unemployment increased. In 1852 a move was afoot to send a delegation to England to impress upon the British government the distressful plight of the island. A letter to the press urged whites to emigrate to Australia. Another commentator, bemoaning the departure of experienced musicians, blamed it on the state of poverty in the island: "Even the Philharmonic Society has given up the ghost . . . the civilization of a people may be known by their knowledge and cultivation of music; if such be the test, Kingston and its vicinity must be fast verging to barbarism."[1] Important shifts in perspective were taking place as new leaders came to the fore. Under the chairmanship of the mulatto Edward Jordan, mayor of Kingston, a public meeting was held in 1852 to consider the political and social condition of black Americans and a resolution was passed inviting them to settle in Jamaica if they were expatriated by hostile state governments in the United States.

The theatre revived sufficiently in the early 1850s to host productions by several new amateur groups, an Italian opera company of reduced size that had difficulty recruiting competent musicians for its orchestra, and, as advertised, the world-renowned Heron family of artistes and vocalists. Since the new theatre opened its doors, only the Davenport family with their prodigy daughter had made money, so it is no surprise to learn that the Heron family comprised a father, mother, and three daughters. Their month-long residency of high comedy and farce was undistinguished, however, and a financial flop. By way of consolation the young ladies enjoyed the usual gallant support in their productions from gentlemen amateurs and other admirers.

Competition among Kingston amateurs flared with new vigor. When the Union Amateur Association presented *George Barnwell* in the Theatre Royal, detractors in the house almost wrecked the show: "Calling of names, hissing and throwing of pindar shells from the boxes on the persons in the pit, continued throughout." The raucous element was headed by two or three otherwise respectable young men, one in particular "who played the character of Beauseant in Bulwer-Lytton's *The Lady of Lyons* was most obstreperous in calling out at the pitch of his voice during the performance."[2]

The rambunctiousness of Kingston audiences, referred to earlier, was a recurrent source of irritation through the end of the century. In 1850 at the Kingston Dramatic Society's staging of the ubiquitous *George Barnwell*, "there were present the most blackguard set of men and boys that ever disgraced a place of public amusement with their attendance." While most of the audience were apparently moved by this moralizing drama that Charles Lamb once referred to as "a nauseous sermon," rowdies in the upper boxes behaved abominably. Calling for the theatre to be closed rather than witness a repetition of such "brutalizing scenes," the critic explained that although Justices Salom and Qualo were present and tried their best to command order, "nothing they said or did had the least effect in calming the raging torrent of Billingsgate expression and disreputable conduct which were exhibited by the lawless assemblage who seemed to have been the very scum of the city of Kingston."[3] Despite such severe rebuke in the press, when the performance was repeated two weeks later the disturbances recurred and were eventually calmed by the prudent intervention of several justices.

There were repeated calls for more policemen to be posted in the house in order that offenders might be arrested on the spot; and, in fact, in 1873 five persons were fined sums of 5s. to 10s. each for creating a noise inside and outside the theatre. Even as late as 1900 at a local dramatic performance there were complaints of disorder and lawlessness in a section of the house:

> The opening of the doors of upper boxes is the signal for the greatest uproar and blackguardism on entering, and after seats are taken, the screaming and yelling, blowing of whistles and bicycle horns, is something terrific. Then the calling of each other's names across the room and even of those in the Parquette . . . others have had to leave the building on account of the scenes that have taken place even while the plays have been at their height.[4]

How can one account for this persistently boisterous behavior in the Kingston theatre? It should first be understood that Jamaicans were not singular in this regard. The Drury Lane Theatre in London witnessed the Gordon Riots in 1730, after which a company of Guards was posted nightly at the theatre until 1896. At its sister house of

Covent Garden, when John Philip Kemble in 1808 tried to raise prices to pay rebuilding costs, there broke out the Old Prices Riots that kept the theatre in nightly turmoil for about two months. Over in America, New York witnessed the tragic Astor Place Theatre Riots in 1849, triggered by a dispute over the relative merits of rival American and English actors, that resulted in twenty-two people being killed and another thirty-six injured. Nothing remotely resembling the violence of these events ever marred the Jamaican stage. By comparison, Kingston playgoers appear to have been lively and boisterous, but not intemperately so.

If, as seems to be the case, the misbehavior was confined to patrons of the upper boxes and gallery, which were occupied by the colored and black working class, it is quite possible that, apart from intergroup rivalry, most of the plays witnessed were irrelevant to their lives and thus unable to hold their attention. Going to the theatre would then become a social occasion to meet and greet friends and acquaintances, rather than to be inspired, moved, or entertained by the play on stage. It is equally possible that, for the group in question, the customary manner of responding to a live performance was much more active and participatory than for the sedately appareled and decorous members of the audience in the higher-priced seats. Nor were all productions of an acceptable standard. In 1873, for instance, when an indifferent company was in residence there were repeated complaints of unseemly audience behavior. At the same time, reviewers berated several of the productions: "The music was again wretched . . . simply painful to listen to the miserable scraping and discord"; or, "The play is not immoral—but it is illogical, incongruous and inconsistent."[5] Faced with such exhibitions for which they had paid hard-earned money, is it any wonder that members of the audience expressed their disapproval stridently?

The most important development of mid-century was the staging of original Jamaican plays including two by Charles Shanahan, a reporter for the *Colonial Standard* newspaper and president of the Amateur Roscian Association. Since Jamaican playwrights will be discussed in chapter 7, Shanahan's titles are simply mentioned here: *The Mysteries of Vegetarianism*, a farce, and *The Spanish Warrior*, an historical drama. They were presented at the Theatre Royal to large and respectable audiences in September and December 1853. For the next several years, though the records are woefully incomplete, it appears that no major company of professionals came to Jamaica. The amateurs were in command, at least those that had survived the recent internecine skirmishes.

Basking in its recent acclaim for staging Jamaican plays, the Amateur Roscian Association mounted five productions at the Theatre Royal, including a benefit performance in 1855 for the orphan daughter of Dias, the theatre agent, who had recently died. D. M. de Cordova was appointed to succeed him. That year another Italian opera troupe of seven or eight vocalists played an ambitious three-month season at the Royal during which twenty-six performances of opera selections *sans* choruses were rendered. October brought news of the fall of Sebastopol in the Crimean War to brighten a dull Kingston season with rejoicings and to set the mood for the "astonishing feats" by the Abdala family of gymnasts at the theatre. Numbered among the acts were a Drunken Sailor on Stilts, Mme Abdala on the bottles or a glass pyramid or representing Joko the Brazilian Ape, the whole to close with "a serious pantomime, so-called."[6] The Kingston theatre was becoming anemic. Fresh blood was needed.

At this point Jamaica-born Aaron Tavares, more familiarly known as Morton Tavares, returned to his homeland after spending some years in the United States as an actor. (His career will be discussed fully in the following chapter on native professionals.) His return inspired the leading Kingston troupe, the Amateur Dramatic Association, to come out of hibernation. At the Theatre Royal, with Tavares playing lead roles, the group staged a number of renowned tragiromantic dramas such as John Banim's *Damon and Pythias*, Edward Bulwer-Lytton's *Richelieu*, Mrs. G. W. Lovell's *Ingomar the Barbarian*, and *Othello*. The programs for the latter two plays give the names of gentlemen belonging to the association, the majority of whom were Jews. Such names are still familiar to Jamaicans today: A. de Cordova was president, E. Delgado was treasurer, and J. D. Naar, secretary. Committee members included William Girod, S. Melhado, S. D. Lindo, C. Campbell, and E. Lucas. In the cast, in addition to Naar and Delgado, were M. de Cordova, F. de Souza, R. de Leon, Noel de Leon, N. Alberga, A. A. Hart, and others. There were no women in the productions. Desdemona was played by M. de Cordova and Emilia by R. de Leon. As well as playing Ingomar and Othello, Tavares was listed as "Acting and Stage Manager" or, as we should term him today, play director.

The announcement that a dramatic company would visit Kingston in 1859 was welcome news to playgoers, despite lingering doubt that the country in its penurious state could support a full-scale repertory season. When the Lanergan company arrived in April of that year, it was the first full company to visit the island since the de Cordova troupe fourteen years earlier, and only the third since the Theatre

Royal was built back in 1840. James West Lanergan, born in Massachusetts in 1828, ran his own Dramatic Lyceum in Saint John, New Brunswick, where he produced legitimate drama during the summer months. In the winters he either took his company on tour or disbanded it and himself joined a repertory troupe. His wife, Caroline, was a fine actress and together they constituted the "chief ornaments" of the company. Lanergan had begun his Saint John summer theatre in 1857 and would continue the operation for twenty years, gaining a reputation as a man of good taste and judgment who strove to present high quality productions.[7] He was, however, not that well established when his company came to Jamaica.

Their first visit was a short one. Over a four-week period, the company gave only twelve performances, an average of three a week. The repertoire consisted of the usual romantic melodramas such as Bulwer-Lytton's *Lady of Lyons* and Knowles's *William Tell*, comedies like Tom Taylor's *Still Waters Run Deep*, and the conventional farces that filled out an evening's bill. At popular prices ranging from 2s. to 4s. good houses were anticipated but in fact attendance was discouraging. Of the acting talent, only Mrs. Lanergan's performance in the title role of Alexandre Dumas's *Camille* stirred the critic to unstinted praise. In his view, her personation was "the most finished and perfect we have witnessed on the Jamaican stage . . . chaste and beautiful, utterly defying all attempt at criticism." Other productions were creditable but unimpressive. Francis Burnand's *Alonzo the Brave*, for example, was only "an old nancy story dramatized, one would imagine, specially for the 'Gods.' "[8] In an effort to win greater public support, the company produced as afterpieces two farces of local authorship. Neither piece excited critical comment though some trifling improvement in public attendance was gained. After a disappointing stay, the company left the island in early May, conveniently avoiding competition from Chiarini's Grand Circus of twenty-six performers and eleven horses, with credentials that boasted appearances at the famed Astley's Royal Amphitheatre in London. The circus provided two weeks of visual entertainment in Kingston, playing to pretty full houses before moving on to Falmouth and other parts of the country.

Lanergan's company spent the next two winters in the Caribbean, visiting Jamaica in February and March 1860, and again from December 1861 to February 1862, trying its best to live up to audience expectations. On his second visit Lanergan secured the services of Morton Tavares, with the result that his repertoire was strengthened by the addition of Shakespeare and other heroic dramas in which Tavares starred. Lanergan himself attempted *Hamlet* and was repaid with a crowded house. He managed the role "with great judgment," the reviewer conceding that it was not as easy to play Hamlet as to criticize it. Again it was Mrs. Lanergan who scored in *The Stranger*, excelling all her former efforts, not excluding *Camille:* "Nothing has yet surpassed on the Kingston boards the exquisite acting of this favored lady and Mr. Morton [i.e., Morton Tavares] in the closing scene. . . . It would have won the ovation of tears from any audience in the world."[9]

On the departure of Lanergan's company in 1860, Tavares went to New York and recruited a modest group of professionals for a season of his own. Among his players was G. K. Dickinson, who stayed in Jamaica when the tour was over and was engaged by Lanergan as leading man for the company's third trip in 1861–62. By now Lanergan realized that Kingston audiences were partial to serious drama, and he needed a strong classical actor on his team. His list of plays on this occasion contained *Othello, Hamlet, Richard III,* and *Macbeth,* in addition to Friedrich von Schiller's *The Robbers,* Dion Boucicault's *The Octoroon,* and others. However, Lanergan did not have the resources to mount these pieces fittingly. In Sheil's *The Apostate,* a tale based on the conquest of Granada in which a Moorish prince betrays his countrymen for a woman's love, not only was the acting inadequate but also the prince was "so badly dressed as to become repugnant to the audience." Costumes were generally poor, stage directions confusing, and supernumeraries notably absent, prompting the reviewer to deplore "the shabby manner in which it was placed on stage."[10] Other offerings fared much better, in particular those that featured Dickinson and Mrs. Lanergan, who continued to impress in parts suited to her talents.

Dickinson was an English actor who had played the provincial circuit from 1848 to 1851 before migrating to the United States. Once there, he began by giving public readings at the Tabernacle in New York on October 8 and 10, 1851. He is next found in the company of the renowned actor-manager Laura Keene, where he played important secondary roles in her 1856–57 and 1857–58 New York seasons. He came to Jamaica, presumably accompanied by his wife and two children, with Tavares's troupe in 1860, signed up with Lanergan the next year, and appeared again with Tavares and the Kingston amateurs in 1862. His principal stage roles were Hamlet, Othello, Claude Melnotte in *The Lady of Lyons,* and Elmore in George Lovell's *Love's Sacrifice.*

Critics treated his work with respect. It is all the more regrettable that, in commenting on the paucity of the house at his performances, he allegedly derided the Jamaican public, saying that he was "throwing pearls before swine." In a letter to the editor of the *Morning Journal*, Dickinson strongly refuted this published allegation, which he termed a slander. The incident moved the editor to comment on the duty of the theatre critic in the following terms: "The critic, whilst doing justice to the actors, has a stern duty to the public to perform which he cannot discharge faithfully and with impartiality unless he makes it a rule always to keep in front of the curtain." This was a reference to other so-called critics who "enter into alliance with the denizens of the Green Room." The editor continued: "It is only by the opinions of the newspapers that the public can judge whether the actors are worthy of patronage, and if the writers for the papers prostitute their mission and give false reports, they not only deceive the public and sacrifice the confidence that had been reposed in them, but in the end damage the actors whom they had gone out of their way to serve."[11] Dickinson joined the list of stage readers in Jamaica, where, accompanied by his wife as vocalist, he will be encountered again in chapter 8.

Traveling companies were constantly seeking plays that dealt with topics relevant to Jamaica. As well, they were quick to introduce playgoers to new works that had won approval abroad. There was, however, one play that qualified on both counts yet was kept off the Kingston boards for well over half a century. This was the musical melodrama in two acts entitled *Obi; or, Three Fingered Jack*. When it was finally produced in Jamaica, it played for a single performance and then apparently disappeared from the stage for the rest of the century. Written by John Fawcett, the play had its first London performance in 1800, playing in New York the following year. Thereafter it became a staple on both sides of the Atlantic.

The melodrama is a fanciful dramatization of the true story of a runaway slave named Jack Mansong, who in 1780–81 waged his own guerrilla war from the mountains against Jamaican plantation society.[12] He had lost two fingers in a previous encounter with Maroon slave hunters. Armed with musket and cutlass and protected by obeah charms, Jack terrorized the countryside until the government was forced to offer rewards for his arrest that included freedom to any slave effecting his capture, dead or alive. Eventually Jack was tracked down by a party of Maroons and killed in a ferocious battle on the road to Morant Bay. Although the play contains the usual stereotyped characters, archaic language, and improbable scenes of happy slaves engaged in merrymaking, implicit in the dialogue is a strong condemnation of slavery. In earlier times such a speech from the Kingston stage might have inflamed passions in a country where the peculiar institution existed for over two hundred years. In one scene Jack captures a planter's daughter who begs for mercy. His retort has all the pent-up fury of a race that has borne centuries of oppression:

> You whites are ever ready to enforce for one another that civilized, that Christian law of mercy which our dusky children never yet partook of. . . . I had a daughter once; did they spare her harmless infancy? Where is my wife? was she spared to me? No! With blood and rapine the white man swept like a hurricane o'er our native village and blasted every hope! Can aught efface the terrible remembrance from my soul, how at their lordly feet we begged for mercy and found it not. Our women knelt, our infants shrieked in vain, as the blood-stained murderer ranged from hut to hut, dragging the husband and the father from their homes to sell them into bondage! No more, no more! the vext spirits of my wife and child hover o'er me like a holy curse, and claim their due revenge.[13]

Obi; or, Three Fingered Jack was produced at the Theatre Royal, Kingston, on September 16, 1862, by J. Thompson, supported by amateurs. It was a benefit performance for Thompson, a former member of the Lanergan troupe, who had elected to remain in Jamaica when the company moved on. Unfortunately, available records are silent on the public reception of the play, nor did it ever reappear in the record of Jamaican theatre through the end of the century.

Early in the 1860s amateurs were again active in Kingston and Spanish Town, the American Civil War having stemmed the flow of touring professionals from that continent. Occasionally these dilettantes attained a high level of performance even when their choice of material remained pedestrian. The all-male Amateurs of Merit, for instance, were especially good in the perennial *George Barnwell*, which was presented at the Theatre Royal in April 1864. The young man who played Barnwell was dubbed "quite a genius." He had a clear, musical voice, distinct articulation, and acted "perfectly natural" without rant or exaggeration. The difficult role of Millwood was also convincingly portrayed, considering that the young gentleman in this part "labored under the additional disadvantage of having to play in petticoats." The roles of Lucy and Maria were also taken by young men in crinolines. "Altogether," wrote the critic, "this entertainment was highly successful. It gave proof that among the natives of this country, there exists a vein of talent which only requires to be developed to reach the most splendid results. . . . We do not remember to have seen anything better even from gentlemen of much higher pretensions."[14]

Earlier that year a small French troupe had arrived at the Royal playing in their native tongue, but after a week of performances that did not draw audiences they quietly packed their bags and left. They were succeeded by the cantatrice Mme Garbato, who came from Cuba. Assisted by Bandmaster Doorly and Sergeant Beardhall of the 14th Regiment, this hopeful lady announced a vocal and instrumental concert at the Kingston Court House that attracted only a sparse audience. Her second appearance, this time at the Theatre Royal, fared no better and a subscription concert had to be arranged by the Kingston Volunteers for her benefit. Only the circus, it seemed, did good business in these lean times. Two of them invaded Kingston, capping their gymnastic and equestrian exhibitions with pantomime acts that were highly diverting: "Mr. Orrin's excellent personifications of the old woman as well as the comicality of the several actors provoked shouts of laughter. Indeed, Wednesday evening's performance was excellent and we would recommend everyone to visit the Royal Circus where they cannot fail being amused."[15] Laughter was obviously the desired tonic for times that were grim.

The year 1865 was momentous for Jamaica. No relief was in sight from grievous economic conditions characterized by high unemployment, low wages, rising prices for imported food, and increased taxation. Hardest hit were the peasantry, who needed arable land to cultivate and whose crops had been ruined by a series of recent droughts. Protest meetings were called and petitions drawn up for submission to the governor for forwarding to the queen. But Governor Eyre was known for his bias toward the plantocracy and lack of sympathy for the workers. His advice to Her Majesty was predictable when the queen responded that the peasants should work harder and show greater industry in order to improve their lot. This haughty rebuff did nothing to allay the anger of the peasants.

Meanwhile in April an Italian opera troupe managed by Signor Barrattini came from New York for a season of twelve nights. A subscription had been taken up by Kingston citizens as a guarantee against loss, and the troupe opened at the Theatre Royal on April 3 in *Il Trovatore*. With an ensemble consisting of seven men, four women, and two pianos for accompaniment, the performance failed to win support. Members of the Kingston Military Band came to their aid, the orchestra was strengthened, and the singers with heightened spirits were in excellent voice for their next offering of Rossini's *Il Barbiere di Siviglia*, to the delight of their audience. Tickets for nonsubscribers had at first been advertised at 6s. and 8s., but they were quickly dropped to 6s. flat for first-time performances and 4s. for repeats. In early May at the end of its contracted run the opera company opened a second subscription list at £6 for twenty-four tickets, that is, 5s. per ticket. This offer must have proved popular for the company continued playing three times weekly through the end of the month.

A new dimension in popular entertainment was introduced when the first quartet of minstrels to visit Jamaica arrived from New York in July 1865. Led by Frank Hussey the foursome presented a variety program at the Royal, but at cut prices of 2s. and 3s. failed to raise a good house until they hit on the strategy of a benefit performance in aid of beautifying the central park in the city. For this occasion Hussey wrote and sang a new song entitled "To Walk in Central Park" dedicated to the people of Kingston. Although the so-called Negro Songs had in the past been rendered as supporting items to dramatic plays, this quartet was the first professional group to introduce Jamaica to the blackface minstrelsy that had become immensely popular in America during the second half of the nineteenth century. Other troupes would soon follow: the Original Georgia Minstrels in 1869, the Christy Minstrels in 1872, and Edwin Browne's Minstrel and Novelty Company in 1884. They established a tradition of blacking-up to portray comic stereotypes of the black man that Jamaican comedians of the populist theatre adopted and maintained into the Bim and Bam era of the 1950s and 1960s.

In August 1865 a deputation of peasants from Morant Bay journeyed forty-five miles on foot to Spanish Town to lay before Governor Eyre their complaints against the planters and local magistrates who continued to victimize them. Heading the deputation was deacon Paul Bogle of Stony Gut, a supporter and friend of the mulatto assembly-man George William Gordon, himself an outspoken critic of Eyre and his administration. The governor refused to see the delegation and the men were forced to trek back to Stony Gut, their determination to take matters into their own hands stiffening with each step. On October 11, after some initial skirmishes between the police and the Stony Gut men, and with warrants of arrest issued against many of them, Bogle brought a band of armed men to the Morant Bay courthouse where the vestrymen were meeting under the protection of local volunteers. When the volunteer captain was hit by a missile thrown from the crowd and gave the order to open fire, the riot began. The toll from that cry of the common people for social justice was grisly. Twenty-one whites were killed by blacks; in retaliation, 439 blacks were killed; 600, including women, were scourged; and one thousand homes were destroyed. Nineteen of the people's leaders, including Gordon, who was ill at home in Kingston at the outbreak of the rebellion, were hanged without trial from the yardarm of Her Britannic Majesty's gunboat *Wolverine* drawn up in the harbor of Morant Bay. The findings of the royal commission sent out from London to inquire into the rebellion were that:

    (i) martial law had continued longer than necessary;

    (ii) punishment of death was unnecessarily frequent;

    (iii) floggings were reckless and at Bath positively barbarous;

    (iv) the burning of one thousand houses was wanton and cruel.[16]

Working-class Jamaicans, driven to revolt in order to gain the attention of the British government for their suffering under an inflexible and inhumane governor, had been savagely chastised.

In a belated attempt to ameliorate the injury, the *Wolverine* and her sister gunboats, the *Bulldog, Nettle,* and *Aurora,* began a series of theatrical performances by their officers and crew, aimed at winning friends among the people they had recently crushed. They had been sent to the Jamaican station to protect the people against capture by foreign forces. Instead they had become instruments of terror in the hands of a sadistic governor. Both the *Bulldog* and the *Wolverine* had combined to stage productions of farces aboard the former vessel at Port Royal, merely a month before the outbreak of hostilities. At the first performance, over one hundred guests were wined and dined. Following the riot, amateurs of the *Wolverine* appeared at the Theatre Royal in March 1866, with the band from the *Aurora* in attendance. The performance was given for the benefit of Kingston reformatories. Commenting on this further evidence of their public-spiritedness, the editor of the *Colonial Standard* newspaper representing the Planters' party, praised the officers and men of the *Wolverine* for saving the unfortunate fugitives from Saint Thomas from a fearful death through their courage, care, and disinterestedness.[17] Building on this goodwill gesture, the amateurs from the *Aurora* appeared in April for the benefit of a sailor's home and presented *The Corsican Brothers, Nigger Delineators,* and a farce, *The Irish Tiger.* In May, the Military Amateur Dramatic Society gave its first performance at the Royal of a bill comprising a comedy, interlude, and farce. No charity is identified as beneficiary but the production received the patronage of the acting governor, Sir Henry Knight Stokes, who had temporarily replaced Eyre and was present in a show of solidarity with the community. These military amateurs, combining later with players from the navy, would eventually stage seven different productions in Kingston through October 1868. Their programs consisted mainly of farces and musical burlesques. Sometimes they would invite a local female actress to join their casts.

In November 1866, while the Circuit Court was in session in Morant Bay, Commander Jenkins of the *Nettle* staged the melodrama *Robert Macaire* in a large room of the temporary barracks of the town where the rebellion had started a year ago. A stage was erected at one end of the hall; the scenery and seating arrangements, designed and executed by a member of the ship's company, were effective and tasteful. Sailors playing women's parts were dressed in crinolines. Between the acts a genuine "darkie" danced in correct style a pleasing Virginia breakdown, which was greeted with thunders of applause. Then came the master stroke. After the first act, "Cmdr. Jenkins ordered free admission of persons of whatever class who should desire to see the performance, and in a short time the back part of the room became crowded to suffocation with numbers of the unwashed, whose genuine expressions of wonder and pleasure at what was going on made up to the remainder of the audience for the inconvenience and discomfort otherwise occasioned by their invasion."[18] Military and naval amateurs continued to perform intermittently through 1869 when the situation in Jamaica had calmed sufficiently to permit troops to return to barracks and lead the life of peacetime soldiers. In a situation of grave social unrest, the live theatre had been called upon and had helped to heal the wounds.

Apart from productions by the military, theatre in the years following the Morant Bay uprising was at a low ebb. No major professional company came to the island until 1873, giving local amateurs another opportunity to fill the breach. A group of senior thespians, who had originally performed back in 1846, came together again to stage a number of productions at the Kingston theatre beginning in 1866. Occasionally they combined with a few resident professionals and produced Shakespeare, but mostly their choice of plays was commonplace. Among these older actors were F. Brodhurst, J. V. da Costa, A. C. Henriques, J. G. Lewis, and Messrs. de Pass, Duperly, and Hylton. Their musical director was Mr. Abendana.

A much younger group, calling themselves the Juvenile Thespians and clearly belonging to another generation of amateurs, made their bow to the public at this time with a performance of Home's *Douglas*. Directed by D. M. de Cordova, agent for the theatre, the show played at the Royal on September 3, 1868. The cast comprised the following actors, who were most certainly mere teenagers: Eustace Abraham, Charles Alberga, Clarence P. Alberga, S. P. C. Henriques, Henry J. Isaacs, W. de Mercado, and Robert Nunes. Thrilled to recognize budding talent that would ensure the continuity of the Jamaican theatre, the critic for the *Colonial Standard* went into ecstasies of praise, calling their performance "one of the greatest theatrical successes, if not the greatest, that has in our recollection been put before the public on the Kingston boards, especially when the youth of the actors is taken into consideration."[19] He had to admit, notwithstanding, that the audience was "very thin."

Understandably, given the depressing state of public affairs, the smallness of audiences is a recurrent theme in theatre reviews of this period, despite constant urgings from the press on the superior quality of performances. Often visiting performers wound up in debt for lack of box-office receipts and had to be rescued by local amateurs who mounted benefit performances in their behalf. Even a superb company of Japanese gymnasts and magicians—artists of a caliber never before seen in Jamaica who "leave one spellbound amidst breathless admiration of the truly astounding and dangerous acts performed by the troupe"[20]—even such skilled showmen had trouble maintaining good houses for a two-week run at the Theatre Royal in March 1868.

Not all amateur shows at the Kingston theatre merited warm commendation. Guardians of Jamaica's long theatrical heritage, while sympathetic toward local efforts, would not tolerate shoddy, ill-prepared productions regardless of their origin. Above all, standards must be maintained for the sake of the paying public. In 1872 a new corps of young actors calling themselves the Kingston Amateurs twice ventured into the arena of the Theatre Royal. On each occasion they were so roundly berated by the critics that the group had no alternative but to disband. Their first production took place on June 27, when John Courtney's play *Time Tries All* was offered, an unpretentious domestic drama in two acts with a single interior setting and eight characters. Even so, the production was deemed by one writer to be "a dismal failure. Nobody understood what went on—the Amateurs spoke in whispers, moved about the stage as if they were so many mechanical toys." A lady played one of the principal roles, and "her presence on the stage was the means of preventing a manifestation on the part of the audience at the absolute failure and ridiculousness of the entertainment."[21] Were this the only published review, one might be tempted to attribute its harshness to a partiality of the critic toward the regular Kingston Amateur Dramatic Society whose turf was being invaded by this upstart group. But the review carried in a second paper was just as severe, calling the production "one of the greatest inflictions a small though respectable audience was ever called upon to undergo. Not one of the Amateurs understood the character he had undertaken and none but the poor lady seemed to have realised the position of affairs."[22]

About six months later, on December 3, the Kingston Amateurs again dared to face the public. This time they had picked a known favorite for their play, *La Tour de Nesle* (The chamber of death) by the elder Dumas, a romantic-historical melodrama set in medieval France. It was an ambitious choice, but the Amateurs had strengthened their ranks by adding a few seasoned players such as George McCaddon and Augustus Brodhurst, and advance publicity had attracted a large and expectant audience. Sadly, the performance was once again painfully inept, probably owing to the lack of a knowledgeable and skillful stage director. Memory lapses occurred frequently, while the defaulters tried in vain to cover them with grotesque overacting, to the laughter and jeers of spectators in the upper boxes. After a "fearfully amputated" second act, a young gentleman came forward with an excuse but "the respectable portion of the house rose *en masse* and left the theatre, thoroughly disgusted with the exhibition." Not so easily appeased, the gods began "a regular chorus of shouting, yelling and hooting amidst which the curtain rose for performance of the farce; but as the drama had already been turned into a farce, this part of the programme was unheeded."[23] The review ended with an expression of sympathy for Brodhurst, McCaddon, and Simons who were "amateurs of no mean order." After this second fiasco, the Kingston Amateurs were heard from no more.

The discussion of Jamaican theatre thus far has tended to focus on Kingston, which maintained a proper playhouse and a steady stream of professional and amateur activity and where press reports of performances are available. This focus, however, should not tempt us to ignore other parts of the country that were visited by traveling shows, and where local players performed periodically. The town of Falmouth, for instance, had a reputation for amateur theatricals. The editor of the *Falmouth Post* had himself acted professionally for some years and had retained an interest in local theatre. In 1868 we find a notice in the Kingston papers to the effect that it was not His Excellency the Governor who ordered the Trelawney Amateur Theatrical Association to discontinue performances at the Falmouth courthouse but the custos, who acted to protect government property that was being destroyed.[24] That His Excellency should wish publicly to dissociate himself from the suspension of amateur theatricals testifies to the depth of resentment inspired by the action of the custos.

The situation was eventually resolved in favor of the players, and during the year 1872 the Corps Dramatique of the same Trelawny amateur group performed at the courthouse. They produced a series of seven evenings of theatre consisting of some sixteen comedies, melo-dramas, and farces, with comical and orchestral interludes as well. With tickets costing 3s. and 1s. and children at half-price, a typical program might comprise an orchestral overture followed by a farce as the curtain raiser, then a comedy or melodrama, then an interlude of song or recitation, and finally another farce to round off the evening's program. These performances were always well attended, for they represented one of the principal ways of bringing all members of the rural community together for edification and enjoyment.

Ten years having passed since the last troupe of professional actors had visited the island, it was with profound relief that Kingston play-goers welcomed the arrival of the Holland Dramatic Company in March 1873. Conditions favored a successful season. The events of 1865 had precipitated action on much-needed improvements in the country and, under the firm and enlightened governorship of Sir John Peter Grant (1866–74), known as "the architect of modern Jamaica," noted reforms were being carried out in education, health, agriculture, and transport. The transfer of the seat of government from Spanish Town to Kingston in 1872 meant that greater attention would be paid to improving amenities in the new capital.

Actor-manager W. M. Holland, moreover, was supposed to be expe-rienced in management and an astute businessman.[25] His troupe had been touring the Caribbean area for at least a year before coming to Jamaica. Prior to that, in 1871, Holland had managed the great Ameri-can actor Edwin Forrest in his farewell performances of *King Lear* and *Richelieu* at the Fourteenth Street Theatre in New York. Holland kept his company to a manageable size of eight men and four women, which required some doubling of parts in plays with large casts, or, as likely, some tampering with texts to eliminate minor characters. In the company was Holland's wife, the attractive and talented Effie Johns, whom he billed as "the Elfin Star." The sobriquet was taken from the actress Alice Kingsbury, who had been given the title in 1867 after her performance in *Fanchon the Cricket* at Maguire's Opera House in San Francisco. To cap his arrangements, Holland had en-listed the services of George Levy, publisher of the *Colonial Standard* newspaper, as his agent, a move that he felt would assure him healthy publicity and a sympathetic press.

Holland's first Jamaican season lasted seven weeks from March 24 to May 14 at Kingston's Theatre Royal, during which the company staged twenty-two plays and thirteen farces, with occasional revivals. The repertoire was varied with an emphasis on plays that provided stellar roles for his featured actress, Effie Johns. Shakespeare's *Romeo and Juliet* was performed along with standard romantic dramas such as *Camille, The Lady of Lyons, East Lynne,* and *Leah, the Forsaken.* There were in addition the musical burlesque of *Pocahontas,* the fairy burlesque of *Cinderella,* Watts Phillips's comedy *Lost in London,* Augustin Daly's thriller *Under the Gaslight,* John Haines's military drama *The French Spy,* and William Pratt's temperance drama, *Ten Nights in a Barroom.* Also introduced to Jamaica for the first time were two contemporary realistic dramas by the English playwright Tom Robertson. Titled *Caste* and *School,* these plays had premiered at the Prince of Wales Theatre in London merely six and four years earlier.

The season opened with Schuler's melodrama *Fanchon the Cricket.* It provided a starring vehicle for Miss Johns, who completely enchanted the crowded house. Miss Johns "reaches the sacred region of sterling genius," wrote the critic of the *Colonial Standard.* "Possessing a lithe and graceful figure and gifted with a winsome beauty in which spirituality is the predominating feature, she also evinces the accurate conception and expressiveness which are the soul and substance of dramatic art." In her songs she displayed a voice of rare power and sweetness. She was repeatedly applauded during the performance, and at the end received numerous curtain calls. The third production saw Miss Johns in the title role of *Lucretia Borgia,* a part strongly contrasting with *Fanchon.* Here she was self-possessed and confident in the "calm self-sustained power with which she essayed the working out of the terrible tragedy of a voluptuous, cruel and sin-polluted life."[26] In *Romeo and Juliet,* her Juliet was played to perfection while Holland as Romeo mustered only the noncommittal "true to the best interpretations of the part" from the critic. As Richelieu, however, he was "triumphant."

If the actors were, on the whole, treated kindly, not all the plays escaped censure. *Ten Nights in a Barroom* was dismissed as being inapplicable to Jamaica, and the manager was advised to be more sensitive to the tastes of the community before placing on the boards dramas that were well suited to large communities but that could never find favor with a Jamaican audience. Phillips's *Lost in London* was not immoral but illogical, incongruous, and inconsistent, and the intervals between the acts were too long. Nevertheless, the house was moved to tears, some incidents and situations being impressive and stirring.[27] The reviewer's most severe criticism was reserved for the locally recruited orchestra, which performed execrably. It was simply painful to listen to the miserable scraping and discord, and the promised improvement did not materialize during the season.

Toward the season's end when audiences began to wane, Holland rekindled their interest by staging a number of plays in which local amateurs were given important roles. Audiences came to see how the Jamaican players would measure up beside seasoned professionals. *Richelieu*, presented on April 29, 1873, had Jamaicans Solomon de Cordova as Mauprat and Reginald de Leon as Baradas. This was followed on May 1 with John Tobin's comedy *The Honeymoon*, in which four amateurs appeared: de Leon, Samuel Lawton, Solomon da Costa, and Augustus Brodhurst. Three amateurs including a female appeared in Boucicault's *The Colleen Bawn* on May 8, and de Leon was again cast in the final play of the run, *Leah, the Forsaken*, on May 12 and 14.

According to *Gall's Newsletter*, not altogether an impartial source, Holland's company netted £1,000 from their first twelve performances and, after their unprecedented run of seven weeks, left the island for Panama carrying over £5,000 net profit. The involvement of the press in this success story did not go unnoticed by the caustic Gall, who seems to have had his quarrels with the *Colonial Standard*. In an article on public amusements, he pointed out that usually it is the theatrical agent who makes money on touring shows while the entertainers wind up "with a long bill or suit in the Kingston District Court." If a manager goes to one printing office, Gall contended, the other will have nothing whatever to do with his company. If he goes to the other, he will get any amount of newspaper "puffing" just in proportion to the orders he gives for printing and advertising. Holland, in Gall's view, was an astute manager who acted according to his own judgment and kept his proper position among the competing printers.[28]

Whether or not Gall's figures were accurate, Holland must have done fairly well on his first Jamaican visit for the following year he brought back his company, including the ineffable Effie Johns, for an extended stay. He seemed not to mind that, just prior to his opening at the Royal, the Eureka Dramatic Combination of fourteen actors from America had closed out its month-long season at a distinct loss. This company had even staged two plays on the racial issue, Boucicault's *The Octoroon* and the long-running American classic, *Uncle Tom's Cabin*. The latter was presented for the first time in Jamaica, but did nothing to bolster the Combination's fortunes. Of their failure, Gall commented that "the indefatigable printer, something like the lawyer, enjoyed the oyster while he apportioned the shell."[29]

Billing his new program "Fourth Season in the West Indies," Holland opened his run on August 25, 1874, with J. B. Buckstone's comedy *Married Life* and the farce *Man, the Good for Nothing*. The company played four weeks in Kingston giving three performances a week, before embarking on an extensive tour of country towns, appearing in Savannah-la-Mar, Lucea, Montego Bay, Trelawny, Saint Ann's Bay, and Linstead. The players were universally acclaimed: "So excellent were their delineations of character that on several occasions the audience were moved to tears, particularly in the plays of *East Lynne* and *Leah, the Forsaken Jewess.* . . . The power of Miss Effie Johns is something more than wonderful."[30] The company returned to Kingston and reopened at the Royal on November 2. With short breaks in its schedule, the troupe played through mid-June 1875, in the course of which seven of Shakespeare's plays and other familiar pieces were presented. It was an ambitious season and a test of the country's ability to support year-round professional theatre offering three new productions a week in Kingston with intermittent trips to the outlying townships. The country failed that test; stage devotees were probably no more than two thousand to three thousand in the city, and there was a limit to their support of any one troupe. By the end of June 1875, Holland was unable to maintain his program. The company broke up, some members remaining on the island either by choice or necessity. Toward year's end and in January charitable performances were sponsored by local citizens to help players "left in a strange land under very trying circumstances."[31]

In January 1875 Holland had applied to the Kingston Municipal Board for a reduction in the fees charged for rental of the Theatre Royal but his application was denied. In November, still seeking to raise a new season of plays with resident professionals, Holland again petitioned the board for the use of the theatre gratis for a month, basing his application on the claim that he had contributed nearly £500 to theatre revenues since his return to Jamaica. He argued that his company had met with "a singular want of success" in consequence of which he had lost £2,500. Supporting the application, board member Alberga submitted that to grant Holland's request would be "an act of charity and the means of preventing the applicant from becoming a pauper." The board agreed, without prejudice to any other company desiring the use of the theatre, and on condition that the agent's fee of £1 for each performance would be paid.[32]

One might question the propriety of the board's action. Holland had shown himself to be an able entrepreneur, and it is hard to understand what led him to persevere in Jamaica once it became obvious that his company had exhausted the generous support of its patrons. Possibly Holland had decided to settle in Jamaica and was intent on making theatre a paying proposition. Domestic trouble might also have en-

111

tered the picture at this time, as might be deduced from coming events in the unfolding saga of Holland's dealings.

Early in 1876, Effie Johns left for New York, ostensibly to recruit a new company to be managed by Holland. Before this venture materialized, other developments occurred. In May 1876, the *Falmouth Post* reported the sudden death in New York of Mrs. Holland, known as Effie Johns the Elfin Star, and that Holland had left for America immediately on hearing the news.[33] As it turned out, the light of this particular star was not so easily extinguished for Miss Johns returned to Kingston the next year with a touring company of her own. Holland meanwhile had heard of a project to bring an English opera company to Jamaica and had agreed to act as the local manager. The troupe was expected to appeal to a broad cross section of cultivated society, rendering well-known serious and comic operas in English for a season of twelve nights before proceeding to South America. Subscribers were invited to purchase tickets in advance at a cost of £3 for the season. It was later alleged that Holland had received £400 in subscriptions before the company reached Jamaica.

While Holland was engaged in negotiations to underwrite the opera company's visit, yet another professional troupe, the May Fisk Dramatic Combination, made its bow to the Jamaican public on December 19, 1876. It performed for seven weeks without exciting much interest. Most of its standard offerings were by now "old hat" to the regular playgoer. Twice the company had to drop prices from 4s. and 2s. to 4s., 3s., and 1s.6d., then to 4s., 2s., and 1s., in order to entice people into the theatre. At the performance of *London Assurance,* one of the actresses refused to go on for the fourth act because she had not been paid her week's wages, and the curtain had to be rung down on an unfinished play. Then the actor James Lowery became ill and died. The company then advertised special performances, the proceeds from which would help defray the expenses of his illness and death.

Holland had traveled to New York to assist in recruiting the English Opera Company, which was under the leadership of H. W. Ellis. With Ellis were his wife Carolina, their sixteen-year-old daughter and the troupe's prima donna, Florence, and eleven others. Advance notices had described them as the most talented artistes who would give a season of twelve operas in a style superior to anything ever heard in Jamaica. However, when the company gave its first performance of Michael William Balfe's *The Bohemian Girl* to a capacity house in the Theatre Royal on May 1, 1877, it was immediately apparent that the singers were not only ill prepared but of inferior quality. After three weeks only five operas were staged with little noticeable improvement and Holland was forced to disband the company. The debacle caused a stir in theatrical circles. Company members left stranded on the island were constrained to make public appeals for assistance in meeting their expenses and paying for their return passages. Holland absolved himself of responsibility, contending that the artistes had broken their contract; Ellis charged that Holland had pressured him into forming the company quickly and embarking from New York before it had been properly rehearsed; subscribers demanded that Holland return their money, or at least that portion of it that represented the seven canceled performances. To compound the predicament, immediately following the opera fiasco, Effie Johns brought out her own dramatic corps of fourteen actors, most of them being variety performers who had been engaged to play legitimate comedy. They opened at the Royal with *Our Boys* and played with gusto for two or three weeks but failed to draw houses, and for the third time in two years players were abandoned in Jamaica penniless.

These disastrous ventures coming one after the other were reported in the *New York World* with additional grisly details that graphically portrayed the hazards faced by the touring professionals. On their voyage to Jamaica, which took eight days, the opera company had encountered a hurricane that greatly endangered the ship, which took in seven feet of water. One of the women gave birth while they were at sea; the child, being stillborn, was thrown overboard as the vessel approached the harbor. But the body floated ashore causing much consternation among the local populace. Upon cancellation of the opera season, several of the performers began giving individual recitals to earn their keep and to raise money for the trip home. The Ellis family formed a quartet and toured the island offering "Drawing-room Entertainments" until Mrs. Ellis contracted yellow fever and died. Some of the men shipped home as common sailors; two women had their passage paid by subscription from Kingston benefactors, while a third, "driven to desperation by her impoverished condition, took to drink and was left in a wretched condition by her companions."[34] Miss Florence Ellis was taken in and cared for by a Jamaican family.

Stranded members of the Effie Johns troupe published a pathetic appeal in the local press, saying they had been living on bread and coffee furnished by their landlady, who could no longer support them. They had fed on bananas until their money ran out. They had perforce to throw themselves on the benevolence of the charitably disposed citizens of Kingston. Noting that a bill was being introduced in the Legislative Council to prohibit the entry of any theatrical company to the island unless its members were provided with return passage

113

tickets, the *New York World* concluded its article with the observation that "good singing and acting are appreciated and supported in Jamaica, but a company to succeed must be such a one as would succeed in New York or London."[35]

Effie Johns went back to New York, where she appeared as the Elfin Star at Brooklyn theatres in 1878 and 1880,[36] after which her name is no longer mentioned in New York stage records. The irrepressible Holland remained in Jamaica and continued to act whenever opportunity offered. In 1879 he was a jester in the Carlos Brothers Circus at a benefit performance given on his behalf. The next year he appeared with gentlemen amateurs in a couple of productions in Kingston and Spanish Town. He joined the E. A. McDowell Company for part of their 1881 season in Kingston when he earned a benefit night, and he was with them again on their return visit in 1886. Thereafter he fades from the scene.

The spate of dramatic companies visiting the island between 1873 and 1877 could not continue unchecked after the adverse report in the *New York World* and the stories of failed enterprises and hardships endured that were carried back to America by returning players. Kingston audiences too needed a respite from the emotional anxiety generated by the comings and goings of luckless troupers. For the next three years, 1878 to 1880, the theatrical scene was governed by amateurs, gentlemen and military, with the addition of a new element, school plays. These latter were presented by students in schoolrooms, church halls, occasionally at the Theatre Royal or a town hall, and advertised as open to public, paying audiences. Among the active amateur groups at the time were the Kingston Amateur Dramatic Society, the Cosmopolitan Dramatic Association, the White Cravats of Kingston, and the Blue Cravats of Spanish Town, the Pioneer Dramatic Association, the revived Philo-Dramatic Society, and the Lilliputians. Even sports associations temporarily abandoned the playing field for the stage when members of the Kingston Cricket Club presented Morton's farce *The Three Cuckoos* at the Theatre Royal on September 4, 1880, to raise funds for their new pavilion at Sabina Park. The next year the Rugby Cricket Club, with assistance from the Lilliputians, staged two plays at the Royal, the melodrama *The Idiot Witness* and the farce *The Obstinate Family*. Among the leading players were names we have already encountered: Joshua R. de Cordova, Leonard de Cordova, Julien C. Henriques, and Isidore de Pass. Others in the cast were Charles de Cordova, Charles da Costa, Joseph Morrice, S. J. Nunes, George Patterson, and Clifford C. Henriques in a female part.

The emergence of school plays into the public forum was primarily due to two teacher-clerics, the Reverend John Radcliffe and the Reverend Father Xavier Jaeckel. Radcliffe had arrived in Kingston from Northern Ireland in 1849 and was associated with the Collegiate School, where he became principal during his long residence of over forty years on the island. Active in extracurricular pursuits, he gave public lectures, wrote and published poems, formed in 1871 the College Debating Society from among his former pupils, and in 1875 organized monthly literary and musical entertainments at the school, where, for an admission fee of one shilling, the public would be regaled by amateur performers, male and female, with song recitals, recitations, and lectures. Radcliffe also wrote and published an original burlesque growing out of a religious controversy on biblical interpretation in which he was involved. He died in Jamaica in 1892.

For three successive years beginning in 1874 Collegiate students presented a major production in the school hall, the most notable being *The Merchant of Venice* on June 14, 1875, to mark the closing of the academic year. Directing the production was Collegiate graduate G. McCaddon, who played Shylock, all others in the cast being students. These productions, written up in the press, doubtless inspired other school clubs to come forward, among them Father Jaeckel and his students. Jaeckel ran the Mary Villa College, a classical secondary school for boys, which annually presented plays at the Theatre Royal beginning in 1878. At least two of his productions were Molière's comedies in English translations: *The Rogueries of Scapin* was given in 1880, followed by *The Bourgeois Gentilhomme*, adapted by Jaeckel and retitled *The Citizen Nobleman*, the next year. As shall be seen, these school efforts were to result in the writing and production of original Jamaican plays before the end of the century.

Three years devoid of professional players was punishment enough. The wanderlust to which troupers were addicted brought them once more to Jamaican shores. In the last two decades of the century, nine dramatic troupes and three opera companies played a sum of thirteen seasons in Kingston for a combined total of ninety-five weeks of theatre. Their visits were the more meritorious since during this period the aging Theatre Royal was in need of restoration and a noisy press campaign was under way to pressure government to provide funds for its rebuilding. The companies and their periods of sojourn were:

E. A. McDowell Company, December 18, 1880, to February 23, 1881.

Charles Arnold Comedy Company, October 30, 1881, to December 7, 1882.

Burroughs' New York Ideal Combination Company, October 23, 1882, to December 9, 1882.

Josephine Cameron's Dramatic Company, August 2 to September 21, 1884.

Slavin Standard Opera Company, January 20 to February 24, 1885.

E. A. McDowell Company (second visit), December 19, 1885, to February 2, 1886.

Morris-Fuller Dramatic Company, January 15 to March 25, 1889, later billed as Campbell Golan Company, April 3 to May 2, 1889.

London Dramatic Company, January 27 to April 18, 1891.

E. A. McDowell Company (third visit), February 3 to May 18, 1891.

Hamilton and Rial's English Opera Company, March 12 to April 18, 1892.

Empressa Ferrer's Grand Opera Company, February 16 to March 24, 1897.

Alfred De Lisser Stock Company, March 16 to April 24, 1897.

Inevitably, there are similarities in the composition and experiences of these companies, and it is therefore unnecessary to examine each tour in detail. Trends in programming and performance are of interest, however, as well as an indication how each company fared.

Given the dilapidated state of the playhouse, most of the visiting troupes were forced to spend time and money refurbishing the interior of the building before opening their seasons. This outlay put a strain on marginal finances, constraining managers and local agents to do all in their power to attract good houses. Next, it was obvious from recent experience that the optimum season for which a reasonable patronage could be sustained should not extend beyond two months. Companies therefore scheduled three and sometimes four performances a week over a period of from four to eight weeks, then left for another country. A third development was the introduction of new contemporary realistic plays into the repertoire. Works by authors such as Tom Robertson and Augustin Daly, along with Dion Boucicault's Irish plays, seldom seen before, now shared the stage with old-fashioned romantic melodramas. These contemporary pieces required a more natural and restrained approach to acting than hitherto, which in turn was reflected in performances of the earlier plays and of Shakespeare. Finally, the realistic dramas called for greater emphasis on scenic decoration to approximate verisimilitude than had been customary in the past. Companies now traveled with their own scene painter and machinist. These developments can be illustrated by reference to certain productions.

The McDowell Company of eleven men and six women, including a scenic artist and master carpenter, was a well-knit troupe, the core having worked together for years. Eugene McDowell was born in New Jersey, but along with his wife, the actress Fanny Reeves, had been managing a stock company in Canadian cities from Halifax to Winnipeg. His company made three separate trips to Jamaica beginning in 1880. For his opening performance at the Theatre Royal, McDowell chose Lester Wallack's military extravaganza *Rosedale, or, The Rifle Ball*. The performance was under the joint patronage of the governor, the commander of the forces, and the custos of Kingston. This was a tactical move to demonstrate wide support from leading authorities on the island, and to enlist participation of the Jamaican Regiment, a detachment of which appeared in the play. This novelty was such a hit that it was thrice revived: first with the production of Gilbert and Sullivan's *H.M.S. Pinafore* on January 15, 1881, when a portion of the crew of HMS *Urgent* took part; then on January 20 with *The Geneva Cross*, a romance on the Franco-Prussian War that used troops from the Newcastle station in a grand military tableau; and once again on February 12 with Robertson's *Ours*, when troops were shown departing for the Crimea accompanied by the regimental band. Moreover, three of these productions were repeated, making a total of seven performances that incorporated military and naval personnel.

The review of *Rosedale* noted that, while the play was not suited to display all the talents of the company, many of whose best members had little to say or do, yet "a better mounted, better dressed, better rendered play has not been seen here for many many years." The company performed with easy, fluent, natural acting; they were word-perfect; entrances and exits were managed amazingly well in view of the cramped accommodation on stage; and scene changes were rapidly executed. Here then was a well-managed, efficient company that knew how to please an audience by offering attractively mounted productions of both old-fashioned spectacles and contemporary pieces. Resounding applause greeted the end of W. S. Gilbert's *Engaged*, presented on December 22, and Mr. Abjon, scenic artist, was called before the curtain for recognition of his work. For the duel-in-the-snow scene of Boucicault's *Led Astray* on December 30, Abjon had "painted a beautiful landscape showing a forest after night snowstorm, the first steel streaks of dawn breaking in with almost ghastly effect through the avenues of leafless trees."[37]

In their repertoire the company offered five plays each by Gilbert and Boucicault, and three each by Robertson and Daly, all playwrights established in the latter half of the nineteenth century.[38] At the end of the final performance in their season, a deputation of townsmen presented an address on stage, thanking the company for their excellent production of no fewer than twenty-five celebrated pieces, given "with care, skill, taste, accuracy and disregard of expense." A gold watch was presented to Mrs. McDowell. With its Jamaican tour a complete triumph, the company left for Barbados and Guyana in February 1881, returning to Jamaica in 1885–86 and again in 1891. It is painful to report that, when McDowell died in his forty-eighth year in 1893, his obituary notice indicated that in the summer of 1891 he had taken a company to the West Indies, "where he had a disastrous season's business. The result so preyed on him that his mind gave way."[39] He entered a sanatorium in New York and did not recover.

Compared with the McDowell troupe, the Charles Arnold Comedy Company, which arrived late in 1881, was inferior both in its choice of plays and in the quality of acting and staging. American regional accents of some actors were pronounced and particularly disturbing. The company failed to draw audiences and departed after a disappointing season of five weeks.

Next came one of the most talented dramatic corps to visit Jamaica during this period. This was the William F. Burroughs' New York Ideal Combination Company, comprising fourteen men and six women. Actor-manager Burroughs had shown a penchant for Shakespeare ever since he had played in the 1864–65 New York seasons with the great American tragedian Edwin Booth, whose Hamlet had a record run of one hundred performances. Burroughs was also an experienced comedy actor, and his repertoire contained a wide range of offerings from *Rosedale* to *London Assurance* and from *Richelieu* to *Patience*. Shakespeare contributed no less than five dramas to his season: *Hamlet*, *Macbeth*, *Othello*, *Romeo and Juliet*, and *The Merchant of Venice*. Burroughs undertook all the leading roles except Othello, electing instead to play the more theatrical character, Iago.

Burroughs managed a uniformly good ensemble whose acting style was distinctively modern. This quality was nowhere more evident than in the will scene from Bulwer-Lytton's *Money*, as observed by the critic:

> This scene gave the entire cast an opportunity for natural realistic acting which was turned to best advantage. The strong cupidity and envious suspicion—of confident expectation and ferocious disappointment—were expressed by the several actors with an energy and truth that presented a revolting though powerful picture of human selfishness and rapacity. Throughout the entire piece, the acting was natural, easy and effective, showing that Mr.

118

Burroughs has been fortunate in securing the services of a clever all-round Company.

Burroughs's Hamlet, doubtless influenced by Edwin Booth's, "was marked by profound penetration, subtle analysis, and intense realistic expression." The soliloquies were delivered "with exquisite modulation, warm appreciation, unstrained effort, and quiet but potential effect." In the ghost scene, "he seemed studiously to guard against a not uncommon tendency in actors to exhibit violent and even angry excitement, preferring instead to let his surprise and fear be absorbed by the stronger emotion of filial love."[40] The production was a brilliant success in which the whole ensemble shared.

The company concluded its season on December 9, 1882, with a repeat performance, by popular demand, of *Uncle Tom's Cabin*, replete with beautiful stage pictures. The theatregoing public of Kingston had hardly time to congratulate itself on the tour's all-round success when, three days later, disaster struck. Kingston was engulfed in a great fire that destroyed most of the business section of the city. The Theatre Royal, situated in the northern environs, escaped the flames though some may have considered its survival a mixed blessing, believing that, had the old playhouse perished, a new theatre would have risen as part of the general rebuilding of the city.

In August 1884 Josephine Cameron's Dramatic Company arrived for a packed five-week season playing four performances a week. Miss Cameron and her leading man, Barton Hill, had visited Jamaica briefly the previous year on their way back to America from the disbanded Slavin Dramatic Company, which had been on tour in the Caribbean. Cameron was an actress of modest talent whose previous experience was largely provincial. She had, however, assembled a skilled company led by the seasoned Barton Hill, who had launched a busy career at the Broadway Theatre in New York over thirty years earlier. Despite an appealing repertoire that accented familiar plays of sentiment and passion and some Shakespeare, Cameron's company failed to attract strong patronage. One possible explanation for the poor response was that commercial interests in the city were still recovering from the losses sustained in the fire and could not give the usual generous support to the theatre.

The 1889 visit of the Morris-Fuller Dramatic Company was even less successful. The deteriorating condition of the playhouse was a serious handicap; in one instance scenery suspended from a rotten overhead beam collapsed during a performance. More damaging was the fact that the principals of the company had, probably unintentionally, alienated a section of the public who refused to patronize them, despite a gifted cast of players and a season that included such favorite works as *Romeo and Juliet, As You Like It, Hamlet, School for Scandal,* and *The Count of Monte Cristo.* (Records do not disclose the cause of the contretemps.) The usual strategies were employed to entice audiences. Local players were brought in to act with the professionals, and the regimental band appeared on stage to no avail. When William Morris and Lois Fuller finally left the island, remaining members of the troupe tried to redeem the situation by changing the company's name and giving a performance in aid of the Jewish Alms House building fund. Those compromises failed to placate disaffected audiences, and houses remained empty.[41] Eventually the Kingston amateurs were persuaded to stage a benefit performance for company members and chose the suggestively titled *Two Orphans* for their production.

The advent of the Jamaica International Exhibition, which lasted for three months in early 1891, put Jamaica on show as never before. Appropriately, the theatre came alive with gusto. These were not primarily local performers as might be expected; the prospect of providing sustained entertainment of acceptable quality to locals as well as foreign visitors during the trade fair was considered too risky for amateur players. Vocal and instrumental concerts were given at the Conversorium by the Kingston Choral Union under their director T. Ellis Jackson, but for dramatic performances two visiting troupes of professionals were installed respectively in the temporary Exhibition Hall theatre and a hastily refurbished Theatre Royal. They were the London Dramatic Company led by Warren F. Hill and E. A. McDowell's enormously popular company, with its favorite star Fanny Reeves, on its third visit to the island. Playing an average of five performances a week over the exhibition period, these two companies presented some seventy different plays for a grand total of 128 performances.

As the festival was meant to brighten the spirits and unlock the purses of nationals and foreigners alike, the plays chosen for production were mostly lighthearted: comedies, melodramas, and historical romances by such authors as Boucicault, W. S. Gilbert, Victorien Sardou, and Arthur Pinero. These rival companies from England and America competed by occasionally staging the same piece, for example, *The Private Secretary* or *The Colleen Bawn,* on the same evening or within a few nights of each other. When the London troupe presented that old favorite *East Lynne* by Mrs. Henry Wood, the American players countered with *Sara Multon,* which they billed as "the new *East Lynne."* This good-humored jousting must have kept audiences agog in discussion on the relative merits of the actors. Hill's London company completed its tour on April 18, two weeks before the official end of the exhibition, and McDowell audaciously moved his troupe into the Exhibition Hall, where he revived several of his earlier successes at the Royal. Then, as the exhibition grounds closed on May 2, he moved back to the Theatre Royal for two more weeks, playing an extended season of fifteen weeks in Kingston.

It would have been encouraging to record that these companies enjoyed box-office success, but a report on McDowell's returns indicated that, while the tour began promisingly, business was on the whole considerably less than expected. Only in the final weeks, when there were no other attractions and the company had elicited the patronage of the governor and Lady Blake, did business improve substantially. On closing night, with the house packed "from pit to dome" and with Their Excellencies in attendance, McDowell gave a farewell speech in which he hoped, on his return to Jamaica, "to find a new theatre, large and comfortable and suited to the requirements of a large and important city such as Kingston. . . . The speech was received with prolonged and vociferous cheers, showing a desire on the part of those present for a new and elegant place of amusement."[42] Kingston eventually got its new playhouse in 1897, but McDowell did not live to see it. As reported earlier, he died in New York in February 1893.

The ambition to supply Kingston with quality theatre through visits of first-rate professional companies continued to occupy the minds of native enthusiasts. It was clear that such an enterprise would be financially feasible only on the basis of a subscription audience that would reserve a good part of the house for the entire bill of plays. Lewis Hallam had tried this plan a hundred years earlier with some success, and in 1877 there was the ill-fated Holland subscription season of English operas that was abandoned midway through the run. Now a Jamaican actor working abroad came up with his own proposal. In a letter to the *Colonial Standard*, Rudolph de Cordova of the Lyceum Theatre in Baltimore offered a five-week season of fifteen plays at a cost of £2 10s. (or 3s.4d. a ticket) for seats in the parquette and dress circle. The season would begin about June 1, 1893. Twelve of the plays would be new to Jamaica, the other three would be well-known classics. Contemporary authors whose works would be presented would include Henry Arthur Jones, Arthur Pinero, Bronson Howard, Sydney Grundy, and possibly Tennyson.

De Cordova argued that the expenses involved in outfitting a company with scenery and costumes, along with paying round-trip transportation and the salaries of competent actors, were too heavy for an enterprise of this kind to be undertaken on a speculative basis. Companies recruited without the necessary capital outlay were apt to be substandard, their poor performances usually resulted in poor audiences, and this was "the surest way to degrade Art and to bring its followers to a financially early grave." He promised to select his company carefully, and that the core of them would comprise colleagues currently engaged with Mme Modjeska at the Lyceum Theatre, Baltimore. Having played together over a season they had created a harmonious ensemble, thus obviating the need for the star system. A scenic artist and a stage electrician would be engaged as part of the troupe to ensure that the visual quality of the productions would be of the highest. De Cordova ended his proposal with an appeal for support stating: "The motive which inspires me to offer this season of Drama to the inhabitants of Kingston is not that of mere gain. . . . Far beyond money will be the pleasure for me, a son of Jamaica, to work for the enjoyment of the people among whom I was born . . . and to win a place in their hearts so that I may return every year for a short season and produce for them the best plays which have been seen since the previous year. This would be a pleasure I cannot over-estimate."[43] De Cordova's plan had the virtue of keeping the Jamaican theatre up-to-date with contemporary plays, presenting them by a closely knit professional company over a short season that playgoers could support, and doing so on an annual basis. His offer, however, was ill timed, and the project failed to materialize. The old playhouse had to be pulled down, and until a new building was ready, professional troupes could no longer be properly accommodated.

The new Theatre Royal opened its doors in 1897, and the first company installed in it was managed by another Jamaican professional actor, Alfred de Lisser, who had recruited his troupe of nine men and five women in New York. He had received a guarantee of £400 subscribed by several leading Kingston citizens, and in return he undertook to present, over a four-week span, twelve plays, "mostly emotional dramas [that] have been carefully selected from recent favorites in London and New York."[44] Six years had passed since the McDowell Company last visited the island, and theatre enthusiasts were in a state of high expectancy, having the added incentive of supporting a Jamaican actor-manager. They were to be bitterly disappointed. Totally ignoring Jamaica's long tradition of theatre based on established plays of merit, de Lisser presented five ephemeral dramas in a truncated season of three weeks, during which he shared the new theatre with a children's opera troupe. Because he belongs among the

Jamaican professionals, further discussion of this tour will be deferred to the next chapter.

Noting the dismal record of several professional dramatic companies toward the end of the century, it is comforting to turn to the three visiting opera troupes, which fared much better. The Slavin Standard Opera Company of 1885 consisted of twenty fine vocalists, a violinist, and a pianist. Other musicians were recruited locally. At Kingston's Theatre Royal and in Spanish Town the opera company presented eleven operas with nine revivals for a total of twenty performances. Houses were usually crowded and SRO (standing room only) notices had to be posted for some of the shows. Gilbert and Sullivan's *Patience, Pinafore, Pirates of Penzance,* and *Iolanthe* featured prominently in the repertoire, the last named earning praise as "the gem of the season," but the works that appealed most to audiences were Robert Planquette's *Chimes of Normandy* and Edmond Audran's *La Mascotte*. A distinct favorite during their six-week stay on the island, Slavin's company may have inspired the formation of a local amateur opera group.

Hamilton and Rial's English Opera Company of 1892 made less of an impact. With fifteen singers this was a smaller troupe than Slavin's and one hampered by the illness of its prima donna, Miss Beatrice Golde, who was left behind to recuperate in Jamaica when the company continued its tour to Barbados, Trinidad, and Demerara. Houses, nevertheless, were mostly filled during a five-week season that included comic operas, concert versions of full-scale works, and medleys, which were presented at various locales in the city.

The real novelty in this genre of theatre was the so-called Empressa Ferrer's Grand Opera Company that occupied the Theatre Royal in 1897 soon after it had been rebuilt. This intrepid band consisted of about fifty juveniles who rendered, in Spanish, cut versions of popular operettas and short original pieces that had been specially composed and arranged for them. Their performances were vociferously hailed by the scores of Cuban refugees on the island, who had been displaced from their homeland by the prolonged independence war against Spanish rule. More objective criticism noted that, while the eye was gratified and the ear amused by the youthful singers, the pulse remained unstirred. The Spanish dialogue of the operas was too prolix, few could understand it, and the music was too trivial, yet "a certain respectful admiration remains to rescue the productions from the fatal reproach of feebleness."[45] Among the works presented were the now familiar *Chimes of Normandy* and *La Mascotte* that had already been made popular by the Slavin company.

Ten years prior to the arrival of the Empressa's troupe of youthful singers, history was made when the first Jamaican opera company, numbering fifty vocalists, adults as well as juveniles, presented *La Mascotte* at the Royal in Kingston on October 6, 1887. Acclaimed an outstanding triumph on all sides, the production received three additional performances on October 11 and 18 and December 12. The amateur company had been carefully coached by J. J. Lewis, with Miss Carmen taking charge of the younger actors. Lewis would later emerge as the leading stage director on the island, responsible for directing the productions of several amateur groups. Filling the title role in the opera was Miss Lurline Nunes in her stage debut. Her delightful voice and vivacious stage personality stole the hearts of the audience. She continued to enliven amateur theatricals in Jamaica for many years and was still appearing in dramatic productions in 1900. Other leading players in the opera also performed creditably while the choruses were capitally rendered. The enraptured critic remarked that although allowances were usually made for amateur effort, this production required neither exceptional consideration nor traditional indulgence. His feeling of personal gratification had been succeeded by the proud reflection: "In no part of the world was it possible for a community of the same size to bring forward a better display of musical and artistic talent."[46]

Encouraged by their accomplishment, the company formed themselves into a new association called "La Mascotte" for the production of comic operas. In May 1888 they presented *The Little Tycoon* at the Royal for two performances. This opera, being new to Jamaica, was not so popular as *La Mascotte*, nor was it as skillfully rendered, two or three of the vocalists, including Miss Nunes, having been afflicted with colds on opening night. However, the shows were well attended and the company preserved its reputation for a handsomely mounted production. In September of that year the group again appeared at the Royal, this time in Gilbert and Sullivan's *The Mikado*, which earned four performances; then *La Mascotte* was revived in December for two more showings. The strain of rehearsing and presenting six performances of two operas over a two-month period may have been too strenuous for an amateur group. After 1888 they are heard from no more. Nevertheless the success of their efforts must have emboldened other amateurs to attempt musical theatre, for in the years ahead no less than eight different operettas were produced. Two of them proved popular enough to warrant repetition: *The Frolic of the Flowers* in 1892 by the Children of Alpha Cottage, and *John Bull and His Trades* in 1899 by the Lilliputians. Each piece received three performances at the Theatre Royal before reasonably well-attended houses.

As with lyric theatre, so with the dramatic: some of the most impressive work of the period was provided by amateurs. In productions as diverse as Sheridan's *The Critic*, Gilbert's *Box and Cox*, Robertson's *Caste*, Pinero's *The Magistrate*, the comedy-drama *Alone* by J. P. Simpson and H. C. Merivale, and Garrick's military drama *Neck or Nothing*, local players entertained audiences with skill, energy, and a variety of subject matter. They played not only in Kingston but also traveled to outlying towns, many of which were supporting their own groups of thespians. Thus the last two decades of the nineteenth century witnessed theatricals in Black River, Falmouth, Lucea, Mandeville, Montego Bay, Port Maria, and Spanish Town as well as Kingston. The military amateurs were also active in this period. At Up Park Camp in the city, they opened the Garrison Theatre, which continued to serve as a performing space into the mid-twentieth century. But perhaps their most enduring contribution to the Jamaican theatre was in the introduction of the modern English pantomime.

Traditional English pantomime had been part of the theatrical fare offered as popular afterpieces by Hallam's American Company in the eighteenth century. In its 1780 season, for instance, the *Genii*, billed as "the very pleasing pantomime," was played no less than six times. The last pantomime staged by Hallam's troupe during its final season in Jamaica was *Robinson Crusoe; or, Harlequin Friday*, billed to follow Home's *Douglas* on April 16, 1785. Thereafter, one finds the odd pantomime appearing on bills until about 1820, when they seem to have gone out of fashion. The next time we hear of pantomimes in Jamaica they are the closing attractions at circus exhibitions and are dumb-mimes. Thus the Mathir Circus during its run in 1838–40 offered a series of different pantomime acts such as "Harlequin Skeleton," "Harlequin Doctor," "Harlequin Statue," and "Harlequin Protected by Magic."[47]

These silent mimic performances accompanied by music and dancing usually brought the circus performance to a lively end, to the great delight of spectators. On one occasion in 1877, when the so-called Russian Athletes brought their animal and gymnastic show to Kingston, their leading pantomimists appeared in the farce *A Bad Night's Rest*. This innovation scored a hit, sending the audience into roars of laughter and educing the critical comment that the institution of a speaking drama for a pantomime was a great improvement.[48] Hence it may be presumed that any pantomime performance that comprised broad characterization, expansive gesture, music, dance, and spicy dialogue was likely to be genuinely popular with a broad-based Jamaican audience.

In 1898 naval and military officers at Port Royal reintroduced the English pantomime in its modern form when, for Christmas entertainment, they gave *Alladin* at their station. This was followed the next year with four performances of *Dick Whittington and His Cat*, the last two showings taking place at the Theatre Royal in Kingston on January 6 and 17, 1900. The Christmas pantomime, based on a familiar English legend, with gorgeous scenes and dresses, songs, dances, transformations, and magical feats, was irresistible to children, but adults were also captivated by the "bright, witty libretto" adapted by T. H. Millet that "teems with local hits which do so much to make a pantomime, and its allusions to the War Fund found quick response in the soldiers and sailors of the audience and prompted many an outburst of splendid patriotism."[49] Two scenes in the production were set in Jamaica, which must surely have enhanced its appeal; one was aboard the Port Royal Guard Ship and the other took place along the Palisadoes that lined the isthmus between Kingston and Port Royal. For the Kingston performances, a special train was arranged to bring patrons to the show from Old Harbour and Spanish Town and take them home at its conclusion. This form of festival theatre caught on in Jamaica and was repeated every Christmastime by amateur players. Eventually its focus changed and a lively transformation occurred in which a foreign product planted on Jamaican soil was turned into a truly indigenous and popular theatrical event.

6

Jamaican Professional Actors

 In the late eighteenth century, Jamaica enjoyed an international reputation for having quality theatre. Actors advertising themselves in the New York Press would boast "from the Theatre in Jamaica."[1] As most actors making this claim had come originally from Britain, there is nothing that tells us about Jamaican-born professionals and their contribution to the theatre at home and abroad. As we have seen, local amateurs shared the stage with career thespians from an early date and frequently appeared in productions mounted by touring companies. As a result, the island began to produce its own cadre of career actors who journeyed abroad to work in metropolitan theatres. This chapter will introduce a number of these professionals and attempt to trace their careers through the end of the nineteenth century.

When the reorganized American Company under David Douglass returned to America after its first visit to Jamaica (1755–58), the young Lewis Hallam, then eighteen years old, took back with him "a West Indian girl" whom he had married.[2] The new Mrs. Hallam was an actress and appeared occasionally with the company, playing mostly small parts such as the Player Queen in *Hamlet*, in the 1761–62 New York season. Her most ambitious role was probably that of Polly in *The Beggar's Opera* at the Chapel Street Theatre on January 1, 1762. The union had produced two sons: one, L. D. Hallam, Jr., studied medicine and died prematurely in Jamaica in 1780 at age nineteen; the other, Mirvan Hallam, became an actor and appeared regularly on the American stage. The marriage, however, was not successful, and the couple apparently lived apart for many years. Mrs. Hallam died in the 1790s sometime prior to her husband's remarriage to Miss Tuke, an actress with the company. The younger Mrs. Hallam was thus the first on record of several Jamaican actors to appear on the foreign professional stage.

Well known and invariably billed as coming from the Jamaican theatre were the Storer sisters: Ann, Fanny, and Maria, who appeared with the American Company both in Jamaica and America at different periods from 1766 to the end of the century. Although they were recruited in Jamaica by the insatiable actor John Henry, who married two sisters and mated a third, the Storers were actually not native to the island. There were four sisters in all: the three named above and Helen. Their mother, Frances Storer, was a singer at the Covent Garden Theatre in London in the 1761–62 season and came to Jamaica the following year, bringing her four daughters with her. She probably hoped they would catch the eyes of wealthy Jamaican planters. Henry first married Helen, who perished tragically with her two children in a fire on board ship in 1766.[3] He then turned his affections to Ann, who billed herself as Mrs. Henry and gave him a son before she settled into proper matrimony with John Hogg, a minor actor many years her junior. Eventually, Henry married the youngest daughter Maria, an actress and singer, with whom he lived until his death in 1794. Maria died a year later.

Perhaps the most reputable eighteenth-century Jamaican professional was Frances Barnet Woollery (c.1764–1810) [fig. 10]. Her father, Edward Woollery, was a native Jamaican and a member of the island's assembly in 1770–71. Frances was sent to England for schooling, where her fledgling histrionic talent attracted the attention of the manager of the Haymarket Theatre, London. She was cast in James Thomson's tragedy *Tancred and Sigismunda*, which opened at that house on July 12, 1784. According to the playbill, this was her first appearance on any stage, yet she was assigned the title role of Sigismunda. The anxiety felt by the actress facing her first public audience and in a principal role was sensed by the Haymarket manager, the elder George Colman. In a prologue to the play spoken by John Bannister, who played Tancred, he begged the audience for their sympathy:

> You, who can judge a young adventurer's fears,
> You, who've oft felt a female's sighs and tears,
> Will hear a suppliant, who for mercy sues,
> Courting your favour through the Tragic Muse.
> Across the vast Atlantic she was led,
> With blank verse, blood bowls, daggers, in her head!
> And as she passed in storms the Western Ocean
> Felt her rapt soul, like that, in wild commotion!

Expanding his nautical image, Colman prayed the audience to allow this Sigismunda to "spread her little sail" despite the perils of "Critic shoals and Actor-marring rocks," since "Britain ever hails the cloth unfurled / And opens her free ports to all the world."[4]

10. Frances Barnet Woollery

Colman had good reason to be concerned. Only a few months earlier in the season, the two patented London theatres, Covent Garden and Drury Lane, had both produced this play, with the experienced and acclaimed actress Sarah Siddons playing Sigismunda in the Drury Lane house. How would the neophyte Jamaican fare against such mighty competition? The *London Magazine* gives this appraisal of her performance: "She possesses very great requisites for the stage. Her figure is one of the most genteel and elegant we ever remember to have seen. Her features are expressive. Her action is mostly just, but requires regulation; and her voice has but little compass or power. She appears to have great judgement, sensibility and passion. . . . She was well received by the audience and, allowing for the depression of a first appearance, promises to become an acquisition to the stage."[5] The production was repeated three times, the last performance on July 24 being a benefit for Miss Woollery. She also appeared as Lady Russel in another tragedy, *Lord Russel,* by William Hayley, which played at the Haymarket five times during the short summer season.

Returning to the Haymarket the following summer, Miss Woollery was seen in six productions, including revivals of the two mentioned above. Among her roles were Desdemona in *Othello,* Maria in *School for Scandal,* and Harriet in the elder Colman's comedy *The Jealous Wife,* thus displaying for one so young an unusual competence in both tragic and comic roles. Having served her apprenticeship in summer fare, Miss Woollery was recruited by Richard Daly as principal tragedienne for the winter season at his Theatre Royal in Smock Alley, Dublin. There she opened in November 1785 in a verse tragedy, *Elfrida,* and later appeared in the title role of *Jane Shore,* a performance that stirred one critic to assert: "Those spectators who were unmoved and sat with dry eyes must have had more stoicism and less feelings than usually attend the human breast."[6]

However, her career on the Irish stage was abruptly terminated by circumstances beyond her control. It happened that manager Daly was attacked in a local paper for his tyrannical attitude toward the players. In rebuttal he drew up an advertisement testifying to his honorable conduct, which he asked company members to sign. They all did, even those who had privately complained of Daly's actions, except for Miss Woollery. She took a principled stand expressing indignation that a theatre manager should have to declare publicly he is a gentleman, and arguing that her acquaintance with Daly was too short to justify her signing the declaration. Although she was a favorite with audiences, her refusal to sign so offended the manager that her engagement was promptly canceled.

Miss Woollery returned to the Haymarket Theatre in London in the summers of 1786 and 1787. In her final season from May 25 to September 14, she appeared in twelve plays, five of them being comedies, four farces, and three tragedies. In May 1788 she married James Cottingham, a clergyman's son, and retired from the stage. In her brief professional career she had performed in some eighteen productions, starting out as principal actress, a position she never relinquished. An Irish critic supplies this pen portrait of the young woman: "Her figure neat and delicate, her conception strong, her feeling exquisite and very aptly expressed, her tones soft and melting, her powers [i.c., forcefulness] rather too weak."[7]

The next figure of note was Jamaican by adoption rather than by birth. Born in Guyana in 1802, he arrived in Jamaica a teenager and began acting immediately. He played several seasons in the course of which he acquired a memorable reputation and a distinctive stage name. He then traveled to the United States to perform for a period of years, finally returning to Jamaica where he settled into a respectable career as a newspaper proprietor and journalist. He may therefore be thought to have earned his place among the Jamaican professionals. To grasp fully the relevance of his precocious career, however, it is necessary to introduce briefly a distinctly non-Jamaican wonder by the name of Master Betty, otherwise known as "the Infant Roscius."

The original Roscius was the most admired actor of the Roman stage in the first century of the Christian era. Over 1800 years later the Infant Roscius made his first appearance on the Belfast stage in Ireland. William Henry West Betty, to give him his full baptismal name, was actually born in Shrewsbury, England, of Irish descent and had received early training in fencing and elocution. In 1803, at the age of only twelve, he began playing leading roles in the major theatres of Ireland and Scotland to the utter idolatry of audiences and critics. While principal actors might draw up to £20 a week for their services, the Infant Roscius was offered £50 a night to play at Covent Garden Theatre in London. His appearance for twenty-three nights at Drury Lane brought that house £12,000 in gate receipts. So great was the public clamor created by this extraordinary young actor that in 1804 the British House of Commons, on a motion by the younger William Pitt, adjourned its business in order that members could visit the theatre to see the Infant Roscius as Hamlet! Happily the Betty madness was short-lived, at least in London, and though he continued to play in the provinces for years thereafter, reason had returned to the public who saw him for what he was—a promising young actor with an amazing memory, an elegant manner, and a natural acting style

131

that was marred by his habit of dropping his *h*'s (incidentally, a speech defect common to many Jamaicans).[8]

This brings us to the West Indian Roscius. It was common practice for Jamaican newspapers to reprint notable theatre items from the London Press, so the literate public would be familiar with the Betty phenomenon. They would also know that when the Infant Roscius played the leading role of Young Norval in Home's *Douglas, or, The Noble Shepherd* (a play at that time highly popular in the West Indies), the author himself was present and exclaimed that he had never till then seen Young Norval acted as he had conceived it. Picture then the reopening of the theatrical season in Spanish Town in October 1816. Manager Adamson announces that he has engaged several able performers who are expected to arrive in time for the regular season in Kingston, but in the meantime "a young gentleman has already joined him, whose early excellence as a performer, being only thirteen years of age, may justly entitle him to the appellation of the West Indian Roscius, being a native of Demerary."[9] The young man's name was John Anderson Castello, the play chosen for the opening was none other than *Douglas*, and the role assigned to Master Castello was of course that of Young Norval.

The review of the production published in the *St. Jago de la Vega Gazette* was very flattering to Castello. The writer was astonished at the chasteness and accuracy of his performance and pronunciation. Throughout the play, he displayed neither rant nor affectation but was true to nature, and in the dying scene he was excellent, the critic affirming that it could hardly have been better acted. Castello also appeared in the farcical afterpiece that concluded the evening's entertainment and which he performed "with such animation and propriety and, notwithstanding the necessary rapidity of utterance of this character, such was the distinctness and the power of his voice, that not a word or syllable was lost; he is really a wonderful boy."[10]

His career launched with high praise, Castello continued to play regularly as a full member of Adamson's company, enjoying the favor of Jamaican playgoers. In 1818 he took the role of Lothair in Monk Lewis's tragedy *Adelgitha*, which was witnessed by the author. As Lewis records, Castello's voice at the time was breaking (i.e., becoming more masculine), "which made him pipe and whistle in the sound. His action was awkward, and altogether he was a sorry specimen of theatrical talent."[11] Lewis's disappointment with this production of his work, already referred to, inclines one to view his acidity with indulgence. Oblivious to any loss of appeal among his admiring audience, the West Indian Roscius continued to regale Jamaican audiences with his boyish charm and precocious talent until the death of his sponsor, manager Adamson, in mid-1818 wrought a change of circumstance.

The new company manager, Mr. Burnett, was not as enthralled with the young man's talent. Facing a financially lean season, Burnett attempted to renegotiate his players' salaries. Castello, despite his juvenile status, insisted on being paid the same as adult actors, who, he maintained, received £10 a week. However, he was willing to accept a reduced amount, to be determined by arbitration, whenever house receipts fell below standard expenses. The upshot of this dispute, as aired in the local press, was that Castello was dropped from the roster, his last recorded performance with Burnett's company taking place in December 1818.

Castello is next found in July of the following year at the Pavilion Theatre in New York City where he appeared in one of his favorite roles, Caleb Quotem, in the farce *The Wags of Windsor*. For this relatively minor part he received special billing as "his first appearance in America, formerly designated the West Indian Roscius, and late of the Jamaican Theatres."[12] The production ran through August 13, and that is the only notice found of his career overseas. How long he stayed abroad it is difficult to surmise, but Castello was back in Jamaica by July 1828 when he appeared at the Kingston theatre in George Stevens's satiric monologue *The Lecture on Heads*. This performance was exceptionally well received, testifying to Castello's comedic talent. When in April 1829 the locally recruited English Company took up a five-month residency in the Kingston theatre under the management of Mr. Jones, Castello was the leading male actor and Mrs. Monier the leading female. In a season of light comedies, melodramas, and farces, the precocious young actor had become the self-confident performer. He had developed a flair for character parts in which he was often acclaimed, at times chided for overacting. For instance, playing the role of Glenalvon in Home's *Douglas* in 1829, Castello "exhibited too much bluster—shaking of fists—beating of bosoms—to depict the wily, haughty, and designing character."[13] When the English Company disbanded, Castello may have performed on subsequent occasions, for he was very popular with audiences. Newspapers, however, are missing for this period. Though he loved the stage and the applause it brought him from an early age, Castello was evidently not prepared to invest his future in the precarious profession of an actor. About 1836 he purchased the *Falmouth Post*, a weekly newspaper of which he became publisher and editor up to the time of his death in 1877.

The *Post* had been established to promote full freedom for the slaves who had to serve a period of forced apprenticeship after their liberation in 1834. This paper's political stance brought the editor into open conflict with the proslavery party, but Castello would not be silenced. Always a fighter for what he believed to be right, once full Emancipation was achieved, Castello also took a firm position against the perpetuation of slave masquerades, such as the Jonkonnu and the Set Girls. As a justice of the peace and church warden of his parish, he once attempted to suppress the so-called street orgies that were traditionally held at Christmastime, but which he viewed as a desecration of holy days. A serious riot erupted, the ringleaders were brought to trial with Castello, erstwhile friend of the Negro, now appearing as one of their chief oppressors.

Throughout his life, Castello's affection for the stage persisted, prompting him to give generous support to theatrical activities in his town. The indelible impression he had made as a young actor lingered in the minds of older Jamaicans. In a letter to the editor of the *Daily Advertiser* in 1857, two writers recalled "the days of yore when John Castello was really the 'West Indian Roscius.'" They declared that "if we have theatricals in Jamaica, it will be owing to the goodwill and efforts of the just mentioned Veteran Star of the West, [there being] few to surpass the versatile tragic and comic powers of the present Editor of the *Falmouth Post*."[14]

Castello's overseas record may be maddeningly skimpy but that of Joseph Gabay is downright elusive. He is included in the catalog of Jamaican professionals for the sake of completeness and in the forlorn hope that at some future time information might surface about his performances abroad. Searches for this study have proved fruitless. The Gabays were an old Jamaican family whose forebears arrived on the island some few years after the English conquest of 1655. In theatrical annals, Joseph Gabay (fl.1860–74) is first mentioned in a notice of an upcoming 1860 production at Kingston's Theatre Royal when he was part of a rather incompetent troupe assembled by Morton Tavares. He received a benefit performance and was referred to as "our countryman."[15] Next, in the role of Valcour he gave an effective and pleasing performance in a local production of *The Point of Honour*, a military drama that was staged at the Royal in March 1864 to raise funds for the Drum Corps of the Kingston Artillery. In a report of that production, Gabay is again referred to as "a native of this island," but on this occasion he is one "who has, we understand, taken to the profession and performed with success in the United States."[16]

Further references to Gabay occurred ten years later when in 1874 he was called upon to direct a benefit performance of *Uncle Tom's Cabin* for a member of the touring Eureka Drama Company, which had enlisted the assistance of Kingston amateurs. This performance took place at the Theatre Royal on August 20, and in return the Amateur Dramatic Society gave Gabay a complimentary benefit production of *Camille* at the Royal, in which he played Armand Duval to the Camille of Zoe Gayton of the Eureka Company. The announcements state that Gabay, a fellow townsman who had been away for twenty-five years, had "lately been connected with the principal theatres in New Orleans, Memphis and St. Louis."[17]

Attempts to track down Gabay's engagements in these cities and elsewhere in North America have been largely unsuccessful. An actor listed as J. Gobay was in the 1858 summer company of the Varieties Theatre in New Orleans, and his contract apparently carried over into the 1858–59 season of Placide's Variety Theatre in that city. This is probably the Jamaican Gabay, but without further information it is not possible to report on the parts he played or what impression he may have made on audiences and critics. The fact that even on home ground his stage appearances were sporadic suggests that Gabay did not rely on acting for his livelihood. He may have inherited a small patrimony that he supplemented by claiming occasional benefit performances when he acted. One assumes that in his youth he was another stagestruck amateur who, when opportunity offered, went to America to test the waters for an acting career. He apparently worked abroad for some two-and-a-half decades with periodic visits home when he would perform on the local stage. Eventually he returned to settle in Jamaica, where he continued to dabble in the theatre, perhaps working as a stage director and mentor to amateur companies that rewarded him with benefit nights. Unable, as we are, to give a proper eyewitness report of Gabay's skill as a professional actor, it is necessary to rely on a secondhand account. Writing of his coming performance in *Camille*, the *Colonial Standard* remarked: "Of Mr. Gabay as an actor we know little save the frequent and high commendation which the American Press has bestowed on him, but we have been informed by those who have seen him on the boards that he possesses considerable merit."[18]

Yet another Jamaican to embrace an acting career is Lewis Morrison (1844–1906). Unlike Gabay's, Morrison's record was wholly overseas with no evidence of stage appearances on his native island. According to the *Jewish Encyclopedia*, Morrison left Jamaica for America "before his twentieth year." Had he performed on the local stage it would have been as one of those eager amateurs whose names were not at the time mentioned by the critics. Certainly his name could not be found among Jamaican theatre records. The *Encyclopedia* further states that at the outbreak of the American Civil War (1861–65), Morrison enlisted in the Federal Army in which he served as an officer for four years. On leaving the army he went on the stage, his first engagement being at the Varieties Theatre in New Orleans where he appeared in 1865 with Lawrence Barrett, then gaining recognition as an actor and producer. Finally, the *Encyclopedia* reports that Morrison subsequently played Iago to the Othello of the Italian actor Tommaso Salvini and assumed supporting roles in productions featuring some of the leading actors in America such as Edwin Forrest, Edwin Booth, and Charlotte Cushman.[19]

Further research supplies details to the foregoing summary. Morrison spent three seasons at the Varieties Theatre of New Orleans from 1863 to 1866. During this period he married a dancer and newcomer to speaking parts, Rose Wood. By the end of his engagement in New Orleans he was deemed to be a competent secondary actor who was partly responsible for the success of his final season. He then went to San Francisco where he played leading characters at Baldwin's Theatre. By 1874 he was in New York taking part in a double bill at Booth's Theatre, followed by appearances at the Park Theatre in Brooklyn. His first significant role in the city occurred at Booth's Theatre in December 1880 when he supported the romantic actor James O'Neill in the melodrama *A Celebrated Case* from the French of MM. D'Ennery and Cormon. Morrison took the part of the villainous Lazare, prompting one writer to remark that his saturnine appearance doomed him to villains.[20] He played the role intermittently for the next three years in various theatres in and around New York.

Other important roles undertaken by Morrison at this time were Count de Maubraye in *The Legion of Honour* at the Park Theatre where he is noted for "a careful performance,"[21] Creon in *Oedipus Tyrranus* at Booth's Theatre to the Oedipus of George Riddle, and Armand in *Camille* at Daly's Theatre with Eugenie Legrand in the title role. In 1882–83 Tommaso Salvini made one of his periodic visits to America to present a season of bilingual performances in which he spoke in Italian while the rest of his cast spoke English. In his repertoire were Shakespeare's *Othello* and *King Lear*, along with more contemporary dramas like *The Gladiator* by Robert Montgomery Bird. In this series of plays the supporting players were intelligently led by Morrison and Marie Prescott, two of the roles taken by the former being Iago in *Othello* and Edgar in *King Lear*. As to Morrison's alleged performances with Edwin Forrest, Edwin Booth, and Charlotte

Cushman, available records are silent. He could have worked with these luminaries of the American stage when they were on tours across the country.

By 1890 Morrison was considered to be "a star of some note, particularly 'on the road.' "[22] He was now married to the actress Florence Roberts who had a thriving career of her own. He had formed his own company and had launched into production of the play with which his name would be associated for years to come. This was a spectacular version of *Faust* that must have rivaled in its setting and effects the operatic productions of this famous work, which were then in vogue. Morrison took the role of Mephistopheles and as Marguerite he introduced to the stage Rosabel Morrison, a daughter from his first marriage. She appeared with her father for two seasons before moving on as the principal character in a little-known play titled *The Danger Signal*. After her father's death Rosabel starred at the head of her own company in *Faust* and in a dramatic version of *Carmen*.

For at least five years, from 1889 to 1894, Morrison presented *Faust* in one-week stands primarily at the Brooklyn theatres of the Grand Opera House, Amphion Academy, the Empire Theatre, and Holmes's Star Theatre as well as at the Opera House and Columbus Theatre in Harlem. His decision not to bring his production to the New York city theatres suggests that he was conscious of the inadequacies of his company and perhaps himself in facing the major critics. His last-mentioned season was in 1904–05 when he appeared with a stock company at the Grand Opera House in Brooklyn, apparently working up to the year of his death.

The next group of theatre professionals all belong to one of the most celebrated Jamaican families, the de Cordovas. Members of this family were theatre owners, promoters, producers, actors, readers, playwrights, and stage managers, both professional and amateur. At least five of them were professionally engaged in the nineteenth-century theatre for long or short periods. The de Cordovas came originally from Amsterdam (where they had traditionally been printers) via Curaçao, whence the eldest de Cordova arrived with his family in the middle of the eighteenth century to serve as rabbi to the Jewish community of Kingston. Because the family observed the timeworn Jewish tradition of naming children after deceased elders, it is often difficult to establish an authentic genealogy; but we know that in 1834 two half-brothers, Joseph Raphael and Jacob, founded the *Gleaner* newspaper, which the family owned and operated through the century and beyond. This paper played a vital role in keeping the Kingston theatre alive in its darkest days and in fighting for the restoration of the building when it was no longer suitable or safe to house productions and accommodate patrons.

First among the de Cordovas to be professionally associated with the stage was Solomon, but which Solomon remains an open question. At least two Solomons of Jamaican birth were involved in the nineteenth-century theatre. The first, born in 1813, was the son of Raphael de Cordova. At his death in New York at age sixty-four, he was reported to be in every respect a most estimable gentleman and highly connected socially, being with the New York firm of S. Cordova & Co., West India merchants, and a member of the Produce Exchange.[23] He had come to the city twenty-six years ago (i.e., in 1851) and had been in business from that time. Could this gentleman have been the Solomon de Cordova who, in 1845, a few years after the new Theatre Royal was opened in Kingston, had left Jamaica for New York to recruit a professional company, which he then brought back to Kingston? He had leased the playhouse for a full year from July 15 and had planned an ambitious season of performances. Regrettably, few newspapers have survived from this period and no records exist of the company's productions, but it is a fair guess that Solomon functioned as actor-manager and appeared in a goodly number of shows. He had doubtless participated in amateur dramatics in his youth, although the etiquette of those days that precluded mention of amateur players by name in newspaper reviews makes it impossible to detail his involvement. In any event, by May of 1846 his venture into professionalism had proved to be a financial blunder causing him to apply to the Kingston City Council for relief from paying one quarter's rent. Assuming that we have the right Solomon, he must have decided to abandon the theatre as a profession after that experience and set up as a New York merchant, at which business he was evidently more successful.

The other Solomon of record was a nephew of the first and primarily an amateur player with strong professional aspirations. He was born in Jamaica in 1835, eldest son of Aaron de Cordova, a wealthy Kingston merchant, and was accounted "a wild dissipated young man who could not be brought to settle down quietly in life." He too had played on the Kingston boards in his younger days and must have gone to North America seeking a professional career. He obviously failed to secure gainful employment, for in a lawsuit he brought against his brother over nonpayment of his father's legacy, he informed the court that he was so financially distressed in a foreign country that "thinking he had a turn for the stage he changed his name to Frederick Leopold and sought work as an actor; but every effort failing he managed to get back to Jamaica in September 1869."[24] When in 1857 Morton Tavares mounted a series of productions at the Theatre Royal in Kingston with amateur support, Solomon de Cordova was on stage playing at least two roles: de Mauprat in *Richelieu* and Cassio in *Othello*. Years later, in 1873, he was one of two experienced Jamaican players invited to match their skills with the professionals in the W. M. Holland touring company's production of *Richelieu*. Solomon was again assigned the role of de Mauprat, eliciting from one critic the comment that he "had lost the physique of sixteen years ago but not his fine conception of the part."[25]

If a cloud hangs over the professional aspirations of the two Solomons, no such sign darkens the luminous career of Raphael J. de Cordova, another nephew of the first Solomon. In 1848, at age twenty-four, Raphael also went to New York, where for twenty-five years he managed a large import business. He was in addition a journalist and wrote leading articles for the *New York Daily Times*. But his true love was the stage. Beginning in 1858 and for some thirty years Raphael J. wrote and recited original humorous stories on public platforms across America. Since a separate chapter is devoted to solo readers and storytellers as distinct from actors in full stage productions, we shall return to Raphael J. in his proper place.

The fourth de Cordova to pursue a stage career was a thoroughgoing professional who became an actor, reader, and playwright in England, the United States, and Jamaica. Rudolph de Cordova [fig. 11], born in Jamaica in 1860, was the first son of Altamont de Cordova and nephew to Solomon. His father was a respected Kingston merchant who had served for many years as president of the Kingston Dramatic Association and must have introduced his son to theatricals at an early age. Rudolph was sent to England to study medicine and was actually enrolled at London University College Hospital for a time before he abandoned his studies and took to the stage. He began by forming, with George R. Foss in the spring of 1885, the Dramatic Students' Society, whose lofty aims were "to give further opportunities of practice to the junior members of the theatrical profession, and to promote the study of dramatic literature by the production of the best plays in the English language, especially those little known to the stage."[26] Foss would later become a Shakespearean actor and a reputable theatre director for the Browning Society, the Oxford University Dramatic Society, and the Old Vic Theatre.

The Dramatic Students' Society gave periodic entertainments that were attended by theatre critics of leading metropolitan papers. In addition, the young members received some benefit through contact

11. Rudolph de Cordova. Photograph © reserved,
National Library of Jamaica.

with the organization's patrons, among whom were eminent theatre
personages like W. S. Gilbert and Herman Vezin, while well-wishers included Henry Irving, Wilson Barrett, and Augustus Harris. With such
connections de Cordova gained a short engagement with Irving's Lyceum Theatre Company in the spring of 1885, and in September of that
year he was with Frank Benson's touring Shakespearean and Old English Comedy Company, playing a week at the Theatre Royal in Windsor when they offered *Hamlet, Othello, The Merchant of Venice,* and
Goldsmith's *She Stoops to Conquer.* In the last named de Cordova had
the secondary role of Falkland, which he played "with finish and taste."[27]

Rudolph must have known of his elder cousin's success as a public
reader in the United States, for very early in his career he too attempted solo recitals of plays, to which reference will later be made.
He continued to perform through the end of the century, even as he
developed other talents in play writing and cinema script writing in
collaboration with his author-spouse Alicia Ramsey. He was in the
highly acclaimed *Winter's Tale* production that played at the Lyceum
Theatre, London, in 1888 for a record 150 nights, after which it was
brought to Broadway, New York, for a six-week run. Leading the cast

was Mary Anderson in the double role of Hermione and Perdita. Four years later de Cordova was again on Broadway as a member of Madame Modjeska's troupe at the Garden Theatre, playing the part of Suffolk "uncommonly well" and supporting other roles in a repertoire that also included *As You Like It, Much Ado About Nothing, Cymbeline,* and Schiller's *Mary Stuart.* That de Cordova was consistently associated with some of the finest acting of the time can be gleaned from a *New York Times* review of Modjeska as Mary Stuart. It spoke of her "admirable talent" and concluded, "there is no worthier actor with us now, and we are not likely to have one in our time . . . her acting was never better than it is now."[28]

Rudolph de Cordova lived a good long life, dying in 1941 at the ripe age of eighty-one and adding to his acting credits a respectable number of original dramas and melodramatic sketches for the old Hippodrome Theatre in London, as well as a biography of the actress Dame Madge Kendal and several cinema scripts. The 1916 screenplay of *Romeo and Juliet* on which he worked as assistant director and probably acting coach was hailed at the time for its faithful rendering of Shakespeare's play "contrary to usual practice," a reference no doubt to the cut versions that were previously put on film. It was deemed to be "a great production and one that will easily rank with the best."[29]

David M. de Cordova was the last of the clan to be professionally engaged in theatre during the nineteenth century. According to his tombstone in the Jewish cemetery on Orange Street, Kingston, he was the son of Moses de Cordova and died on July 4, 1876, aged seventy years. He apparently never worked outside of Jamaica. As an actor he was frequently referred to as "an old and favourite amateur," having in his younger days played a number of female characters. He is included here in his capacity as agent of the Kingston Theatre, a position he held for twenty years from about 1855 (after the death of Dias) until his own death. These were difficult years for the theatre in Kingston, and anyone in direct charge of the playhouse must have been sorely tried. As Agent, de Cordova derived his remuneration from the fee paid by users of the building; at the time of his death this was £1 for every performance. It was therefore important to him that the house should be regularly occupied. It was also the agent's responsibility to see that the building was kept in good repair and to insure that the required bond against possible damage was posted by occupants before they were permitted to begin rehearsals. However, the dilapidated condition of the building and the lack of interest displayed by a governor-appointed committee after the 1865 riot made proper maintenance virtually impossible.

An agreeable and knowledgeable building supervisor was also important to visiting professional troupes of all kinds, and de Cordova filled this role admirably. Because he was himself an actor, he saw to it that actors were accommodated as comfortably as possible and he encouraged Jamaican players to use the theatre regularly, coaching them himself (probably for a small fee), assisting in providing scenery, and sometimes performing with them. He was always willing to contribute his expertise to productions that were mounted for charitable organizations or to relieve the predicament of stranded players and others in distress. In recognition of his services, amateur groups would periodically produce a play for his benefit, thereby providing another source of income for his labors. On January 21, 1857, Kingston amateurs gave him the first of these benefit performances, having "received much kindness from him as their Manager and desirous of testifying their gratitude."[30] The plays presented were Sheridan's *Pizarro* followed by the farce *Fortune's Frolic*, popular pieces that could be expected to draw a good house. For his assistance to Tavares's first series of productions with amateurs, de Cordova received another complimentary benefit on August 25, 1858, when the bill was a disappointing *Othello* and the time-honored afterpiece, *The Wags of Windsor*, in which he appeared as Caleb Quotem, the same character that had introduced Castello to the New York stage.

The Philo-Dramatic Society publicly recognized de Cordova's voluntary effort as stage director when they mounted the tragedy of *Barbarossa* in September 1862 to raise funds for several local charities, including the Jewish Benevolent Society. In March 1864 de Cordova was persuaded to take the lead role of the Chevalier Saint-Franc in Kemble's *The Point of Honour*, having previously played the role at the opening of the Theatre Royal twenty-four years earlier. Proceeds from the production were donated to the Drum Corps of the Kingston Artillery Company. As may be expected, the review of his performance was full of goodwill: "A veteran Amateur . . . proved himself, in spite of his advancing years, quite as able as ever to enlist the sympathies of an audience by his energetic acting and spirited reading." A month later de Cordova directed amateurs at the Royal in Lillo's tragedy *George Barnwell* in aid of the Widows and Orphans Society. "Stage management will be under the special direction of the veteran father of Amateurs, Mr. D. M. de Cordova," the notice read.[31]

In April 1868 when the Brooke's and Fyffe's Combination failed to draw audiences to their performances, amateurs came to their support in a production of *Pizarro* that was criticized as "shameful." De Cordova, his powers evidently waning, could not have drilled his youthful players thoroughly and was himself inadequate in the part of Rolla. He continued to serve for several more years as agent for the theatre, however, and in December 1869 the Juvenile Thespians mounted *Douglas* at the Royal for his benefit. The next year he was complimented for taking charge of the stage and other arrangements, which were perfect in the decidedly successful presentation by Kingston amateurs of *Lady Audley's Secret,* the proceeds going to help families that had been bereaved by the loss of HMS *Captain.*[32]

These various productions have been enumerated to indicate the range and scope of activities pursued by this Jamaican man of the theatre in the prime of his life. As agent for the Kingston Theatre, his compensation would not begin to match the duties he was called upon to perform. The point should be emphasized that it was not only the star actor, admittedly the most visible participant, whose contribution was crucial in keeping the Jamaican theatre active and healthy. There were many others including the old theatre agent who functioned also as stage manager, director, scenic artist, building supervisor, and sometimes actor. D. M. de Cordova had been all of these by the time he died in 1876.

None of the previously mentioned Jamaican professionals amassed a record of performances as spectacular as that of our next thespian, Morton Tavares [fig. 12]. His life graphically illustrates both the slim rewards and enormous sacrifices that are often the lot of those who follow the actor's calling. His stage career spanned five decades; he played on four continents; he undertook leading roles in Shakespeare and other English classics in major metropolitan houses. Yet in spite of extensive travels and wide critical acclaim, he came home to Kingston to play with rank amateurs, reinterpreting his greatest roles with inexperienced supporting players and in shoddily mounted productions. In the end, poor and half-blind, Tavares entered the Public Hospital to die in 1900. Tracing his career presented special problems for the researcher. He would disappear entirely or turn up in unexpected places. He changed his name two or three times, first from Aaron Tavares to Tavares Morton, then to Morton Tavares. In addition, he was sometimes billed as A. Tavares Morton or A. T. Morton, courting confusion with a contemporary American comedian of the same name. At one time he reportedly shared the stage in New Zealand with his wife, but it has not been established that he was ever married.[33]

He was born Aaron Tavares in Jamaica on December 1, 1823, his father Abraham Tavares being a small Kingston trader. Little is known of Aaron's early life but, like so many other young Jamaican Jews, he

12. Morton Tavares

144

was attracted to the stage and took part in amateur dramatics, allegedly making his first appearance on the Kingston stage at age eleven. The family home was at 37 Church Street in Kingston, a short walk from the theatre on the Parade, which he must have often visited. After attending a performance, Tavares was wont to visit the Kingston Race Course, where he would pour forth Shakespeare's soliloquies in the dead of night beyond earshot of neighboring residents. Just when he left Jamaica for his first trip abroad is difficult to determine. His obituary notice reveals that he set sail in a schooner for New York "unknown to his parents and with scarcely any money, his capital on arrival in New York being fourteen shillings."[34] On the night he arrived he spent two of the fourteen shillings to see Edwin Forrest at the Broadway Theatre. Forrest was at the Broadway first in 1848, when he had a very successful run playing *Hamlet, Macbeth,* and *King Lear,* along with several of his famed nineteenth-century roles. If, as seems likely, this was the year Tavares decided to become a professional actor and left home for America, he would have been a mature adult, being then twenty-five years old. His move represented a firm decision, not the rash action of a stagestruck youth. It is said that an American actor named Morton, long resident in Jamaica, had helped to train Tavares and had procured him an engagement in the United States. Out of gratitude to his benefactor Tavares adopted Morton as his surname and was first billed in American productions as A. T. Morton. One feels he may also have thought it politic, during his early peregrinations, to screen his identity by changing his Hebraic name until his career was well established.

As A. T. Morton he is found during the 1854–55 season in the stock company of the Charleston Theatre, South Carolina, reestablishing with that historic American city a theatrical link that had first been forged by the Hallam and Douglass Companies a century earlier. In August 1856, as Travers Morton, he made his New York debut at the Summer Garden Theatre (old Wallack's), then moved to the Bowery Theatre, and next to Burton's New Theatre (previously the Metropolitan), where he played with the Davenports, being advanced to leading man in Boucicault's *Genevieve* when E. L. Davenport left the company. The Davenports were in Jamaica in 1840, and it is a happy thought that Tavares may have been among the youthful Kingston amateurs who supported their company at that time. Now he had become a professional colleague, skilled enough to replace the veteran actor. Of this first American visit we have only fragmentary records. Along with Charleston and New York, Tavares is said to have played a season under Bateman in Saint Louis, with Dion Boucicault's Company in Washington, D.C., and with Bates's company in Cincinnati, as well as in Canada. He may also have played a few seasons in New Orleans. If he accomplished all that over a period of some eight years he must have been a very busy actor indeed on his first venture overseas.

By July 1857, now called Tavares Morton, he was back home ostensibly to make arrangements for bringing an acting company to Jamaica. Kingston amateurs marked his return with a complimentary benefit performance of *Damon and Pythias* in which he played Pythias, entrusting Damon to a well-known and talented amateur who had previously played the role. This production took place at the Theatre Royal on August 6. The afterpiece was the fifth act of the melodrama *The Hunchback* with Tavares in the title role of Master Walter. The review of the production left no doubt that Tavares had become an accomplished actor. He was "undoubtedly a master of the stage. . . . His renderings of the principal passages of the author were extremely chaste [and] his delineation of the whole character was perfect as was testified by the plaudits of an approving and delighted audience."[35] This was praise indeed, and it confirmed Tavares in his intention to present a series of productions with amateur support, a practice he pursued on each of his subsequent trips back to Jamaica from distant lands, not always with the same happy result.

With his amateurs in a state of high expectation, Tavares next attempted *Richelieu*, followed by Gilbert's *Box and Cox* for two performances at the Royal on August 31 and September 12. He was accounted "great" in the title role of the Cardinal, but the disparity between his professional polish and the gaucherie of eager amateurs was glaringly evident. The actor who played Count Baradas, for instance, was a complete failure, and the critic made no bones about saying so: "A worse performance we do not think we have ever witnessed on the part of any amateur whose name has been modestly kept from the public."[36] He hoped never to see him again on the stage. Clearly, Tavares had to gather a stronger cast if his aim to produce regular theatre with Jamaican players were to succeed.

Tavares therefore persuaded a group of influential Kingston gentlemen, many of them Jewish and with theatrical connections, to form themselves into the Amateur Dramatic Association. This gave him the financial and logistical support needed for his enterprise. He undertook to produce a play a month at the Royal using the finest local talent available. Under this arrangement, Tavares mounted four productions over the next five months: *Othello*, Mrs. Lovell's *Ingomar the Barbarian*, the comedy *Time Tries All*, and Sheridan Knowles's

Love, each of them followed by an amusing short farce or melodrama. He was not seen to advantage as the noble Moor, the amateurs in the parts of Iago and Desdemona (played by a male) being the hit of the evening. In *Ingomar*, however, an admirably dressed production, "nothing could exceed the beauty of his acting." With *Time Tries All* strains were beginning to show in the company. The production received a carping review—it seemed to have been a hastily mounted show—and with *Love* the Amateur Dramatic Association dissolved itself "due to lack of strength and want of liberality in the management."[37]

Tavares was not the kind of man to allow this setback to thwart his plans. He was an actor and he would act at all costs. Seeking support from other sponsors, he presented three more full productions in Kingston. *The Hunchback* had two performances on July 22 and August 4, 1858. A revival of *Othello* took place on August 25, this time with himself as a brilliant Iago. A hapless amateur cast as the Moor was so "imperfect in his part he could not take the stage as he ought to have done but clung to the wings that he might be nearer to the prompter whose voice, at many parts of the piece, was more audible than that of Othello."[38] The third production, Knowles's *Virginius*, opened on October 31 after three postponements and played to a scandalously noisy audience that required police intervention to quell it. Tavares had advertised for twenty-five supernumeraries to take part in the production, and it is entirely possible that the disturbance was triggered by disgruntled aspirants whose applications had been rejected. For his final performance of the season, Tavares avoided further controversy by relying wholly on himself in a solo reading of *Richard III* on November 6 at the Theatre Royal. In the fifteen months since his return home, he had produced and performed in seven major plays and an equal number of afterpieces, had staged two revivals, and given a public reading. Considering the burdens involved in producing, recruiting, and directing amateurs, as well as acting lead roles in plays of such magnitude, this was a herculean accomplishment.

Tavares had been thinking of leaving the country once more and had given several farewell performances, advertising his reading as "positively his last appearance prior to his departure from the island."[39] Then he disappeared from view for over a year. Wherever he went it could not have been very far or for very long. On February 9, 1860, he resurfaced as one of the principal actors in J. W. Lanergan's touring company that occupied the Theatre Royal for a six-week season. Still billed as A. T. Morton, Tavares would at last be seen among peers at home on the stage of his beloved Kingston theatre. His roles for the

147

season, according to incomplete records, included Richelieu, Shylock, Kotzebue's "Stranger," and Macbeth, in which he took a benefit performance. Playing against Mrs. Lanergan in *The Stranger*, Tavares could only feel comforted to read an ecstatic press review comparing him favorably with the much-lauded actress. His overall conception of the role was considered to be brilliant.[40]

At the conclusion of Lanergan's visit and to capitalize on his excellent notices, Tavares announced that he would travel to America and recruit his own company of professionals. In July 1860 he returned to Jamaica with a small band of four or five players that included Mr. and Mrs. Browne, Mr. Mills, Mr. Dickinson, and Mr. Gabay (who was recruited locally). Kate Edwardes, who had agreed to join the company as leading lady, decided at the last moment against coming because of an alarm over the incidence of yellow fever in the islands. A regular dramatic company performing a classical repertoire requires a core of about fifteen players (Lanergan traveled with fourteen plus two scenic artists), so Tavares was shorthanded at the start and had to rely on local amateurs to strengthen his troupe. His new season, running from mid-July to the end of August (when there is a gap in available newspapers) was anything but distinguished. The old standbys were there: *The Stranger, Virginius, Pizarro, Othello, Richelieu,* and *Macbeth,* as well as *Hamlet* and *She Stoops to Conquer.* But one could not find a single glowing review of any of these productions. Newspaper reports were divided between soliciting support and understanding for Tavares and voicing criticism of inadequate performances that cheated subscribers. Tavares must have been relieved when it all ended.

For the next eight years, Tavares again became a mysterious figure, emerging into the limelight for brief stage appearances in Kingston before receding into the shadows. He dropped from view in 1861, had a brief turn in three productions with Dickinson and the Amateurs in mid-1862 when he was about to leave for England. In December 1866 he read Shakespeare on a concert program in Kingston, and with amateurs helped out stranded players of the Brooke's and Fyffe's Combination in three indifferent productions at the Theatre Royal in April–May 1868. Attempting *Hamlet,* he failed miserably. In November of that year he added *Richard III* to his repertoire with amateur support, and the following March he took a benefit as Richelieu. During this period Tavares may have paid his first visit to England, being "in straits there for want of continued employment."[41] Yet, when in November 1869 he was engaged to play at the Sadler's Wells Theatre, it was advertised as his first appearance in England. His obituary indicated that he was with Boucicault at his Broome Street Theatre in New York and with John Brougham at the Bowery Theatre after taking a company to Jamaica. These New York engagements would have had to occur some time after the end of the American Civil War, probably around 1865–66 or more probably 1867–68.

Of this admittedly dark period of his life, one of the darkest moments may well have been the day that the following notice appeared in the obituary column of the *Morning Journal* in Kingston on May 15, 1868. Tavares had been tempted to play Hamlet, for which he was both unsuited and ill prepared, with a cast composed of stranded professionals and amateurs. The notice read:

> Died, on the night of the 11th instant, at his official residence, Parade, Kingston, by the hand of ruthless assassins, William Shakespeare, dramatist. The deceased was formerly well known in this community, but of late years had not appeared much in public. He was induced, however, against the wishes of his friends, to leave his usual seclusion on the night in question, and was murdered in cold blood, as already stated. His sufferings were great and protracted, and drew groans from the breasts of the few true friends, who surrounded him in his dying moments. It is believed that plunder prompted the deed, as the sum of nearly £100 in silver was removed by some of the assassins.

"The darkest watch of the night is the one before the dawn." Dawn broke for Tavares on November 21, 1869, with the following announcement in *The Era*, London: "Mr. Morton Tavares from the West Indies will make his first appearance in England at the Theatre Royal, Sadler's Wells, on Tuesday 23rd inst., as Richelieu, Wednesday as Shylock, and Friday as Iago." He had finally reverted to his original surname of Tavares. The Wells was a small but distinguished playhouse in the working-class district of Islington outside of London. Tavares shared the stage with Edmund Phelps, whose father, Samuel Phelps, had become renowned at the same theatre for productions of Shakespeare that respected the text while enhancing it with visually exciting settings. By 1862 Samuel had retired and the theatre had lost much of its fame. Indeed poetic drama was on the wane in London. The great nineteenth-century English actors had had their day. The majestic Kemble had given way to the mercurial Edmund Kean, who was supplanted by the pedantic Macready and the younger, historically correct Charles Kean. Henry Irving was just gearing up for his spectacular rise at the Lyceum Theatre, while at the Prince of Wales Squire Bancroft and Marie Wilton were introducing a more restrained type of acting that was in keeping with the new realistic dramas that Tom Robertson was writing for them. In truth, the style of acting was changing, especially for Shakespeare and the classical drama. Old-fashioned oratorical readings were no longer acceptable, nor were the rant and tear of melodrama. In this transitional phase, how would the newcomer Tavares from Jamaica fare? The reviews speak for themselves.

Of his performance as Richelieu, *The Era* of November 28, 1869, wrote: "He is a far better actor than any new arrival we have seen for a considerable time. In everything he does the superior intelligence we have a right to look for in a performer of high class characters is apparent." The critic went on to describe particularly felicitous moments in his performance such as the Cardinal's expression of fatherly affection for Julie, his confrontation with de Mauprat (played by Phelps), and his defiance of Baradas. The report continued: "The newcomer makes all the traditional points, though with no slavish adherence to precedent. . . . Nothing could have gone better with the public than Mr. Morton Tavares's Richelieu. At the end of the first act the audience seemed to know they had an actor before them of very exceptional talent. The tragedian was called forward every time the curtain fell, and we heartily congratulate him on having made a very decided and palpable hit." There could be no better vindication of his talent and training than this, but more was to come.

Heading its column "Triumph of a 'New Iago,'" *The Era* of December 5, 1869, lauded Tavares's interpretation of this embodiment of villainy. Tavares had divested the arch plotter of everything that was unnatural, and was "unquestionably the best representation of Iago that modern days have seen. It was essentially Shakespeare's Iago . . . shown with an ease which was not constrained, and a power which was not forced." Calling Tavares "unsurpassed" as a tragic actor in characters that display artfulness and design, the review concluded:

> At a time when Iago is so seldom well played, and Shakespeare so little understood, it is refreshing to find that there is still on our boards an actor who is capable of restoring the fallen fortunes of the legitimate drama, and making some of the finest productions of our language acceptable, even to an age which has lost the taste for everything which is not "sensational." Such an actor is Mr. Tavares whose performances we view with gratification and surprise.

Tavares had left old Jamaica to rescue the classical English drama from neglect and degradation in its native land. No wonder the critic was surprised. Even the staid *Times* of London could not withhold its enthusiasm for the visitor, finding his face replete with "Southern" fire and animation, and his delivery possessed of a sudden and spontaneous freedom that set him apart from the ordinary run of conventional declaimers. With Tavares, the *Times* reviewer wrote, one is always aware of the thought that suggests the word, as well as the word itself.[42] After Sadler's Wells, Tavares played at the Surrey Theatre in London, the Theatre Royal in Dublin, where he redeemed himself in *Hamlet*, and in the autumn of 1870 was invited to appear at Drury Lane, then considered to be the national theatre of England. The play was *Amy Robsart*, a dramatic adaptation of Sir Walter Scott's novel *Kenilworth*. Adelaide Nielson had the title role and Tavares played the part of Edmund Tressilian, a Cornish youth devoted to her, in a quick, earnest, and chivalrous manner that the critic considered worthy of commendation.

Why at the pinnacle of his career Tavares should decide to leave London for distant lands is another of those mysteries that defy rational explanation. He had made a favorable, even triumphant, debut in the quest for histrionic honors at the very center of English-speaking theatre. There were other challenges to be won before he could claim true eminence in his profession, but he had the skill and energy to meet them. He had not exhausted all the roles in his repertoire, far less attempted new ones. Nevertheless, after less than two years in Britain, Tavares left in 1871 for Australia and New Zealand, where he remained for over ten years. In those countries he traveled and performed in many towns and cities: in Adelaide, Brisbane, Melbourne, Sydney, and Toowoomber in Australia; and in Auckland, Canterbury, Christchurch, Dunedin, Littleton, and Otago in New Zealand. To his list of Shakespearean characters that included Hamlet, Iago, Macbeth, Richard III, and Shylock, combined with the Victorian heroes Richelieu, Virginius, and Master Walter from *The Hunchback*, he added a number of lighter contemporary pieces such as *London Assurance, The Two Roses,* and *Still Waters Run Deep.* These comedies certainly helped to create a balanced repertoire, but they may also have been added to provide leading roles for an actress called Miss Surtees, reputedly Mrs. Tavares, who apparently had traveled out to Australia with the actor. Miss Surtees, an attractive young woman with but limited stage experience (one report indicated she had not appeared more than ten or twelve times on the public boards), received good notices for her performances in comedy but was far less comfortable in performing Shakespeare. Nevertheless, she and Tavares journeyed through cities and the interior playing to appreciative if unsophisticated audiences.

They performed with resident companies at urban theatres and joined others on tour to outlying areas. At the Prince of Wales Theatre in Auckland, Tavares played Iago to the Othello of William Hoskins, then reversed their roles at the next performance, causing the puzzled critic to wonder whether they were indulging their own whims rather than giving the public the best entertainment possible. Tavares's Shylock was ranked with his Iago (by all accounts his most successful role in Shakespeare), although not quite as powerful. At Christchurch he broke his engagement and was fined £5 in damages, which he happily paid, explaining that he could no longer tolerate his fellow actors who pronounced Shakespeare's words incorrectly. One said, "Launcelot is *diseased* and gone to Heaven" instead of "Launcelot is deceased."[43] After leasing the Victoria Theatre in Brisbane, Queensland, for six months in 1873, Tavares bought the building, renovated it, and reopened it as the Queensland Theatre in April 1874. There he installed his own acting company and was looked upon as a public benefactor for bringing high-class entertainment to the colony. He also bought house property with elaborate gardens and grape arbors in Brisbane, where he settled down for a period of years.

One assumes that Tavares had a successful tenure as proprietor-manager-actor in Brisbane. But once again he was drawn to a new country, and in February and March 1882 he is found in southern Africa. Perhaps a sudden and serious change in his domestic affairs may have occasioned his departure from Brisbane, for now he was traveling alone minus Miss Surtees.[44] In any event, he sold off his property in Australia, realizing a tidy sum of between £1,500 and £2,000. Supported by local players, Tavares appeared for a short period at the Theatre Royal in Capetown, then moved to the Trafalgar in Durban, Natal, for a truncated season of three performances, and finally to the Theatre Royal in Pietermaritzburg. Conditions for dramatic theatre were fairly primitive in these towns. Tavares's visit was beset with problems, not least of which was the unbearable heat that required the installation of noisy cooling fans in the auditoriums. When this heat was relieved by inclement weather during a performance, the sound of rain falling on the corrugated iron roofs drowned out the actors' voices. Added to these impediments were inept house management that resulted in several quarrels with audience members and a disaffected company that included many weak amateurs.

Of the Cape Town season we have only the puff that Tavares achieved success "in spite of obstacles thrown in his way." Plays presented on this tour included the familiar *Richelieu, The Stranger,* and *Othello,* an occasional *Macbeth,* and the usual farcical afterpieces. *Richelieu*, an "unqualified success" at the Trafalgar Theatre in Durban, could raise only a small audience. *The Stranger* that succeeded it was a disaster, with one of the leading female roles being read by a lady because the regular actress didn't show up. There had been a quarrel over salaries. Tavares decided to cut his losses and, although billed for twelve nights, for his third appearance he announced a final performance at the Trafalgar of *Othello*. He received high praise as Iago as did Harry Miller in the part of the Moor. Eliza Thorne as Desdemona was barely adequate. So effective was the murder scene when Othello forced the pillow on Desdemona's face that an outraged voice from the audience cried out: "Give her a chance, you scamp!"[45]

In Pietermaritzburg, Tavares again had to cope with poor audiences, such playgoers as there were showing partiality toward the rival house of the Gaiety, which offered variety programs, minstrel shows, and farces. Tavares revived *Richelieu* before the governor of the province, followed by *Othello*, scenes from *The Stranger*, *The School for Scandal*, *Macbeth*, billed as "a great spectacular musical play," *The Merchant of Venice*, and, for his benefit performance, selections from several of his Shakespearean roles, which finally brought him a decently filled house.

It is doubtful that his pioneering visit to these southern African towns was rewarding, professionally or financially, but perhaps Tavares needed a new challenge. The critics were impressed with his natural style of acting and his lack of staginess and exaggeration, but apparently his audiences were not ready for him. As one reviewer remarked of his *Macbeth* production:

> The audience, taken as a whole, was not prepared thoroughly to appreciate a play of this description. . . . It is not likely, for instance, that any persons present in the Theatre on Saturday night could unravel the meaning, and properly appreciate such a passage as the following one, indistinctly heard as it most probably was, at the lower end of the building: "if the assassination could trammel up the consequence, and catch with his surcease success."

The same critic quoted a response from "one of the Gods: who, on leaving a performance of *Othello* was asked by a friend what sort of a piece it was. Having paid a shilling to see the production, this worthy replied in an injured tone: 'A confounded fraud. There wasn't any singing or any fun in it.' "[46]

Leaving southern Africa, Tavares returned to England in 1882, a year short of his sixtieth birthday. Of this return visit little is known. His friend Alfred Cork says simply: "Though he met with some little favor [he] could no longer win the hearts of his audience. So he resolved to return and spend his last days in Jamaica."[47] Certainly he was in Kingston on March 7, 1883, when he gave what was supposed to be his farewell performance at the Theatre Royal on the Parade. Tavares had decided to retire from the stage and he chose to go out as Richelieu rather than Iago. The choice was appropriate. Richelieu, as one of his reviewers had written, was "an enfeebled old man, tottering on the verge of the grave, yet whose mind is as strong, as fresh, and as active as when the body was young and healthy—a mind towering far above that of any of his compatriots."[48]

With the little fortune he had made, Tavares bought a small banana plantation in an eastern parish of Jamaica but, ignorant as he was of banana culture, his venture soon collapsed and he came back to Kingston to seek work. The last fifteen years of his life must have been the most painful, being rejected as too old to follow his only true passion, the stage. But Tavares was never one to admit defeat. Cork mentions a trip to England when Tavares brought and won a lawsuit for slander "against a traducer who had embittered his life abroad,"[49] an action that quite likely took place on his earlier trip in 1882. For the most part his declining years were spent between heroically trying to maintain a small business—making soap and syrups—to provide a steady income and, in defiance of growing weakness, periodically assembling a band of loyal but inexperienced amateurs once more to tread the boards of the Theatre Royal and rekindle the excitement of his earlier triumphs.

What was he like, this world-class Jamaican actor, consummate devotee of the stage, whose entire life was spent in the service of his art? Born a Jew, he assumed a sardonic agnosticism toward the faith yet was proud of Jewish achievement and generous to a fault. In his prime, he was seen as "a zealous, brilliant, reckless, dare-devil and dare-Heaven" man who, as the years pressed upon him, was described as "moderately tall, dusky of hue, pronounced in features, with iron gray hair, dark-brown eyes, keen but sombre, a good fine head, a great curving nose, a firm, straight, bitter mouth, a strong chin, a well-knit frame, a quiet, grave yet slightly wearied courtesy."[50] Perhaps the quality that shone most brightly was his robust enthusiasm for life that would not be dimmed despite the trials of a nomadic actor's career. In the closing years of his life, as Alfred Cork observed, growing blind from cataracts, living in dingy surroundings with rickety furniture and an old box for a side table, he would gather a few close friends around him for an appetizing meal and a discussion of philosophy. Although in straitened circumstances himself, he could still find sustenance to help a fellow creature in need, whether friend or stranger. Tavares died at the Public Hospital in Kingston on June 15, 1900. A goodly gathering attended his funeral and laid him to rest.

It may seem ungallant to turn from the heroic Tavares to a distinctly minor actor and company manager, but the record of Jamaican professionals would not be complete without mention of the last name on our roster, Alfred de Lisser. When he first claims attention, de Lisser has arrived back on the island in February 1897 after an absence of some twenty years during which time he has, by his own account, been employed as actor, manager, and author in North America: "There is not a city or town in the United States of America that I have not been in, or in Canada."[51] He has returned home to make arrangements for the first professional dramatic company to occupy the newly rebuilt Theatre Royal in Kingston. His company is to consist of fourteen members, nine men and five women, recruited in New York from English and American actors. There are to be no 'stars' so as to avoid controversy, and de Lisser plans to present about twelve plays in the first instance. They will all be pieces never previously staged in Kingston, but which have already had long runs in England or America, thus establishing their stageworthiness. To underwrite the venture, he was guaranteed financial backing from Messrs. Andrew and G. F. de Lisser, Kingston merchants. In his meeting with the Theatre Committee of the Kingston City Council, de Lisser succeeded in persuading that parsimonious body to spend up to £80 on the purchase of a new green cloth to serve as a stage carpet for interior parlor scenes, and on improvements to the lighting fixtures in the playhouse.

Had he kept his promise regarding the choice of plays, the tour might have begun on a more positive note. As it was, he opened his season on March 16 with a completely unknown and untried vehicle, an original melodrama titled *The Golden Hope*. One of the joint authors was Henry Bagge, his leading player who took a prominent role in the production. By all accounts this was a most ill-advised decision, it being a theatrical canon that new scripts by novice playwrights seldom succeed on first airing. The choice suggested a lack of appreciation by the manager of the sophistication of Kingston playgoers and a pandering to the ego of his leading actor. The end result was a disappointing start to a season from which much had been expected. In a review that strove to be supportive, the *Gleaner* found the first act to be "somewhat dull," many parts of the play to be "wholly unintelligible," and the plot "certainly hackneyed." But its tone of manliness and honesty saved it and "with a few trimmings and occasional explanatory additions the play may become a success."[52] More forthright was the critic of the *Jamaica Post*. Declaring, "we have developed unmistakable intellectual feebleness and a brilliant aversion to all but the most vague and arid pleasures," this writer judged the play to be "among the most insipid melodramas it has been my misfortune to witness. . . . [It] bristles with inadequacies and absurdities and has failed to satisfy even the most depraved taste of the local public."[53] Nor did the acting rise much above the play, except for de Lisser's performance, which was accounted a splendid impersonation.

This initial error in judgment was hardly responsible for the early cancellation of the tour, but it certainly depressed company morale and may have contributed to a general feeling of malaise. The first production took place on Tuesday; the next scheduled for Thursday was postponed to Saturday, and the bill was changed as the company was not ready to play the announced drama. The Saturday performance, only the second by the company, was *The Burglar* by Augustus Thomas, a play whose plot "entered the Ark with Noah" but which was saved by the strong performance of Henry Bagge in the title role. Also in the cast was a child actor from Kingston whose presence on stage may have helped to bolster the size of the audience, but in fact the whole effort could not rise above the mediocre.

The second week again witnessed only two productions: Sydney Grundy's *Snowball* and another postponed piece, David Belasco's *The Wife*, known in Jamaica from previous productions. This performance represented the best effort of the troupe. By the time the fifth production occurred, Edward Rose's *San Diablo*, the company had split into two factions and the tour had to be aborted. Thereafter the inevitable benefit performances were mounted by one group or another of company members to try raising funds to pay their passages back home.

What had gone wrong? As aired in letters to the editor of the *Gleaner*, the tour's demise was due to management's refusal to pay the actors their proper salaries at the end of the second week.[54] For their part, the managers contended that the actors had contracted to play three times a week but owing to their own negligence they had performed only twice each week. It does seem as if the company lacked a strong core of experienced players and had not thoroughly rehearsed their productions before embarking for Jamaica. Throughout the whole debacle, de Lisser maintained a stony silence in public. His own participation as an actor in the company's five staged productions was curiously marginal and suggests some misgivings on his part with the quality of the company from the start. He had come to Jamaica five critical weeks before the rest of the troupe, and must have left the preparation of the team in New York in the hands of others who failed to carry out thorough rehearsals.

De Lisser himself was a good character actor but he appeared in only two productions, both times as a miner from "out west." In *The Golden Hope* he was convincing in the minor part of Big Joe, whose "bluff, hearty style was a pleasure to see after so much gentleness, for the villain was not a low scoundrel but a gentleman, so Big Joe carried the palm as a big honest miner." In *San Diablo* de Lisser had a more prominent role as Nevada Jim, "the happy-go-lucky, honest, upright miner, the man in whom you could trust your life, who revenged a blow with a blow, and stood up like a man against chicanery and villainy. . . . Mr. De Lisser must be congratulated upon his exposition of Western life and sentiment."[55] From this distance in time it would seem that the actor-manager, with his professed wealth of experience in both areas, was unaccountably remote from the center of operations and must be held responsible for the tour's premature end.

Despite his professed overseas credentials, de Lisser's name could not be found either as actor or playwright among the companies that played in most of the principal theatres in the United States during the last quarter of the century. He could have worked as a stage manager or at minor theatres whose records are not readily available. His principal actor, Henry Bagge, did appear as a supporting player in several plays in the New York area. The most that could be said of the abbreviated season in Jamaica was that the plays were pleasant and agreeable but in no way taxing the mind or engaging deeper sympathies. They fused old motives with situations of mild farce and melodrama, colored with a touch of truth, while the performers lacked the polished skills to bring them off successfully. "So far as progress is concerned," lamented the *Jamaica Post,* "1897 must hang its head and confess that the seventies and eighties had the best of it."[56] Only in the early decades of the twentieth century, with annual visits by the Florence Glossop-Harris Company from London and the W. S. Harkins Dramatic Company from New York, was the dream of regular professional theatre of high quality finally realized.

An attempt has been made to show the level of competence achieved by leading Jamaican theatre artists of the nineteenth century. The country had hosted many world-class acting troupes and supported vigorous and active cadres of amateur performers. The maintenance of a strong theatrical environment inevitably produced young worshipers of Thespis who desired to make a career for them-

selves on the professional stage. To do so, travel abroad was imperative. That some were able to succeed on foreign boards is testimony to
the quality of the grounding they had received in their amateur efforts
at home.

Their experiences were not always happy or successful. Those who
attempted to bring companies back to Jamaica for theatrical seasons—actor-managers like Solomon de Cordova, Tavares, and de Lisser—failed in their ventures, primarily because the players they chose
were not skilled enough or adequately prepared to satisfy the theatrical intelligence and sophistication of Jamaican audiences. Even experienced touring companies, such as W. M. Holland's, had to be reminded that "the public of Kingston are better judges of Dramatic Art
than to accept representations such as we have had for the past few
weeks of *Romeo and Juliet*, *The Lady of Lyons*, *The Hunchback*, and
Richelieu as specimens of good acting."[57] Nothing but the best would
suffice.

7

The First Playwrights

Hamlet calls actors "the abstract and brief chronicles of the time," and, addressing a company of players, he reminds them that the purpose of playing is to show "the very age and body of the time, his form and pressure." In giving Hamlet these words, Shakespeare, with characteristic modesty, is not describing the actor's craft so much as he is defining the playwright's role since actors should "speak no more than is set down for them." It is thus the task of the playwright to capture the shape, texture, and pulse of contemporary life and reveal them to the audience through the medium of the actor. In discussing the work of the first playwrights of Jamaica it may be worth considering how well they have carried out this duty.

The first original plays written and performed in Jamaica came from members of Lewis Hallam's American Company during its second stay on the island. Later, resident playwrights emerged. Some appeared as newspaper columnists who adopted the dramatic form to air their views on issues of social and political import. Others wrote plays to be presented by amateur groups. Altogether, by the end of the nineteenth century, these authors produced some thirty-eight pieces of dramatic writing, from short skits to full-length dramas, which represent the earliest known group of Jamaican plays so far identified [Appendix B].

On February 16, 1780, the American Company presented a farcical afterpiece called *Theatrical Candidates* at the beginning of its new season. In the published announcement, the farce was described as "a home-made production revealing the troubles and merry experiences of the company on the opening and alteration of the theatre."[1] Among the characters were Mercury, Harlequin, Punch, Pierrot, and the Comic and Tragic Muses. It happened that the Kingston theatre had been appropriated by government in August 1779 to house Maroon troops during a national emergency. When the emergency passed and the American Company was allowed to reoccupy the theatre, it was in such a state of disrepair that the players were hard put to make it ready for their opening performance. Hallam, in fact, petitioned the assembly for damages and received £125 in recompense. The exercise no doubt produced some memorable experiences, which the company apparently fashioned into a lighthearted piece that was presented, along with the evening's principal offering, *The Lyar* by Samuel Foote, to open the season. This assumption, however, is only partially correct.

In London five years earlier, on September 23, 1775, David Garrick had written and produced a curtain raiser with the identical title, *The Theatrical Candidates,* to mark the opening of his season of plays in the refurbished Drury Lane Theatre. The play contained under two hundred lines of rhymed verse in dialogue and song lyrics, with characters similar to those in the American Company's production, but for the omission of Punch and Pierrot. Garrick's play was subtitled "a musical prelude, upon the opening and alterations to the theatre."[2] Obviously Hallam had got hold of a copy of Garrick's work and staged it with modifications for his 1780 opening. He added two more comic characters, Punch and Pierrot, and also made appropriate adjustments in the text to make the farce relevant to the Jamaican scene. There was nothing illegal about this; adapting the work of others was acceptable theatre practice before the days of strict copyright laws.

The next year, in 1781, another company member, John Henry, wrote for his benefit performance on August 25 a four-act drama called *School for Soldiers; or, The Deserter.* This play was thought to be an adaptation of a musical drama, *The Deserter,* by the English playwright Charles Dibdin. Henry was quick to refute the charge, claiming full authorship of his work, which was "totally different in every respect from a piece of the same name, for which it has been mistaken."[3] Henry need not have been so squeamish. Dibdin's play had itself been taken from *Le Déserteur* by Michel de Sedaine, and even Henry himself may have chosen his main title from another of Dibdin's plays entitled *School for Fathers.* In any event, Henry's play was printed in Jamaica in 1783 and went into a second edition, but the script has apparently not survived.

Henry's experiment of presenting an original play for his benefit may have been quite successful. It prompted a similar effort some months later by another company member known as Miss Cheer, whose full name was Margaret Cheer Cameron. Her farce, an afterpiece called *A West Indian Lady's Arrival in London,* met initially with some resistance when, prior to its opening, objections were voiced by some who feared that it was designed to ridicule Jamaican society since its heroine "assumed the dialect peculiar to a few in this island." To allay such concerns, Miss Cheer hastened to explain that her Jamaican heroine "for a time lay aside the elegance of her character and assumed an awkwardness" in order to rid herself of three English fortune hunters who were after her money.[4] The sensitivity of West Indians to the use of dialect in stage plays persisted until the mid-twentieth century. In 1955 a secondary schoolmaster in Trinidad protested vehemently against the use of what he called "broken English" in West Indian plays. "Any educated person," he avowed in a letter to the press, "found speaking broken English should be thrown in jail and anyone daring to introduce it into the higher forms of literature like the drama should be hanged."[5] Miss Cheer's innocent little farce was presented on October 6, 1781, on a bill with Colman's *Jealous Wife*, she and Lewis Hallam taking part in both plays.

The American Company was responsible for the production of two more plays of local interest. One was an adaptation by the company of *The Liverpool Prize* by Frederick Pilon. Rechristened *The Kingston Privateer* in its new version, it was presented on December 8, 1781, with a cast of ten in a benefit performance for Hallam, then Master of the Revels. Apart from his prediction that it "cannot fail of pleasing," we have no further information of this effort. Finally, on February 7, 1782, the company staged an original piece entitled *Scandal Club; or, Virtue in Danger*, written by a "West Indian Lady," thus making it the first known play by a Caribbean writer to be presented on the Jamaican stage. Unfortunately, the script has not been preserved, but from its title and cast of characters—Tindar, True Love, Bareface, Lucher, Tatter, Sneak, Fidget, and others[6]—the play seems to be indebted to Sheridan's *School for Scandal*, which Hallam's company had produced in Kingston the previous year.

The five plays mentioned above were generated through the efforts of a group of practicing professional actors who performed them in the Kingston theatre. All but one of the playwrights were not native to the region and were concerned primarily with commercial success rather than with truthfully depicting island life. The next four plays are very different. They were written by local residents who submitted them for publication in Jamaican newspapers and journals. They were not intended for performance although they were quite stageworthy. Authors' names were withheld, the dialogues were subscribed with initials or pseudonyms, or they carried no attribution whatever. Above all, all but one of the plays dealt with issues that were relevant, even crucial, to conditions obtaining on the island.

First among this group was a brief *Dialogue Between a Poet and a Doctor*, comprising some fifty lines of rhymed verse that appeared in the *Daily Advertiser* in 1790. The scene is a piazza above Wit's Corner, the time is forenoon, and two characters, a Poet and a Doctor, who symbolize the faculties of arts and science, are in close discussion. They upbraid the Trustees of Wolmer's Free School for inadequate supervision of students and for improper use of funds:

POET: True, my kind sir, the copy-books
          Should once a quarter claim our looks,
          We ought to hear the children *read*
DOCTOR: And find where figures best succeed.
          Know, if the Masters teach the scholars
          And duly earn John Wolmer's dollars.
          In general that care be shown
          As tho' the children were our own.
POET: You're right; but mind me (if you please)
          (*Whispering*) We never shall be made Trustees.
          (*Parting different ways. The Poet, recollecting
          himself, runs after* The Doctor)
          I ask you pardon, Sir. I've thought
          We should inspect the *funds* . . .
DOCTOR: We ought.
POET: You know full well, when money's lent
          At lawful interest, six per cent.
          The lender cautiously proceeds
          And asks their worth who signs the deeds.
DOCTOR: The bonds you mean; but let them rest
          Earl Effingham will do his best.[7]

Obviously, the school in question was not being properly administered and there was a question concerning the use of funds to which the Earl of Effingham, then governor of Jamaica, had referred in a speech to the legislative council. Dramatizing the topic in the columns of the press would bring it before the public in an entertaining way yet make the point that reforms were needed. Drama begins to serve a corrective purpose.

The remaining three plays in this group were printed in successive issues of the *Jamaica Journal and Kingston Chronicle* in 1824–25 and were written by a member or members of the planter class. Very probably, there was a single author of all three. The first playlet, *The*

Exile, little more than an exercise in dramaturgy, was introduced by the following note: "Any attempt at the Drama is a novelty in Jamaica. Few planters are 'Theatrified.' The following is written, from the recollection of a Tale in Voltaire's works, which I read some years ago in France. [Signed] G."[8]

The little drama tells the story of an exiled Count and military officer who has been pardoned and recalled by his sovereign. On his homeward journey through a foreign country he falls ill and is taken into the home of a beneficent Countess where, by odd chance, his two children whom he has not seen for many years are guests. A reconciliation takes place when the children notice a resemblance between the Count and a miniature of their father that they carry. The dialogue observes the decorum of sentimental drama, and there is some attempt to characterize the Count's faithful servant, an old Irish soldier, through the bluntness of his speech. The discovery scene is, however, suddenly contrived and unconvincing. Apart from the repeated homily that loyal military service to one's country should not go unrewarded, there is nothing in the play that bears the least relationship to conditions in Jamaica. The writer, obviously a man of culture and a member of the plantocracy, seemed to be flexing his muscles for further composition.

The second playlet, titled *A West India Scene,* was published in the next issue of the weekly paper and preceded by a letter from the author to the *Journal's* editor requesting publication of his play. This letter was signed by "A Planter," and though the two plays have nothing in common, it is a fair guess that they issued from the same pen. The coincidence of finding two planters who were budding playwrights in pre-Emancipation Jamaica seems highly unlikely.

A West India Scene is a pungent satire on the question of whether slaves ought to be whipped to make them work harder. The issue was timely in view of the gathering momentum toward the abolition of slavery. By 1824 there were insistent demands to ameliorate the conditions under which slaves labored, one such demand being the cessation of needless whipping. With clever wit, an ear for authentic speech, and remarkable objectivity in the treatment of his characters, the author presents the dilemma faced by a concerned proprietor who wishes to institute reforms on his estate. He will abolish whipping, he will change the name "Negro Driver," with its connotations of barbarity, to "Bailiff," a person who oversees work; and in future he will have his slaves referred to as people, not Negroes. He conveys these orders to his Negro Driver, the dialect-speaking Quashie:

QUASHIE: Me no for make neger work again then?

PROPRIETOR: Fie Quashie! Do you a negro say neger?

QUASHIE: *Neger!* No for name *neger* den? You no for name
             Buckra?

PROPRIETOR: I am a white man, you are a black man.

QUASHIE: Me for *man* den like-a you? Me glad—me joy for
             yearee so!

PROPRIETOR: I do not mean to say that you are to be *like* me.

QUASHIE: Me bin think so. (*Sighs.*) Then make me name
             neger like-a before. Make me name Quashie too, te
             me dead. Quashie name fit me.

The central problem—how to make the slaves work industriously
without using the whip—is still unsolved. Quashie believes it cannot be done; his master insists that it must be done and says he will be
angry with his driver if the latter has to resort to beating. Quashie
replies that he too will be angry with the laborers and will *fum* them.

PROPRIETOR: Flog them? No, Sir! I shall not allow you to flog
             them.

QUASHIE: Then massa won't flog *me?*

PROPRIETOR: I shall not. But I shall be *very angry.*

QUASHIE: (*shrugging his shoulders*) Me no care.

PROPRIETOR: What do you say, Sir! Are you losing your respect
             for me, Sir!

QUASHIE: Me see massa no spec work for done.

PROPRIETOR: I shall put you to the field, Sir!

QUASHIE: Me will tan up. Which driver going to make me
             work if him can't *fum* me!

The proprietor is astonished to learn that most slaves feel this way.
He believes they need to be taught the virtue of honest labor, that
pride and satisfaction come from a duty well performed. If only the
planters had been considerate of their slaves and treated them kindly,
how grateful the laborers would be for the comforts they enjoy. After
all, buckra had brought everything good in the country: every fruit,
every animal, the pig, the fowl, at their door. Quashie responds that
the same buckra had brought the Negroes from afar to work the land,
and if they hadn't brought something to feed them, the Negroes
would have died out long ago. "Yet," insists the proprietor, "you feel
the good and ought to thank buckra for it." Quashie's uncompromis-
ing retort explodes the myth of gentle master and obedient, hard-
working slave:

> We feel the bad too. And, for tell massa true, we curse buckra
> sometimes. No, no, no, massa. Massa must not think say neger
> going to work for *coxing*. When neger know say, them *must* work,
> them work very well; but if them think say, if them no work,
> nothing won't trouble them—*them no care for buckra, none 'tall.*

Upon which declaration Quashie turns on his heel and exits, leaving
his master in great perplexity.

This is the first Jamaican play on record to deal directly with
an issue affecting the lives of thousands of Jamaican people. While
couched in a humorous vein and written from the point of view of the
planter class, it unintentionally reveals the silent resistance of black
slaves to their condition. The play also suggests why, with freedom
won, former slaves were unwilling to continue working on the estates
as paid laborers. Were the play performed today, it would be viewed as
a valid reflection of the feelings and attitudes current in Jamaica prior
to Emancipation.

In his letter to the editor, "A Planter" promised to bring back honest
Quashie and give him a pension, if the editor wished to hear further
from the author and would commend the play. It is most probable,
therefore, that the third drama to be published anonymously in succeeding issues of the *Jamaica Journal* was penned by the same author.
Called *Jamaica: A Comedy*, it appeared serially in three issues of the
paper. It was much longer than the earlier scripts, but was never
completed. It too is set on a plantation and focuses on the working
conditions of the slaves. It reintroduces the character of Quashie in a
peripheral role, but without the threat of the gallows. This time,
however, the author is less objective than before and the play can be
read as an apology for the antiabolitionists.

Toogood, a naive young master of Happy Valley estate, arrives in
Jamaica on what he calls "a sacred mission in the cause of humanity."
He has come from England "where the voice of truth is heard" and is
full of bizarre notions about the way in which plantation slaves live.
He pictures them as wretched creatures kept locked in dungeons, ill-
fed and ill-clothed, toiling day and night, and trembling at the sight of
their white masters. These slaveholders are all tyrannical with countenances that mirror evil, fear, and suspicion. Toogood's visit is to
confirm these impressions and to alleviate the suffering of slaves on
his estate.

Journeying incognito to Happy Valley, he refuses to believe that
workers whom he observes singing in the fields or those who pass by
and greet him civilly are really slaves. Slaves do not sing or walk about

unsupervised. When he reaches his estate in the evening, he is even more surprised to find his own slaves in fine clothes and jewelry, singing and dancing. He believes they are impostors and accuses Grinder, his overseer, of deception. Harsh words are traded as the slaves gather to defend their overseer against this upstart stranger. Fearing for Toogood's safety, Grinder discloses that he is indeed master of the estate. The slaves are taken aback at this news and puzzled by their master's behavior, but they give him a rousing cheer nonetheless.

Toogood remains convinced that he is the victim of an elaborate hoax. He thinks Grinder is a villain who has hired a set of maskers to replace the real slaves who have been imprisoned. When a single dirty and ragged Negro passes by, Toogood goes into a transport of joy, believing that here at last is an authentic slave who must have escaped incarceration. He rushes to embrace the urchin and to learn where the other Negroes are hidden, but the boy runs off in confusion with Toogood in hot pursuit as the slaves shriek their merriment at the ridiculous spectacle enacted before them.

A new concern seizes Toogood. He considers that the apparent happiness of the slaves is hollow. He aims to "strip off the outward covering of cheerfulness which tyranny has forced on [them] to cloak real misery." The overseer warns him against this course of action. To make the slave truly sensible of his wretched condition could lead to incalculable harm. This interesting line of argument is not pursued. According to custom, the slaves have been promised a merrymaking to mark their master's arrival, and they come to claim it:

NEGRO: Me never yearee say one massa come in-a country before, no gie him neger dance same time.

TOOGOOD: Tell me, what makes you so anxious to dance.

NEGRO: Dance make me joy; dance sweet.

TOOGOOD: That is because you are not happy without dancing.

NEGRO: Dance make we happy, any time.

TOOGOOD: You must tell me what makes you not happy, without dancing.

NEGRO: No, nothing can make me happy without dance.

Of note is the fact that slaves usually referred to their dances as plays, precisely the term used by West Africans to characterize their dance exhibitions. The usage suggests the centrality of dance in the theatre of African-derived people. The scene indicates how profoundly the slaves relied upon expressions of their culture through music, dance, and song to sustain them in their struggle for survival in an alien country. Nor should it be expected that a subject people, whose spiritual sustenance inhered in these cultural expressions, would readily abandon them with the achievement of freedom.

To return to the play. The Negroes will be given drink, a steer will be slaughtered and roasted for them, and they go off to prepare for the festivities. Toogood, meanwhile, remains unpersuaded. He fastens on the diminutive and witty Quashie, as unlike the stereotype of the vicious Negro Driver as imagination can conjure, and plies him with questions about flogging. Quashie is keenly embarrassed, especially when in the course of conversation he is called a villain and a barbarian. As the second act ends, Toogood's nagging doubts remain:

> Are these people happy? And is this a Driver? Impossible! It is all a deception! I have seen none of the things that I have heard of in England. Yet, I am certain that they do exist. They *must* exist. Here I see, outwardly, all mirth and cheerfulness—but do I yet know what is in the heart? Do I know what tortures are in secret gnawing the inmost souls away?

To his troubled mind, the overseer is responsible not only for deceiving him but also for the misery of the slaves. He decides to dismiss the tyrant immediately. At this point the play ends, unfinished. It was due to be continued in a later issue of the *Journal*, but no further episodes were published.

Incomplete as it is, *Jamaica: A Comedy* is by far the longest of the texts so far considered. Were it completed it might well have been a full-length play of some two hours' duration on stage. Although the plot is not developed to any degree, it is full of incident, the scenes are varied, and the dialogue sprightly. Unfortunately, the obtuseness of Toogood strains our credulity almost as much as the happy condition of the slaves contributes to his and our disbelief. The author's objectivity, applauded in the previous drama, is here subverted in defense of slavery, and the opportunity is missed for a piquant examination of issues surrounding the "peculiar institution." Nevertheless, we must be grateful for two quite entertaining and somewhat insightful plays about slavery from this unknown Jamaican playwright.

Before we proceed to the next group of Jamaican plays written in the 1850s, mention should be made of two items produced in the Kingston Theatre and about which little is known. The first is a melodrama titled *Rudolph* and billed as "the production of a gentleman of this city." It was staged by the remnants of Mr. Burnett's Company of Comedians on February 23, 1822, and repeated on March 2. The music that accompanied the piece was "composed, selected and arranged by

a [resident] professor of music."[9] Because the melodrama was subtitled *The Calabrian Banditti*, presumably the plot was wholly fanciful and in no way relevant to Jamaica. The second item is a play
manuscript lodged in the Jamaica National Library. Titled *Pelham*,
this drama in five acts containing a cast of eighteen men and two
women is apparently a stage version of Bulwer-Lytton's 1828 novel of
the same name, which carries the subtitle *Adventures of a Gentleman*. The author is unknown, but seeing that the manuscript was
dedicated to "the acting members of the Kingston Amateur Theatrical
Association, 3 April, 1847," it was probably produced in Kingston at
that time when the association was most active. In addition, careful
excisions and annotations on the manuscript suggest that it might
have been used as a production copy, which enhances its historic
value. However, as nothing in the story remotely pertains to Jamaica
or the Caribbean, there is no need to dwell further on this item.

We come next to the first named Jamaican playwright, who had two
plays produced by an amateur company to which he belonged. The
plays are original and, in the absence of scripts that have not been
traced, we must rely on press reviews of productions to reconstruct
them. Charles Shanahan, the author, was a young reporter on the staff
of the *Colonial Standard and Jamaica Despatch* newspaper when he
wrote his first play, a one-act farce called *The Mysteries of Vegetarianism*. It was staged at the Theatre Royal, Kingston, on September 20,
1853, by the Amateur Roscian Association of which Shanahan was
president. On the program were two plays, Edward Young's verse
tragedy, *The Brothers*, followed by the comic relief of Shanahan's
rollicking farce. With praises ringing in his ears for his first essay in
play writing, the young author completed a longer historical tragedy
entitled *The Spanish Warrior, or The Death of Vasco Núñez*, which his
amateur troupe produced on a bill with the aforementioned farce on
December 14 of that year. The evening was a triumph for the author
and his company. With this production it is possible to say that the
Jamaican theatre took a first step on its long journey toward home-
coming.

The Mysteries of Vegetarianism was a spirited satire on what one
reviewer described as "the vegetarian and hydropathic system which
has lately been preached in this city." The plot focuses on an enterprising bachelor named Fourdice who is in search of dietary truth. He
has lost his appetite for food and his health continues poorly despite
(or because of) his experiments with innumerable glasses of grog. He
is advised to try a new dietary plan, namely, "the vegetarian and
cold water system to the abnegation of animal food and spiritous

liquors."[10] This new regimen has allegedly cured one Allwood of a complication of complaints centering on delirium tremens, and this worthy gentleman is promoting the system in the community. In truth, Allwood is a humbug who pretends in public to be a paragon of abstinence but who, in private, imbibes copiously.

Fourdice decides to try the new system. He is opposed by a group of drinking companions who get into all kinds of trouble and land in jail. Eventually Allwood is unmasked and forced to confess that the mysteries of vegetarianism consist only of pretending to be abstemious to the public eye while privately imbibing to the fullest. "The piece was rapturously and deservedly applauded throughout," wrote the reviewer as he lavished praise on the amateurs, most of whom belonged to the printing trade. J. T. Dias, manager of the Theatre Royal, received credit for supplying the elegant scenery and costumes, "considering the difficulty, almost impossibility, of procuring necessary materials for stage costume." Very probably it was also Dias who supervised the production of the play. This glowing review of Shanahan's first effort ended by exhorting him further to cultivate his talents.[11]

Within three months the fledgling dramatist was ready with a more ambitious play, *The Spanish Warrior*. It depicted the adventures of the early colonizers of the new world as illustrated by the career and lamentable death of the explorer Vasco Núñez de Balboa (1475–1519). The play may have been modeled on Sheridan's 1799 tragedy, *Pizarro, or, The Death of Rollo*, which was itself based on the drama by the German playwright August Kotzebue and was well known in Jamaica. Sheridan's play was first produced in 1813 for an unprecedented five performances in Kingston and one in Spanish Town. It was revived in Kingston in 1819 for two performances, in Spanish Town in 1820 and 1821, and again in Kingston in 1841. Amateurs had a crack at it in 1829 and twice in 1847.

This first attempt by a Jamaican to write an historical drama set in the Caribbean is a matter of some importance. The history of the region is replete with tales of sacrifice and heroism that cry out to be recreated on stage. Others, but perhaps not enough of them, considering the richness of the material at their command, have followed Shanahan's lead. Tom Redcam, pen name for Thomas Henry MacDermot, wrote his play *San Gloria* (c.1919) about Columbus's shipwreck on Jamaica's north shore, but chose to examine the admiral's state of mind rather than the effect of his and his crew's presence on the native peoples. Other dramatists took a broader view of history. One thinks of C. L. R. James's *Toussaint L'Ouverture* (1936), rewritten as *The*

Black Jacobins (1967), on the Haitian revolution; Roger Mais's *George William Gordon* (published 1976), martyr of the Morant Bay rebellion in Jamaica; Douglas Archibald's unpublished *Defeat with Honour*, on the surrender of the Spanish governor of Trinidad to the British forces; Aimé Césaire's *The Tragedy of King Christophe* (1969), Derek Walcott's *Henri Christophe* (1950) and his *Haytian Earth* (1984), all dealing with aspects of the Haitian revolution; and Freddie Kissoon's *God and Uriah Butler* (1967), on the Trinidad labor leader during the 1937 disturbances.

The reviewer of *The Spanish Warrior* considered that, while the play was by no means perfect, it was "a piece of composition that many an older litterateur than its youthful author might well be proud of." The writer went on to applaud the correct delineation of characters. Among them were Vasco Núñez, a chivalrous protector of the Amerindians who were being abused by treacherous Spanish gold hunters; Caonabo, the noble savage, whose son was murdered by the cowardly assassin Garabito; and the trusting Indian maiden Carata, who forsook her tribe to wed a pale-faced warrior. As a rule theatre critics of the time were very supportive of serious amateur effort. They did not dissect individual performances too closely and seldom, if ever, did they refer to players by name. The hero of the play, Vasco Núñez, was well sustained but the actor had "a peculiar difficulty" that the critic thought it indelicate to identify. (As subsequently revealed, the role had been written for a different actor, who was unable to appear owing to ill health. He did, however, perform the role successfully when the play was revived.) Other leading characters, including the women, who were all played by male actors, were admirable. The costuming was magnificent and agreeable to the historical period in which the play was set. The only major criticism was leveled at what the writer called "the management" of the production, by which was meant the stage direction of the piece. It was "most wretched—about every scene appeared to be bungled—and the exits and entrances confused." However, the closing scene of the execution went far toward making amends for all inadequacies. As the band played the "Dead March in Saul" (from Handel's oratorio, *Saul*), the tragic figure of Vasco advanced in solemn procession toward the place of execution and "the curtain fell amidst thunders of applause, when at the call of the audience Vasco Núñez, Garabito, and Micer Codro [the Astrologer] successively advanced to the footlights and returned thanks for their reception to the audience."[12]

Here, despite some staging difficulties, was a thrillingly inspiring evening of theatre: a play in the tradition of romantic melodrama, of teeming incident, bold characterization, noble sentiment, arresting plot, historically pertinent to its audience, written and performed by Jamaicans before an elated and admiring public. This was a milestone in the history of the Jamaican theatre. One would like to think that the two plays do not represent the total creative output of the talented Shanahan, but if he wrote and produced anything else, the records are silent about it.

There follows now a duologue of substantial length, titled *The Two Governors: A Dialogue Between the Living and the Dead*, which was published in three parts in *The Morning Journal* in 1853.[13] The author, calling himself "Asmodeus" (which in Jewish demonology means an evil spirit), set out to discuss public affairs in Jamaica from the viewpoint of two of its chief colonial administrators, one recently dead and the other about to relinquish his post. Normally, a colloquy of this sort would attract no more than passing notice as political commentary couched in dialogue form. This two-character debate, however, excites more than cursory interest for several reasons.

First, it deals comprehensively with the crucial years of Jamaican history immediately following the end of slavery when the country had to adjust to a completely new relationship between proprietors and former slaves. That these two groups were further differentiated by race—white European and black African descendants—with the emancipated blacks clearly in the majority, only exacerbated the problem of creating harmonious relations in the citizenry. Next, the drama, written in palatable blank verse, contrasts the administration of two governors, one of whom was successful and the other not. Dramatic interest is engaged through character revelation, particularly when the unpopular governor seeks to justify his actions in dealing with an intractable legislature. Finally, the play forecasts with frightening accuracy violent events that would come to pass in Jamaica twelve years after it was written.

Part One has the ghost of Sir Charles, afterward Lord Metcalfe, paying a visit to his old Etonian schoolmate, Sir Charles Edward Grey. Grey is concluding his governorship at a time of great distress and political ferment in Jamaica. The treasury is empty; sugar and coffee, staple export crops, are in decline; planters have been ruined; commerce has slowed down; buildings, roads, and bridges are decaying; the island legislature is disaffected. Metcalfe, whose regime was also troubled at the start but ended in harmony and signs of progress, wishes Grey to defend his stewardship, to explain why conditions have declined and why he became such an unpopular governor.

Some historical background will bring the issues into focus. Metcalfe was governor from 1839 to 1842. He arrived the year after Emancipation. The planter-controlled assembly was on strike over the question of ensuring cheap labor for the sugar and coffee estates, previously worked by slaves. The former slaves, many of whom were now small peasant farmers, were reluctant to return to estates where wages were low and working conditions abhorrent in memory. Playing the role of conciliator, Metcalfe was able with great diplomacy to defuse the class animosities and instill a feeling of cooperation, for their mutual interest, between estate owner and laborer. When he left Jamaica in 1842 to become governor-general of Canada, Metcalfe was universally admired, and a statue was raised in his memory. He died in 1846.

Sir Charles Grey's term of office was from 1846 to 1853. He too had to contend with a recalcitrant assembly, this time incensed over the free-trade act of 1846 that had removed preferential tariffs on Jamaican sugar in the British market against the slave-grown product from Cuba and Brazil. The Jamaican planters felt, with some justification, that they had twice been betrayed by the British government. First their slave labor had been denied them on humanitarian grounds without, in their view, adequate compensation or provision of an alternative work force. Now their protected market had been abolished in favor of British support of a slave economy in foreign lands. Their fury against the official representative of the British crown was unmitigated if understandable. In view of the impoverished condition of the island, the assembly sought to cut official salaries (including the governor's) by 25 percent. When this bill was rejected by the governor-in-council, the assembly again went on strike, paralyzing the government and causing a loss of revenues that were sorely needed by a depleted treasury.

These were some of the stormy issues underlying the play as the Ghost of Metcalfe questions Grey and the latter describes the predicament he faced on assuming office:

GREY: Princely means
        You had at your command, and generously,
        Munificently, you dispensed your wealth
        And won a host of golden-leafed opinions.
        But did you after all restore the Isle
        To wealth, contentment, and prosperity,
        And give Jamaica permanent repose?
GHOST: I hoped to do so. Tell me, did I fail?
GREY: You put your seal on the Judicial Bill.
GHOST: Well, what of that?

GREY: Why, that's the *marrow* bone
        Of fierce contention they have fought about,
        I mean the "Council" and the "Lower House",
        Since '46, and I have had the blame
        Because I would not stultify *your* act
        And make the Council sanction its repeal!
        The Bill was one you never should have passed
        Much less *suggested*, but I found it Law.

At the end of Part One, after the discussants have mocked the absent Lord Elgin (whose governorship intervened between the two principals) for his plebeian gastronomical tastes and for playing up to the planting interests, Grey again compares his policy to Metcalfe's:

        You lived and govern'd for the day alone
        I've had the future constantly in view,
        You've had your share of living men's applause,
        Posterity will tender theirs to me.[14]

In Part Two, Grey's successor (Sir Henry Barkly, 1853–56) has arrived in Jamaica. Grey and the Ghost of Metcalfe discuss his prospects. Grey would like him to be firm and keep the leaders of the House on a tight rein, but Metcalfe is more tactful. The new Governor should "pat them as I did, and scratch their ears / And feed them; they will take the collar then / And work like bricks; I know the fellows well." Since spirits have the ability to foresee coming events, Grey asks the Ghost whether the new governor will be able to work with the council and Metcalfe predicts that the legislature will be granted a loan of £500,000 from Britain.

Grey, chafing under what he considers to be the slanders of his opponents, whom he identifies as the Planter's party and the Jews, would rather tax the land one shilling an acre and put a duty on all goods imported in the country. Those who threw the revenues away should themselves be made to pay the penalty. Moreover, he says, the lands that now lie waste were acquired by agents and attorneys who made their profits first and now hold the land ruinating, while they seek to reduce the salaries of officials. He prophesies apocalyptically:

        The day of retribution will arrive,
        And that ere long, when sorely they'll repent
        The madness of their present policy.
        What answer will they, can they, make to those
        Who, with avenging power, arise en masse,
        And thunder in their ears "NECESSITY!"

173

"We want your lands, your goods, your merchandise!
We can't afford to leave you in the free
And peaceable enjoyment of your wealth
While we are houseless, landless, unemployed . . .
Talk not to us of justice, private rights,
Or laws of property! We want your land,
Your stores, your houses, and we'll have 'em.
Who will step between us and our lawful prey?
Lawful according to your previous act.
We're ten to one in numbers, desperate,
United, and resolved! Deny us not—
Our argument is yours—NECESSITY!"[15]

Twelve years after that speech was written the Morant Bay rebellion erupted, as a result of which the island's constitution was suspended and direct rule was imposed from Britain. The new governor was empowered to make all decisions autocratically, subject only to approval from the Colonial Office.

Part Three of this absorbing disquisition is by far the longest. It consists less of the give-and-take of argument found in the preceding episodes than of perorations by the two characters. The intemperance of Grey's language and his ill-concealed wish for revenge depict a character well meaning and self-righteous, but in sharp contrast with Metcalfe's urbane and reasonable disposition. Grey contends that the £5 million paid by the British government to Jamaican planters for freeing their slaves had been either squandered, absorbed by absentee proprietors, or used to pay mortgages. Little of it had been prudently invested "in the labor requisite to fill the gap Emancipation made." He pressed home his argument:

Had but a tenth of that enormous sum
But been applied in introducing free,
Intelligent, and useful laborers;
And had you but have had the sense to keep
The people whose condition had been changed,
Upon their old localities, by kind
And liberal attention to their wants,
You might have had a village peasantry
Now living on and tilling your estates,
Whose labor might have been relied upon . . .
Such are the counter charges to the bill
Of plaints and grievances made out by some

Who call themselves, although improperly,
The "people" of Jamaica. Save the mark![16]

Grey defends his appointment of a number of Jews "to places of high confidence and trust" when as a body their actions were inimical to his administration. Although he had been abused by them and hated their propensity "to make the world we live in a mere higgling shop," it was ridiculous to say he despised the Hebrew people. His policy was that religion should never be a barrier to advancement. The Jews had many admirable character traits, among which were their boundless charities to all in need and their firm adherence to a venerable faith. With these sentiments Metcalfe's Ghost warmly agrees, adding that the Jews were inferior to none in mental powers and had shone in Philosophy, Arts, Science, and Literature, wherever freedom permitted their genius to express itself.

The conversation turns once more to the future. By this time Metcalfe is persuaded that the "party of Obstructives" must be curbed or they will bring the country to ruin. They had even tried to slur Grey's memory in their address to the new governor, a paltry and contemptible act. As dawn approaches, the Ghost takes leave of his old schoolfellow, bringing the play to an end:

'Tis on the stroke of four, I must away,
But as to thee, old Warrior of the State,
Betake thee to thy slumbers, and repose
As well thou mayst, upon thy laurels. Sleep,
Aye, sleep, old man, nor dream of aught but rest,
And on the morrow or some early day
Depart. Let England have her faithful son
And England's Queen smile gratefully upon
Her old and long-tried servant. Fare thee well.[17]

One may wonder whether a duologue of such length, expository in style, static in external action, and with little obvious conflict, should be considered a drama. True, the play was not written for the stage; and, apart from its serious tone, dialogue format, and archaic iambics, there seems little to recommend it as a *pièce de théâtre*. Yet, it is eminently performable. Its coherent theme is explicated through the character of Grey, a wronged public official who, at the end of his commission, desperately needs to satisfy both his friend and himself that he has done his duty by his sovereign, that he has honestly served the people he was sent to govern in the face of hostile factions interested only in their own aggrandizement. If the play lacks variety of action, we should remember that Reader's Theatre was very much in vogue at the time it was written and that audiences were more accustomed than we are today to listen to a single actor recite a story or play from the platform for a whole evening's entertainment and edification.

Next in the catalogue of nineteenth-century Jamaican playwrights is Philip Cohen Labatt, a Kingston native, who was a member of the Literary Society and published a weekly miscellany called *The Echo*. His little drama is a one-act farce, *Next of Kin, or Who Is the Heir?* which was published posthumously in 1855 in a collection of his works.[18] As its name implies, the play deals with the perennial theme of finding the rightful heir to a legacy, in this case an inheritance left by one John Smith who had died in Jamaica. All the action, however, takes place in London, where various claimants descend on the lawyer who, by advertisement, invites the next of kin of the deceased to communicate with him. The play says nothing about Jamaica, was apparently not produced, and needs no further explication here. Whether Labatt was capable of producing more substantial work we will never know. He died at the early age of thirty-one in 1854.

Several more original pieces were composed and/or produced in the 1850s, a decade that witnessed increased amateur activity on all fronts. On December 1, 1855, at the Theatre Royal, an historical drama in three acts was presented under the title *Edinburgh Castle, or The Last Days of Hutchinson, the Assassin*. According to the announcement, it had been written "by a gentleman of this city."[19] No additional information is available about this effort except that the first performance was a success and the play was repeated four days later. There was in Jamaica a strong Scottish community whose support for a play about the home country could be taken for granted, one of the most constantly produced plays by professionals and amateurs being *Douglas, or, The Noble Shepherd*, the Scottish tragic melodrama by the Reverend John Home.

Next were two original farce comedies presented during the 1859 visit of the Lanergan Company to boost box-office sales. One, entitled *The Man of My Own Choice*, was written by a Kingston gentleman and produced at the Royal on April 29. The next evening the company presented *Did You Ever Send Your Wife to Spanish Town?* an afterpiece described as a farce that had been arranged and localized for the occasion. One unfinished play of the decade is another newspaper drama published serially in four issues of the *Jamaica Tribune*. Captioned *Political Roguery Unmasked; or, The Plotters Confounded*, the anonymous author describes his effort as "a short political drama based on the origin, progress and final completion of a horrible plot concocted at the 'Public Jobbery Institution' of King's Town."[20] The action of the play takes place in five scenes that are set at various locales in Spanish Town and Kingston, the chief characters being the Czar (an obvious pseudonym for the island's governor), the Honorable Edward Crafty, a wily counselor to the Czar, and Greedy Grasp-All, a venal newspaper editor and sometime supporter of the Czar, now his mortal enemy.

As far as can be discerned from the excessively verbose, mock-heroic prose of the dialogue, Grasp-All is furious because the Czar has declined to appoint him either as Road Commissioner with a stipend of £100 a year, or to the more prestigious and lucrative office of Custos or Chief Magistrate of Kingston. He vows vengeance and repulses Crafty, who visits him on a peacemaking mission. Crafty reports back to the Czar, urging that some means be found to restore Grasp-All's allegiance, or at least to keep him quiet, "the fellow's devilry and mischief to avoid." The Czar is persuaded that something must be done, and Crafty is left to devise a scheme to win back the editor, fearing that the price will be great. Scene Five ends at this point, but no further episodes were published.

Much of the dialogue consists of circumlocutory solo speeches by Grasp-All and Crafty, who admit their wrongdoing without seeming to show any remorse. They simply explain, somewhat repetitiously, why they act as they do. Even the Czar realizes that his decisions are often self-serving. This he attributes to the influence of his evil counselor: "Crafty! your jobs so dirty which to me you oft propose, my sanction I do quickly give to, because a power strange I feel, I can't describe, that o'er me you do exercise."[21] Most notable in this otherwise unremarkable fragment of political satire is that the author wrote with a deliberate attempt to disguise transparently the identity of the officials being censured. He seemed assured that his readers would be thoroughly acquainted with the schemes and machinations of political payoffs in high places.

Two skits that warrant passing attention were published in 1868 in the Morning Journal. The first, under the caption "Dramatic," is set in "a city in an island of the West Indies" and was obviously intended as a burlesque of a local incident, details of which are now lost to us.[22] In the billiard room of a hotel, a "Volunteer Inspector" who has fallen from high estate insults a Colonel by first charging him with cheating during the game and then with bearing a title he has not earned. The Colonel insists on a duel but the Inspector is a coward and, quoting

Hamlet's apology to Laertes in the duel scene, begs to be pardoned. When the Colonel in anger discharges his pistol through a window, the Inspector is so terrified that he suffers a heart attack and dies, still quoting Shakespeare. The final scene shows a grand tableau of spectators around the corpse and an interment "with all due solemnity and in conformity with ancient rites." The burlesque concludes with an epitaph that is also from Shakespeare: "Oh! what a noble mind is here o'er thrown." There is a suggestion in the text that the real-life model for the cowardly Volunteer Inspector may have been Jewish and an amateur player of note; he was also probably a commissioned member of the Kingston Volunteer Militia.

The second skit, titled *The Modern William Tell,* takes place in the Portland courthouse where William Tell, representing the *County Union* newspaper, and a fellow journalist from the *Morning Journal* are attending court. Three Supreme Court judges are also there along with attorneys, overseers, and bookkeepers, all eagerly awaiting some exciting event. Presently, another newspaper editor called Sarnem enters. He is from the *Colonial Standard* and carries a pole on top of which is a Planter's Hat. He comes before the assembly and commands the judges to bow before the Hat: "the emblem of your masters' power / And will! . . . let all bow down to it / Who owe it love and loyalty."[23] The judges comply; they step forward individually and, to the consternation of the two onlooking journalists, make humble obeisance to the Hat.

At this stage a character Michael, representing Judge Masheder, enters and takes his seat on the Judges' Bench. Commanded by Sarnem to bow to the Hat, he refuses saying, "I'll bow to Planters, if you please / But not to Planters' law set up in Hat / Nor Hat of any man in Planterdom."[24] This defiance leads to a fracas when Sarnem calls on the officers to seize Michael, and William Tell leaps to his defense. Tell strikes Sarnem, who rushes off shrieking in pain. Then Tell throws down the pole, tramples on the Hat, and embracing Michael, strikes an attitude as the curtain falls. Once again with thinly veiled sarcasm, the author of this skit castigates all but one of the High Court judges, who, in league with the *Colonial Standard* newspaper, demonstrate their spineless deference to the interests of the Planters' lobby instead of upholding the country's laws fairly and objectively.

A letter to the editor of the *Colonial Standard* in 1870 provides the next item in this record of Jamaican plays. The writer, signing himself "Thespis," reports on a performance he attended in Kingston by invitation. It was given by young gentlemen of the Athenian Dramatic Club and took place in a drawing room without stage or proper scenery but with a large audience present. The main offering was the tragedy *Barbarossa* by John Brown. According to the writer, the amateurs surprised their auditors with the quality of their performance, excellent readings being given the roles of Zephira and Selim. The evening's entertainment was rounded off with a one-act farce entitled *Women's Rights*, which had been written for the occasion by one of the club members. The topic was timely in view of the current agitation taking place in England and America for the introduction of women's suffrage. The play, however, supported the conservative side:

> The story turned on a medical practitioner called Dr. Rattlebones, a decided advocate of "Women's Rights" who, impressed with the idea that women should not be deprived of the enjoyment of the same liberties as the other sex, refused to allow his daughter to marry any other than a man who went in for women's rights. In the course of the piece, however, Dr. Rattlebones discovered his error, renounced his infatuation, admitted that women are best at home in the fulfillment of social duties, and sanctions the marriage of his daughter with a gentleman of the same opinions.[25]

The writer, evidently delighted with the achievement of the young amateurs, hoped their success would spur them to greater efforts. However, while there were many future productions by unnamed amateurs, the records show none by the Athenians.

Early in the year 1872, the Reverend John Radcliffe, minister of the Church of Scotland in Kingston, delivered a sermon that provoked a lively religious controversy in the city. The bone of contention was the doctrine, attributed to Radcliffe, that the righteous man could achieve salvation on the strength of his works alone. Ten churchmen, including the archdeacon of Kingston, opposed this view. They prepared and circulated a statement denouncing Radcliffe for preaching an unsound doctrine and ignoring many scriptural truths. In reply, Radcliffe asked for proof of their accusations and charged them with misquoting and perverting Holy Scripture. He was a writer and poet, and in March that year an advertisement appeared in the Kingston Press for the sale of a new publication by him titled *Ye Opening of Ye Ten Seals*. The work was described as "a second miracle play or mystery suggested by correspondence between the Reverend J. Radcliffe and his Reverend Brethren," the latter being the ten churchmen who opposed him. (There may have been a first miracle play by Radcliffe of which we have no information.) The advertisement provided a few more details of the second play: "This amusing burlesque of the religious controversy that has for some time been going on among our

Kingston clerics is now ready for sale at this office. Price 3*d.* a copy. The play is replete with good-natured badinage and sly raillery. Those who read it will, we are assured, agree with us in considering the 'Mysterie' a clever production and very creditable to the literary capabilities of the country."[26] The burlesque was never publicly performed, though it was no doubt read avidly by hundreds of parishioners on both sides of the issue. Regrettably, the published texts of Radcliffe's plays have not been found.

As noted above, newspapers of the day would from time to time print short dialogue scenes intended to enliven their commentary on local issues. The characters in these pieces were often well-known public figures, sometimes disguised by transparently obvious aliases, at other times boldly identified by their proper names and offices. Often their speeches would be phrased to reveal glaring character traits and to hold them up to ridicule. The 1870s witnessed a number of these short political burlesques in the columns of the press for reasons that will shortly be revealed. No attempt has been made to enumerate every one of these skits. Some are much too short and obscure to be counted in a listing of Jamaican plays. An example of this type of dramatized scene is a short dialogue that appeared in the *Gleaner* of November 29, 1879, as a brief conversation between a white gentleman and a black constable in which buckra complains of nightly noises from a wake or revival meeting that disturb his sleep. The constable, responding in dialect speech, explains why he is powerless to stop the noise.

One newspaper playlet that should not be overlooked appeared in 1872 in the *Colonial Standard* with the lugubrious title, *We Are All Honorable Men, or How They Play Their Parts in the Back Room of the Treasury.* It was written by "the Spirit of an Old Receiver General," with a cast comprising three honorable gentlemen who are market commissioners with the names of Scrape Penny, Guinea Chick, and Roll Keep, and four Printer's Devils who represent contemporary newspapers and speak in chorus. The commissioners meet to decide which paper should be awarded the printing contract for the market and find reasons why the paper with the lowest bid, the *Colonial Standard* of course, should be passed over in favor of another:

> Tick-a-tuck. I'll be grilled, bedevil'd and toasted,
> But name me not *Standard* by which I am roasted.
> Tick-a-tuck, I'd e'en enter Pluto's hot wicket
> And allow all my Clerks to hold Easter-day cricket

Than pay the vile *Standard* who calls me a Grundy
Who opens her shop upon Easter Monday.[27]

Evidently the *Standard* believed it had been denied the printing contract by the commissioners for being too outspoken. The final comment on this piece of chicanery is given in the last line of the skit:
"Alas for Virtue gone and Jobbery new-born."

In 1876 the *Colonial Standard* also published four political dialogues in rhymed couplets, upwards of 150 lines each, in which the
writer (most probably the editor, George Levy) takes to task the government of Sir William Grey. Grey had succeeded Sir John Peter
Grant, the first of the Crown Colony governors, following the 1865
rebellion. Although many needed developments had been carried out
under their rule, the cost of these projects had resulted in sharply
increased taxes. Moreover, not all of the changes seemed essential in a
hard-pressed economy. Dissatisfaction arose in certain sections of the
community, and these dissenting voices were championed by the
press in articles and dramatic dialogues. In fact, although the Jamaican constitution had been willingly surrendered after the Morant Bay
outbreak, autocratic rule by English governors had become irksome,
and sniping away at administrators was really a way of calling for a
return to representative government. When in 1884 a new constitution was granted allowing for some elected representatives, political
burlesques all but disappeared from the columns of the newspapers.

The four dialogues in the *Colonial Standard* attacked Grey on a
number of issues, including costly public works and high taxation, in
particular the newly imposed water rates. They can be treated as four
scenes on a single theme for they were clearly written by the same
author. The governor appeared in the cast of all four episodes along
with his inner cabinet: the colonial secretary and attorney general.
The names of these two characters, Sir Edward Neddy and Baron
Charles O'Malley, were slight alterations of their real names, Edward
Everand Rushworth and Edward Loughlin O'Malley. Other characters
appeared in each episode as needed. The first dialogue, titled *The
Almighty Dollar*, denounced the devaluation of the Jamaican cur-
rency. The second dialogue, titled *The Tropical Aquarius*, condemned
tax increases. The third, called *Scene on a Jamaican Sugar Estate*,
showed the governor and his cronies disguised as bailiffs visiting an
estate to spy on its output in order to fix a stiff government levy. They
were frightened off by the ghost of a poor Indian coolie who had died
when the government's doctors refused him a certificate of relief. The
fourth skit, called *Passing the Estimates*, took place in a legislative

council meeting where several budget items were challenged as contributing to waste and official patronage while heavy taxes were placed on the citizenry:

> My country on her neck is made to feel
> The cruel impress of the despot's heel,
> Her fields lie barren since no fertile brain
> Can crown with smiling crops each hill and plain.
> Her waning wealth is lost in spendthrift waste,
> Crushed is her spirit, and depraved her taste;
> Crime with a giant stride stalks through the land,
> While want and woe rise up on every hand.
> Nothing is done to chase the gathering gloom,
> No statesman's prudence stays the threatened doom.
> I raise my voice to rouse, beyond the sea,
> The rage of Freedom that such things should be.[28]

The skits are for the most part polemical. The characters discuss issues of public concern, give opinions, and quarrel with each other before a final ruling is made. Three of the scenes take the form of a council meeting. There is little dramatic incident or even interior action to sustain interest once the events they reflect are no longer pertinent. Only comedy and wit remain, and they are insufficiently employed. The pieces, therefore, are of historic value and suggest the penchant of newspaper subscribers for reading argument couched in dramatic dialogue, but they are hardly suitable for the stage.

A similar criticism applies partially to the last of these political diatribes, *The Old Year (1879) at the Gate,* which was published in *Gall's Newsletter* in December 1879. In this case, a fictional plot is attempted. The Old Year has died and seeks admission at the Gates of Heaven. A committee of four intelligent Shades has been appointed to interview the applicant and report on his eligibility. They are Lord Elgin and Sir William Grey, both former governors; the Honorable Alexander Heslop, a former attorney general, and the Honorable Edward Rushworth, a former colonial secretary and lieutenant governor. Grey finds the Old Year cheeky and would keep him out since he "may start a journal, who can tell / And if he did, why Heaven were worse than Hell."[29] But he is overruled, and the petitioner is allowed to tell his story, during which he recounts the government's failings and the added burdens that have been placed on the people. The tone of this skit is lighter and more satiric than occurs in the earlier pieces, although it too does not merit repetition today.

Gall published another satiric sketch in 1882, which he called *The*

Smuggled Shawl: An Infernal Revenue Play. In four short scenes, the vignette told of a Collector of Customs who persuaded a sea captain to bring him goods from London, the captain having to advance money for the merchandise. Since the articles did not pass through the Custom House, the Collector paid no duty, yet when the time came to repay the captain, he received even less money than he had advanced. The captain complained to his friend, Fish, but the latter offered no consolation: "Serve you right. Why did you bring out anything for the fellow. I am only astonished he paid anything. He is a pest to every Captain that comes here." In his preamble to the sketch, Gall stated that it was "acted in a Northside port some little time back. The performers deserve credit for the manner in which it was put on the boards."[30] Knowing Gall's impish character, one might question whether his play actually saw stage life or was simply composed by the author from a real-life incident and published in his *Newsletter* in order to expose the swindling customs officer.

Reference has been made to Father Xavier Jaeckel of Mary Villa High School, who staged plays with his students at their annual "breaking-up" exercises. We know of two plays that Jaeckel wrote or adapted. The first, an unnamed comedy that was "arranged by him," has the following plot outline. A young lady on a visit to England marries a marine officer without first securing her father's consent. He disapproves of the marriage and, while the marine is on duty overseas, he obtains fraudulent divorce papers and compels his daughter to remarry. On the day of the second marriage, the marine officer returns. The play was staged in December 1879 as part of an evening's entertainment given by the High School. Jaeckel's second play was *The Citizen Nobleman*, an adaptation of Molière's *Le Bourgeois Gentilhomme*, which was performed by students to an admiring audience at the Theatre Royal on June 22, 1881. Between the acts of the comedy, ladies and gentlemen contributed instrumental music to enhance the evening's offering. These plays were apparently not published.

Another unpublished play, under date 1880, resides in the manuscript collection of the Jamaica National Library. Titled *Malcolm and Alonzo, or, The Secret Murder of Leonard* by John Duff Spraggs, it is a revenge melodrama complete with male and female ghosts. It is also written in rhymed couplets, which seem to be the literary fashion of the time. Although the action of the drama is supposed to occur in Jamaica, there is little evidence of locale in the script except for one minor character who provides a sense of place. The time is some years after the end of slavery. Tobie is a laborer living on a pen (a small enclosed farming area) two miles from the city. He speaks in the vernacular and is meant to be a comic figure. The author, however, is not insensitive to the condition of the black estate worker, and, while Tobie's dialect may be considered quaint, what he says is important to his and his country's welfare. Asked by the son of an old white planter how he is getting on, Tobie replies:

> Me work ya, sa, till all my han' kin peel,
> If you see dem sometime, you ha't wi' feel . . .
> Me work fe true an' true, but pay is small,
> Money is mek, but massa keep mose all;
> Him put am up da Bank, say it fe tan
> Till when Miss Mora get one good husban,
> And den him gie 't fe him and fe de man.

If Tobie speaks true, and he has no reason to do otherwise, it is understandable why the ex-slaves chose to work their own farm grounds rather than continue as paid laborers on their former estates. He does not reappear in the play, for the author is more interested in bloody and supernatural dealings. For all that, there is no record of performance and therefore no report on a public reception of this full-length Jamaican play.

In the last decade of the century five plays were written and performed. Once again there is cause for regret that scripts have not survived, and we are forced to rely on newspaper accounts of productions to reconstruct the theatrical events. In April 1892, an entertainment billed as an operetta was given at the Theatre Royal, Kingston, before Their Excellencies Sir Henry and Lady Blake and a large audience, with the band of the West India Regiment in attendance. The performers were colored orphan children of Alpha Cottage, a Roman Catholic charitable home and school. They were presenting a spectacle called *The Frolic of the Flowers*, which had been prepared for them by one of their instructors. The children, some as young as three or four years, were dressed as forest flowers; they sang pretty choruses and danced, executing "various graceful movements and evolutions, remarkable from the general harmony and unison which were obtained."[31] The girls danced a Maypole, performed sketches from Red Riding Hood and Mother Goose, while the boys, dressed as soldiers of the West India Regiment, went through military drills. The occasion was considered to be "simply marvellous," and the operetta received two more performances. Great credit was given to the Mother Superior and Sisters of the institution for their accomplishment.

Alpha Cottage nuns continued periodically to present plays with their students, gaining their most memorable production with an original chronicle play, *In Stormy Days, or, The Vow That Saved Jamaica.* It was written by one of the Sisters and performed by their high school girl pupils at the Theatre Royal on June 29, 1897.[32] The play recalled an event in early Jamaican history when a large contingent of French forces from neighboring Hispaniola, led by Jean Du Casse, attempted to capture the island then governed by Sir William Beeston. The colony had been enfeebled by the devastation caused two years earlier by the great earthquake of 1692. The French forces made several landings on the island, were engaged by local militias, and were eventually driven back, but not before they had inflicted severe destruction to life and property. The play even had the governor captured by the invaders and rescued through the efforts of a gypsy queen.

Reviews were highly complimentary to both the play and the production.[33] The drama was a worthy beginning "full of dramatic power and literary merit of a high class." It was well written for acting and required little or no pruning. The production had life, power, and energy. Scenery and dresses were superb, and the acting "sustained the reputation of the Convent Sisters as teachers." In another Maypole scene, which revived customs of olden times, the grouping of figures was excellent. The only criticisms were directed at poor pronunciation, a tendency to shout instead of projecting the voice, and scenes of violence in which the all-girl cast was hardly effective. With Shanahan's previous efforts in play writing dimmed by the passage of time, the most significant critical comments focused on the fact that *In Stormy Days* opened possibilities for a serious native drama and theatre. Noting that the play was about Jamaica, one reviewer affirmed, "We are of those who believe that in Jamaica life, in Jamaica history, in Jamaica scenery and customs, lie hidden treasures which the poet, the dramatist, the novelist, and the historian will one day bring into the range of the world's attention."[34] It remains only to say that this play and Shanahan's earlier *The Spanish Warrior* were the two most ambitious and successful Jamaican dramas staged for Kingston audiences during the whole of the nineteenth century.

The catalog of Jamaican plays concludes with references to two farce-comedies and, finally, to a production organized by Cuban amateurs in Kingston. The first, *Cupid's Delight,* author unknown, was a humorous farce staged by an amateur group on June 13, 1892, in the auditorium of the Lunatic Asylum, under the management of Dr. McCormack. Part of a music and drama program, it was likely no more than a single act. The plot is not revealed, but from the review it is clear that it centers on a domestic intrigue in which several characters assume disguises by blacking up and playing servants. Mrs. Mc-Cormack, for instance, was seen in two contrasting roles as Mrs. Williams, a householder, and Nancy, a maid. In such scenes, jokes are usually made at the expense of the poorer class. Hence the comment that E. W. Astwood's performance as Blowers, "who is Cornwall blackened and disguised as a dispenser, was nothing short of excellent. His ridiculous jumble of medical phraseology and his curious manner of conducting the duties of his post . . . was sidesplitting."[35] Miss Blake took the part of a maiden lady "whose ancestors came over with the conqueror and who had a deep disgust for anyone not possessing 'blue blood,' " a fine bit of acting that nothing could surpass in the estimation of the critic. However, it was all meant in good fun and the large, fashionable audience, as well as a number of patients from the asylum, enjoyed the performance immensely.

The second light comedy was the work of J. S. Brown, a writer of lively wit and a composer of topical songs, who produced *The Demon Academy* at the Theatre Royal in January 1898. This was another play based on deception and mistaken identity. The maidservant Janet, played by Dr. Ragg, turns out to be a man in disguise who is in love with Betsy Demon, the lady principal of a girls' academy. The play was longer than the one-acter discussed above, but may have been less well structured for it contained a school concert and a wedding banquet with the usual amount of speechifying as part of the action. Many of the actors were making their first appearance on stage, yet the comedy was enthusiastically received by a fairly full house of about five hundred patrons.

For the final item on the Jamaican play list, we turn again to the Theatre Royal where on February 17, 1898, an entertainment was given by Cuban refugees to commemorate their country's declaration of independence while the war with Spain was still being waged in their island home. Despite threatening weather, the theatre auditorium was densely crowded with people of all classes. The program was a mélange of various items. A military band played nationalist music, comic songs were sung, and *tableaux vivants* represented the death of the Cuban patriot Antonio Maceo and a free Cuba. There were stirring patriotic orations; one by Charles Campbell took for its subject: "Resistance to Tyrants is Obedience to God."

The central attraction of the evening was a thrilling one-act drama entitled *A Las Armas*, describing the outbreak of the war. It is not certain that the author of this drama was indeed a Jamaican, but that question loses significance when it is viewed in the wider context of Caribbean solidarity and Caribbean destiny. The fate of the two neighboring islands had been intertwined for generations and will doubtless continue to be so, regardless of changing fortunes and big-power politics. Reporting on the performance, a reviewer called the play

> a dramatic allegory of the great moral and physical sacrifice, male and female, that characterized the movement. The acting was worthy of the best dramatic stars. In fact, as many remarked the performers were not acting at all. Lost in patriotic enthusiasm, they forgot the stage and were, for the nonce, living their parts. The result was an intensity of realism never before achieved on the Kingston stage—the best proof of this is that the audience themselves were carried away by it.[36]

During the nineteenth century, there emerged in Jamaica playwrights who sought to make the drama intensely relevant to the Jamaican experience. They knew that to be meaningful and vigorous, the theatre must reflect the reality of the lives of people it purports to serve and must cater to their noblest aspirations. The best playwrights did this with skill and passion, using English prose and verse, but also exploiting the Jamaican vernacular speech when it was fit to do so. They employed the range of dramatic forms as they sought material from history and contemporary life. They realized, as one reviewer stated forcibly in 1897: "Too long has the foreign environment encircled the stage in Jamaica; often and often [sic] have we watched the weary, long-spun plots of strange countries whence no good springs, in the hope that a touch of homeliness might drag us, even against our will, to an appreciation of the play, but how often in vain."[37] The Cuban pageant went one step further. These exiles with a longing to return home, side by side with their Jamaican supporters, saw theatre as a source of national inspiration, as fundamentally an act of celebration uniting a community and giving it a sense of purpose, of hope and faith in its destiny. In presenting their pageant, the Cubans captured the imagination of their audience and transported them with feelings of patriotism and sacrifice for the good of country. Jamaican playwrights today can learn much from their precursors of long ago.

8

Readers, Reciters, Storytellers

The blind Greek reciter of epic tales of war and sacrifice and the African griot weaving his stories of the mischievous Spider Anansi are kindred spirits. They share a common heritage in the urge of human beings everywhere to recount, to rapt auditors, tales of wonder, daring, and suspense. The Homeric sagas, collected and written down, became the source of dramas that have held audiences spellbound since the days of Thespis, 2,500 years ago. But the solo recitation survived in these dramas, notably in messengers' speeches that related the most fateful moments of tragic events. The Anansi tales, crossing the dread Middle Passage with African slaves bound for the New World, retained their oral form to offer lighthearted respite from grinding labor, and perhaps to suggest survival strategies to those skilled in discerning their hidden message.

The solo recital has never quite left the professional stage. In the hands of a gifted reader and interpreter, it can move audiences to laughter or tears as much as any full-scale dramatic production might do. Charles Dickens was apparently one such reader, as was Mark Twain (Samuel Clemens), both delivering their own narratives for a full evening's entertainment before entranced listeners. At other times, when playgoing was banned by nervous authorities, as in puritanical New England towns prior to the nineteenth century, actors would advertise their performances as edifying "lectures" or "poetic addresses" and would simply give readings of selected passages from popular dramas. There were also pieces specially composed for the single performer. One of the most enduring of these was *The Lecture on Heads* written by George Alexander Stevens.

Stevens, a mediocre English actor, writer, and lyricist of the eighteenth century, first presented his *Lecture* in 1764 at the Little Haymarket Theatre in London. He stood behind a long table that was covered with a green baize cloth. On the table were arranged papier-mâché busts of varied characters from Alexander the Great to a Cher-

188

okee Indian, from a Billingsgate Fishwife to a Methodist Parson. The *Lecture* consisted of a two-hour monologue in which Stevens satirized one character after another, using the head as a point of reference. It was immensely popular, and at a time when copyright laws were nonexistent, the *Lecture* was promptly imitated and adapted, original characters being replaced by new ones that were more topical. For ease of transport, painted portraits were sometimes substituted for molded busts. As Gerald Kahan wrote: "The *Lecture* became a staple of the one-man (or -woman) entertainer and brought many back from the brink of penury."[1] The vogue continued for half a century, eventually fading out in the early nineteenth century.

In the Jamaican theatre, the earliest reciters appeared in 1781, when two members of Hallam's American Company offered *The Lecture on Heads.* William Wignell performed it in January at the Ranelagh House auditorium in Kingston, and later that year William Moore gave the *Lecture* to audiences in Kingston, Spanish Town, and Montego Bay. So successful was Moore with his recital that he took the piece on tour to several sugar ports on the west and north of the island where it was a clear favorite with audiences. The following year, when military thespians on the island offered a benefit performance for the American Company, one of the officers attempted parts of *The Lecture on Heads* as an entr'acte diversion between the two plays on the bill. In 1783 Moore again performed it at the Kingston Theatre, and the year after Thomas Wignell presented parts of a new *Lecture on Heads and Hearts* at a variety entertainment that was taken on tour of the island.

A rival monologue, *The Lecture on Hearts,* written in imitation of its popular antecedent, appeared early in the new century as part of the repertoire of J. P. Cussans. He first offered a mixed bag of recitations and songs at the Kingston theatre on March 4, 1803, and later in the year presented his *Hearts* lecture on separate occasions in Kingston and Spanish Town while the courts were in session. This new monologue failed to catch on. Stevens's original *Lecture* continued to be revived in the years ahead. In 1816 Mr. Hitchener, who with his wife had recently joined Adamson's Company, performed it at Spanish Town in a benefit performance for himself, his wife, and a Mr. Cummins. Hitchener must have expected a bumper house to enable him to share the profits three ways. When Adamson died in June 1818 and his company disbanded, Hitchener took to the road with the *Lecture on Heads,* "with many variations and additions, interspersed with Scotch, Irish, and English songs by Mrs. Hitchener." His announcement noted that the *Lecture* had previously been delivered "with general approbation" in Kingston, Spanish Town, Clarendon, Vere, Black River, Savanna-la-Mar, Montego Bay, Falmouth, Rio Bueno, Dry Harbour, Saint Ann's, Ocho Rios, Port Maria, and so on, at standard theatre prices ranging from 13s.4d. for lower boxes to 5s. for the gallery.[2] Two further entries will close the logbook for Stevens's *Lecture* in Jamaica. Mr. Blake, one of the comedians then active in the city, scheduled a performance for March 1, 1823. He alleged that the "Heads," all fifty of them to be used in his recital, had been executed in a style of elegance seldom witnessed. The final performance was by John Castello, the erstwhile West Indian Roscius, who in 1828 presented the *Lecture* at the Kingston theatre on his return from a spell of acting in America. That Castello attempted to add local flavor to his lecture is evident from the reviews that cautioned him to avoid party politics and all allusions to the private amusements of the governor.

A hiatus follows for solo reciters. The 1840 opening of the new Kingston theatre brought a spate of productions, local amateur and imported professional, but no monologuists. Toward the end of the decade, however, three events occurred that had a significant impact on native literary and musical pursuits. In October 1849 the Colonial Literary and Reading Society was formed in Kingston with the Reverend R. A. Johnson as president and H. Ryder Waldron as secretary. While by no means the first of such literary clubs, it was one of the more important ones. Occupying rooms on the southeastern corner of the Parade, it sponsored lectures and readings in Kingston over the next twenty and more years. In November a philharmonic society was established "to regale subscribers once a month with a concert of vocal and instrumental music."[3] The philharmonic promised to employ professional artistes and to invite talented amateurs to assist at these concerts. The president was Dr. MacFayden. And in December 1848 the Reverend John Radcliffe arrived on the island to minister to the Presbyterian community. He was destined to play a significant role in the promotion of the storytelling art.

Meanwhile the country continued to host a fair sampling of career readers from abroad whose visits punctuated the ensuing decades. In May 1858, Mrs. Mary E. Webb gave a series of three dramatic readings at the new courthouse in Kingston and one in Spanish Town. She hailed from Philadelphia and had read to large assemblies in the United States and Britain. Her readings were "sanctioned by multitudes whose religious scruples would prevent them giving any patronage to theatrical representations." Doubtless the choice of the courthouse rather than the Theatre Royal was a more appropriate venue for this quite proper lady from Quakertown who offered a program that included selections from *The Maniac* by Monk Lewis, *Uncle Tom's Cabin, Romeo and Juliet, King John*, and Tennyson's *May Queen*. She also read two homespun stories written in Yankee and Irish dialects. Her opening recital, billed as a benefit for the boys' and girls' reformatories, was well attended, although the reviewer's admission that ticket prices at 4s. for men and 2s.6d. for ladies were high reflected the depressed state of the island's economy. *The Maniac* proved to be the "gem of the evening" with the dialect pieces also receiving high praise. In the opinion of the critic, however, Mrs. Webb's forte did not lie in her readings of Shakespeare.[4]

While Mrs. Webb was hoping to instill "proper and correct habits of reading . . . for mental and intellectual enjoyment" among her Jamaican audiences, Jamaica was returning the compliment by having one of her own sons, Raphael J. de Cordova [fig. 13], embark on an illustrious career as a humorous reader in the United States. De Cordova's first public appearance of record took place at Clinton Hall, New York City, in October 1858, when he announced three evening readings of Charles Dickens's Christmas books: *A Christmas Carol*, *The Chimes*, and *The Cricket on the Hearth*. In his advertisement he informed potential auditors: "These beautiful works are not generally known among us as they should be. They are perfect gems of humorous and pathetic writing, adorned throughout with a tone of pure religion and universal charity, and, when properly read, are among the most attractive literary jewels in our language."[5] It was the first time that Dickens's Christmas stories were read publicly in America. The readings attracted appreciative audiences, including a number of distinguished clergymen who were impressed and entertained with the reader's clear and well-modulated voice, which convincingly expressed the range of emotions that the stories required.

Solo performances of this type were well established in America ever since the noted English humorist Charles Mathews brought his "At Home" performances to New York's Park Theatre in 1822. The exslave and abolitionist William Wells Brown read his own antislavery plays on lecture platforms throughout New England beginning in 1856. By mid-century the field was so crowded that one had to be a fine elocutionist to survive. Take, for example, New York in the winter of 1859. The admired actress Fanny Kemble announced her final series of public readings at Dodsworth's Saloon on Broadway. She was retiring after ten years of recitals. On Monday, January 31, she offered *Much Ado About Nothing*, on Tuesday, February 1, *The Merchant of Venice*, and on Friday 4, *Richard II*. Admission was $1.00, with $1.50 for reserved sofa seats. In the same season Mr. and Mrs.

13. Raphael de Cordova

G. Vandenhoff read *As You Like It* and the trial of *Bardell* v. *Pickwick* from Dickens's *Pickwick Papers* at Hope Chapel, 720 Broadway; Professor J. W. Tavernier read *Macbeth* at Clinton Hall; H. R. Ball gave his second dramatic reading of *The Hunchback* at Niblo's Saloon; Robert Raymond, an English professor at Brooklyn Polytechnic Institute, read *The Merchant of Venice* and extracts from *Much Ado About Nothing* at the institute's chapel; and Miss A. M. Freeman was at the Lyrique Hall in various literary selections from Robert Browning and others, at an admission price of fifty cents. There was even a complimentary benefit performance for "the wonderful child reader," Little Ella Burns, four years old, at the Academy of Music on February 10.

De Cordova's contribution to this winterfest of readings was a humorous lecture entitled *The Arabian Nights*, which he delivered at Clinton Hall on February 10. This was probably a selection taken from a recent translation of this admired work. It might have been adapted by de Cordova and it immediately placed him in a special category as a reader of new works, mostly of a comic tenor, that nevertheless offered commentary on affairs of public interest and concern. Later that month, de Cordova gave another lecture at Hope Chapel to accompany an exhibition of twenty-four original and colossal historic paintings, executed by John M'Nevin, depicting memorable events in the American War of Independence.[6]

From here on de Cordova would write his own lectures, composing about forty pieces over the next eighteen years, some in rhymed verse and others in prose. All of them remained in his repertory, the most popular recitations being frequently revived. One of his first successes was *Broadway*, in which he described an omnibus ride up that main artery of Manhattan. There was such a demand for it that in December 1860 de Cordova announced he would read *Broadway* for the last time. Yet he was forced by public entreaty to revive it in 1861 and 1864.

In the fall of 1860 the British Prince of Wales, Albert Edward, came to the United States. This was the first visit of a member of the royal family to America since it had won independence from the mother country. To mark this event, de Cordova produced a humorous epic poem in rhymed verse. It ran to seventy printed pages when published. He recited this poem, called *The Prince's Visit*, fifty times in two months prior to an engagement in London. On his return to America, he traveled with it throughout the country, modestly admitting that "its success in most of the principal cities of the Union, North and South, has been unequivocal, which is doubtless to be attributed more to the effect produced by the oral delivery of the rhymes, than to the intrinsic excellence of the 'Poem.'" The following two extracts will provide a sample of de Cordova's style. The first is taken from his introduction:

> Sound the trumpets! Beat the drums!
> The Princely Heir of England comes!
> Years of hateful anger past,
> A softer feeling rules at last;
> And George's great grandson shall find
> A greeting warm, a welcome kind.
> Write the letters! Sweep the halls!
> Erect the arches! Deck the walls!
> Charge all the guns! Subscribe for balls!

Warm though the reception might be for the English prince, its very extravagance is treated with a slight tone of absurdity. The second selection makes this point more vividly. It describes the attempt by policemen to clear a dog from the path of the prince's procession through Manhattan:

> Their means were few and their hopes were fewer,
> The dog was too big to squeeze into the sewer;
> The street was full, all the crossings were blocked
> And all the front doors of the shops were locked;
> The second-floor windows were full of the fair,
> You never could hurl the great brute up there,
> And 'twas no use to cast him up into the air—
> He'd be sure to come down—for what did *he* care?
> There was nothing in prospect but Madison Square.
> So a squad of policemen, quite red in the face,
> Were deputed to manage this new dog chase,
> 'Mid the jeers and the shouts and the laughter loud
> Of the greatly delighted, applauding crowd.[7]

When the Civil War broke out in 1861, de Cordova penned two sober lectures entitled *The Soldier* and *The Rebellion and the War*. For the latter piece, a historical poem, he returned to the format of his earlier presentation on the Revolutionary War. He hired Hope Chapel on Broadway, where his nightly recitals were illustrated by "dissolving views of the principal events of the campaign, after designs by several of the most eminent American artists, and with appropriate music." Commented the *Tribune* newswriter: "His poetical notes . . . are doomed to carry dismay to many a Rebel's heart, while they help, with the efforts of the regular theaters, more than many wise heads imagine, to sustain the spirit and confirm the resolution of the loyal."[8] His loyalty notwithstanding, de Cordova was primarily a humorist, and nothing could for long subdue his irrepressible comic view of life. During the war years he produced some of his most enduring pieces such as *Courtship and Marriage*, and its sequel, *Our First Baby*, *Mrs. Smith's Surprise Party*, and his satire on amateur dramatics titled *The Amateur Theatrical Association*. First delivered in 1862, these lectures were still being presented twenty years later.

In 1877, 1886, and 1888, de Cordova returned to Jamaica on periodic visits during which he recited his compositions. His performance of *Mrs. Grundy* on his first visit was considered an intellectual treat of a very high order. The reviewer for the *Colonial Standard*, a rival to de Cordova's family newspaper *The Gleaner*, described the piece as a dramatic sketch of modern life and character in which several interesting and typical leaders of society were introduced "not as insensate dummies, but actual living, breathing, speaking, erring human beings." In the tradition of the solo performer, de Cordova peopled the stage with a cast of imagined characters "with whom he laughed, and talked, and pleaded, and remonstrated, never for a moment losing his identity, or making confusion among his lively, motley company." His dialogue was spritely, the incidents amusing, and the plot clever. He possessed a magnificent voice and pleasing presence with which he combined histrionic and mimetic ability to impart to his delineations a variety and charm that kept his audience spellbound. More than an exhibition of brilliant wit and racy humor, the lecture "was pervaded with a deep, uninterrupted current of serious sentiment and sound philosophy, so that the audience were not only amused and entertained, but instructed and improved."[9]

Toward the end of his career, de Cordova was persuaded to appear in regular stage plays produced by amateur groups in New York, to which younger members of the de Cordova clan belonged. He stage-managed and played Sir Harcourt in *London Assurance* at the Brooklyn Academy of Music in 1878; wrote and appeared in a drama called *Constancy*, which the Amaranth Society presented at the academy the next year; and played Dogberry in *Much Ado About Nothing* for the Kemble Society to mark Shakespeare's birthday on April 23, 1884. His last known appearance, according to available records, was in Kingston, Jamaica, on June 16, 1888. He lectured on *The Law in re Midge vs. Pidge* at the Mico School Room to raise funds for repairs to the Jewish Alms House. His son, Julian, in 1939 edited a collection of six of his father's lectures under the title *The Wit and Humour of the '70s.* He was not unduly eulogistic when he called de Cordova "the most noted humorous lecturer in the United States."[10]

Dominant though he was on the lecture circuit in the United States, de Cordova had appeared for only brief spells on the Jamaican stage. Other readers came along to keep alive the art of oral recitation and storytelling. One of these was G. K. Dickinson, whom we have already met. After a short career of some three years as an actor in England, Dickinson traveled to New York, where he performed both as reader (*Hamlet* and *Othello*) at the Tabernacle in 1851 and with Laura Keene's company in a number of roles at the Varieties Theatre in 1856. By 1860 Dickinson and his wife, Emma, a mediocre actor and singer, were domiciled in Jamaica. Within months he was recruited into Morton Tavares's company and later performed with the Lanergans, but he also began to present readings "in character."

Lanergan had opened his season at the Theatre Royal on December 5, 1861, with Bulwer-Lytton's comedy *Money*, which was well received. The following August, Dickinson offered a dramatic reading of the five-act play at the courthouse in Kingston. His next recorded reading was at the New Buildings in Spanish Town, in January 1863, when he was supported by his wife's soprano singing. He was by this time considered to be "an old acquaintance of the enlightened portion of Jamaica," and it was deemed unnecessary to add anything further in his praise. Particular mention, however, could not be withheld on his rendering of Tennyson's "The Charge of the Light Brigade" and the will scene in *Money*, these being considered excellent specimens of the grave and humorous.[11] With this upbeat notice, Dickinson's future never looked brighter, but whatever star led him across the oceans to Jamaica was about to be extinguished. Six months later he was dead, in Mandeville, presumably a victim of the Jamaican fever. His wife and two children were left in destitute circumstances. A subscription was proposed to help the family return to England and in August Kingston amateurs, in another of their charitable acts, staged a performance of Sheridan Knowles's *The Wife; or, A Tale of Mantua* as a benefit for Mrs. Dickinson, who played the lead role of Marina. One hopes that the production realized a tidy sum.

The news in that fateful year of 1865 that the British actor Charles Kean and his wife, the actress Ellen Tree, would visit Jamaica must have raised the spirits of all true lovers of theatre on the island. They were scheduled to come for two weeks and to give Shakespearean readings and ballad recitations. This was still January; the Keans were expected in February, and it would be October before the Morant Bay rebellion occurred that would have such a profound effect on the future history of the island. Charles Kean, son of the great romantic actor Edmund Kean, had built his reputation as actor-manager of the Princess's Theatre in London during the 1850s. There he had staged extravagant productions of Shakespeare's plays with an emphasis on historical and pictorial accuracy in sets and costumes that far surpassed anything yet attempted on the English stage. While not approaching the electric magnetism of the elder Kean, Charles was also an actor of repute and, with his contemporary Samuel Phelps at Sadler's Wells, was considered the leading actor of his time. His visit to Jamaica was therefore an historic event. The Keans were slated to give two performances at the courthouse in Kingston on March 2 and 4. A third was later added on March 9 at the larger Theatre Royal to accommodate demand.

For their first program, given under the joint patronage of His Excellency the Governor and Mrs. Eyre, the Commander of the Forces Major General Ashmore, and the Bishop of Kingston Reginald Courtenay, the Keans read before a large and enthralled audience scenes from *King John*, followed by a number of poetry and prose selections that included Aytoun's "Execution of Montrose," Wordsworth's "We Are Seven," and Macaulay's "Legend of Horatius Cocles." For their second night the Shakespeare play chosen was *Henry VIII*, coupled with a different set of shorter recitations. The program for their third reading is not known. Calling the visitors "the greatest luminaries of the world," the reviewer for the *Jamaica Tribune* felt that their reputation was so well established as to render comment from a Jamaican journalist unnecessary. Their readings were an intellectual treat enjoyed by all; they were chaste, elegant, and expressive.[12] An equally glowing review in the *Colonial Standard* found that the two world artistes surpassed even the expectations that had been formed on the island of their talent.[13]

The Keans' visit was unquestionably an inspiration to all theatre people, artistes and audiences alike, and especially to those bright young aspirants to the stage who attended the island's secondary schools and performed at the end-of-year prize-giving exercises. Elocution and public speaking were much encouraged at these institutions, and from time to time both male and female schools sponsored debates and staged plays. At the Collegiate School prize-giving function, it was customary for leading reciters to compete for the Elocution Medal. In December 1865 one of the young men, George McCaddon by name, chose a passage that had been on Kean's program earlier that year. McCaddon's rendering of this excerpt was so impressive

197

that he emerged winner of the medal by a wide margin. The review of his recitation deserves to be quoted at length:

> Those who had the privilege of listening to Mr. Kean's reading of the death of Montrose can never forget or outlive the thrilling influence produced by the keen analysis and depth of passion displayed by the greatest of living actors. It is not to be expected that a boy of 14 could make the same display as an artist of such experience and genius as Kean, but in addition to the ease and grace which McCaddon throws into his gesture and action, his performance is characterized by great clearness of conception and spirituality of expression. . . .
>
> As he gave the last touching incidents of the martyrdom, the small, thin, palefaced boy expanded for a moment into the very hero of the piece, as he thrilled with the emotions of a thorough identification with the terrible tragedy, and over his pale, spiritual features there seemed to flash something of the light and glory that encircled Montrose upon the scaffold, that strange, mysterious lighting up of the human face which is a visible reflection of the deep emotions of highly intellectual natures—a light seldom seen and when it comes and goes, ever leaving us in doubt whether it proceedeth from within or from above—whether it is a lustre from the soul or a spark from heaven.[14]

The next year McCaddon again recited at the prize-giving function, but having already won the medal he was barred from competing. After he left the Collegiate School, he continued to grace the Kingston amateur stage in the capacity of actor, director, and reader. In September 1872 he returned to his alma mater in a reading of scenes from *Richard III* and other pieces, and in June 1875, to close the midsummer term, he directed students in an ambitious production of *The Merchant of Venice*, taking the role of Shylock himself and winning for his young actors admiration and praise from their elders. His reputation among local players was such that a rhymester writing in the press about Kingston amusements penned this verse:

> And if for reading you may care,
> I think you should M'Caddon hear,
> Who with conception bold and grand
> The subject grasps with master hand
> Making the reading of an hour
> The vivid scene of tragic power.[15]

Taking McCaddon's achievement as an instance of the quality of preparation provided by the secondary schools of Jamaica, one can confidently assert that beginning in the mid-nineteenth century they were the nursery of the country's serious histrionic talents.

After the high tone achieved by the Keans' visit it is not inappropriate to illustrate the range and reach of thespian fancy by turning to "the celebrated and gifted monologuist Mr. Watty Wallack," as he introduced himself to readers in the daily press. In his inflated notice Wallack, "the greatest representative of the numerous characters of the world," undertook to appear for one night only, on May 13, 1867, at Kingston's Theatre Royal in his monologue entertainments that had been "patronised by the representatives of royalty and the elite of fashionable society, and performed over five hundred nights in the West Indies to delighted audiences."[16] This unusual pot pourri was titled "All the Year Round" and purported to represent the career of man from infancy to old age. There would also be fifty marvelous instantaneous changes of costume, forty sentimental and comic songs, dances, anecdotes, recitations, and so on, with delightful and pleasing music. A feast for eye and ear surely, all offered to the public at prices ranging from 4s. to 2s.

Wallack seemed like an old-fashioned carnival showman with his bag of tricks and quick-change routines, and it may be that his act belonged rightly to Orrin's and Luande's Grand Combined Circus then playing in Kingston rather than to the temple of Thespis on the Parade. He had come originally from Liverpool and contended that he had made his stage debut at age twelve in his native town, before embarking on worldwide travel. He was nothing if not ambitious, and his "highly interesting and mirthful performance with versatile delineations of character" in Kingston was greeted with continuous and warm applause, prompting him to announce a second performance on May 21. This performance he advertised under the intriguing title "Wallack's Negro Comic History of England in 199 chapters with stirring local hits introducing the whole of the Jamaican oddities."[17] Regrettably, no details exist of exactly what this program consisted, but it may have touched a nerve of familiarity in the Jamaican public, for Wallack not only gave a third performance in Kingston, in which he imitated various characters like a Nurse, School-boy, and Opera Dancer in appropriate costumes, but he then took his acts around the island.

When next we encounter him three years have passed. Wallack is back at the Royal on December 7, 1870, with Mrs. Fanny Wallack, a

Kittitian lady whom he had married while on tour of the islands. She sings in Italian and English to add variety to his recitations of "Dog Tray," "Captain Jinks of the Horse Marines," "Not for Joseph," and his "great monologue" with forty costume changes. Five additional appearances with program changes that add operatic selections and a farce take the couple through January 7, when Wallack has a farewell benefit performance. But we have not seen the last of him. He returned to the Theatre Royal in May 1872 with a scratch company composed of his wife, a concert singer named Frank Mellon, and gentlemen amateurs in a variety program that included a comedy and a farce. As this production was billed for his benefit, one assumes that he had already given a run of performances not mentioned in the records. Another island tour took place the next year, but by the time he reached Morant Bay and Yallahs, "they have long since ceased to draw audiences. Mrs. Wallack commands much of sympathy and good feeling in Kingston."[18] The Wallacks then left for the Turks Islands to replenish their purses.

Shortly thereafter Wallack is back in Jamaica. He opened the Gallery of Illustration on Harbour Street and promptly raised complaints about the propriety of the entertainment it provided. The venture did not last long, for by 1879 the building was referred to as "late Wallack's Gallery." Wallack had the habit of suddenly reappearing on the scene when least expected. He turned up in November 1883 to give four performances at the Theatre Royal with his wife and a supporting actor, J. A. Rider, who was his cousin. His variety program on this occasion was titled "Tripologue" and consisted of short plays, readings, and songs. Rider won approval as a first-class comic, Wallack was clever and amusing as ever, and Fanny Wallack "adds to the charm of a talented actress the grace and talent of an accomplished singer."[19] Two years go by, then Wallack announced a revival of "Tripologue" at the theatre in Kingston on October 16, 1885, to be followed by appearances in Spanish Town, Linstead, and Old Harbour. These engagements were peremptorily canceled, however, when his wife became ill. She died in Kingston later that year.

Wallack's final visit to Jamaica occurred in January 1893 when he returned from the United States as manager of a musical family comprising Professor Joseph Heine, a blind violinist and composer, Mme Heine, a pianist, and Miss Evelyn Heine, soprano and violinist. They performed several evenings at the Theatre Royal, holding audiences spellbound. Then Wallack announced his own benefit performance at the Royal on April 5, 1893, "to celebrate his fiftieth anniversary of service to the profession." The governor's patronage had been solicited, the theatre was to be lit by electricity for the first time, and Wallack would appear with Rider and a host of amateur talent in a brilliant comedy. The program turned out to be a burlesque opera by the Heines and a comic scene enacted by Wallack and company. A "samfie" artist surely, this Wallack, as the Jamaicans would call such a schemer, but not without talent and a sense for locally flavored entertainment.

In a vain attempt to follow the fortunes of Watty Wallack as monologuist, discussion has strayed from the strict subject of this chapter. Despite fulsome advertising, Wallack's notices have added little to our enlightenment, and it is time to regain the high ground. The two decades of the seventies and eighties witnessed a clutch of reciters from abroad, not to mention local professionals. The depressed state of the economy favored the single reader over the traveling troupe, as slim gate receipts would not have to be shared with a large company. The dilapidated Theatre Royal could be avoided by using any suitably large hall, and when performances had exhausted the potential Kingston audience, travel to country towns could be readily undertaken at minimal expense. Moreover, the visit of the Keans had raised oral recitation to a high art and stimulated public interest in the genre. In Hanover and Old Harbour, for instance, Penny Reading Societies were formed, where for the fee of one penny it was possible to gain admission to the courthouse of an evening and listen to local gentlemen read passages of literature. Above all, the emergence of popular Jamaican storytellers presenting Jamaican material and using the local dialect developed a following for the professional reciter that has been equaled only in the second half of the present century.

To mention first the professionals from overseas: John E. Ince, with a program consisting of selections from Shakespeare, Dickens, Edgar Allan Poe, and others arrived in November 1870 and stayed several months. He gave readings at Kingston school halls, the Spanish Town Court House, at Newcastle, and in country towns. His audiences were said to be "thoroughly appreciative." In 1873 Frank Mellon, who both sang and recited, gave an entertainment at the Gallery of Illustration and for three hours kept his audience in perpetual laughter. He traveled to Vere and Clarendon for performances and also appeared at the Theatre Royal in support of Watty Wallack. James Leslie Main of Ipswich, England, "celebrated lecturer, elocutionist and vocalist," came to Kingston in September 1880. He offered three literary concerts at the theatre embracing "A Night with Tennyson," "Our Great Poets and Singers," and "Among the Muses, Grave and Gay." His final performance concluded with a ventriloquist's sketch in which he imitated the sounds of animals and other creatures. His press reviews were generally positive; *Gall's Newsletter* found it extraordinary that he occupied the stage for three consecutive hours, "a solitary artist, without the aid of showy accessories or sensational fanfaronade, has held multitudes spellbound by the potential charm of the 'living voice' and the eloquent rendering of some of the most beautiful selections from the musical and literary anthology of the English tongue."[20] Main then embarked on an island tour, touching some dozen towns before returning to the city for several more readings at the theatre, the courthouse, and Mico College prior to his departure for Barbados. He was billed for a return engagement in June 1883, but arrived from New York in poor health and died on July 6 without once again taking the stage.

Occasionally actors from a touring company might offer reading concerts at the end of their company's season of performances. If the company did poorly at the box office and disbanded in Kingston, actors would be forced to find the means to pay their passages home. At other times company members might choose to stay on in Jamaica at the end of a season or to return to the island on their own. The next two groups of readers belong to this vagabond breed. In December 1881, Messrs. Gilmour and Sidman of the Charles Arnold Company presented a Literary and Musical Evening at the town hall in Kingston, their program comprising readings from *Henry V* and *As You Like It*, along with piano and cornet solos and singing. Gilmour had been a popular leading man in McDowell's Company from the previous year, and his name alone would have attracted a crowd of admirers. The evening, described as a rich intellectual treat, was a decided success. The program was probably repeated more than once in Kingston and may have been taken on the road. Several months later, on March 4, a booking at the theatre for Gilmour's benefit was canceled owing to his imminent departure for New York.

In October 1883 Barton Hill and Josephine Cameron, originally members of the Slavin Dramatic Company, arrived from the island of Saint Thomas. On the dissolution of their troupe they had teamed up to give dramatic readings and had already visited Barbados and Demerara. Of particular interest was their practice of inviting local amateurs to share the stage with them. They opened at the Theatre Royal on October 17 with "An Evening with Shakespeare," which they generously billed in aid of the Leslie Main Memorial Fund, thus honoring the memory of a fellow reciter. The Regimental Band was in attendance to play Sullivan's "The Lost Chord" and other songs made popular by Main. This recital was succeeded on October 18 and 19 by

"An Evening with the Poets," both presentations incorporating gentlemen amateurs. *Romeo and Juliet* and *Macbeth* were the two Shakespeare plays from which scenes were read, along with selections from *The Lady of Lyons* and *Ingomar.*

The teaching of oratory received a boost with the arrival on the island in June 1885 of Professor J. Warburton Taverner to present a series of lectures on "Elocution as a New Science." Taverner was a practiced public reader and had appeared more than thirty years earlier at Clinton Hall in New York, when he recited *Macbeth.* In Kingston he delivered five lectures at the Mico Hall, his topics being (1) "On Movement of Time," (2) "On Emphasis," (3) "The Inflections of the Voice," (4) "The Culture of the Voice," and (5) "Antagonism of Grammatical Forms." Having discoursed upon the theory of oral recitation, Taverner decided to demonstrate his expertise in a number of dramatic impersonations. This he did at the Mico Hall on July 1, at St. George's Schoolroom on July 6, and beginning on July 20 with three entertainments at Wolmer's School. This parade of foreign readers ends with "the eminent English elocutionist" Arthur Huntley, who recited *Karl the Martyr* at the town hall on April 14, 1887, under the patronage of a galaxy of officials that included the governor, Lieutenant Colonel Ward, Colonel Talbot, and officers of the West India Regiment. Huntley gave two further readings with a change of program and then announced a tour of country districts, of which no further information is presently available.

Before turning to the resident Jamaican storytellers, one more reciter should be mentioned, the Jamaican Rudolph de Cordova, a graduate of the Collegiate School who lived abroad and whose theatrical career has already been discussed. Comment will be given here on his solo recitals. His professional debut in this area took place at Steinway Hall, London, in 1885 when he recited from memory W. S. Gilbert's fairy play in verse titled *Broken Hearts.* As the *Pall Mall Gazette* observed: "To recite a three-act, six-character piece from memory, and without the aid of scenery or other assistance, and to keep an audience interested in it from beginning to end, is a task of no ordinary difficulty."[21] Despite de Cordova's "sympathetic voice and admirable elocution" he was not equally successful with all the characters. Yet the overall performance was effective and merited approval. De Cordova would seek to refine it in succeeding years, not always with satisfactory results.

In August 1886 Rudolph de Cordova came back to Jamaica for a visit of several weeks' duration. During his stay he gave public readings in Kingston, Spanish Town, and in country areas. His repertoire consisted of *Broken Hearts* and a selection of pieces from Sir Walter Scott, Tennyson, Thackeray, Browning, and others, "from grave to gay, from lively to serene." The lengthy reviews accorded him in the local press were mostly ecstatic in their commendation. At the Theatre Royal on October 4, 1886, his recital of *The Merchant of Venice,* in which he spoke the text from memory, assuming the roles of some eighteen characters, was a prodigious feat in itself apart from the demands made on the actor to present different characterizations in rapid succession. De Cordova, however, was up to the task; he "inspired an entire cast of diversified, complex and in several instances elaborately constructed characters with the vital warmth and the distinct individuality, without which the delineations of the actor or the creations of the artist, though possibly fair of form, lack the soul of a living, breathing, sympathetic human interest."[22]

Leaving Jamaica, de Cordova journeyed to New York where he spent some months before returning to London. His recital of *Broken Hearts* at Chickering Hall in New York on November 3, 1886, was coolly received by the *Times* critic, who felt that the task of memorizing the play was "scarcely worth undertaking." De Cordova wore conventional evening dress and had an assistant seated close by to read the entrances and exits of the characters. Other than that, the stage was bare. The critic, clearly unimpressed with the performance, found de Cordova's attitudes to be "queer and quaint." Conceding that "his voice is of fair quality, as the voices heard on the stage nowadays go," the writer felt that de Cordova's gift for impersonation was not strikingly manifested and that he was not likely to make a fortune as a public reader.[23]

This discouraging review is in marked contrast with the report of de Cordova's recital of the same play at Steinway Hall, London, several months later. Whether the young actor had considerably improved his performance or whether his English auditors were more attuned to his material and the manner of its presentation than were those in America, one can only surmise, but the review in the London *Saturday Review* was comparatively flattering. Not only was de Cordova's voice resonant and full of varied intonations, but also "his histrionic ability was so great that he was able to keep his audience interested for an exceptionally long time, winning and deserving considerable applause."[24] In this critic's opinion, de Cordova would without question be an acquisition to the London stage, a prediction that subsequent history confirmed.

With Henry Garland Murray and his two sons, Andrew C. Murray and William Coleman Murray, we come to a most important development in the history of oral recital in Jamaica. Except for Raphael de Cordova, all previously mentioned readers and reciters took their material from abroad; the Murrays wrote their own. De Cordova's original pieces were set in a foreign country; the Murrays' stories were Jamaican. None of the previous speakers employed the Jamaican vernacular; the Murrays used dialect regularly and copiously. If the foregoing readers or reciters represent the Western tradition of oral delivery that began with Homer, the Murrays represent the West African tradition exemplified by the Anansi storyteller.

Henry G. Murray, a black man, came from Montego Bay and completed his education at Mico School in that town. As a youth he showed a talent for writing and started a tiny newspaper that he called *The Juvenile Journal.* After a short spell of teaching, he became editor and proprietor of the *Cornwall Chronicle* on the death of its former owner. This venture was not successful, and Murray moved to Kingston, where he worked as editor of the *Morning Journal* before again publishing for a short time his own paper, *Murray's Daily News.* On a visit to Panama he caught the local fever, which apparently caused his death in Kingston on January 28, 1877.[25] For the last eight years of his life, Murray devoted the greater part of his time to writing humorous stories that he referred to as "Manners and Customs of the Country a Generation Ago." These he read to public audiences throughout the island. His appeal was immediate and electric. Nothing like that had ever been offered to audiences before, and they never tired of hearing him.

Murray penned almost forty of his narratives. With repeated recitals on his regular country tours he may well have given several hundred performances. Since each performance represented a full evening's reading and singing of appropriate songs that were incorporated into the text, the physical strain on the speaker's voice must have been considerable.

The elder Murray had been writing a book of these character sketches and had completed four chapters when he was encouraged to offer his first reading at Wolmer's Girls' schoolroom in the city on January 27, 1869. His presentation covered the following topics: "Cropover rejoicings; Sketches of the Walkfoot Buckra; the Sets; John Canoes; Actor Boys; Fishermen; Bakerboys; Bugaboos, etc.," with songs of the period. By the time he had given his third reading on "Muster Day in Older Times" some definition of this new phenomenon was called for: "We have heard the name of Lectures and of Readings applied to these delightful entertainments, but neither, to our opinion, is an accurate designation. They are rather a series of charming character-etchings executed by a masterly hand—a string of varie-

205

gated and priceless brilliants, hung together with a free, careless negligence which often produces grander effects than the most studied art, and the most consistent harmony."[26] This was storytelling at its dazzling peak.

Murray was aware that his pieces should be heard rather than read, and he was particularly concerned at the appearance in print of the vernacular passages. He was at first reluctant to have his stories published, and when he later bowed to demand and printed some sketches, he admitted that he had anglicized the native idiom for the benefit of readers not to the manner born. The reviewer of *Muster Day*, in attempting to quote sections for the reader, was also sensitive to this problem: "We are conscious of having rendered but scanty justice to the easy delivery, and the interminable drolleries that marked the performance. No mortal pen can successfully transcribe the pure vernacular, with its pungent shrewdness, and caustic humor, any more than it can portray the natural acting and elastic facial expression of the lecturer. The laughter and enjoyment produced by the more telling passages were unbounded, and at times almost painful."[27]

Murray's style was described as simple and natural, devoid of bombastic heroics or highly labored, inflected descriptions. He regularly introduced Anansi tales and native proverbs in dialect form to illustrate a moral; and although most of his characters were taken from the black working class, he also gave striking portraits of authority figures such as overseers and military officers. He was most often compared to Charles Dickens, "whose inimitable combinations of touching tenderness and genial humour have similarly affected us." The risk of offending some element of the population by the sting of satire directed at members of the poorer classes was an ever-present danger in these addresses. The elder Murray was never accused of such insensitivity as was his son William C. Murray, but he must at times have cut close to the bone. Witness, for instance, this description of the character Jackey, who had a passion for guava fruit:

> But a dis brown man ya dem call Jackee-ya! Aow! When him go fe nyama guaba, ef a ripe eh, ef a green eh, all a de same to him. Den come hearee de seed na him jaw na go ya "Cooroodoop-cooroodoop" de same likee when horse da nyam corn. Den when him done nyam, him knockee him mout-ya! Paow! de same like alligator, when dem catch fly. Den come yerry him teeth go "copoop" de same like a jawbone raker.

In contrast there is the following description of Ellen, an ignorant, forlorn girl falling in love for the first time: "In the meantime, a visitant had entered her heart. He had come in tenderness and sweetness; come with hands of velvet with which he patted her cheeks, and with a breath as of the incense of the morning or the sweet south over a bed of violets. Joy waited on his every step, and when he shook his wings the incense of pleasure that rose exhilarated the heart beyond description. This was Love."[28]

After almost four years of constant and unrivaled appearances in Jamaica, Murray was encouraged to visit Boston, Massachusetts, in the hope of joining the lecture circuit in that part of the United States. He left Jamaica in September 1872 and gave three auditions in Boston to which journalists and producers were invited. They were very impressed, but Murray found the Lyceum Bureau circuit booked up and was told he would have to wait until next year unless, as one manager said, he had about £30 to spare when the thing could be done. Having no such funds at his disposal, a disappointed Murray returned home and gave three serialized readings on "What I Saw in America." Thereafter a distinct falling off occurs in the regularity of press reports on his presentations. He was no longer a novelty and, with the rejection in Boston, had lost his chance of celebrity status. In May 1874 Murray suffered an extended illness, and a benefit variety program was organized on his behalf. He had been most generous in giving readings in aid of charitable causes; this, and his immense personal popularity, made the benefit a success and £75 plus a leather attaché case were donated to him. His last known reading took place on July 3, 1876, at Saint George's Schoolroom in Kingston, when his topic was "Spelling Bees in the Olden Times." By the following January Murray was reported to be seriously ill at his residence, 142 Princess Street, in the city. He expired on January 28. He left a wife and five children, two of his sons being close to maturity.

The first to succeed his father as a professional storyteller was Andrew C. Murray, who commenced his career in May 1879 with a reading entitled "Some Men Does Ded Befo' Dem Time." Described as a discussion between two country Negroes on the question whether death doesn't visit some people prematurely, the younger Murray may have been using laughter to soothe the pain of a father's early demise. Young Murray delivered this reading several times in Kingston over the next two years along with other original pieces such as "Timbo, the Quadrille Instructor" and "Dong Quima, or The Curious Sayings of the Old School." On one occasion his performance so moved an auditor that it prompted a letter of appreciation to the press: "This young man has inherited his father's genius for telling Negro stories and for delivering Negro character, and bids fair to equal, if not sur-

pass, his much lamented father. . . . He kept the room in one continued roar of laughter from beginning to end of the entertainment."[29]
The writer praised the younger Murray's versatility of talent that
could at one moment depict settings in the choicest language and
richest poetry, and at the next, convulse an audience with his broad
humor and inimitable imitations of Negro language and gesture.

Newspapers of the time did not carry as detailed reports of these
appearances as had occurred with the elder Murray. Over the next five
years the titles of only ten different stories were traced. These were all
presented in the city, although it is quite probable that, like his father
before him, young Murray made extensive speaking tours to country
districts that have gone unrecorded. Indeed, only one appearance in
1882, none in 1883, and two in 1884 have been traced. Then, after the
entry for "Puss Twenga" delivered at the Saint Joseph's School in
Kingston on November 18, 1884, all readings by Andrew Murray
ceased and his name dropped from the records.

Yet another Murray appeared to carry on the tradition. Some two
years later William Coleman Murray announced a reading at the town
hall in Kingston on January 26, 1887. Two stories were presented:
"Dead Man's Socks" and "How Alligator Mek 'Lection." By the end of
the century, some sixteen new titles were recorded for him, with only
one delivered out of town at the Old Harbour Court House. Since it is
obvious that performances in rural areas were seldom reported in
Kingston papers, the likelihood is that a number of original stories by
the third Murray may also have escaped notice.

This latest Murray seems to have focused his jibes on the Jamaican
peasantry and the black underclass, more so than his predecessors did.
He also spoke on contemporary subjects—one lecture being on a fire
at the Solas Market in Kingston, another on the 1891 Jamaica Exhibition, and a third on a recent mayoral election. Two of his readings were
published. "A Day with Joe Lennan, the Rosewell Duppy Doctor"
went into print in 1891 and was inscribed "to the memory of my
beloved mother"; and "Tay Bambye, We All Wi' See," describing in
"Negro English" scenes and incidents related to the Jamaica Exhibition, was issued in 1893. Based on the Joe Lennan booklet that sur-
vives, this Murray's prose style, compared with his father's, seems labored: "Following the course of a swift, transparent, gurgling stream,
born of the spring floods and nourished by the sweet soft rains of
yester-night, you are brought in the midst of rock and trees which
form a basin or reservoir by the sides of which the lovely pink, wild
okro and other plants, fanned and invigorated by the pure mountain
air, impregnated with the perfume of innumerable aromatic herbs and

flowers, infuse new life into your veins and you deem yourself a very Oberon."[30]

In his preface to this booklet, Murray declared that the chief incidents in the story were actual facts and that the people described were real people who had either lived or were then living. Here, too, the youngest Murray was breaking new ground and doing so dangerously. It was one thing to poke fun publicly at people from an earlier era who were no longer alive, as his father and brother had done. It was quite another to satirize living folk who were known and possibly respected in the community. This Murray had, in one of his readings, made fun of his old schoolmaster, "Mass George," who apparently had a penchant for using malapropisms. Doubtless aware that his remarks might give umbrage in certain quarters, Murray inserted the following defense in his prefatory note: "It is surely possible to depict the peculiarities, manners or eccentricities, either of individuals or of communities, in language which, if slightly satirical, is wholly untinged by any ill-humour, any offensive suggestion, any word or thought which is likely to cause a moment's pain. Such at any rate has been my aim."[31]

Like his father before him, W. C. Murray was a newspaperman. He worked for a time on the staff of the *Gleaner* and then acquired his own paper, the *Cornwall Herald* in Savanna-la-Mar, of which he was editor. In this capacity he invoked the wrath of a fellow journalist, the eminent Dr. Robert Love, editor of the *Jamaica Advocate,* a race-conscious paper devoted to uplifting black Jamaicans. Murray had testified before an education commission in May 1898 and condemned the notion of free education at state expense beyond the "3 R's" of Reading, 'Riting, and 'Rithmetic. He had urged instead the establishment of trade and farm schools for the children, whose parents would be expected to contribute toward their education. Angrily, Love dismissed as not worthy of consideration "the stupid objection recently made in a paper edited by a Negro in Savanna-la-Mar that the State who kept the Negroes in absolute ignorance whilst they were slaves, should not educate them freely now they are free men and citizens."[32]

Love had earlier commented on Murray's reading at the Conversorium in Kingston on February 8 of that year. Granting the reading's success from a commercial viewpoint and the incontestable amusement it generated in the audience, Love came away saddened by the experience: "For ourself, we cannot say that we enjoy these lectures for the simple reason that in them, our race is held up to ridicule and lampooned. When this is done by a member of the more fortunate race, it makes us angry; when done by one of our own race, even the humour does not take away a feeling of sadness from us."[33] At no time was there a direct allusion to the elder Murray's race. These references to W. C. Murray being a Negro and an earlier reference to Andrew Murray, who was once described as "the popular Negro lecturer," make it clear that the Murrays were a black family.

During slavery the Jamaican population was clearly structured. There were black slaves, free blacks and coloreds, and whites of whom those of Jewish persuasion formed an influential minority. After Emancipation, however, the lines of demarcation were obliterated, partly by design and partly by intermarriage. Whites, retaining privilege and power but now grossly outnumbered by free blacks and coloreds, seemed reluctant to identify persons by race for fear of being swamped by a black tidal wave. As a result, when black leaders like Robert Love and later Marcus Garvey came on the scene and began to preach black solidarity, they were usually vilified as revolutionaries. Black intellectuals were expected to join the ranks of the ruling class, politically if not socially, rather than seek common cause with their working-class brethren. This attitude often makes it difficult to identify clearly the race of Jamaicans who formed the cultural elite of the late nineteenth century. The Murray sons were an exception in this regard. Revealing their race was equal to conferring a badge of authenticity since their readings depended for their humor on the speaking of black Jamaican dialect. The problems that the young W. C. Murray encountered were due to the pressures of society on him to conform to prevailing modes of thought. Despite these larger issues he remained a popular entertainer of the people. Appearing on a concert program in 1893, he was billed as "Funny Murray." The appellation stuck, especially after an island tour the next year. As Funny Murray he (no longer differentiated from his father and elder brother) entered the twentieth century and is dimly remembered by older Jamaicans today.

The success of the Murrays was partly due to an upsurge of interest among intellectuals in Jamaican creole as an expressive medium of wit and wisdom. This new interest surfaced around mid-century and was inspired mostly by leaders of the Presbyterian community in Kingston, chief among whom was the Reverend John Radcliffe [fig. 14], minister of Scot's Kirk and for several years headmaster of the Collegiate School. He had in fact presided at many readings by the elder Murray. Radcliffe spent forty-four years in Jamaica, from his arrival on December 7, 1848, to his death on September 7, 1892. He involved himself energetically, and as we've seen sometimes controversially, in the intellectual and cultural life of the island. He wrote and published poems and plays, gave and sponsored public lectures on

14. Bust of the Reverend John Radcliffe at Saint Andrew's Scots Kirk.
The inscription reads: "A Preacher, Teacher and Poet, who died on the
7 Sept., 1892, after a residence of 44 years in this island. Erected by
some admirers of his brilliant genius and personal worth, as a slight
mark of their high esteem." Reproduced from the collection of the
National Library of Jamaica.

211

a wide variety of topics, formed the Collegiate Literary and Debating Society from past pupils of his institution, and was a founding member of the Institute of Jamaica.

In July 1852 while fellow speakers were lecturing smug audiences on such topics as "Whether Shakespeare or Milton Was the Sublimest Genius" or "The Poetry of Robert Burns," Radcliffe showed his preference for studying the folklore of his new country of residence by speaking at the Kingston Polytechnic on "Serpent Worship Illustrative of Obeahism." In 1859 he gave a series of six lectures on Jamaican proverbs, which he published serially and then compiled together in a single volume. As foreword to this volume, Radcliffe reprinted the text of a paper on Negro literature previously submitted for publication in an organ of the Royal Society of Arts and Agriculture. He had written: "We have no National Literature in Jamaica" (since it has no race that can be regarded as sons of the soil), but

we have the Literature of a race—the Negro race. . . . The people of Europe are sporadic; the people of Africa are aggregated. The one leaves behind them their old national traditions; the other preserves and perpetuates them. . . . The exploits of *Anansay* [*sic*] are transmitted from one generation to another; and one of the pleasantest pictures to be seen in Jamaica, of peasant comfort and enjoyment, is that of a circle of youngsters seated around some village story-teller, as he recounts the cunning and the exploits of *Anansay*. What the legends of Hercules were to the peasants of Greece, and the tale of the She-wolf to those of Rome, are the *Anansay* legends to the African. What was Literature in the one case must be regarded as Literature in the other.[34]

In his analysis, Radcliffe saw this Afro-Jamaican literature existing in three areas: the mythological, represented by Anansi tales; the proverbial, represented by Negro proverbs; and the lyric, represented by Negro songs. He ended his essay by urging the collection of this Negro literature as a worthy and useful undertaking. "It would be a gauge," he wrote, "of the intellect of the people to whom it belonged, and would be a mental standard higher than many dream of. It would reveal the idiosyncrasy of the African, and thus give some direction for his training—a thing much to be desired amid the grim uniformity of stereotyped education, which forgets that every individual mind and every race follows the laws of his own development."[35] The proverbs that inspired his six lectures were (1) Greedy choke puppy, (2) John Crow tink him pickney white, (3) When cockroach give dance, him no ax fowl, (4) Rock tone da riber bottom no know sun hot, (5)

When trouble catch bull-dog, monkey breeches fit him, and (6) Pass long, okro poil.

Radcliffe had thrown down a challenge that others took up. A month after his address J. M. Young advertised a lecture on "Peasant Literature and Mythology of Jamaica, or Anansay Stories, illustrated." He promised early publication of his lecture. In 1862 James Gall offered a lecture at the courthouse, Kingston, on a popular Negro proverb similar to one used by Radcliffe: "Trouble catch you, pickney breeches fit you." Knowing Gall's prickly nature, this lecture was likely a hit at some of his detractors. Then in 1866 a dialect poem, the first encountered in reviews of the columns of the daily press, was published in the *Colonial Standard.* Titled "Mr. Holt," it was allegedly written by a black woman. It happened that Holt, himself a black, on a visit to England to find markets for Jamaican small farmers had been asked by the white ladies there whether or not black men in Jamaica married white women. In recounting this experience at an address in the city, Holt reportedly commented that he was ashamed to reply in the negative, whereupon he recommended his people to dress in such a manner as to make them acceptable husbands to the white ladies of Jamaica. One of the verses by the outraged folk poet reads as follows:

Him tun him back pon we—him no wanty black wife—
Tick yah him no hab fe hide from Maroon and Colonel Fyfe;
But we wi' wait till him cum back no Black Ribba, yerry,
Den tick yah dem no teck him from bilbo room go bury.[36]

Thereafter to the end of the century, specimens of Afro-Jamaican literature were published in the island press, in occasional local publications, as well as in the United States and England. *Gall's Newsletter* published two Negro sermons, the first drawing a wry comment from the editor of the *Morning Journal* that the writer by his misuse of the vernacular could not be a Creole. The editor, Robert Jordan, allowed that Radcliffe had tried to promote Creole literature but considered that his 'nancy (Anansi) stories were far from being pure. As to collecting this literature, Jordan felt that such work could only be properly undertaken by a Creole as a labor of love. He, Jordan, knew any quantity of set songs, mule songs, shasha songs, myal songs, and so on, which he offered to furnish to anyone qualified for the task of compiling them "as illustrations of the morals and manners of days that are past in our country."[37] The notion that this literature could form the basis for a system of education designed to capitalize on racial and intellectual characteristics, as Radcliffe envisaged, completely escaped Jordan, who thought of it in terms of a dead language. Nor, despite the remarkable success of the Murrays as popular performers, was it ever dreamed at the time that this folk literature might contain the raw elements of a national drama and theatre. It would take several more decades before such a development would occur.

Meanwhile Jamaican proverbs and Anansi stories continued to claim attention at home and abroad. In 1873 Charles Rampini published in Edinburgh *Letters from Jamaica . . . with Negro Proverbs,* and the Reverend D. J. Reynolds in 1890 wrote an article in *Timehri,* the Demerara journal, entitled "Jamaica Proverbial Philosophy." Also in 1890 Mary Pamela Milne-Holme published in London a collection of Anansi tales under the title *Mamma's Black Nurse Stories.* More *Jamaica Proverbs and [a] John Canoe Alphabet,* written by Violet Heaven, appeared with a Kingston imprint in 1896; and by the end of the century Anansi stories were appearing in Sunday editions of the New York *Herald.*[38] This summary listing of publications is not exhaustive. It is meant to illustrate a growing interest beyond Jamaican shores in the native vernacular that was pervasive throughout the black communities on the island.

As professional storytellers, the Murrays played a central role in winning appreciation of the folk literature, but their influence on an emerging indigenous drama is more difficult to trace. One possible link exists through H. G. Murray's serial story published in the *Jamaica Instructor,* a fortnightly paper aimed at a black reading public. Titled "Jim Purdy: A Tale with a Moral," the story ran in episodes from May 1871 through at least July 1873, when subsequent issues of the paper became unavailable. Employing simple standard English and Jamaican creole, the story might well have been eagerly read and recounted in the Jamaican countryside. According to one source, it also provided material for some of the earliest folk plays:

> Jamaican drama paralleled the evolution of the English theatre. At first they [i.e., the villagers] acted passages from the Bible, especially the Old Testament, that they adapted for the stage. Later on highly moral stories were acted. Finally, they learned to produce very amusing short plays based on daily life. One source of many of these farcical local efforts was a book dealing with the adventures of an ambitious but completely illiterate cane-piece labourer named Jim Purdey [*sic*].[39]

Storytelling has become an honored profession in Caribbean life, and our age has been blessed with several preeminent practitioners of this art. There is the folk poet and actress Louise Bennett, who, in a recent public opinion poll, was voted the most outstanding woman in Jamaica.[40] In Guyana, the late, much lamented Bill Trotman was of this breed, as are Shake Keane of Saint Vincent, Paul Keens-Douglas of Trinidad, Derek Burrows of the Bahamas, and the ubiquitous calypsonians (ballad singers) who were originally attached to the Trinidad carnival band but now inhabit all the territories as solo artistes. Many unsung heroes exist. Long may they reign.

9

Slave Performances

Discussion of the Murrays' readings and of the aroused interest in Jamaican folk literature leads to a consideration of types of performances by blacks who were not part of the literate theatre community. Up to the first third of the nineteenth century, most of them were in fact slaves; when liberated and joined with other free blacks, they constituted almost 80 percent of the island's population. They had come originally from West Africa and, despite the disjuncture of slavery, had retained aspects of inherited African traditions, adapted to their new environment and conditions of livelihood. As the overwhelming majority of the population whose physical links to an ancestral African home had been irrevocably severed, these Afro-Jamaicans produced a performance culture that would eventually come to be considered native Jamaican. The task here is to record instances of performance events generated by this black underclass, to describe their format, trace their development, and examine attitudes regarding their display.

For reports on formal theatrical and other Western-type public entertainments, one could rely mostly on the columns of the daily press. Performances by slaves, however, were seldom so publicized. Occasionally slave exhibitions that had been sanctioned as part of a recognized festival might receive passing mention in newspapers. But indigenous performance, religious or recreative, that was enacted by blacks on their own volition was ignored. Worse, if such performance involved nighttime beating of drums, choral singing, and dancing, as it invariably did, this was viewed by the authorities as a potentially hostile act to be curtailed by laws, and the beating of drums was restricted to certain hours.

Although surviving newspapers lack sufficient data, it is fortunate that several descriptions of various slave entertainments exist in books published in the decades leading up to Emancipation. British parliamentary debates on slavery in the late eighteenth century focused attention on the plight of blacks on the sugar plantations and generated a number of publications from both residents in Jamaica and visitors. The account was often biased, its tone depending on whether the writer supported or opposed the abolitionist movement, but with the cessation of the slave trade by the British in 1807, it was obvious that the days of slavery were numbered. Even among the plantocracy there were few responsible individuals who could any longer find valid arguments in defense of slavery in the manner it existed. As De La Beche wrote in 1825: "I can truly say with Bryan Edwards, 'that I am no friend to slavery in any shape, or under any modification,'" yet for him the real question was "how the existing state of things in our West India colonies can be changed with justice and safety to all parties interested."[1] Both Edwards and De La Beche had extensive planting interests in Jamaica and both wrote of the conditions of slaves there. Edwards's *History of the West Indies*, published in 1793, is a celebrated text.

Before turning to descriptions of slave entertainment in Jamaica, it may be helpful to consider the variety of performance events indigenous to blacks in their African homeland, prior to their capture and transport to the New World. Many of these events took the form of vegetative rituals performed in connection with the planting and growing seasons of food crops. Others, like the masquerades, were festivals to praise or petition the gods or to worship ancestors. Still other performance events took place in celebration of victories in battle or other daring feats. One gets the impression that such public celebrations were a common occurrence, as Olaudah Equiano, the Ibo ex-slave, wrote in 1789:

> We are almost a nation of dancers, musicians, and poets. Thus every great event, such as a triumphant return from battle or other cause of public rejoicing, is celebrated in public dances, which are accompanied with songs and music suited to the occasion. The assembly is separated into four divisions.... Each represents some interesting scene of real life, such as a great achievement, domestic employment, a pathetic story, or some rural sport.... We have many musical instruments, particularly drums of different kinds, a piece of music which resembles a guitar, and another much like a stickado [i.e., a xylophone].[2]

The traditional African theatre evolved from tribal and national beliefs, according to Bakary Traore, and the appointed repositories for these beliefs were the griots, "who at the festivals perpetuate the memory of heroes. Their role is to recite the legends and so keep alive heroic narratives." Traore proceeds to cite M. Delafosse, who, having witnessed performances by the griots, wrote: "They make their he- roes come alive as they speak and, in their rendering, become full- scale theatrical scenes with several characters all represented by a single actor."[3]

There is yet one further type of performance in precolonial Africa that has received little attention. Taking his cue from the journals of Hugh Clapperton and Richard Lander, who, as guests of the King of Oyo in 1826 witnessed an exhibition by professional performers, J. A. Adedeji has researched the traditional Yoruba traveling theatre. The company, having emerged from the egungun masquerade in the 1650s, was at the time attached to the court; but there were other troupes, each one being identified with certain artistic specializations, such as poetry and dance, acrobatics and dance, sketches, and tableaux vi- vants. The actors were costumed; they played under carved masks, and were accompanied by the bata (i.e., drums) orchestra and a chorus of singers.[4]

These are but a few examples of the types of performance African slaves would have known when they arrived in the New World. The exhibitions could be ritual, festival, or secular, they could be per- formed by amateurs or professionals, and they could include music, dance, song, chant, speech, mime, and acrobatics. They would take place out of doors and would involve the whole village or town. The meaning of these exhibitions would depend on each tribe's history, beliefs, language, and common bonding—characteristics that would be destroyed by the slave trade and slavery. But a residue of their heritage lodged in the consciousness of the slaves would inform their efforts at self-expression in their new environment.

On the Jamaican plantation, life for the slaves was one of monoto- nous drudgery. Up before dawn, they worked at prescribed and repeti- tive tasks, with short breaks for two meals, until sundown, day after day. In Robert Dirks's pithy description: "A plantation distinguishes itself on two counts: the repetitive nature of the tasks of its work force and the close watch kept over them. These features give the planta- tion its singular character, one that might best be described as highly routine and thoroughly regimented."[5] Relief from this regimen oc- curred on Sundays, when slaves were allowed, on some plantations, to work a piece of ground that provided their food. For recreation, the slaves made music, sang, and danced on Saturday nights before their day off. They also enjoyed special holidays at Christmas, New Year's Day, Easter Monday, and at Crop-over. During croptime, however, no free time was allowed on Sundays. Seven-day work weeks around the clock were the rule as the harvested cane had to be milled before it rotted.

Lacking musical instruments for recreation as well as their rituals, the slaves fashioned their own from local materials. Hans Sloane, who was in Jamaica in 1687–88, wrote of "several sort of instruments, in imitation of Lutes, made of small gourds fitted with necks, strung with Horse hairs, or the peeled stalks of climbing Plants or Withs." Others were made of "hollowed Timber covered with Parchment or other Skin wetted, having a bow for its Neck, the Strings ty'd longer or shorter, as they would alter their sounds." Sloane noted "Rattles ty'd to their Legs and Wrists, and in their Hands," and one enterprising musician answered the rattles with sounds made from the mouth of an empty gourd or jar with his hand. Sloane's description of slave musical instruments was somewhat limited because, as he observed, trumpets and drums that had been allowed the slaves at their festivals were prohibited as "too much inciting them to rebellion."[6]

Charles Leslie, writing in 1740, found that the Negro slaves regularly used two musical instruments, like kettledrums, for each company of dancers. Other instruments named by him include "a Bangil, not much unlike our lute in anything but the Musick, the Rookaw, which is Two Sticks jagged; and a Jenkoving, which is a way of clapping their Hands on the Mouth of Two Jars."[7] More instruments were named by Edward Long in his massive *History of Jamaica* (1774), in which he too reported a rustic guitar of four strings, made from a sliced calabash over which a dried bladder or skin had been spread, and with a handle fastened to it. He called this guitar a "merry-wang" and said that the slaves took great pains to ornament it with carved work and ribbons. He further identified the "goombah," a hollow block of wood covered with sheepskin, and described how it was played: "The musician holds a little stick, of about six inches in length, sharpened at one end like the blade of a knife, in each hand. With one hand he rakes it over a notched piece of wood, fixed across the instrument, the whole length, and crosses with the other alternately, using both with a brisk motion; whilst a second performer beats with all his might on the sheep-skin, or tabor."[8] By the end of the century the Jawbone and the Dundo had been added to the catalog of musical instruments, the former being the lower jaw of a horse with teeth over which a piece of wood was drawn quickly up and down, and the latter another kind of drum.[9]

Coming from various tribes and speaking different native languages, the slaves probably attributed different names to instruments that were essentially alike. Thus in the early nineteenth century Monk Lewis found that the slaves' music consisted of "nothing but Gambys

(Eboe drums), Shaky-shekies, and Kitty-katties: the latter is nothing but any flat piece of board beat upon with two sticks, and the former is a bladder with a parcel of pebbles in it."[10] John Stewart advised that "the drums of the Africans vary in shape, size, etc. according to the different countries."[11] He might have added that the drums varied also according to the particular sound each was designed to produce as well as the function each was constructed to serve. Finally, Michael Scott mentioned flute players, horn blowers, and fiddlers.[12]

The fiddles were, of course, Western instruments. Among slaves on the estates were often found two or three expert fiddlers who would be required to provide music for the reels and country dances held at the great house. The horns came from oxen or they might be conch shells. The flutes were apparently less prevalent. The sole description found of the Afro-Jamaican flute comes from an unidentified source quoted in a lecture given in Kingston in 1913 by the Jamaican musician Astley Clerk:

> The Caramantee flutes are made from the porous branches of the trumpet tree, are about a yard in length, and of nearly the thickness of the upper part of a bassoon; they have generally three holes at the bottom; are held, in point of direction, like the hautboy [oboe]; and while the right hand stops the holes, in the left is shaken a hollow ball which is filled with pebbles. I have frequently heard these flutes played in part, and I think the sounds they produce are the most affecting, as they are the most melancholy, that I ever remembered to have heard. The high notes are uncommonly wild, but yet are sweet; and the lower tones are deep, majestic and impressive.

In his lecture, Clerk referred to the extensive list of musical instruments of the African Negroes with an accompanying drawing provided by Captain J. G. Stedman in his *Narrative of a five years' expedition against the Revolted Negroes of Surinam . . . in the years 1772 to 1777*. In this drawing the full panoply of drums, horns, flutes, rattles, sounding boards, a finger piano, guitar, and harp found in another Caribbean country are illustrated [fig. 15]. Clerk submitted that most of the slave instruments were "decidedly primitive," but he cautioned his audience against a tendency to deride or scoff at them because of their rude construction or curious appearance: "It is from just such beginnings that the present day, and almost perfect, musical instruments of the world have descended. I have no doubt that if the evolution of certain instruments was studied you will find that the world owes something to the instruments of Afro-Jamaica."[13]

Instrumental music was invariably accompanied with singing carried out mostly by women. Edward Long observed that the slaves had good ears for music and that their songs were generally impromptu, while the tunes "consist of a *solo* part, which we may style the recitative, the key of which is frequently varied; and this is accompanied with a full or general chorus."[14] Regarding subject matter, the singers, he felt, showed a preference for songs of derision, "not infrequently at the expense of the overseer if he happens to be listening." In the crop season when work continued nonstop, those slaves feeding the mill during the night were wont to entertain themselves with such songs in order to stay awake.

Edwards echoes Long in noting that the songs were improvised and derisive, but adds that they were also fraught with obscene ribaldry and accompanied with dances that he claimed were "in the highest degree licentious and wanton." On the other hand, he observed in many of the songs, most likely those couched in the minor key, a predominant melancholy that was very affecting.[15] Monk Lewis considered the vocals to be the principal element in the music for dancing, one girl singing two lines by herself and then being answered by a chorus in the call-and-response mode so prevalent in African performance. He declared that at one of the slave dances the singing began about six o'clock in the evening and lasted without a moment's pause until two in the morning.[16]

An illuminating analysis of the performance of black music is given by the Nigerian scholar Laz. Ekwueme in his article "African Sources in New World Black Music." He contends that there are at least two parts to African and black cultural expression: an outward visible part that appeals to the visual senses and an acoustic part that appeals to the aural senses. He argues,

> No one, whether in Africa or in the New World goes merely to hear black music; people go to *see* it. . . . The point here is that black people do not make music, or for that matter any creative art, only for one of the senses. A drummer is not just beating out rhythms; you have to see him do it in order to appreciate in any sense what he is doing. His costume, his facial contortions, his gestures, are all part and parcel of his art of drumming. This extra-acoustic (visible) motion is as essential a part of drumming as the sound produced.[17]

If the slaves showed a fondness for singing and music-making, their passion for dancing was boundless. They were known to walk ten or twelve miles to attend a dance, or as they called it, a play; they would

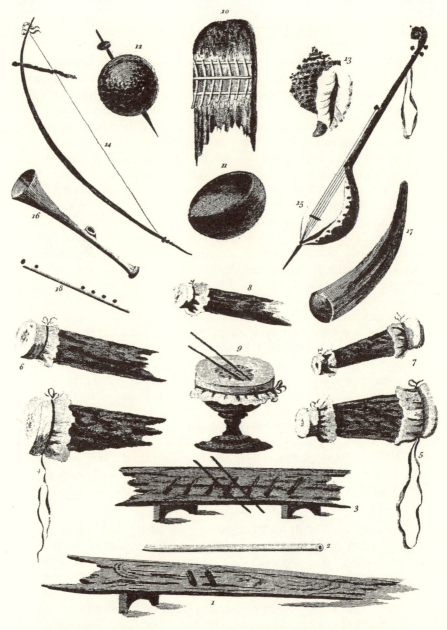

15. Musical instruments of the African Negroes. The instruments
identified by number are: (1) qua-qua or sounding board; (2) nasal flute;
(3) dulcimerlike sounding board; (4) to (9) sheepskin-covered drums of
different types; (10) and (11) finger-piano and sounding gourd; (12) saka-
saka or gourd rattle; (13) conch shell horn; (14) benta or harp;
(15) guitar; (16) trumpet; (17) ivory horn; (18) flute.

stay up all night enjoying themselves and yet return to the plantation in time for work the next morning.[18] One might infer that their songs and music were created to be put in the service of the dance since it was the dance, more than any other activity, that provided a temporary escape from the reality of their enforced servitude. The close correspondence that existed between music and dance was well captured by Long in the following account:

> Their tunes for dancing are usually brisk, and have an agreeable compound of the *vivace* and *larghetto*, gay and grave, pursued alternately. They seem also well-adapted to keep their dancers in just time and regular movements. The female dancer is all languishing, and easy in her motions; the man, all action, fire, and gesture; his whole person is variously turned and writhed every moment, and his limbs agitated with such lively exertions, as serve to display before his partner the vigour and elasticity of his muscles. The lady keeps her face towards him, and puts on a modest demure look, which she counterfeits with great difficulty. In her paces she exhibits a wonderful address, particularly in the motion of her hips, and steady position of the upper part of her person: the right execution of this wriggle, keeping exact time with the music, is esteemed among them a particular excellence; and on this account they begin to practise it so early in life, that few are without it in their ordinary walking. As the dance proceeds, the musician introduces now and then a pause or rest, or dwells on two or three *pianissimo* notes; then strikes out again of a sudden into a more spirited air; the dancers, in the meanwhile, corresponding in their movements with a great correctness of ear, and propriety of attitude, all which has a very pleasing effect.[19]

Calling their dance "a play," which several writers noted, would seem to imply that the blacks viewed the occasion as a form of theatre during which certain pantomimed actions were performed by the dancers toward each other, no doubt in response to suggestions made by the drums and in the lyrics of the songs. Thus a dynamic relationship would be established between all the performers not unlike that of characters in a drama.

A vivid description of a pantomimic dance appears in the 1790 book *A Short Journey in the West Indies*, written by an anonymous planter whose visit to his Jamaican estate brought out the Negroes to dance in his honor. The singers formed a ring with the dancers within it. A female dancer was approached by a "beauman," sometimes by two men, and they "exhibit all their powers of grace and activity." The men follow her, fan her with their handkerchiefs, court her, and eventually leave her, conveying to the audience "as perfectly as any ballet dancer in Europe, what they mean."[20] When the principal dancers have completed their act they are replaced by a new group and the next pantomime begins. This "love-dance" was also witnessed by Stewart in 1808 and by Williams in 1823. As well, Monk Lewis observed dances that he at first thought were improvised on the spot until he was informed that "there is a regular figure, and the least mistake, or a simple false step, is immediately noticed by the rest."[21] Paying closer attention, he fancied that one story represented an old duenna guarding a young girl from a lover; and another showed a young woman pursued by two suitors. He was further informed that there were dances that not only represented courtship and marriage but also "being brought to bed." An illuminating sample of Negro dance figures on the island of Trinidad about 1836 is given by Richard Bridgens in his book *West India Scenery, with Illustrations of Negro Character*. His sketches are reproduced in this book in figure 16.

While the focus has tended to be on the dances created by Afro-Jamaicans, it must not be thought that the slaves did not also participate in Western-style dances such as were held by whites and mulattoes on the estates. As already shown, some slaves had become proficient in playing the violin, and this process of acculturation was extended to the dance. One of the occasions for jubilation by the whole estate was the day of Crop-over when, the last canes having been cut, the grinding stopped, and the boiler house fires doused, flags would be displayed in the fields, rum shared among the slaves, and general rejoicing begun. In the evening, there would be a large assembly in the hall of the master's or manager's house, where, with fiddle and tambourine, dancing would commence. As Barclay observed: "Here all authority and all distinction of colour ceases; black and white, overseer and bookkeeper, mingle together in the dance."[22]

One of the fullest descriptions of a Crop-over ball is given in *Marly*, whose author took part in the event. Overseers, surgeons, and other white people from neighboring estates had been invited to dinner and dancing. There was a sumptuous feast, much punch was drunk, and as evening approached the houseboy was dispatched to call in the Negro fiddlers:

> This was the signal which the negresses were impatiently awaiting, for all the finery which they possessed, had been put into requisition, and was actually on their backs. They knew there could be no ball without them. They required no special invita-

tion to attend, for all came as fast as they were able, and before the party at the dinner table arose, the hall was nearly filled with black belles, for only four brown beauties graced the plantation. They were attended and followed by a number of the negro men, the sable fops of the estate, in their gala dresses, of which a white neckcloth forms a prominent part.

When the fiddles struck up the whites left the table, and on choosing their sable partners, the reels commenced. The ladies, nothing loth, never rejected a partner because he had previously danced with others. All Buckras who offered, came alike to them, and all were apparently equally well received.

The negresses danced barefoot, and Marly was concerned that their toes might be crushed by the Buckras' shoes, but as this seldom happened everyone had a grand time. There were occasional intermissions in order to allow the black men to display their prowess in dancing. When supper was called, the Buckras left the hall only to return later "when country dances commenced, in which the negro girls performed their part extremely well. They were very fond of the amusement, and among them there were numbers pretty well dressed, with pleasing countenances. . . . After continuing the dance to an early hour in the morning, the party broke up, when all departed."[23]

As the blacks became familiar with the music and dances of their white masters, a reverse process was subtly taking place. One instance of the penetration of European culture by that of the Afro-Jamaican occurred with the publication in the 1820s in London of musical arrangements by J. F. Edelman under the title *West Indian Pot Pourri*. Among the pianoforte selections were several "Creole Airs as sung and danced by the Negroes of Jamaica," which carried the intriguing names of "Kalimba or Pepper Pot," "The Horse's Head," "The Jackass with the Long Tail," and "The Jaw Bone."[24] These airs had been collected by Francis Egan, music master of the Kingston Militia and organist of the Kingston Church. He published the compositions in London and sold them at his Circulating Library in Kingston. Other titles advertised by him in 1835 as the fifth set of Creole apprentice tunes included "Prentice's Song of Liberty Addressed to his Pickninny," "The Pinda Boy," "Lady Mingo Flew Away," and "St. Mary Sha Sha."[25] That the Creole airs enjoyed a wave of popularity is evident in the announcement by Prospere Robert that he had rented a house in the city to teach dance and, "as the Creole airs have become so fashionable and are sometimes introduced in the first circles [of quadrilles], regular Steps and Figures are arranged to each . . . with written information of all the figures in the English and French languages."[26]

Storytelling is another kind of slave entertainment that encompasses performance. The art of storytelling is, of course, universal, but there may be features in this African-derived species that are unique to Afro-Jamaicans. In 1790 a planter in Jamaica found the language of Negroes not only more expressive than he had imagined, but also apt to convey their ideas forcibly. His slave, Cudjoe, related old stories with humor, his remarks being often proverbial and his allusions keen and novel.[27] The tales told by the slaves were all called 'Nancy Stories, referring to the spiderman trickster Anansi who, being the weakest creature in the forest, must live always by his wits. Louise Bennett has written: "Everything that happened in the world was started by Annancy,"[28] so there were also tales of magic and adventure in which the spiderman did not appear but which were also called by his name. In 1873 the *Colonial Standard* published excerpts from a manuscript entitled "Characteristic Traits of the Creolian and African Negroes in this Island." The manuscript, written by a Kingston gentleman some twenty years earlier, dealt with the period of slavery, for in it the author referred to Negroes who ran away from their owners to live in the hills and others who worked in their masters' kitchens. On the subject of storytelling, the manuscript described the "little fictitious histories" told by blacks to amuse themselves at night:

> Most of these memoirs have a strong resemblance to our ballad operas; the relation being frequently interrupted by songs; the words and music of which they well remember. They often seem intended to convey or enforce morality by a summary comment or exposition with which they conclude. The incidents are simple and the language inelegant. Many of their stories have the same imaginary personages, not unlike our exhibitions of pantomime characters in various adventures.[29]

Monk Lewis recorded six of these stories from the slave era, comparing them to "quaint old nursery tales" such as "Jack the Giant-killer" and "Little Red Riding Hood." One of them was set in Africa where a king who practiced Obeah tried to thwart the marriage of a young suitor to his daughter. After many trials, the young man succeeded in vanquishing the evil king and married the princess. Lewis also reported that the stories were both spoken and sung, and that the moral was an indispensable part of the plot. He provided this sketch of an old woman storyteller whom he met on his estate:

226

She is so truly picturesque in her short cloak, her dapper red petticoat, and the strip of white calico so exquisitely rolled about her head, from beneath which, her shrewd black eyes twinkle towards the proffered rum, so expressively; then the short pipe, stuck in the corner of her mouth; and the scarlet string of palm-berries round her shining throat . . . [she] appears wonderfully adroit in her profession (and I may with great propriety term it so) as she trots about with her marvellous budget, reminding one forcibly, though in more humble grade, of the Eastern story-tellers of certain renowned "Hunchbacks," "Wonderful Lamps," etc. . . . a most irresistible little woman.[30]

One can imagine such a woman, sitting on a rough stool at sunset under a spreading tree, children crouched around her eagerly while weary adults recline in the shadows behind them. She begins her story with a salutation that brings a ready response from keen young throats, then she eases into the plot, impersonating all the characters herself, acting out the events, creating graphic pictures out of air with word, chant, and song, altered tones and rhythms, expressive gestures and body movements, "with such vigour, dexterity and adeptness that the presentation may sometimes be seen in the light of either a drama or farce. . . . The use of these various techniques strengthens the plausibility of the performance which takes on an increasingly musical and rhythmic nature."[31] The children join in singing some of the refrains, which are deliberately repetitive to encourage their participation. At times the storyteller will pause at a critical moment of her recitation and ask a question, designed to elicit from listeners their version of how a particular difficulty might be overcome. Finally, the story reaches its climax and ends, a short proverbial moral being its epilogue: "Jack Mandora, me no choose none!" (I have not sided with anyone in the story).

Other areas in which slave performances occurred were religious rituals. These were mostly held in private and illegally, the authorities being concerned that secret meetings bred rebellion. As a result, eye-witness accounts of slave religious ceremonies are almost nonexistent. There are some descriptions of dead-wake rituals and much speculation on obeah and myalism, but little informed writing. We know now that black slaves as a rule belonged to either one or the other religious cult, such as Kumina or Pukumina, but analyses of these religions have only recently been undertaken and are properly discussed in the subsequent chapter. It may not be amiss, however, to introduce what we know of slave practices at this juncture. In his book on African roots in Jamaica folk tradition, Leonard Barrett explains that for the communicant Kumina and Pukumina represented the soul of his community, the former being still performed as a dance in Maroon communities while the latter was the most important of the typically native religions of the island. Barrett notes further: "The possession crisis in Kumina is known as *myal*, that stage of Kumina when the spirit of an ancestor actually takes control of the dancer's body, at which time the dancer loses control of speech and faculties and is actually the ancestor."[32]

Two activities associated with these religions—healing and divination—were usually classified as "obeah" and were strictly prohibited by law. In the minds of the ruling class, all such practices were not only heathen but also illegal, since obeahmen exercised power over their supplicants and often caused sickness and death. Writing in 1818, Monk Lewis explained that obeahmen and their assistants were subject to hanging or transportation. He gave a vivid description of a myal dance during which, he said, a person was killed and restored to life in order to convince spectators of the obeahman's supernatural powers. The ceremony he described has overtones of a drawn-out theatrical performance:

He sprinkles various powders over the devoted victim, blows upon him, and dances round him, obliges him to drink a liquor prepared for the occasion, and finally the sorcerer and his assistants seize him and whirl him rapidly round and round till the man loses his senses, and falls on the ground to all appearance and the belief of the spectators a perfect corpse. The chief Myal-man then utters loud shrieks, rushes out of the house with wild and frantic gestures, and conceals himself in some neighbouring wood. At the end of two or three hours, he returns with a large bundle of herbs, from some of which he squeezes the juice into the mouth of the dead person; with others he anoints his eyes and stains the tips of his fingers, accompanying the ceremony with a great variety of grotesque actions, and chanting all the while something between a song and a howl, while the assistants hand in hand dance slowly round them in a circle, stamping the ground loudly with their feet to keep time with his chant. A considerable time elapses before the desired effect is produced, but at length the corpse gradually recovers animation, rises from the ground perfectly recovered, and the Myal dance concludes.[33]

Having thus established his credentials, the obeahman was open for business and, Lewis surmised, was on occasion prepared to substitute poison for the narcotic powder used on the test victim.

Some fifty years earlier Edward Long had reported that obeah was universally practiced in Jamaica among both African and Creole Negroes who "revere, consult and fear" the obeahmen, resorting to them on all occasions and with implicit faith, "whether for the cure of disorders, the obtaining revenge for injuries or insults, the conciliating of favour, the discovery and punishment of the thief or the adulterer, and the prediction of future events."[34] Some of the paraphernalia used in these ceremonies were listed by Stewart in 1823 as grave dirt, human blood, a piece of wood shaped like a coffin, crows' feathers, a snake's or alligator's tooth, eggshells, and other nameless ingredients, all constituting a regular witches' cauldron from *Macbeth*, which produced "the fatal mixture."[35]

In respect of dead-wakes, the Africans' belief in a world of spirits persuades them to take especial pains with burial ceremonies so as to satisfy the spirit of the departed, which, thereafter, can become a benign protector of the family or community. That an individual has lived a long and useful life before dying is cause for rejoicing tinged with sadness at his passing from the material world. The pouring of libations, drumming, dancing, singing and speech making take place at these ceremonies. Bryan Edwards found the dancing to be "warlike," with bodies "strongly agitated by running, leaping and jumping, with many violent and frantic gestures and contortions. Their funeral songs too are all of the heroic or martial cast."[36] Stewart mentioned the sacrifice of a fowl over the grave of the deceased as well as the practice of placing one's ear against the lid of the coffin to hear what the deceased wished to say. This communication often consisted of complaints and upbraidings for various injuries suffered, particularly the nonpayment of debts. In the latter case, the coffin would refuse to proceed to interment past the door of a debtor until the debt was paid.[37] Three nights and nine nights following interment, additional ceremonies would be held as a final benediction and to ensure that the spirit of the dead was satisfied with the observances.

To turn from private ceremony to public festival, the most prevalent form of black public entertainment in Jamaica during the nineteenth century was the masquerade known as Jonkonnu (one of several alternative spellings much in use during the period being "John Connu").[38] Similar masquerades were observed in other Caribbean lands such as the Bahamas, Saint Kitts, Nevis, and British Honduras. A "John

Kuner" masquerade was also reported along the eastern seaboard of North Carolina and suggests a strong African tradition that was carried by slaves to the territories where they were finally deposited. The masquerade appeared as part of the Christmas holiday revels. On the plantation, late December was an interim period between the planting and growing season of the sugarcane and the harvesting season that began in January. Once cutting the ripened stalks commenced, a grueling round-the-clock regimen was imposed of trimming, stacking, transporting, grinding, and boiling until the cane juice was turned into sugar. This routine went on for months on end. It was therefore sound policy to allow slaves two or three days off prior to the start of harvesting. On most estates work stopped at midday on Christmas Eve and resumed at daybreak on the second or third day after Christmas. The slaves were free to tend their provision grounds, which were often some distance away from the estate, to go to market and trade their produce for meat and articles of clothing, and generally prepare themselves for reveling. They were also allowed to be off on the first day of the new year.

The Jamaican Jonkonnu, probably first seen by Sloane in 1687–88, reached its most elaborate form early in the nineteenth century. It came under attack after Emancipation but continued to be held sporadically in various parts of the country. The masquerade went into decline in the early decades of the present century but was revived as a Jamaican art form for competitive festivals in the 1950s. It has since entered the dance repertoire of native performing troupes. Associated with the Jonkonnu were two other types of masquerade, the Actor Boys and the Set Girls. Each will be discussed in turn.

In his all-too-brief account, Sloane mentioned that the Negroes danced and sang "at nights and on Feast days," and, without attaching a name to the disguising or indicating the time it occurred, he noted: "They very often tie Cows Tails to their Rumps, and add such other odd things to their Bodies in several places, as gives them a very extraordinary appearance."[39] Almost a century later, Edward Long provided a full description of the masquerade:

> In the towns, during Christmas holidays, they have several tall robust fellows dressed up in grotesque habits, and a pair of ox-horns on their head, sprouting from the top of a horrid sort of vizor, or mask, which about the mouth is rendered very terrific with large boar-tusks. The masquerader, carrying a wooden sword in his hand, is followed with a numerous crowd of drunken women, who refresh him frequently with a sup of aniseed-water, whilst he

230

dances at every door, bellowing out *John Connu!* with great vehe-
mence. . . . In 1769 several new masks appeared, the Ebos, the
Papaws, etc. having their respective Connus, male and female,
who were dressed in a very laughable style.[40]

Here, the imitation of the bull figure is more expressly defined than
in Sloane's brief account. It is possible that this representation was
analogous to a generic and cultic African masquerade, since it was
supported by a number of different tribes and made its appearance
throughout the Caribbean region. The Africans invested all things,
animate and inanimate, with a resident spirit that they were wont to
placate through imitation and various other rituals, especially if they
wished to acquire the attributes of the object or were forced to kill an
animal for food or clothing. Thus the Yoruba leather workers of Old
Oyo are known to chant praises before beginning their workday to the
spirit of the beast whose hide they are carving as well as to the god of
iron whose metal they have fashioned into knives. Failure to carry out
this exercise is to risk the hide's resisting efforts to turn it into a
beautiful and useful object, or the knife's slipping and cutting the
carver. But there is another and deeper significance than this. Observing reverence for the elements of nature makes man an equal partner
with, rather than an exploiter of, earth's riches. Thus also in Trinidad
the cow masquerade, presented by butchers who worked at the city's
abbatoir, was until recent years a regular feature of the annual carnival.

The Jonkonnu performed a vigorous dance with many twirls and
twists, stops and starts, to music provided by a small accompanying
band of musicians playing on homemade instruments and with singing by a chorus of women. The wooden sword held by the masquerader
was typical of the sort of "weapon" carried by leading carnival characters who saw themselves as combative warriors, prepared always to do
battle with sword, stick, or whip. While the assembled group paraded
through the streets dancing and singing, they would stop from time to
time before houses or in front of clusters of spectators to give a special
performance in the hope of receiving a handout in return for the
entertainment provided.

By the first two decades of the nineteenth century, the Jonkonnu
performance had developed into a regular ballet with several more
characters and a variety of costumes among which animal skins were
heavily favored. Quasi-military dress was also in evidence. The performance was seen by Michael Scott, a young Glaswegian who came to
Jamaica in 1806 and was employed at a mercantile house in Kingston

from 1810 to 1817. He then returned to Scotland briefly but was soon back in Jamaica, which he finally left in 1822. Scott recorded his experiences in a diary, or "log" as he called it, which he later turned into a series of magazine articles for *Blackwoods* and then a book titled *Tom Cringle's Log*. He gave a lengthy and detailed description of the Butcher's Jonkonnu Party, which he witnessed at one of the Christmas revels:

> The prominent character was, as usual, the John Canoe or Jack Pudding. He was a light, active, clean-made young Creole negro, without shoes or stockings; he wore a pair of light jean small-clothes, all too wide, but confined at the knees, below and above, by bands of red tape, after the manner that Malvolio would have called cross-gartering. He wore a splendid blue velvet waistcoat, with old-fashioned flaps coming down over his hips, and covered with tarnished embroidery. His shirt was absent on leave, I suppose, but at the wrists of his coat he had tin or white iron frills, with loose pieces attached, which tinkled as he moved. . . . His coat was an old blue artillery uniform one, with a small bell hung to the extreme points of the swallow-tailed skirts, and three tarnished epaulets, one on each shoulder, and . . . the biggest of the three stuck at his rump, the *point d'appui* for a sheep's tail. He had an enormous cocked hat on, to which was appended in front a white false-face, or mask, of a most Methodistical expression, while Janus-like, there was another face behind, of the most quizzical description, a sort of living Antithesis, both being garnished and overstopped with one coarse wig, made of the hair of bullocks' tails, on which the *chapeau* was strapped down with a broad band of gold lace.[41]

The introduction of military apparel in the Jonkonnu costume deserves attention. The recent past had been a very anxious time for Jamaicans, ever since the slave uprising in neighboring Saint Domingue in 1791, followed by the Maroon insurrection in Jamaica in 1795–96, and the failure of the British military expedition against Saint Domingue in 1798. There had, in addition, been a slave revolt in the parish of Saint James in 1803, and unrest among the Negroes at the Christmas holidays in 1807 had necessitated calling out the militia. The country was again put under martial law in 1805 when attacks were expected from French and Spanish forces. As a result of all this military activity, troops and militia were frequently seen in Kingston and ships of the fleet in the harbor, so that it is entirely possible that discarded uniforms would find their way into the Jonkonnu. As a

matter of fact, as we shall presently see, the introduction of the Set
Girls masquerade into the Christmas revels was a direct consequence
of the presence of military personnel in the city.

Having portrayed his principal figure who carried a white wand,
Scott explained that the Jonkonnu suddenly sprang on the back of a
nondescript animal that capered and jumped about in grotesque fashion. This signaled the start of the music:

> The performers were two gigantic men, dressed in calf-skins en-
> tire, head, four legs, and tail. The skin of the head was made to fit
> like a hood, the two fore-feet hung dangling down in front, one
> over each shoulder, while the other two legs, or hind-feet, and the
> tail, trailed behind on the ground; deuce another article had they
> on in the shape of clothing except a handkerchief, of some flam-
> ing pattern, tied round the waist. There were also two flute-
> players in sheep-skins, looking still more outlandish from the
> horns on the animals' heads being preserved; and three stout
> fellows, who were dressed in the common white frock and trow-
> sers, who kept sounding on bullocks' horns. These formed the
> band as it were.

The gigantic figures presumably played drums, which with the flutes,
the horns, the jingling bells on Jonkonnu's costume, and the singing
constituted the music. In addition to the band, the masquerade consisted of about fifty of the butcher Negroes, all neatly decked out in
blue jackets, white shirts, Osnaburgh trousers, and carrying their steel
knives and cases at their sides. There was also the animal character,
supported by the head of the butcher gang on whose back the Jonkonnu had climbed:

> He was clothed in an entire bullock's hide, horns, tail, and the
> other particulars, the whole of the skull being retained, and the
> effect of the voice growling through the jaws of the beast was
> most startling. His legs were enveloped in the skin of the hind-
> legs, while the arms were cased in that of the fore, the hands
> protruding a little above the hoofs, and, as he walked reared up on
> his hind-legs, he used, in order to support the load of the John
> Canoe who had perched on his shoulders, like a monkey on a
> dancing bear, a strong stick, or sprit, with a crutch top to it, which
> he leant his breast on every now and then. After the creature . . .
> had capered with its extra load, as if it had been a feather, for a
> minute or two, it came to a standstill, and, sticking the end of the
> sprit into the ground, and, tucking the crutch of it under its chin,

it motioned to one of the attendants, who thereupon handed, of all things in the world, *a fiddle to the ox.* He then shook off the John Canoe, who began to caper about as before, while the *Device* set up a deuced good pipe, and sung and played, barbarously enough, I will admit, to the tune of Guinea Corn, the following ditty:

> "Massa Buccra lob for see
> Bullock caper like monkee—
> Dance, and shump, and poke him toe,
> Like one human person—just so."

And hereupon the tail of the beast, some fifty strong, music men, John Canoe and all, began to rampage about, as if they had been possessed by a devil whose name was Legion.[42]

After rendering more verses of the song with the dancers circling around the Beast figure at the end of each verse, the performers were paid off and left, cavorting up the street.

Another pantomime party observed by Scott represented "the work-house people" or common jail, whose act was simply to show how a prisoner would be beaten. One fellow, dressed in lawyer's gown, bands, black silk breeches, wig, and cocked hat, resembled the island's chief justice. He carried a cat-o-nine-tails, threw the prisoner on the ground, and walloped him with the whip, this worthy having his body wrapped in hide to shield him from the blows. Attendant musicians and chorus were also costumed "to give a tolerable resemblance of the Bar broke loose."[43] Scott claimed that other crafts and trades also brought forth their own "Gumbi-men, Hornblowers and John Canoes," the Gardeners having an incomparable Jack-in-the-Green, covered with the superior bloom of large flowers such as are found in the tropics.

Scott had spent some twenty years in Jamaica, and we must give credence to his report as coming from someone who had carefully observed the annual Christmas revels over a considerable period of time. Monk Lewis, on the other hand, saw only one exhibition and that in the town of Black River, Saint Elizabeth parish, on New Year's Day 1816, the very day of his arrival in Jamaica to visit his estate. Yet he too was a thoughtful observer with an inquiring mind. He describes a procession of the Set Girls that greeted him as he disembarked, mistakenly calling them the Jonkonnu procession although he does later admit that "John-Canoe made no part of the procession but . . . seemed to act upon quite an independent interest, and go about from house to house, tumbling and playing antics to pick up money for

234

themselves." The character he saw was dressed in "a striped doublet, and bearing upon his head a kind of pasteboard house-boat, filled with puppets, representing some sailors, others soldiers, others again slaves at work on a plantation, etc."[44] This houseboat Lewis later discovered had indeed been constructed of pasteboard, with gilt paper, a looking glass and paint by a carpenter on a neighboring estate. He also learned that the Jonkonnus were costumed by rich Negroes who shared the money collected from spectators during their performance, one share being reserved for the performer himself.

A third informant on the Jonkonnu in the early nineteenth century is Cynric Williams, who made an extensive tour of the island in 1823. He spent the Christmas holidays on an estate and described the masquerade exhibited on Boxing Day:

> First came eight or ten young girls marching before a man dressed up in a mask with a grey beard and long flowing hair, who carried the model of a house on his head. This house is called the Jonkanoo, and the bearer of it is generally chosen for his superior activity in dancing. He first saluted his master and mistress, and then capered about with an astonishing agility and violence. The girls also danced without changing their position, moving their elbows and knees, and keeping tune with the calabashes filled with small stones. . . . All this time an incessant hammering was kept up on the gombay, and the cotta (a Windsor chair taken from the piazza to serve as a secondary drum) and the Jonkanoo's attendant went about collecting money from the dancers and from the white people . . . the Jonkanoo man, I am told, collects sometimes from ten to fifteen pounds on the occasion. All this ceremony is certainly a commemoration of the deluge. The custom is African and religious, although the purpose is forgotten. . . .
>
> On all these occasions of festivity the mulattos kept aloof, as if they disdained to mingle with the negroes; and some of the pious, the regenerated slaves, also objected to participate in the heathen practices of their ancestors.[45]

A final eyewitness of the masquerade at this early period is George Marly (probably a pseudonym for the author, whose identity remains unknown), a Scottish bookkeeper on a Jamaican estate who in 1828 published his account of the life of a planter. He did so, he declared, in order "to delineate with truth and fidelity what came under the observation of an impartial eye-witness." During the Christmas holidays he noted that the field Negroes who flocked into town to enjoy the festivities were far from agreeably clothed compared with those

Negroes who belonged to townspeople. The estate Negroes, nevertheless, had their Jonkonnu who was fantastically dressed and accompanied by his wife (a male dancer "metamorphosed into the appearance of a gigantic female, only by the whimsical dress"). They carried
a small imitation of a canoe into which donations from the onlookers
were deposited, and they "danced without intermission, often wheel-
ing violently round, for a great number of times, and all the while
singing, or, in more correct language, roaring an unintelligible jargon,
in true stentorian voices." Marly concluded that "John Canoe and his
lady, with their favourite gumba, were of true African extraction."[46]

It would appear that the Jonkonnu masquerade had been first introduced by black slaves on the estates. Being free to move about during
the holiday period, the slaves took their masquerade into nearby
towns where they could be sure of collecting money for their performances. Before long, blacks in the townships began to portray their
own versions of the Jonkonnu representing types and conditions of
employment in which they were engaged. As time went on the masquerade assumed a more secular and showy aspect, especially after
the appearance of its two principal characters, the Actor Boy and Set
Girl. Flashy costumes and model constructions replaced the skins,
horns, and tails of the animals previously represented. To provide the
new dresses and properties, skilled craftsmen were employed, and the
entire operation was apparently taken over by Negro financiers who
advanced the money and supervised the preparations for the spectacle
in the hope of making a fair return on their investment. The town mulattoes disdained this masquerade, which was limited to black slaves
on estates and in urban areas, and perhaps to some free working-class
blacks.

At first the masquerade carried some symbolic ritual significance,
most likely of African origin. As it developed, the symbols changed.
Military apparel replaced animal skins, models of ships and great
houses were carried on the head instead of horns. Could it be that the
signs became localized but the message remained constant? The new
appurtenances were all symbols of power: military dress with wooden
swords; ships that conveyed the slaves to a strange country from
Africa and might some day return them thence; great houses, the
occupants of which controlled every fiber of their existence. Perhaps by investing themselves with these costumes and properties the
slaves hoped to transfer some of that power to themselves.

One can understand that the Baptist, Methodist, and other nonconformist churchmen who opposed slavery and ministered to the blacks
would strive to convert them to Christianity, away from their heathen

religions and practices. The churchmen would surely view the Jonkonnu masquerade as a desecration of the holy season celebrating Christ's birthday. These efforts met with limited success, however, until the ministers were able to prove the efficacy of the Bible in withstanding the obeahman's power and until they preached freedom from slavery, taking as their text the biblical injunction: "No man can serve two masters." John Stewart compared the West Indian Christmas to the Roman Saturnalia and felt with sadness that the slaves cared nothing for the origin of the festival.[47] On the other hand, Williams's host told him in all seriousness that there would be a rebellion on the island if any attempt were made to curtail the masquerade of the blacks, even on religious principles.[48]

It is time now to consider the Actor Boy masquerade. When this character entered the Christmas revels is a matter of conjecture. He is mentioned in four eyewitness accounts in 1801, 1816, 1823, and 1824, and it cannot be far wrong to place his emergence in the late eighteenth century. Lady Nugent, wife of the island's governor, in her diary for Christmas Day 1801, mentions a party of actors among the revelers: "Then a little child was introduced, supposed to be a king, who stabbed all the rest. They told me that some of the children who appeared were to represent Tippoo Saib's children, and the man was Henry the Fourth of France. What a *mélange!* All were dressed very finely, and many of the blacks had real gold and silver fringe on their robes. After the tragedy they all began dancing with the greatest glee."[49] The reference is to Tippoo, Sultan of Mysore, who opposed the British in India and was killed in 1799. In the Actor Boy enactment Tippoo's heir, the child-king, supposedly took revenge for the slaying of his father. How this story relates to a French king who ruled two centuries earlier, and how the blacks had got hold of the story so soon after the event and decided to represent it in their masquerade, remain a mystery.

On his arrival in Black River on New Year's Day 1816, Monk Lewis also saw a small group of actors as part of the street revels:

A play was now proposed to us, and, of course accepted. Three men and a girl accordingly made their appearance; the men dressed like the tumblers at Astley's [a London, England, equestrian amphitheatre], the lady very tastefully in white and silver, and all with their faces concealed by masks of thin blue silk; and they proceeded to perform the quarrel between Douglas and Glenalvon, and the fourth act of *The Fair Penitent*. They were all quite perfect, and had no need of a prompter. As to Lothario, he was by far the most comical dog that I ever saw in my life, and his dying scene exceeded all description. . . . As soon as Lothario was fairly dead, and Calista had made her exit in distraction, they all began dancing reels like so many mad people.[50]

In this case the actors had selected climactic scenes from two well-known plays, Home's *Douglas* and Rowe's *The Fair Penitent*, that had recently graced the boards of Jamaican theatres. That the actors were word-perfect suggests that they had been carefully drilled in the study of the texts, even though their costumes were more attuned to the carnivalesque nature of the occasion than to the characters represented.

The next two reports are similar in content and refer to the years 1823 and 1824. Alexander Barclay, a longtime resident of Jamaica, spent Christmas 1823 on a friend's estate where he saw "a novelty, never before witnessed." It consisted of a performance by Negroes of some passages of *Richard III* done in a farcical manner. He referred to the actors as "Joncanoe-men, disrobed of part of their paraphernalia," and the two heroes fought not for a kingdom but a queen, whom the victor carried off in triumph: "Richard calling out 'A horse! a horse!' etc. was laughable enough."[51] Barclay was puzzled to know how the Negroes had acquired even the very imperfect knowledge they seemed to have of the play. H. T. De La Beche, on a visit to his Clarendon estates in 1824, records a similar masquerade that came to his house on Easter Monday. The party consisted of musicians, "and a couple of personages fantastically dressed to represent kings or warriors; one of them wore a white mask on his face, and part of the representation had evidently some reference to the play of *Richard the Third*; for the man in the white mask exclaimed, 'A horse, a horse, my kingdom for a horse!' The piece, however, terminated by Richard killing his antagonist, and then figuring in a sword dance with him."[52]

From these reports one might deduce that the Actor Boy troupes were blacks (mostly slaves) whose first encounter with Western drama might well have been from the upper balcony of the theatre where they waited to attend their masters and mistresses in the seats below and drive them home. Those who showed some interest in acting might have been encouraged to appear in a troupe during the holiday masquerades. They would be taught the lines of the play by their master or mistress, who would help to outfit them for the performance. Their dresses might be modeled on the heroic stage costume of an earlier period, complete with plumed headdress, engravings of which were available in published playscripts. Some rivalry might well have existed among estates as to which could turn out the most handsomely appareled and theatrically accomplished Actor Boy troupe. In the towns, Actor Boys might also find patrons among the literate mulattoes or free blacks. If so, it is possible that once again the notion of investing in a profitable masquerade was the incentive, for each performance of a scene would be expected to receive payment from the spectators. In any event, through these acting masquerades, black slaves were becoming personally familiar with Western dramatic texts and beginning to interpret characters after their own fashion.

The third and final type of masquerade to appear in the street revels at the Christmas and New Year holidays was the Set Girls. How this disguising originated is revealed by the indefatigable Monk Lewis, who claims that many years ago an Admiral of the Red was superseded on the Jamaica station by an Admiral of the Blue. They simultaneously gave balls in Kingston to the "Brown Girls," which divided the city into two camps. This division spread to other districts, and at Christmastime thereafter the whole island was separated into rival factions of the Reds and the Blues (the Red representing the English and the Blue the Scottish), "who contend for setting forth these processions with the greatest taste and magnificence."[53]

Lewis, no doubt, reported what he was told, but it is perhaps more plausible that the Reds represented the Red-coats or army soldiers billeted on the island while the Blues represented the Blue-jackets or sailors of the navy. When the masquerade actually started is unknown. It might have begun at the time of islandwide celebrations following Admiral Rodney's arrival in Jamaica in 1782 after his defeat of the French fleet. The whole island had been on alert against invasion, and the relief led to spontaneous jubilation. Soldiers and sailors in the mood for revelry would have repaired to their favorite tavern or hostelry for refreshment, the Red-coats favoring one set of public houses and the Blue-jackets another set. These houses were managed by mulatto women who apparently kept a bevy of black and/or brown women slaves and servants to attend to the needs of the servicemen. Dances held at the taverns or in the homes of these mulatto women as part of the victory celebrations might well have spilled into the streets to begin the spontaneous Set Girls' processions.

At the start, the masquerade was unquestionably a Kingston affair, sponsored and played by women on New Year's Day. It quickly spread to other towns on the island and on to the plantations where it formed part of the general Christmas festivities. Beckford in 1790 was the first to mention it when he said that at Christmas the mulattoes held public balls "and vie with each other in the splendour of their appearance, and it will hardly be credited how very expensive their dress and ornaments are." At the same time he noted: "The negroes upon neighbouring estates are divided, like other communities, into different parties: some call themselves the blue girls, and some the red; and their clothes are generally characteristic of their attachment."[54]

A hiatus of eighteen years then occurred in reports on the Sets. When Stewart wrote about them in 1808, he observed that they were less prevalent than they used to be, no exhibitions having taken place for some years back. As previously noted, the turn of the century was a time of grave concern for Jamaica owing to conspiracies and revolts from within and without. In this unsettled state of affairs, it is conceivable that the Set Girls masquerade suffered a decline; if so, it must have rebounded with buoyancy in the ensuing two decades, when no less than seven authors gave glowing testimony about it.[55] Two descriptions will suffice to show how the masquerade appeared on the plantation and in the city. Alexander Barclay provides the view from the estate:

> The young girls of a plantation, or occasionally of two neighbouring plantations leagued, form what is called "a set." They dress exactly in uniform, with gowns of some neat pattern of printed cotton, and take the name of Blue Girls, Yellow Girls, etc. according to the dress and ribbon they have chosen. They have always with them in their excursions a fiddle, drum, and tambourine, frequently boys playing fifes, a distinguishing flag which is waved on a pole, and generally some fantastical figure, or toy, such as a castle or tower, surrounded with mirrors. A matron attends who possesses some degree of authority, and is called Queen of the Sett. . . . Thus equipped, and generally accompanied by some friends, they proceed to the neighbouring plantation villages, and always visit the master's or manager's house, into which they enter without ceremony, and where they are joined by the white people in a dance. . . . A party of forty or fifty young girls thus attired, with their hair braided over their brows, beads round their necks, and gold ear-rings, present a very interesting and amusing sight, as they approach a house dancing, with their music playing, and Joncanoe-men capering and playing tricks.[56]

Barclay's mention of "Yellow Girls" suggests that the pristine division into Red and Blue had fragmented into other Sets. We know that the French-speaking community produced a band called "Royalists," and there may have been an African Set named "Mabiales," and yet another called "Americans." Whatever the motif, lavish apparel was imperative since the intention was to display one's opulence by extravagant costuming. This is clearly demonstrated in Marly's description of the city masquerade:

> The day was not far advanced before the procession of the negroes commenced. It consisted of at least one hundred of both sexes, and was preceded by a very tolerable band of sable musicians. The dress of the female negroes, besides being elegant and neat, was in general tastefully put on, and many of them displayed a handsome assortment of jewellery, apparently of considerable value. . . .
>
> At this time the negroes were only proceeding for their honorary sable dignities, for these people, during their short span of freedom, must have their king, and queen, and court, to rule over them, and mimic, so far as they are able, a kingly state of society. With these dignitaries at their head, and their court in the rear, followed by all the town negroes who could procure suitable dresses for the occasion, the music soon afterwards announced their approach. It was a gayer sight than the former, the flags being unfurled, and the cavalcade very considerably increased in numbers.

From this and from Barclay's account, what is instanced here is a form of processional theatre in which the element of competition will presently appear. Marly's comment that the Negroes were mimicking a kingly state might appear less snide when we recall that processions such as this were regular events in West African communities where the full panoply of kingly states were not unknown. To continue Marly's description:

> The head of black Luna [the Queen of the Set] was decorated with a profusion of Ostrich feathers, fastened with combs studded with pearls, and gold bodkins, set with precious stones, while her feet were confined in embroidered shoes. Round her neck were several strings of coral beads, and a gold chain, with a locket attached, forming a contrast with the bottom of her gown, which was thickly set with a profusion of spangles; but her gown was studiously allowed to shew that her legs were encircled with silk stockings. She wore an elegant brooch, set with stones, upon her bosom; and at her side dangled her Massa's gold watch, with an additional quantity of appendages. Coral bracelets, with gold clasps, encircled her arms, while her fingers were overloaded with rings, some of them set with diamonds. . . .

241

16. Negro dance figures, ca. 1836.

Marly was informed there was a competition between Miss Strutt, with Miss Pandar, and another acquaintance, a Miss Goodly, relative to who would show on their girls the greatest profusion of jewels on these slave gala days. This is a species of competition which yearly occurs among the native born ladies of the Island, and accordingly the girls display not only finery, but trinkets of considerable value. . . .

With the intervention of slight intervals, the procession of the negroes, according to their gradation of ranks, preceded by their band of music, passed through the principal streets of the town. The greatest number of them were skipping and dancing along, in place of walking, and kept singing . . . in chorus.[57]

Marly observed that Luna was more interested in displaying her dress and jewels than of exhibiting "the royal dignity which she was supporting." In any event, she was the clear winner of the competition

17. Jonkonnu music band, 1837.

and, in consequence, "a dryness of a long continuance" ensued between Miss Strutt and her two erstwhile rivals. The evening ended
with a Negro ball to which white persons were not admitted.

In terms of performance, one can assume that the Set Girls were
fully involved in making their costumes after a predetermined pattern, that each would have added some individual adornment, that the
discipline of the order of procession would have been maintained, and
that the dignitaries would have marched or danced on the streets with
a decorum appropriate to the display of their finery. One source indi-

18. Koo-koo or Actor Boy, 1837.

cated that among individual characters of the company were four
Grand Masters whose duty was to protect the Set, two Adjutants
bearing flags, the Queen, the Ma'am, the Commodore, and bringing
up the rear after the full body of girls all dressed alike, a Jack-in-the-
Green whose function in this particular band was not disclosed.[58] The
Set Girls were the largest and most spectacular of all the masquerade
bands of the Christmas and New Year holidays. Considerable sums of
money were spent on their preparation.

In the year 1837 Isaac M. Belisario, an English painter resident in

19. Queen of the Set Girls, 1837.

Jamaica, prepared a portfolio of lithographed pictures, in color, representing characters from the Jonkonnu, Actor Boys' and Set Girls' masquerades. The prints were supposedly "drawn after Nature" but it is questionable whether they in fact represent the masquerades as they appeared in the late 1830s. Given the history of those times, one might well conclude that the heyday of the Christmas revels had passed and that Belisario probably created idealized portraits based on earlier descriptions, but having his sketches vetted for their accuracy by others who had seen the masquerades in their prime. Belisario's

245

own descriptions accompanying the prints lend credence to this assumption. Whether or not he actually saw the characters as drawn, the plates are magnificent and much admired. They provide a rare pictorial record of a past era [figs. 16–19].

At the Christmastime holiday of 1831, when the slaves were supposed to be engaged in their customary merrymaking, a rebellion broke out in the western parishes. When it was finally crushed by the combined force of the local militia and regular army troops, the toll was twelve whites killed and 160 properties burned, causing damage amounting to over £660,000, as against four hundred blacks killed and another one hundred executed. The leader of the revolt was Samuel Sharp, himself a slave who had been appointed a deacon of the Baptist faith. It was alleged that the rebellion was inspired by Baptist preachers such as Thomas Burchell and William Knibb, who led the slaves to believe the British government had granted them freedom but that the local planters refused to set them free. While Baptist and Wesleyan ministers were not entirely blameless of preaching against slavery, the planters themselves were partly responsible by their firm opposition to the home government and by open talk of secession. The rebellion led to a heightened state of unrest for months, a condition that was not abated by the British government's announcement, a year later, that slavery would be abolished as of August 1, 1834.[59]

These events must have had a dampening effect on the brilliance of the Christmas masquerades, especially the Set Girls who relied exclusively on their mistresses, Creole, white, and mulatto, to bear the cost of outfitting them. Nevertheless, the masquerades did not entirely die out; the Reds and the Blues survived in the Bruckins folk dance of later years, while the Jonkonnu continued in country towns and villages into the present century, with a notable upsurge in the 1950s under the sponsorship of the *Gleaner*. By the same token the role of sponsors was diminished, and the festivities lost much of their former glamour. In the slave era, blacks had developed a performance culture through ritual, festival, and other recreative activities. How this culture fared and what further adjustments were necessary in the new conditions of freedom form the substance of the next chapter.

10

Performance Modes after Slavery

After Emancipation a curious turnabout occurred in white patronage of the Christmas revels. Since the blacks were no longer their property, white planter families had no interest in putting them on show. As a result the quality of spectacle that had distinguished the festival declined while the Jonkonnu returned to what it was always meant to be: a re-creation by the black peasantry of their remembrance of things past with tenuous links to ritual and magic.

Then the economic aspect of the festival became an issue. The British government had paid the planters six million pounds for freeing their slaves, but the slaves had received nothing but freedom for their years of hard labor. The provision grounds from which they had fed themselves belonged to the planters. As free people, they now had to rent or buy the land if they wished to continue farming it. Those who had built modest houses on the property faced the same dilemma. Few could afford to buy outright; to rent usually meant returning to work on the estates for several days each week in lieu of paying cash. The situation was intolerable. Nonconformist preachers from the Baptist and Wesleyan ministries who had fought strenuously in the cause of Emancipation now felt that the only viable solution was for the ex-slaves to occupy freehold land and establish themselves as small peasant communities. They strove to encourage and to instill in the minds of the peasants the necessity for hard work, thrift, and industry.

In this context, time and money spent on frivolities like the Christmas masquerade, regardless of how ingrained it had become after a century and more of observance, were seen as wasteful and injurious. The Wesleyan position on such activities was unambiguous. Dancing, according to a letter from Robert Young to Wesleyan societies on the island, was antiscriptural and evil; it pleased the carnal mind and led to immorality.[1] The year prior to full freedom the Baptist Knibb had applied to the magistrates "to suppress the singing and senseless jargon of the setts," calling them excesses of foppery, vain show, and non-sensical ribaldry.[2] Casting off the chains of slavery was construed as an act similar to baptism into the Christian faith; black Jamaicans were deemed to have renounced everything associated with a barbarous, pagan Africa and had entered the advanced state of free, civilized people. Drumming, dancing, and masquerading bespoke idleness, profligacy, drunkenness, and lascivious behavior that were repugnant to the church and could not be condoned.

As for the civic authorities, Jonkonnu parades no longer controlled by whites became a nuisance. They were noisy and crowd inciting, with the ever-present danger of fomenting serious public disturbances. At the 1839–40 holiday season, Jonkonnu was pronounced defunct on the estates while only a few Jack-in-the-Green figures and stiltmen paraded the city. In January 1840, the *Despatch* editorialized that the black population of Kingston wasted a whole month "drumming, idling, drinking and traversing our streets and lanes until one or two o'clock in the morning."[3] The next Christmas, the autocratic mayor Henry Mitchell gave orders to the police to stop all drum beating on city streets. The police seized the drums from revelers and charged them with disturbing the peace. However, Magistrate Hart, disagreeing with the mayor, ruled that yuletide festivities were a time-honored custom, no law had been broken, and the drums should be returned to the masqueraders.[4]

This skirmish was an omen of serious trouble in the year ahead. On December 17, 1841, the *Morning Journal*, castigating Christmas revelers as "the most idle and profligate servants and abandoned women, dwellers in the purlieus of infamy and vice of every description," warned that the mayor of Kingston was determined to stop all drumming and noisy disturbances. Mayor Mitchell had invoked a clause in an ambiguous statute passed some ten years previously but never enforced. It outlawed horn blowing and drum beating that might cause danger, annoyance, or disturbance. This law, ignored for the slave festivities, had been resurrected by the mayor to support his order. He was seeking a decisive confrontation with the revelers, and the result was an outbreak of rioting in which the police were forced to give way and armed soldiers were called in. The Riot Act was read and the regiment opened fire; two people were killed and others were seriously wounded. In his report to the secretary of state, Governor Metcalfe blamed the mayor for being wrongheaded: "setting at defiance the consent of his colleagues in the Corporation and the Governor's own opinion."[5] Metcalfe said he was forced to support authority although he disagreed with the mayor's reckless conduct. In his opinion it was best not to prohibit the amusements but to allow them to a moderate extent, and to trust for their ultimate discontinuance to the increasing good sense of the people and to the dissuasion and discouragement of the upper classes. Disturbances had occurred also in Montego Bay and in Cornwall when the police tried to take drums away from the masqueraders.

As the 1842 holiday season approached, the inspector general of police wrote to the new governor, Lord Elgin, as follows:

> The mob of that city [Kingston] appear determined to have at this time the illegal drumming and other noisy disturbances called John Canoe, the putting down of which caused such unfortunate consequences last Christmas. From the vast numbers whom I understand already to have commenced the drumming, I am certain that the Police Force in Kingston will be totally unable of themselves to put it down. . . . Nothing but a good military or militia force in addition to the Police will be able to repress the John Canoe without probable loss of life.

The governor's response was to issue a proclamation, in the name of the queen, that allowed public amusements confined to times and places at the discretion of revelers, so as not to cause danger, annoyance, or disturbance to others. This reasonableness won the day. The governor was able to report on a continuing state of tranquility in Kingston, and in Montego Bay the Set Girls reappeared, exhibiting their fineries and parading the streets without interference from the authorities.[6]

There were always well-meaning individuals who considered themselves to be partial to the blacks yet would not tolerate the holiday parades. One of these was John Castello, the West Indian Roscius of earlier days, now a magistrate and newspaper editor of Falmouth. He had people arrested and kept in the lockup for singing and dancing in the streets during the 1846 holidays. At their trial he declared: "I am still their friend. I laboured in their behalf when they were oppressed as slaves, and I now desire to see them behave as free men ought to do."[7]

There followed a period of quiescence when it was hoped that the Jonkonnu would die a natural death. The depressed state of the economy did not allow money for costuming, and such masqueraders as ventured out received little by way of a handout. Then the cholera epidemic in 1850–51 deterred public gatherings. For the 1853–54 holidays, a few so-called discreditable Jonkonnus made their appearance in Kingston to the chagrin of the *Daily Advertiser*, which hoped that the law would finally stamp out such demoralizing scenes.[8] In Spanish Town, Jonkonnus were allowed to proceed from house to house attended by drummers and fifers but were restrained from performing in the streets. In Montego Bay, however, when an over-zealous policeman attempted to arrest a reveler for carrying and crack-ing a whip on the street, a fracas developed. The crowd pelted the officers with bottles and stones causing some injuries. Once again the police were forced to retire, the military was called in, and the Riot Act was read. Calmer heads prevailed; no shots were fired on this occasion and the revelers eventually dispersed.[9]

The adverse publicity occasioned by such incidents may have prompted Montegonians of means to take action to restore the good name of their north-coast town during the annual holiday period and to revive the Set Girls' parade. In December 1858 the *Daily Advertiser* reported that the Reds and Blues were rehearsing for many nights past as "the old time rivalry is gaining fast upon them and we understand that the splendor of bygone days will be revived in a most generous rivalry between the two colors."[10] The paper reassured participants that so long as they were peaceable and decorous, the authorities would not interfere with the amusement and that permission had been granted for the procession and display, accompanied by good music such as Montego Bay could well furnish.

Keen competition between Reds and Blues led to one of the most ambitious and spectacular displays ever mounted for this masquer-ade. It occurred in Montego Bay on January 2, 1860 (New Year's Day being a Sunday), and, although the account in available newspapers seems to be incomplete, enough of it has survived to portray a pageant such as conjures up visions of a sumptuous medieval tourna-ment or the progress of a sovereign through her realm. The following excerpts from the lengthy report describe aspects of the Reds' presen-tation:

> Towards afternoon shouts and hurrahs announced that the "Red Champion" had made his *debut* or, as the population had it, "come out." Sheathed in golden "scale" armour with visor up, lance in hand, mounted on a spirited chestnut, decorated with trappings of gold, the warrior pranced proudly through Montego Bay streets. . . . Arrived at the public square, he threw down his gauntlet and boldly challenged any to do battle against the maj-esty of the Red Sovereign.

As this prologue ended, loud shouts from the assembled crowd proclaimed her most Gracious Majesty Anne I, of Barnett, Queen of the Reds, had made her public appearance. Seated on a chariot and six, with postillions and outriders, Queen Anne slowly drove through the streets of the city—the chariot lined and covered with bright scarlet cloth, profusely decorated with red garden flowers, state coachmen in scarlet livery, rouge bouquet, ruffle shirt bosom and sleeves, together with postillions in the same scarlet livery cut in court fashion, were very well got up and showed great taste in their equipment. Her Majesty wore a blonde skirt over a tissue underdress, the crown imperial on her head, sceptre in one hand and globe of state in the other, with a rich topaz necklace and [was] accompanied by "her Mistress of the Robes, the Duchess of Sutherland."[11]

The Queen's procession eventually arrived at the town square where a scaffold had been erected, ten feet high, and tastefully covered with different colored tapestry. On it stood the throne, draped with crimson cloth, sofas, and chairs of state. Behind the throne were the royal arms while other devices graced the walls around it, the whole being well lighted by a score of lamps. Opposite the throne platform, on the other side of the square, was an arch with the letters v.r. (Victoria Regina) mounted above it. But the most stunning piece of all was an octagonal building called the "lighthouse." The square had been portioned off into an octagon by posts, eight feet apart, connected at the top by rails. Each post was decorated with red flags, and both posts and rails were covered with lamps, some five hundred in number, making a brilliant and tasteful appearance. In the center of the circle thus formed stood the lighthouse:

This consisted of a basement of two stories, in all about twenty feet high and six feet in diameter. The lower story was formed by Gothic arches springing from pillars at two angles, and decorated with rosettes of net ribbon. Inside was the representation of a fountain surrounded by figures of mimic cavalry and infantry. This building was profusely agated, and the whole being covered with pink gauze made a showy and handsome ornament to the ground.[12]

The high point of the pageant was the illumination due to take place at dusk and for which a crowd of some four or five thousand persons had gathered. Just prior to this event, the Queen left her throne and entered the circle where a procession was formed consisting of the Lord High Chancellor in full court dress and bearing a silver wand; the Champion mounted and armed cap-a-pie; two Standard Bearers, one carrying a standard of crimson cloth representing a fountain in full play and the other a white satin wreath encircling the words "Peace to all" written in satin letters; Bellona, the goddess of war, in a dress meant to represent peace; Fame, in a dress of white satin tissue with trumpet, and so forth; Britannia, in half-armor with shield and trident; Peace, in a dress of white satin, bearing two pure white doves; Plenty, in a dress of gold tissue, with a wreath of flowers and wheat, bearing a cornucopia in one hand and basket of gilded fruit in the other; Robe, in white silk, bearing two gold nectar goblets; and finally, four bearers of Chinese lanterns. At this point the report ends abruptly. We are left to imagine the dazzling spectacle that would ensue when the lights were all lit, and in what manner the Blues would offer serious competition to their historic rivals.

This was a pageant whose magnificent display was matched by its significance. By its very size, it required the involvement of a large cross section of the community, bringing together all factions in a traditional holiday revel. (Those who were not involved in the Reds' presentation were no doubt similarly engaged with the Blues'.) Then there was a clear expression of loyalty and homage to Queen Victoria, who, in popular belief, had been instrumental in freeing the slaves. Now with the utmost solemnity in a public display based on slave-time festivities, the community was recognizing the queen who had brought about a free society. Above all, the overriding theme of the event was a call for peace. This was evident from the moment the mounted Champion opened the pageant by announcing his willingness to defend the Queen, until he joined the procession of Peace and Plenty. The community wished to express its desire for an end to the continuing friction between the masqueraders and the authorities over the people's ancient right to hold their street revels in a manner suited to their means and inclination. The appeal fell on the deaf ears of officialdom.

The Jonkonnu kept reappearing intermittently in different parts of the island but, denounced by the church for desecrating a sacred holiday on the one hand and, on the other, harassed by the police for breaking an outmoded law, the masqueraders appeared to shun the towns and confine their activities to country villages. In 1872, the *Morning Journal* correspondent for Old Harbour, reporting on Christmas festivities, found "the inimitable John Canoe" still in existence "in all its semi-savage form and actions" and wondered, "When will this African usage die out? To my mind not as long as Jamaica lasts . . . the evil exists in the encouragement they receive."[13] In Kingston, the

Jamaica Post, commenting on an exceedingly dull Christmas season in 1897, reported the "meteoric appearance on King Street of detachments of alleged 'masqueraders' with their following of vociferous tag, rag and bobtails."[14]

The Jonkonnu masquerade had received a new lease on life with the annual Freedom Day celebrations on August 1. This commemoration coincided roughly with the old Crop-over festivities on sugar estates, but for the ex-slaves it was more meaningful, signifying for them the new liberty to observe their day of freedom as they wished, without restrictions from white masters. Thus, "drumming, fifing, dancing and john-canooing in the demi-savage spirit of olden time"[15] characterized the August holiday, which could stretch into a two-week respite from plantation labor. The churches had tried to make the holiday into a decorous occasion with processions of schoolchildren, tea meetings, and hortatory speeches urging a rededication to the ideals of hard work and thrift; but, having little effect, they ceased to participate in the observance. The authorities kept trying to control the revelry, which they labeled illegal; and a parish magistrate, seeking to put a stop to the "Johncanoeing, dancing and licentious carousing" after they had continued for ten days, was assaulted and had his clothes almost pulled off. Eventually it was economic depression that curtailed the masqueraders from coming out on August 1, the celebrants preferring to wait for the Christmas holidays, when they hoped to get a greater reward from spectators for their appearance. As Higman has shown, by 1860 "the African elements in 1st August festivities . . . had passed into the urban subculture and the country parts, no longer attracting the attention of the elite."[16]

Moving from the public streets to the barrack yard and the village compound, the August 1 celebrants developed other types of events to mark their day of freedom. The "Europeanized black and colored middleclass," to use Higman's phrase, may have had little enthusiasm for observing Emancipation, and the whites had every reason to forget it, but to the black underclass, especially those who still worked the land, it was a day to recall, the day on which Missis Queen had set them free after more than a hundred years of enslavement. They formed ad hoc associations; they erected bamboo sheds with thatch-covered roofs in which they gave banquets, made speeches, sang songs of freedom, played their fifes and drums, and ended with lively dances that were called "Bruckins." Higman explains the origin of the term:

> The bruckins party contains a fusion of many elements. The dance from which it takes its name involves African and English

borrowings from John Canoe. In the 1850s it was reported that in Kingston "shameful dances called Breakings" were common ("bruck"=break). At these "heathenish orgies" blacks meet together, night after night, howling like fiends, and stamping like furies. These elements fused with the church-based tea meeting in the later nineteenth century.[17]

As can be seen the report, taken from the *Falmouth Post*, was highly biased against the bruckins party.

It was stated earlier that West Africans are no strangers to social hierarchies. Many tribal communities have their ruler or king, a court, several degrees of chiefs, warriors, and attendants. It is important that proper deference be shown according to seniority of rank. In Nigeria, for instance, it is not unusual for two strangers upon meeting to try to outbow each other, not knowing who holds the senior position. Despite reports to the contrary in the pre- and postslavery literature, great respect is paid to the titled individual, provided that rank is used wisely for the common good. In forming their associations, the Jamaican blacks elected officers with grandiose titles who took leadership roles in the Freedom Day exercises. One such meeting, called "A Christian Jubilee," took place on an estate in Vere Parish on August 1, 1874:

> They cleaned out one of the Estate's buildings, decorated it with tropical flowers and fruit, and a variety of flags designed and executed by themselves. One had a rough-drawn picture of the Great House on the Estate, another had a picture representing "the Busha" (Mr. John Macgregor), a third had "Papa Grant" (Sir John Grant), others had mottoes. On each of these flags were letters for the "Busha", the Overseer, the Bookkeeper, and the Rector of the Parish, who had seats of honor provided for them at the head of the table which was bountifully supplied with fruit, cakes, ale, porter, lemonade, and old rum. A procession was formed, and the whole Estate's labourers marched passed the Attorney and his Assistants with these flags singing.[18]

After the procession, the laborers seated themselves and the names of the officer bearers were read. There were, as printed in the report, a President and Presidentriss, a Vice and Vicetress, a Controller and Controllist, a Sheriff and Sheriffstress, and a Founder. The titles may seem absurdly pretentious but the sexual parity evident in the list is remarkable. Female officers were clearly important in organizing the assembly. The rules of conduct were read, followed by a program of singing, speeches, and grand marches. No dancing took place, as this was a Christian event; however, a plaintive air was chanted more than once during the marching:

> Suppose me no been come here,
> A who fa shew you how fe dance.
> Jige ding ting, jige ding ting.

The report of the ceremony concluded with these words: "The admission to the jubilee was 1s:6d. each. There were plenty of speeches, chiefly about their forefathers, but all most complimentary to the planters of the present day, and the general happiness of the country under good Governors, when the white men had to pay taxes just as much as the black people."[19] The ceremony was dutifully reserved owing to church influence and the presence of the rector. No bruckins took place, though it is more than likely that the blacks resorted to dancing at night following the formal proceedings.

On the day of the Vere jubilee, there appeared under the amusements column in a San Francisco newspaper catering to a black readership a curious notice. It announced a "Belvedere and Brokins Party" to be given shortly, as soon as the first steamer arrived from Panama in September "with materials and fancy fixins."[20] The notice must have been inserted by members of the Jamaican community of that city, on Freedom Day, in order to advise friends and supporters that their annual festivity was being postponed pending the arrival of necessary appurtenances from Panama. In 1850 several hundred Jamaicans had joined the trek to California at the height of the gold rush. Others went to Panama to work at ferrying gold seekers over to the Pacific coast on their way to California, and still others joined the work force to build the first railway line across the isthmus in the years 1850 to 1854. At this time shortage of estate labor in Jamaica coupled with emigration fever led the *Daily Advertiser* to complain about "the rapid depopulation of this beautiful island by the increasing outpouring of its agricultural laborers to that house of pestilence and proverbial charnel house Navy Bay"[21]—a reference to the bay where the migrant ships off-loaded their human cargo and received a bounty of £1 for every laborer brought to work on the railroad.[22]

When the railroad construction ended, some Jamaican workers might well have moved up to San Francisco, where they helped to establish a thriving Jamaican community, since the newspaper report indicated that the entertainment would be given by "one of the prominent clubs in the city." A foretaste of what was in store for those attending the party was given:

> Belvedere to commence with a comic song. . . . President will be seated on a chair of state on the stage with the Presidentess by his side and his Sergeant at Arms or Marshall will have a huge club, gilt and ribboned for a sceptre, and will do all the work of receiving and escorting. At the close of the ceremonies there will be a grand walk-around during which six maids of honor will hold up the Presidentess' dress, and courtiers to hold the President's clawhammer tail. A little Wolf and a peculiar Fish will be on exhibition who will also assist in escorting the nondescripts.

Since there was no religious or other restraint placed on the proceedings, "a grand Brokins Party" was promised in which "everyone will dance to the laughable extravaganza in true Castillian fashion. The burlesques and grotesques will be assisted by the President and his Knights or other officers, and the funny rhythmical jingle of 'Bakerboy Joe/N'yam firecoal Oh!' will be played by the band to the highly pleasing air of 'Lady Elgin Goat.'" Several new and comic scenes were also to be introduced during the entertainment. The poor American editor of the paper, obviously baffled by the strangeness of the announcement, hoped for further insight into the workings of this mystic entertainment. Some people, he mused, thought it might be a hoax but for himself he felt certain it would come off.[23]

The above report represents a fine example of cultural syncretism. Jamaican blacks, finding themselves in a new environment in California, prepare to hold their Freedom Day observance, in a manner similar to their compatriots at home. However, the expatriates have added several new features to the exhibition. There are to be animal disguises of a Wolf and a Fish in the retinue, whether out of the African respect for the natural world or because these species were prevalent in San Francisco we can only guess. Their dancing will include a version of the Castilian, which may well have been adopted from their Spanish neighbors in Panama or California, and the Walk-Around, which was part of the black minstrel show, then enjoying considerable popularity in America.

In her article on "Emancipation Songs and Festivities," Olive Lewin describes Bruckins' songs as "explicit in their reference to emancipation" and gives several examples of these songs. Noting the penetration of the old Set Girls' rivalry in Freedom Day festivities, she reports that action in the Bruckins' Party centered on two groups of dancers dressed respectively in red and blue:

> De Queen a come in [repeat three times]
> Oh yes, a beautiful sight.
> Red Queen a come in [repeat three times]
> Oh yes, a beautiful sight.
> Blue Queen a come in [repeat three times]
> Oh yes, a beautiful sight.

The nightlong competition included music, dance, skill, and endurance. Each group began by parading/bragging to the chosen venue and round the booth. Leading the procession would be the crowned King and Queen, followed by gloved sword-bearing courtiers and veiled women. Once inside the booth, the competition commenced, the audience egging on performers by their applause and commentaries that would help determine which side had won.

Money for costumes, showbread, and other expenses might be raised by a tea meeting and an entrance fee:

> Jubalee, jubalee, dis is de year of jubalee,
> Queen Victoria gi' we free,
> August morning come again,
> Jubalee, jubalee . . .[24]

Tea meetings, mentioned above, provided another type of performance opportunity for working-class blacks. It was probably the Baptist and Wesleyan Methodist churches that introduced the event to their followers, but they could hardly have anticipated that a sedate social get-together of church members would be transformed into a highly competitive performing occasion, no longer under their control. It is believed that tea meetings were started after Emancipation as a means of combating the traditional festive revelries of which the churches disapproved. In their place, parishioners would gather together in an appropriately decorated church or school hall for pleasant conversation, to sing favorite hymns and anthems, drink tea or lemonade, and eat bread and cake provided by members, for which a small charge was made, thus adding to church coffers. The event would end with a witty but instructive address by the minister or an invited guest speaker. From this inauspicious beginning arose an elaborate variety concert with competitive items promoted by community clubs and individual sponsors.

Tea meetings took place all over the island. In the fourteen meetings for which press reports were found, all were held under church auspices. Five occurred in Kingston, three in Falmouth, two in Spanish Town, and one each in Clarendon, Montego Bay, Port Maria, and Porus.

At the Baptist Chapel in Port Maria, a tea meeting was held imme-diately preceding the watchnight service on December 31, 1864, when tea and cakes were served, hymns sung, and speeches delivered. In Falmouth, that year, so popular was the meeting in the Wesleyan Chapel that the crowd, overflowing into the street and around the church, was reprimanded for its unruly behavior. In 1880, at the Baptist church in Spanish Town, the Reverend Stewart closed the meeting with a lighthearted lecture on "The Eccentricities of the Pulpit." The village of Porus announced that it was becoming so celebrated for its missionary meetings and tea meetings, accompanied by band music, that inhabitants planned to raise subscriptions to build a town hall to accommodate these gatherings and in anticipation of the new railway that would bring in visitors.[25]

The two most ostentatious tea meetings on record took place in Montego Bay and Spanish Town. The north-coast event was held in the court house on April 16, 1855, the purpose being to raise funds for a new instrument to accompany the Wesleyan church choir. The Reverends Geddes and West of the Wesleyan ministry shared the raised platform with Mr. Henriques of the Hebrew faith and several lay gentlemen. Ten tables, each capable of seating thirty to forty patrons, were spread with confectionery, fruit, and preserves. Dis-played on each table were costly china, silver services, and vases filled with flowers. Hundreds of lamps and chandeliers illuminated this "most brilliant spectacle." Over four hundred people attended. A hymn was played on the new instrument, the repast followed with tea drinking in earnest, then the meeting was addressed by the reverend gentlemen, tribute being paid to "those visitors from the lower or-ders—domestics, tradeswomen and the like"—about 150 of whom were present and observed a decorum never excelled by the higher ranks.[26]

The Spanish Town Tea Meeting, organized by the Reverend and Mrs. Russell, took place on March 1, 1892. It was arranged in two parts. The first part was an al fresco fair on the school grounds and, as the evening grew dark, this phase of the event was capped by a variety concert and play inside the schoolroom. For the occasion the grounds were tastefully laid out with evergreens, flowers, and crotons, while the tables, covered with plates, cups, and baskets of eatables, were ar-ranged in hues of pink. The outdoor promenade was embellished with the offer for sale of tea, coffee, cakes, ices, and so on, and "whether you wanted or not, you were bound to have a pink cup of tea, the very contents of which were pink as though the beverage blushed before the rosy cheeks of the maidens who tripped along the lawn with the mild request of 'won't you take a cup, sir?—only three-pence!' " Then there were the elfin Flower Girls carrying on a brisk trade, "only three-pence for a spray and three-pence extra for pinning it on." These were succeeded by irresistible post-boys who greeted visitors with a letter, straight from the post office, containing "trite sayings and apt aphorisms" for which one also recompensed the carrier. The tables were then judged for the best decoration and prizes were awarded the winners.[27]

As evening approached, it was time for the concert. Tickets were sold, and the schoolroom was filled to overflowing. "A neat little stage" had been erected at one end of the school hall for the performers, and the program commenced with a variety of musical items including vocal solos, an instrumental trio, and a comic song that "fairly brought down the house." The side-splitting farce, Who's Who, was performed next and proved to be a total success for the amateurs. The final item was a *tableau vivant* entitled "The Gypsy Camp," which was staged in a manner worthy of professionals and received repeated encores from the highly appreciative audience. Net proceeds from the whole event amounted to £23.[28]

The church-initiated tea meeting underwent significant change once it fell into secular hands. It was still promoted as a money-making affair and the variety concert format was retained, but considerable audience participation was encouraged. Spontaneous bidding for or against concert items occurred, specially made bread or cake was auctioned, a Queen was introduced at a high point in the proceedings, and dancing was allowed. Lacking a nineteenth-century account of a privately sponsored tea meeting, there are nevertheless three sources on which to rely and from which the following composite picture emerges.[29]

A tea meeting has been announced by a social club to raise funds for community development, or it might be given by an individual to help pay the cost of an impending wedding in the family. A bamboo shed is erected and covered with palm fronds. It contains a small platform at one end on which sit the presiding officer, usually the lady president of the club, and the treasurer or secretary-general who serves as cashier. A throne is also placed on this dais. Benches are arranged on three sides of the shed, leaving free a central area for the performers and for dancing. A money tree stands at the entrance to the shed; patrons tie money to the tree and receive a token. This is a form of lottery, and prizes are distributed to the holders of winning tokens during the course of the evening. For the occasion the young ladies have had new dresses made, which they wear with ribbons and other ornaments, all of a prearranged color. Drinks such as ginger beer, lemonade, and rum are sold throughout the night.

When the audience has arrived and the proceedings are about to start, the lady president is introduced and makes a brief, welcoming speech, stating the purpose of the gathering and setting out the rules of conduct. She acts as Mistress of Ceremonies, calling on various people to perform. Her language is deliberately extravagant; one is not quite sure how many of the malapropisms are innocent or intended. Should a scheduled performer arrive late, that person pays a fine. If an act is well received, a spectator might bid to have it repeated; conversely, if an act is being poorly performed, someone might bid to stop it and others, partial to the performer, will bid to have it continue. Most items are not native to Jamaica but have been learned from popular songbooks and literary texts published abroad. Favorite songs such as "Darling, I am growing old/Silver threads among the gold" or "I'll take you home again, Kathleen," will find audience voices joining the refrain, and someone might offer to pay just to have the "long notes" sung again. A commonly spoken poem such as "The boy stood on the burning deck" has to be rendered word-perfect as the audience is familiar with every line. A musical selection by a fiddle, flute, and music box is spirited enough to induce audience members to dance spontaneously in the center of the hall.

About halfway through the program, there is an auction of show-bread and/or cake. These items, molded in various recognizable shapes, are attractive to the eye and delicate to the palate, and the bidding is energetic. The money-tree prizes are announced and distributed at this time. The concert program recommences much as before, but the audience has grown livelier. An Anansi story is told, the crowd joins in singing the songs. Riddles or other guessing games are played. If there is an important visitor from the city or from overseas, this is the time for his or her appearance. The visitor is introduced and makes an appropriately upbeat speech.

After a few more musical items and some dancing, the word is passed around: "The Queen has arrived/Every money must show." She is ushered into the hall, beautifully attired and veiled, and seated on her throne. Men bid to peek at her face under the veil. Then they bid to unveil and to dance with her. District loyalties or personal ambition will push the bidding to the highest level for the evening since it is an honor to win the Queen. The winner is placed in the center of the hall. He receives a cup of tea, which is shared with the Queen. Then he unveils her, kisses her, and has the first dance with her. General dancing and jubilation bring the tea meeting to a close.

What was a docile, spectator-oriented, and sedate occasion under church auspices has been transformed into a joyous, participatory, and climactic event organized by Jamaican blacks.

As already noted, performance elements inhere in the practice of African-derived religions. After Emancipation, authorities of approved religions and civic affairs were as vigilant in their efforts to suppress the non-Christian sects as they had been in respect of the masquerades. The established church described them as "heathenish" while to the police they constituted a public nuisance through their nighttime beating of drums, dancing, choral singing, and chanting. Attacks upon the sects were directed at the eradication of obeahism and myalism. The obeah practitioner, who was invariably a leader of a religious sect, was condemned as a trickster and a fraud at best, a poisoner at worst. Myalism, a form of spirit possession, was denounced as an orgy that had a demoralizing and pernicious influence on its worshipers. Yet, despite prohibition and persecution, the native religions prevailed, and, being pantheistic in nature, they were able to incorporate the Christian trinity, apostles, and saints among their gods and spirits to be worshiped.

Some instances of conflict that arose from this clash of religious cultures will bring the issue into sharper focus. In October 1842 the *Jamaica Standard*, quoting a northside paper, reported on what it called "The Myal Riots" in Saint James's Parish. The disturbances, it noted, had been going on for fifteen weeks. At first overseers and property managers had been lenient, trying to reason with the villagers and dissuade them from participating in "the Myal dances and tumults. Ministers of religion of all denominations took the earliest opportunities of denouncing these superstitious practices from their pulpits, and explaining the folly of them, and in more than one instance were the most riotous expelled from their congregations; yet every effort has been unavailing up to the present time."[30] When estate laborers wished to hold a service, they would take possession of the meeting or prayer houses that were usually found on the properties and begin "their dancing and orgies." The newspaper stated that there were awaiting trial sixty-four cases of riot, assaults with intent, and so on, connected with myalism, as well as a large number of ordinary felonies, and it urged that restrictive measures should be promptly adopted whereby legally qualified persons alone would be permitted to propound religious truths to their brethren.

At the trial occasioned by this outbreak of myalism, the Baptist preacher Knibb was blamed by the prosecutor for having deceived the moral feelings of the multitude by carrying out orgies at his chapel at midnight on the eve of Emancipation: "the theatrical pageants, the almost, if not altogether blasphemous ceremonies then practised—the burying of chains and whips, the planting of trees, and the mummeries then performed."[31] These symbolic acts signifying the end of slavery were felt to have inspired a resurgence of pagan African ritual. But nearly twenty years later the *Morning Journal*, urging the application of corporal punishment for obeahism, was forced to admit that civil law had failed to restrain the obeahman who as a result was believed to have supernatural powers.[32]

During 1860–61 a religious movement known as the Great Revival swept Jamaica, ushered in by the nonconformist churches, of which the Baptist and Moravian missions were foremost. However, as Edward Seaga has explained, the means by which salvation could be achieved in this revival turned out to be more African than European, rooted as worshipers were in myalism and the African belief in a world that unified the material and the spiritual.[33] The Western churches withdrew from the movement and the Great Revival served to reinforce membership in a number of Afro-Christian religious sects such as Pukumina, Revival, and Zion. As late as 1883 *Gall's Daily Newsletter* could publish a graphic account of a revivalist meeting including spirit possession in Allman Town, "one of the healthiest and pleasantest suburbs of this city," which boasted chapels or chapel schools run by the Church of England, the Baptist Mission, and the Wesleyans, and where even the Roman Catholics had commenced building operations:

> Side by side with these denominations, and with too much life and apparent vigour, stand Shepherd Duane and his revivalist flock, who still continue their midnight orgies, especially on Sunday nights, when all other places of worship are closed and all honest people are gone to sleep, much to the discomfort of the neighbors and others. Any one who has not seen these people "working the faith" as they call it, would not believe that such heathenish and pagan scenes could be enacted, in the metropolis of the Island, and at a place so surrounded with Gospel preaching. It is simply shocking, and is an outrage on all decency and morality. . . .
>
> How women, (for there are but few men attending this revival meeting house) and those, too, of the baser sort, can within a few moments work themselves up to such a height of demoniacal frenzy, so as to be beyond the control of their own feelings, and have to be held down and lashed by half a score or more of the

sisterhood—one or two of the brotherhood assisting—is a sad and revolting sight to any person of Christian sensibilities. The grunting, squealing, and screaming like pigs tied together for slaughter, are indeed a piteous spectacle, and all this is done under the socalled "spirit's influence."

But the most troublesome part of their devotions is the monotonous, loud and continuous wailing, miscalled singing, which goes on from beginning to end, to drown the hideous shrieking and tomfoolery that are being enacted . . .[34]

The most notorious of turn-of-the-century revivalist prophets was Alexander Bedward of August Town, who established the Baptist Free Church in 1894 and had himself ordained bishop with the title of Shepherd. Bedward claimed to have cured the sick by having them bathe in the healing waters of a spring in August Town where a pool had been formed. Thousands of people flocked to his meetings to witness this miracle and some hopefuls to benefit from the prophet's special powers: "Dip them, Bedward, dip them/Dip them in the healing spring."

In January 1895 Bedward was arrested on a charge of uttering seditious language. He was handcuffed and taken to the Halfway Tree lockup, followed by some two hundred women. At the trial Bedward was declared not guilty by virtue of insanity. He was then detained in the Lunatic Asylum. On his release he continued his self-appointed ministry, for, when visited by Martha Beckwith in August 1920, Bedward had predicted that he would on December 31 at an appointed time ascend into heaven accompanied by his faithful followers. At the same time the whites who had persecuted him would be destroyed. The day of ascension passed and nothing happened. Bedward said the event was postponed and set another date. That too passed uneventfully. In May of that year Bedward announced that he and his followers would march into Kingston to demonstrate publicly his claims, but on the march he was arrested by the government and consigned once again to the insane asylum.[35]

Whatever else may be said of Bedward's ministry, there is little doubt that his and his followers' conviction that they would ascend to heaven, given the appropriate circumstances, can be traced back to the African belief in transmutation—a state in which the spirit leaves the body and can travel over thousands of miles. Hence in 1833 when the Reverend Knibb was accused of telling the slaves on the night of their Emancipation that he had been to Africa, there was no questioning their acceptance of his declaration. As late as 1888, J. H. Reid, describing the people of Jamaica, asserted: "There are three representative classes. The influential white man, in possession; the progressive coloured man who is pressing to the front; and the struggling negro in his repressed condition, out of whom others manufacture influence and wealth; but who, with here and there an exception, has not yet secured any for himself."[36] Bedward's flock belonged to this third class, who were apparently ready to desert their mortal bodies in order that their spirits might travel to the promised land, where they would find rest and peace from all their troubles:

> If I had the wings of a dove [repeat],
> I would fly, far away,
> Far, far away.

In the present century Afro-Jamaican religions have been investigated by a number of scholarly researchers.[37] They give insight into a complex assembly of spirits and a hierarchy of cult leaders, elaborate ceremony, extensive use of symbols, drumming, dancing and singing, and the all-important and climactic occurrence of possession that provide a treasure house of materials that can be transformed into meaningful theatrical performances. To the somewhat hysterical press accounts, excerpts from which were given above, the following passages from Joseph Moore's essay, "Music and Dance as Expressions of Religious Worship in Jamaica," will serve as a rational corrective. The quotation is extensive as it describes in some detail the performance characteristics associated with indigenous religions:

Cumina is often referred to locally as "African Dance" and for good reason. It is very African in feeling. The drums and other musical instruments, the method and quality of the singing and the dialect spoken during the ceremony, are closer to an African source than to any other. The language used, referred to as "African," has many Bantu sounding words and uses that word order. The only English used was in some songs, called *Bilah*, sung in Jamaican English dialect. On the other hand, Revival, and its closely related groups called Revival Zion and Pocomania, used Sankey or Moody gospel hymns for music and Jamaican English dialect. Both altar and Bible readings are characteristic as well as other Christian religious customs.

In the main, both Cumina and Revival use temporary bamboo and thatch shelters for their ceremonies. In Cumina, the drums and other musical instruments are placed around the center pole, whereas in Revival there is a table for an altar at the center pole and the drums and musicians are seated outside the booth.

Both groups practice spirit possession but their dance forms and movements are quite different, though the possessions themselves have some similarities. In Cumina, the possessing spirits are non-Christian and called *zombies*. . . . There are four classes of *zombies:* skybound, earthbound, ancestral and living *zombies*, the last being those who have been possessed. . . . In Revival the possessing spirits can be divided into three groups: characters from the Old and New Testaments of the Bible, such as prophets, evangelists, disciples, the spirits of deceased cult leaders and officers of the group, and some spirits from Cumina who are believed to come to all services but only possess occasionally.

While drums and rattles are used to accompany the singing of hymns at the beginning of Revival services, after the dancing around the holy table has been going on for a half hour or so, the group begins what they call "trumping and laboring." This involves tramping heavily, bending from the waist, sucking in and releasing the breath while some of the group are still singing hymns. At this point, "trumping and laboring" sounds become the percussion section and the musicians stop playing their instruments.

In spite of great intense movement, dancing and singing, the behavior of both Cumina and Revival groups is orderly. When possessions come, members attend the possessed person with care and consideration. Since these dancers and services are very often memorials or entombment ceremonies for ancestors, all people who come respect the purpose of the ceremony and conduct themselves accordingly.[38]

It may now be helpful to consider how ceremonies such as these may be deferentially translated to stage performance. In the repertory of the Jamaican National Dance Theatre Company, one of the most popular and effective dances, in terms of audience response, is "Pocomania." In an article in *Jamaica Journal,* the company's founder and artistic director, Rex Nettleford, provides a pen sketch of how the ritual is approached in performance:

The dancers had to be aware of the locomotor and dynamic essences of the contraction-release complex in the inhaling and exhaling of air (known as "groaning"), in the stiff-legged windscreen-wiper-like movement of the trunk and head, in the shuffle of the feet in their one-two repetitiveness. The miraculous off-balances of the possessed, the almost lightning transition from tension to a position of total relaxation, the endurance test offered by the flat-back contortion which seems to go on endlessly! . . .

Then how could one forget the Shepherds' wheel? The gowns billow out like dervishes and the pride taken by actual Shepherds in sustaining and repeating the wheel and the billows betrayed a consciousness on their part of the theatrical pleasure their performance gives the onlookers (there are always onlookers at poco-mania meetings). There is, too, a spirit of worldly competitiveness that does not for one moment seem to deflect from the spiritual devoutness of the exercise. The Shepherd's feet are flat on the ground, I was careful to notice, as if the "ground spirits" controlled his destiny or determined his survival. As dance, it is ecstatic, beautiful, and fantastic. As worship, it could hardly fail to please the spirits. For the Shepherd's turns immediately reveal why he is the Shepherd and why his followers are his flock—the movement conjures up strength, agility, command, power.[39]

One of the older traditions that harks back to the days of slavery is the Christmas morning market. It will be recalled that, once they were released from work on Christmas Eve, slaves would journey through the night to town markets with the products from their provision grounds. These they would exchange for clothing and other needed articles. In the course of time, the Christmas morning market became a grand event, none more celebrated than in the capital city of Kingston, where the ladies came out in their carriages and the bon vivants strolled around in high fashion. But there were others too: "High and low; rich and poor; old and young; masters and mistresses; servants and dependants; all became astir on that day, hours before the dawn, and are busy in preparations to take part in the multitudinary procession that, with the first streak of light that ushers in the day, is to find its way to the foot of King Street, where the 'creature comforts' of meat, fruits, and vegetables will be on display to tempt the most fastidious appetite."[40] There were, in addition, useful crafted objects and toys for the children. The market, in fact, assumed the atmosphere of a fairground with decorated booths, flags, and appropriate greetings strung aloft. There was a fine display of beef, mutton, and so on, from prize livestock that had been exhibited earlier at the annual agricultural show, and the supply of meat would be quickly sold out before the morning was well advanced.

This spontaneous coming together of people from all walks of life developed into the Christmas Morning Variety Concert, a popular entertainment that was eagerly patronized through the first half of the current century. How this came about is worth recounting. At the market of 1848, drums and fifes were played to enliven the scene, and by 1870 the City Band, formed earlier that year, was in attendance "discoursing sweet music." Next year the band, its membership increased to twenty, played to large crowds and thereafter a public subscription was raised to hire the band for the occasion.

Toward the end of the century, the King Street music shop of Louis Winkler & Co., managed by Astley Clerk, opened its doors on Christmas morning to patrons who, already in a festive mood, began to play and sing selections fitting to the season. This voluntary concert attracted increasingly large crowds, with the result that in 1898 and 1899 it was decided formally to offer a Christmas morning concert at the music rooms, eventually leading to a variety performance at the theatre in the city. In its heyday the concert offered a medley of items to suit all tastes, including orchestral music, popular songs, stage dances, recitations, conjuring tricks, acrobatic feats, chalk talks, contortions, and comic sketches, ending with an original farce in which the best-known professional comedians would appear. In the 1933 version, the concluding piece employed the talents of the acclaimed comic actor Ernest Cupidon and the then-reigning blackface comedians Racca and Sandy.

As previously shown, blackface comedy was one of two American popular theatre genres introduced to Jamaica in the mid-nineteenth century. The other was the medicine show. Both caught the public fancy and produced homegrown exponents who developed their own styles and local material. Black American music and song had been introduced to the New York stage in the 1820s, when a number of individual blackface performers presented alleged Negro songs and dances between the acts of plays. Their images of blacks as harmless, happy-go-lucky, comical figures helped to salve the conscience of white America about the actual conditions of black slavery in the South. In 1843 four blackfaced white men, calling themselves the Virginia Minstrels, performed an entire evening of "the oddities, peculiarities, eccentricities and comicalities of that Sable Genius of Humanity" in the Bowery Amphitheatre in New York City. They were dressed in striped shirts, white pants, and blue swallow-tailed coats made of calico, and their instruments consisted of a violin, banjo, the bones, and a tambourine.[41] Their performance was an instant hit and began the vogue of blackface minstrelsy that spread across the globe in ensuing decades. Among notable songs produced by the minstrels were "The Old Folks at Home" and "Massa's in the Cold Cold Ground," written by Stephen Foster, and "Carry Me Back to Old Virginny" by James Bland, a black songwriter.

Blackface minstrelsy reached the Jamaican concert stage in 1849 when Mr. Cassares, assisted by resident music professors and amateurs, presented a concert at the New Court House in Kingston that included Ethiopian songs and glees. In 1855 a Kingston bookshop advertised for sale Negro and Ethiopian melodies with choruses. A decade later the first professional American minstrel quartet played at the Theatre Royal and at Spanish Town over a period of two weeks. Members of the troupe were Clinton, who possessed a sweet tenor voice; Collins, who specialized in comic songs and dances; Jake Wallace, king of the banjo; and Frank Hussey, "as droll a fellow as ever shook the sides of an audience."[42] They offered a combination of opera, comedy, minstrelsy, sentimental and comic singing, fancy, clog and Ethiopian dancing, and burlesques. Though not explicitly mentioned in the reviews, they almost certainly wore blackface for they were "of the true Ethiopian minstrel style."

The Original Georgia Minstrels performed next at the Theatre Royal in 1869 and were followed in 1872 by three members of the Christy Minstrels, led by Washington Norton, who allegedly had starred in London, New York, and Australia, and who came to Jamaica after a successful South American tour. The Christy trio opened at the Royal on February 13 with a program in which the "characteristics of plantation life are studiously delineated in many humorous, musical, vocal and terpsichorean selections."[43] After several performances in Kingston to good houses the trio went on a tour of the island until April 8.

The popularity of minstrelsy at this time can be gleaned from two benefit performances presented at the Theatre Royal in 1870. The first was organized by Cuban gentlemen resident in Kingston who wished to raise money for widows and orphans of the revolution then being fought in their homeland. A large and respectable audience attended their variety program on November 1, which included three minstrel sketches: "The Merry Old Man," "The Wise and Refined Negroes," and "The Essence of Virginia: A Grotesque Performance," as well as an Ethiopian dance. Ten days later the officers of HMS *Vestal*, supported by Kingston ladies and gentlemen, staged "The Vestal Minstrels" in aid of widows and orphans of those drowned in HMS *Captain*.[44] The miscellaneous program had several southern songs like

"Going Home to Dixie," a walk-around, and concluded with "the celebrated breakdown" dance.

It was not until 1888 with the visit of the Tennessee Jubilee Singers led by their prima donna, the celebrated Mme Matilda Jones, that Jamaican audiences were treated to the rendering of southern songs by authentic American blacks who had no need for the blackface makeup. The troupe performed to a "rapturously enthusiastic house," which encored every item. The cautious reviewer, obviously unfamiliar with this type of ecstatic song making on the concert stage, wrote: "The camp-meeting songs, though to the unaccustomed ear they seemed at first somewhat grotesque and incongruous, had a quaint charm of tender sentiment and melodious expression which in the end captivated the hearts of the audience. . . . Several of the singers have voices of signal power and compass, and in the several Jubilee Choruses there was an exquisite blending of sweet harmony and clear, effective enunciation."[45] The troupe performed throughout the island from August 11 to October 9 and returned for similarly successful tours in 1889 and 1890.

Jamaican performers developed two branches of the minstrel tradition, both originally retaining blackface makeup. The singing troupes, however, soon dropped the mask as they began to add native folk songs to their repertoires. The comedians, however, kept it as they paired off into a string of duos: Cupes and Abe, Ike and Mike, Harold and Trim, Racca and Sandy, Bim and Bam, and others who produced highly entertaining and original skits, mock trials, and farces using the Jamaican vernacular and making pithy comment on the sociopolitical scene to universal acclaim into the mid-twentieth century. Bim and Bam were known to write their own plays, such as *The Burial of A.B.* (1964) on the funeral of a notably authoritarian policeman, which accounted for a whole evening's performance at the Ward Theatre in Kingston.

That particular slice of Americana known as the medicine show has roots reaching back to Elizabethan mountebanks as portrayed in Ben Jonson's comedy *Volpone* (1605). In act 2, scene 1 of this play, the voluptuous Volpone wishes to make an assignation with beautiful Celia, wife to the lawyer Voltore. Under her window he sets up a stage on which his minions perform while others work the crowd selling potions and expounding on their miraculous curative powers. The American version of this act was brought to Jamaica toward the end of the nineteenth century when the Kickapoo Indian Medicine Company arrived on the island in 1897. Under the manager Doctor Sagwa, the company gave a number of variety shows in the Kingston Town Hall at popular prices ranging from nine pence for the gallery to two shillings for the stalls. At these shows they peddled their main product, the Kickapoo Indian Sagwa, a cure-all for most ailments. Then the company announced a mammoth vaudeville entertainment at the Theatre Royal on February 13, prior to a tour of the principal towns of the island when more shows would be given and remedies sold.

The performance began with a sketch called "An Old Man's Fancy" to set the tone for the evening: "People laughed and ached and laughed again," wrote the reviewer. "It was extremely farcical and proved an excellent curtain-raiser." There followed plantation songs and ditties by two "coons," a fund of irresistibly funny jokes and witticisms by "Jim" and his henchman, a shadowgraph, and other songs and dances, all of which contributed to the liveliness of the audience. Then came the pièce de résistance, a parody on *Romeo and Juliet:*

Nothing half so laughable has been seen on the stage here for many a weary day. The auditorium rang with the shouts of the spectators. Words will not describe the piece; but the idea was that an oysterman was hired to annihilate or exterminate one Romeo, and the adventures of the Goth, in his endeavours to sweep the lover off the face of the earth served to provide the fun of the evening. Laughing was infectious; some people are laughing yet when they think of the herculean exertions of the oysterman to kill the impervious Romeo. There have been performances of a higher class, stamped with the approval of greater minds, but no entertainment has appealed to the imagination of a greater number, or swept away the cobwebs of routine and worry with more thoroughness and despatch, than the entertainment which was given at the Theatre Royal on Saturday by the Kickapoo Indians.[46]

The Kickapoo medicine show left an indelible impression on elements of the Jamaican public. Five months after its advent the Sagwa medicines were still being advertised in the press with graphic drawings of heroic figures who testified to their efficacy. One was James Reuben, allegedly the oldest living Senecan Indian, who attributed his longevity to the use of this medicine. Another was Buffalo Bill, who had used Sagwa for malaria and chills with the best results, and Kickapoo Indian Oil, which had speedily cured his rheumatism.

As with the blackfaced comedians, the medicine show found ready imitators among Jamaica's show people. They developed their own

270

style of farce, using characters, mimetic actions, songs, dances, and vernacular dialogue that were promptly recognized by their mass audience. Because contact with authority figures was most often with the police and court officers, many parodies of real-life courtroom dramas began to be presented across the island. These, along with other indigenous performance events, formed a popular theatre of the underclass. Decades into the approaching century, elements of this popular theatre would merge with the literate drama to begin the process of creating a national Jamaican drama and theatre.

11

Epilogue: A Caribbean Perspective

Few events can be more engrossing than a people's conscious effort to determine and define its identity. Because this effort has encompassed Jamaica as part of a wider Caribbean movement, this chapter will be devoted to a perspective on the emerging drama and theatre of the Caribbean region. The anglophone Caribbean, for centuries culturally dominated by Europe and more recently by America, began its quest for identity in the 1930s when the whole area experienced marked social upheaval. Hard hit by the Great Depression, the export economies of the territories shriveled as sugar prices fell, and wages plummeted. The traditional escape valve of northern migration was shut tight by stringent immigration laws. These conditions prompted the Trinidad calypsonian, "Growling Tiger" (Neville Marcano), to compose his "Workers' Appeal" calypso, which he sang in the carnival season of 1936:

> Many a day persons haven't a meal,
> They're too decent to beg, too honest to steal;
> They went looking for work mostly everywhere
> But saw signboard marked: "No hands wanted here."
> The Government should work the wastelands and hills,
> Build houses, factories and mills,
> Reduce taxation and then we would be
> Really emancipated from slavery.[1]

Between 1935 and 1938 the Caribbean suffered severe labor unrest. There were strikes and rioting by sugar workers in Saint Kitts and British Guiana, charcoal burners in Saint Lucia, oilfield workers in Trinidad, dockworkers in Barbados and Jamaica. At one level these disturbances were a spontaneous outburst of the laboring class for fair wages and improved working conditions. But at a deeper level the riots represented the first concentrated attack upon colonialism, the first stir-

272

ring of a people to assert their readiness for self-determination and nationhood.

By 1958 the British government was ready to relinquish control of its Caribbean possessions, once considered to be jewels in the English crown. Now after centuries of economic exploitation they had become a drain on the British treasury. In that year the experiment in West Indian Federation came into being, but parochialism and self-interest of the larger islands insured that the experiment would fail. It lasted only four years. Nonetheless the event had been marked by the writing and staging of a commissioned drama by the region's premier poet and playwright, Derek Walcott. His drama, titled *Drums and Colours*, attempted to trace the history of the Caribbean lands as pawns in the power struggle between Western imperialist nations, until finally the old sugar colonies emerged into some form of nationhood. But what kind of nation? How to define the identity of Caribbean peoples? That is the quest that has been going on with increasing urgency and passion. It is a search in which the arts—the finest expression of a people's aspirations and sense of belonging—become embroiled and are subject to intense scrutiny and debate. And the theatre, as the most public and lively of the arts, finds itself at the center of attention whenever these issues are disputed.

In its checkered history the Caribbean has been inhabited by many different races and cultures. First were the aboriginal Amerindians, now practically extinct. Then there were the voluntary immigrants from Europe and America, from the Far East and the Near East. Some came for profit or pleasure; others to work the estates for an agreed period as replacements for slave labor. All had the option of returning to their home countries when their work or play had ended. Finally, there were those whose arrival, historically, was *not* voluntary. They came in chains and had to abandon thoughts of returning to an ancestral home across the sea for there was no stated period to their labor. These were the peoples of Africa, known first as slaves, then blacks, then Afro-Caribbeans. They formed the base of Caribbean society. For centuries they constituted that section of the population for whom the Caribbean was the only home they knew; that other home from which their ancestors were torn long ago survived only in racial memory.

Without denying the contributions made by other immigrants, there exists today a significant body of Afro-Caribbean traditions that can be utilized by native dramatists, choreographers, music makers, and theatre practitioners if the theatre is truly to represent the needs

273

and aspirations of Caribbean people. As the Jamaican scholar and cultural leader Rex Nettleford has written: "The African Presence must be given its proper place of centrality in that dynamic process of adjustment, rejection, renewal and innovation. For the products of this cultural process are what constitute the mandates for a national cultural expression."[2]

It is acknowledged that the Caribbean is not a unitary state where a national cultural policy can be adopted and implemented by a central authority. The lands of the region are separated not only by the sea, but also by different governments, languages, and allegiances to metropolitan countries. Yet, in the realm of cultural traditions, one is inclined to the view that these territories will continue to be linked in the future as they have been in the past. The unifying characteristic of Caribbean society is the experience of black enslavement combined with centuries of colonial rule and acculturation by European powers. That experience constitutes a solid bond that will outlast superficial divisions resulting from local environments and social conditions. Hence Astley Clerk, speaking in 1913 on the music of Jamaica could declare: "One must look elsewhere than at home if ever we are to find the musical history of our country . . . it is necessary that we search outside our shores—among the early records of our sister West Indian islands—amid the histories of the peoples of British Guiana, Spain and Africa—then we will arrive at something which will tell us definitely of the Music and Musical Instruments of this island."[3]

Before proceeding to discuss performance traditions for a Caribbean theatre, let us briefly explore the nature of theatre itself. It is generally agreed that the most important single element that distinguishes dramatic performance from other kinds of human activity is *imitation*. Imitation occurs when a person consciously adopts a pattern of conduct that is different from his or her normal pattern and behaves as if he or she were some other person or thing. This activity we commonly refer to as playing a role or acting. So far as one can tell, the basic reason for such performance was originally functional. It ensured the survival of the community to which the actor belonged.

According to one theory on the origin of theatre, the first actor was very possibly our caveman ancestor who, dressed in animal skins, with horns on his head and an animal mask over his face, performed his role in the ritual of the hunt. He became the quarry while his fellow actors played the part of hunters. It was his job to elude them, theirs to capture him. The drama ended when he was killed. From this earliest ritual drama one may draw the following conclusions:

1. Apart from assuming a character, or rather in addition to it, there is always an action to be played that gives to theatre its dynamic force and roots it in the life experience. Theatre is never a static event. The experience that is enacted rises to a climax and achieves a resolution that helps to define the human condition.

2. The purpose of theatre is, in the first analysis, salutary. It began as a rite aimed at assuring the well-being of the tribe. By killing the actor dressed as a stag, his fellow actors were using sympathetic magic to capture the spirit of the real animal. This ritual would ensure a successful hunt, thus providing food for the tribe. The death of the principal actor was a terrible sacrificial act solemnly undertaken by the victim for the good of his community.

3. This theatre appealed to the whole community and was more than a pleasant diversion from the daily routine. It was central to the business of living. Without it life was not simply "stale, flat, and unprofitable," in Hamlet's phrase; instead the community's very existence was threatened. A theatre that approximates its ancient meaning justifies its claim to public recognition and support.

A more recent theory on the theatre's origin is that it began in a different kind of ritual, namely, shamanism. The shaman or protopriest, as the argument goes, is a master of spirits who puts himself in a trance and in this state performs many wonders. With elaborate use of voice, chant, dialogue, gesture, pantomime, and dance, the shaman divines the future, cures the sick, expels evil, and conveys souls to the realm of the dead. In his trance, a phenomenon that Caribbean people recognize as spirit possession, the shaman's body is occupied by a god. He manifests a supernatural presence to his audience, who witness the transformation that is occurring and believe in the efficacy of the god's presence among them. The shaman does not, as is the case with the Hunt Ritual, offer up his life for the good of his people, but he does temporarily surrender his will to the will of the gods for a similarly worthy purpose. In Afro-Caribbean possession rituals, the Shepherd works up the initiates until they are invested by the spirit. Then at the appropriate time he unwinds them back to normalcy.

Regardless of which theory one accepts, it suggests that theatre came from ritual, whose function was to reach an accommodation with powerful forces or gods without whose aid life would be intolerable. As settled communities developed, three principal means were adopted to achieve this basic aim. They were:

1. Petitioning the gods to grant some communal need, be it a bountiful harvest or protection from a threatening disaster
2. Placating the gods against the evil in society that offends them; seeking their aid in purging the evil and asking forgiveness for wrongdoing as well as for reinstatement in the gods' favor
3. Thanking the gods for their gifts and protection, for example, for a year that is free of disease, plague, famine, or wasteful war

Although the reference is to ritual drama, it is possible to argue that all good theatre through the ages retains these fundamental aims. Possibly some of us no longer believe in the power of gods to affect our daily lives. We may scoff at the notion of participating in rituals that seek the active involvement of supernatural beings in human affairs. For such skeptics, we may rephrase the function of theatre in secular terms that are no less essential to our well-being. Suppose, for instance, we were to substitute: (1) for petitioning the gods—the coercive power of the theatre; (2) for placating the gods—the corrective power of the theatre; and (3) for thanking the gods—the celebrative power of the theatre. We would manage to retain the theatre's ancient purpose to secure communal well-being without mention of the supernatural.

The large majority of Afro-Caribbean people are not religious skeptics. Religion continues to hold a significant place in their daily lives. Most important, the practice of religion binds them, consciously or unconsciously, to their African past. Edward Kamau Brathwaite of the University of the West Indies in Jamaica has written pertinently on this topic. He reminds us of the well-documented fact that African culture is based upon religion and that "African culture survived in the Caribbean through religion. . . . There is no separation between religion and philosophy, religion and society, religion and art. Religion is the form and kernel or core of the culture. . . . What we should alert ourselves to is the possibility, whenever 'religion' is mentioned, that a whole cultural complex is also present."[4]

Reference here is to that particular blend of Afro-Caribbean religions that represent the most significant areas of continuities and transformations of African culture through the Caribbean area. As has been shown, under colonialism many of these religions were prohibited or allowed to function only under stifling restrictions with severe penalties for breaking the law. However, with the coming of political independence in the 1960s they have enjoyed a resurgence. Among these indigenous religions in the Anglo-Caribbean are Kumina and Pukumina in Jamaica, Shango and Rada in Trinidad, and Cumfa in Guyana. Associated with them are specific rituals governing rites of passage such as birth, puberty, marriage, and death. A study of the elements employed in the practice of these rites may well reveal forms of expression that, adopted and recreated in the making of Caribbean theatre, would permit the kind of communication and identification with a public audience that is central to the theatrical experience.

One of the major differences between ritual and theatre is that in ritual one communicates with the gods whereas in theatre communication is established with a human audience. In the former case, participation of the audience, often comprising the whole community or sect, could be taken for granted since everyone knew that the enactment was on their behalf and, if properly performed, would achieve the desired result. Members of this audience would be aware of what had to be done and how it should be done. They were vitally concerned it should be done right, and the actors who performed the ritual were expected to live up to their audience's expectations. The dynamics of this situation explain the quality of excellence in ritual performance. Here the celebrant-performers sought perfection, not to please their audience or to boost their egos but because the success of the enactment depended on it—the gods are jealous and will be satisfied only with the best. In a very real sense, the audience were participators in the action. Often they became, or were represented by, a chorus that was involved in the performance through singing, chanting, clapping, or other forms of group response. And there would be music, of course, and dancing. Audience recognition and participation were essential features that contributed to the efficacy of the ritual enactment.

The Nigerian scholar Joel Adedeji has explained the process by which ritual theatre becomes festival theatre, and festival theatre fragments into professional and amateur productions of secular theatre. Over time the religious purpose may diminish but the seasonal enactment continues because people have become accustomed to it as a traditional event. Thus we have the conditions for festival theatre.[5] Examples of this are the multifaceted types of carnival that are held regularly in the Caribbean. The carnival festival may have been transplanted to the region by European settlers; but, once adopted by the Afro-Caribbeans, it was transformed into an expression of surviving African traditions, colored by local experience. Other festivals associated with the vegetation cycle, such as Crop-over in Barbados, or with the liturgical calendar such as the Christmas Jonkonnu in Jamaica, or the La Rose Flower Festival in Saint Lucia, all contain strong traditional expressions drawn from Afro-Caribbean life.

Religious and festival performances by no means exhaust the sources of African continuity that provide ingredients for a Caribbean theatre. To give another example, there is the area of storytelling, previously discussed, that involves idiomatic speech and idiosyncratic pantomime, when the teller of tales assumes the characteristics of all the active participants in the story, whether they be human, animal, bird, or plant, objects animate or inanimate.

After ritual and festival enactments, the next logical phase in the emergence of an indigenous Caribbean theatre should have occurred when gifted individuals began to perform in and out of season for the edification and entertainment of spectators. In constructing their plays and designing their performances, these individuals would normally have built their theatre on the traditions of the past. They would have incorporated the meanings and methods, signs and symbols associated with the religions, rites, festivals, myths, storytelling, and other forms of enactment belonging to their culture. Had this development occurred, the present quest to identify and establish an indigenous Caribbean theatre would probably be unnecessary.

It did not happen that way, of course, for reasons that are now understood. The formal theatre adopted in the Caribbean came neither from Africa nor from Afro-Caribbean experience, but from Europe. It was the product of a culture bent on domination and suppression of African ways. It came as a ready-made package, wrapped in the glory of its acknowledged achievement. It was peddled by touring professionals from abroad and ardently imitated by local amateurs, many claiming links to whatever little European ancestry they could trace. It was admired by the learned and taught in the schools. It became the model on which the Caribbean theatre was wont to be fashioned.

This theatre was *art*. It enjoyed the status of the imported over the homegrown product, which, when not totally banned, was disparaged and relegated to inferior status. Often, the Afro-Caribbean theatre had no buildings other than a backyard shed or a village pasture to house it, no playwrights other than the old storyteller or calypsonian, no professional actors, singers, dancers, musicians, or technicians trained in the academies abroad. What the native theatre produced was deemed to be at the level of quaint folkways, stuff for anthropologists. The art theatre was something quite different: it was the product of a people of greater sophistication belonging to a superior culture.

That this allegation is not mere rhetoric can be instanced by developments that arose in Afro-Caribbean festivities following the end of slavery. Ironically, as we have seen, among those who worked hardest for slave liberation were people prominent in demanding the suppression of so-called slave culture. Reasons given for suppressing the Christmastime masquerades in Jamaica in 1842 were that they obstructed the progress of civilization and were derogatory to the dignity of freemen. At the other end of the Caribbean, similar attitudes prevailed regarding the Trinidad Carnival. Once it was taken over and transformed by the black freedmen, the leading newspaper castigated the festival throughout the nineteenth century in the severest terms and urged its abolition. Rioting ensued. In 1838 the masquerade was called "a wretched buffoonery [tending] to brutalize the faculty of the lower order of our population." In 1846 the carnival was "an orgy indulged in by the dissolute of the town"; in 1857 it was "an annual abomination"; in 1863, "a licensed exhibition of wild excesses"; in 1874, "a diabolical festival"; and in 1884, "a fruitful source of demoralization throughout the whole country."[6] These attacks served only to alienate the revelers and to stiffen their resistance to any form of control. The results, unsurprisingly, were more riots and a widening gulf between government and the people.

In most communities one finds historically two streams of theatre, just as there are two streams of most cultural expressions. These two streams are characterized as the informal and the formal, the subconscious and the conscious, the folk and the art. Informal theatre embraces all types of traditional enactments such as have been identified as deriving from ritual, festival, and other inherited theatre forms that spring from group consciousness. This type of theatre is rooted in customs that manifest a community's ethos.

Formal theatre, on the other hand, represents a conscious attempt to create theatre as an art form. In one sense it is a way of conserving, enhancing, and disseminating the products of folk theatre. In another sense, it represents an attempt by a single individual—the playwright, scenarist, choreographer or musical composer, assisted by the interpreters—to communicate through the medium of the stage some personal vision, insight, or understanding of the life experience as he or she has perceived it and hopes will be of value to audiences. Since the artist is creating, in the first place, for society, the experiences he or she seeks to interpret and those of the audience will coincide. Since the wish is to communicate effectively, the means of communication used will be indigenous to that society—language, movement and gesture, song and dance, patterns and rhythms, images and icons that belong to, and have meaning for, his or her people.

We call this kind of theatre "art theatre" for a special reason. In the realm of art, creators and interpreters are not content simply to represent faithfully the folk forms of expression, but will consciously strive to reconstruct and reinterpret them in a particular style most fitting to the personal vision of the artist or artists involved, and most resonant of the life being presented on stage. The folk theatre enriches the art theatre, gives it validity and meaning, while the art theatre seeks to interpret folk performance, to give what is a communal, traditional form an individual and personal voice and vision.

In truth and in qualitative terms, the distinction between folk and art is often blurred. Many folk artists, so-called, achieve a high degree of individuality in their performances, which can rise to the level of true art. On the other hand, there are professional artists whose work is of little consequence and soon forgotten. But whether we speak of informal or formal theatre, folk or art, the fundamental purpose of both should be the same—namely, to preserve, nurture, and uplift the community to which it belongs and from which it draws its sustenance.

The art theatre of Europe had helped to inculcate a love of stage plays in Caribbean audiences. Dominant in Caribbean playhouses for centuries, it could not, however, fulfill the theatre's essential function as it has just been defined. Although its repertoire included some plays that dealt with universal human problems, such plays did nothing to solve the problem of cultural identity. This theatre was alien to its environment and spoke only to a small segment of the population. The vast majority were ignored. It said nothing of their gods or their religion; it did nothing to enhance, to amend, or to celebrate their lives. It was exclusive, not unifying. It separated the privileged from the underprivileged; the well-educated from the partly or noneducated; the townie from the "country-bookie"; the Creole from the black.

What happened during the period of European cultural ascendancy in the Caribbean testifies to the resiliency of a people's inherited beliefs and practices. Aspects of Afro-Caribbean culture that were outlawed went underground to emerge a century or more later practically unscathed, as for instance the Shango religion of Trinidad. At other times the culture adapted itself to restrictions and impositions, but retained its essential nature and purpose. African gods were paired with Christian saints, and, when the latter were ostensibly worshiped, the former were carried in the minds of the worshipers.

No example of the tenacity of a culture to overcome such depredations is more remarkable than the emergence of the steel band as the popular music of the Trinidad Carnival, now accepted as that country's national music. Imposition against the beating of skin drums in the nineteenth century led to bottle-and-spoon percussive music, then to the bamboo bands; from these to the music from empty tins and discarded pans; and finally in the 1940s to the steel drums that have been hailed as the musical invention of our time. The history of the steel band teaches us that such victories are not won by chance. Left to well-meaning officials, the incipient bands would probably have been crushed out of existence in the name of protecting the populace from the barbarous music of delinquent youths. It took the courage and fortitude of a few influential believers, supported by the perseverance of the youths themselves, to save the bands from extinction.

Three events were critical in gaining acceptance of this new musical phenomenon. The first was a radio program, organized by the Trinidad and Tobago Youth Council, that in 1947 discussed the steel band and its music with one of the band leaders, thus informing the public of the potential in these rustic instruments and of the seriousness with which the youths were developing them. Second was the 1951 appearance at the Festival of Britain in London of a representative group of steel bandsmen in an orchestra conducted by police bandmaster Lt. Joseph Griffith. The band overcame initial skepticism and received high praise for its performances in public and on BBC radio. Third came the writing and production in 1953 of my own play titled *The Ping Pong*.[7] It depicted the jealousies and loyalties of band members on the night of an important competitive festival. The performance in Port-of-Spain, Trinidad, attracted an urban working-class audience into the serious theatre, perhaps for the first time. In ways such as these the educated middle class joined forces with the less-educated underclass in the preservation and appreciation of an indigenous cultural form.

The European and Euro-American drama had for centuries used black characters in subordinate positions. They were the fetchers and carriers, often the villains; only occasionally would one appear as a romanticized noble savage. Thus, the first step on the road to a truly indigenous drama was for Caribbean dramatists to write and present plays about black people as central rather than peripheral figures to the stage action. In this century, two writers provide the earliest examples of this development in the anglophone Caribbean theatre. Marcus Garvey, Jamaican and world-renowned raceman, in 1930 produced three dramatic pageants at his Edelweiss Park open-air stage in Kingston, Jamaica.[8] They predicted the regeneration of black Africa and the expulsion of colonial rule. And the Trinidad historian C.L.R.

James wrote the previously mentioned drama *Toussaint L'Ouverture* about the slave who led the victorious Haitian revolution. It was performed in London in 1936 by the English Stage Society.[9]

A prevailing view in the imported Western theatre was that the concerns of black folk were most suited to comedic interpretation. Thus, a further step for Caribbean playwrights was to choose issues that were part of the common experience of the folk and, not to remove all comedy, but to give these concerns the serious consideration they deserved. The 1938 drama *Pocomania*, by Una Marson, showing the impact of a Jamaican religious cult on a staid middle-class family, is an early witness of this development.

A third step in the effort to bring home the art theatre was the initial experiment with language. At the beginning this took the form of a journalistic recapitulation of vernacular expression, too often employed as a way to ridicule peasant or working-class characters who could not use what passed for standard English speech. This attitude contributed to a further widening of the cultural gap between the educated upper layer and the broad base of Caribbean society. Occasionally, however, an author would capture the rhythm and emotive power of folk language in a way that raised the speaker to tragic grandeur.

The late Jamaican playwright Archie Lindo, in his 1945 dramatization of Herbert De Lisser's novel *The White Witch of Rosehall*, achieves this level of folk speech in a crucial scene of the play. Takoo, the obeahman, and a group of rebellious slaves capture the witch, Annie, who has been accused of killing several of their people. Her white bookkeeper, cognizant of her evil deeds, threatens the slaves with hanging if they should harm her. Takoo replies in his proud, authoritative dialect:

> Who deserve hanging more, she or me? She kill Millicent. I pass sentence on her tonight over the grave of me dead grand-daughter.
>
> I sentence her to dead. You talk about me hang, Mr. Burbridge. It is white man who got to look out for themselves now for we is free tonight. Every slave in Jamaica is free and we is tekking to the mountains to fight. I expec' to die one day but me spirit will live forever. An' before I die, this dam' woman mus' dead . . . no power from heaven or hell can save her.[10]

Delivered in the vernacular, the speech has nothing funny about it.

Use of folk speech can present many pitfalls to the novice playwright. The authentic dialect may be difficult to understand beyond a small group of initiates in the audience; it may often be unnecessarily indelicate; its imagery may be too confused. The mature writer will seek the means to approximate the rhythm, flow, and color of the language, while making it fully comprehensible to audiences. When Derek Walcott, the Saint Lucian poet and dramatist, in 1976 wrote the play *O Babylon!* based on the Rastafarian cult of Jamaica, he recognized both the melodic and rhetorical potential of the native language, as well as the problems it posed for the dramatist. In his introduction he explained the problem he faced:

> In trying to seek a combination of the authentic and the universally comprehensible, I found myself at the center of a language poised between defiance and translation, for pure Jamaican is comprehensible only to Jamaicans. . . . When I considered that, within that language itself, the Rastafari have created still another for their own nation, I faced another conflict: if the language of the play remained true to the sect, it would have to use the sect's methods of self-protection and total withdrawal. . . . To translate is to betray. My theatre language is, in effect, an adaptation and, for clarity's sake, filtered.[11]

A fourth innovation in the drive to establish an indigenous Caribbean theatre is the conscious effort to synthesize dramatic dialogue, music, song, and dance in a single expressive theatrical event, thus challenging the conventional separation of these allied performing skills into specialized types of production. One of the early examples of a successful combination of these different elements in English drama is John Gay's satire *The Beggar's Opera*, first performed in London in 1728. Exactly two hundred years after its English premiere, Bertolt Brecht revived the play in a new adaptation with great success. The American musical comedy comes close to this integrated form, although too much emphasis is often given to musical and dance numbers at the expense of language, and to spectacle to the detriment of story.

The most notable instance of Caribbean integrated theatre happened almost by accident half a century ago. This was the Jamaican Pantomime, first introduced by the Little Theatre Movement in 1941 in imitation of the English version. Two years later, with an original script by Jamaican Vera Bell and titled *Soliday and the Wicked Bird*, the Jamaican Pantomime began to assert its independence. Then in 1949 under the inspiration of play director Noel Vaz and folklorist Louise Bennett, the pantomime produced *Bluebeard and Brer Anancy*. The experiment of moving to the popular folk character Anancy was so successful that he reappeared in successive productions. In the process, the annual pantomime has evolved to become identifiably Jamaican in its use of indigenous material including dance, music, song, drama, improvisation, and pithy commentary on the contemporary social and political scene. As a result, the pantomime has become the most popularly supported annual theatrical event in the region, playing to audiences in the tens of thousands over several months.

Other examples of Caribbean plays that integrate many of the traditional expressive modes are Derek Walcott's *Dream on Monkey Mountain* (1967), and *Maskarade* (1973) by the Jamaican Sylvia Wynter. In the former play, characters from ritual and fantasy are mixed with realistic working-class figures; speech ranges from conversational dialect to oratorical prose to metered verse; folk chants are introduced, both secular and religious; there is a chorus of singers, and groups of dancers and musicians. Yet the theme is serious and meaningful to Caribbean people in search of identity.[12] Similar claims can be made for Sylvia Wynter's drama, which was inspired by events connected with the attempt to ban the Jonkonnu festivities in Kingston in 1841, to which we have already referred. Here the dramatist effectively used the multiple elements in festival enactment, including striking costumes and masks, choral singing, dancing, and staged combat, to weave a story that stressed the importance of traditional performance in sustaining the spirits and aspirations of the dispossessed.[13]

The Trinidad Carnival has produced a number of traditional masquerades, each with characteristic oration, gesture, mime, and dance.[14] In her 1948 show *Bele*, the choreographer Beryl McBurnie of Trinidad was the first to create novel and arresting modern stage dances based on the movements and gestures of the different masquerades. McBurnie, the acknowledged pioneer in Caribbean dance forms, has influenced the work of successive generations of dancers and choreographers throughout the region. In productions of the Jamaican National Dance Theatre Company, which observes the principle of integration of theatrical elements—vocal, choral, musical, visual, and kinesthetic—indigenous dance arguably has reached its highest level of achievement. Carnival is also responsible for retaining the primacy of the mask, an ancient theatrical device that has largely disappeared from the modern theatre. On stage it remains a symbol of tremendous power, more so for audiences that harbor a belief in the efficacy of gods and spirits. Rawle Gibbons, writing on "Traditional Enactments of Trinidad," describes four different types of masking. The mask may be painted on, or it may be worn over the face; it can be carried as an elaborate headdress, or it could be what

Gibbons calls "the inner mask," when the face itself is transformed to a fixed expression under the influence of spirit possession.[15]

Several plays have been written within recent times using the carnival experience as a focal point. Ronald Amoroso penned *The Master of Carnival* (1973), based on a short story by Euton Jarvis, which presents a veteran mask maker who sacrifices his life in his effort to win the carnival crown and regain the supremacy of his district in the annual competition.[16] Marina Omowale Maxwell and Mustapha Matura both have plays titled *Play Mas!* In Maxwell's drama (1968), first presented at the Mona campus of the University of the West Indies in 1974, building a masquerade float becomes a symbol for the political aspirations of a group of youths.[17] Matura's play (1974) contrasts the laissez-faire carnival mentality with an oppressive government regime when the latter lifts a ban on the carnival parade in order to shoot down revolutionaries, who have abandoned their hideout in the hills to "play mas'."[18] The play was staged in London in 1974 and in Chicago in 1981. In *Devil Mas'* (1971), the playwright Lennox Brown has his hero assume the Devil masquerade in defiance of church caveat. Descending into hell, he brings back the bodied souls of ancestral freedom fighters to indict the established religion that continues to enslave the minds of his people.[19] These are but a few of the carnival plays that are currently being written, not merely to give recognition and meaning to a major indigenous festival but also to use the festival experience for formal experimentation in dramatic presentation.

In the matter of spirit possession, it is readily seen how this most significant transformation of an individual's appearance and conduct can be reinterpreted in drama and dance. Summoning the presence of supernatural beings through the trance state speaks to the traditional belief in ancestral spirits who protect the community, and in guardian spirits of all living things who demand to be recognized and reverenced by human beings. Spirit possession places man in his proper context in the natural universe, not as supercreature who abuses nature out of indifference or greed, but as part of the balance of nature, paying his dues and respecting the rights of other natural things to their way of existence.

In his play *An Echo in the Bone* (1974), the late Jamaican playwright Dennis Scott finds an ingenious use for the phenomenon of the trance state.[20] An estate owner has been killed by a peasant gardener who then commits suicide. The celebrants in a dead-wake ceremony want to know why this tragedy occurred. They become possessed by the spirit of the gardener and reveal untold parts of his story. Unconsciously they assume the personas of different people and reenact conflicts and antagonisms that have existed between the races in time past. The moments of possession become climactic episodes. They provide historical perspective and serve as transition points from one scene to another. Time and place are fused and compressed with the present by the force of spirit possession.

No truly indigenous theatre can afford to ignore the role of the audience or, rather, the relationship between audience and performer. We have seen that in ritual drama, audience members are participants in the unfolding action primarily because they have an interest in the outcome of the performance. How may one translate that interest into a communal theatrical experience? Assuredly the performing group needs to have earned the audience's allegiance by the quality and meaning of its work over time and by the recognition that the audience does play an important part in the group's focus and direction. Preserving a sense of audience participation does wonders for the actor, as for the communal psyche.

One area of great relevance to this question is the physical arrangement of the place of performance. It is hardly necessary to state that the old-fashioned proscenium or picture-frame stage with darkened auditorium, inherited from Europe in the last century, is the least suitable arrangement for involving an audience. Indeed that stage grew out of the desire to ignore the audience, to make its members feel as if they were uninvited observers peeping through a keyhole at the private lives of the characters on stage. What this suggests is that those characters were busy working out their own complicated lives, their psychological hang-ups and neuroses, and were not really interested in the public's knowing about their problems. It is an attitude antipathetic to theatre, a public art. Plays need to be addressed to an audience in the firm belief that what they reveal is life enhancing for that audience.

In this century various methods have been used to destroy the proscenium barrier. There have been the thrust stage, the arena stage, and the parallel stage, each defining a different relationship between actor and audience. Bringing actors into the audience now occurs so capriciously as to be almost meaningless. There is as well the environmental theatre, espoused in the late 1960s and 1970s by people like the American scholar Richard Schechner, where the actors play among and through the audience and invite audience members to join them in certain group episodes of the play. Some of these methods are faddish, others represent reasonable alternatives to the outmoded picture-frame stage. In some theatres the auditorium lighting may be

286

dimmed but not entirely extinguished so that the audience may be seen throughout the performance. All such alternatives need to be carefully evaluated for their appropriateness to the Caribbean experience.

An audience needs to be drawn into the atmosphere of a play from the moment of entrance into the theatre. Space staging has become fashionable of late in the Caribbean; a few platforms and boxes painted gray on an otherwise empty and uncurtained stage are often used to supplant costly representational scenery. The problem with this approach, which is usually adopted for reasons of economy, is that the stage space is seldom transformed into a setting that captures the imagination and evokes the empathy of an audience. Area lighting helps, but stage designers and directors need to be more adventurous in creating environments that place actors in evocative and workable settings that will excite an audience's anticipation of the theatrical event to come.

Other aspects of production offer opportunities to enlist audience participation. One of these is the use of the chorus, a device known to the ancient Greeks, passed down to Elizabethan dramatists, and current in African theatre today. The chorus is the communal voice. It ensures that the action on stage is relevant to the body politic. It joins past and present by its recital of historical incidents pertinent to the plot. It invites the audience to consider its point of view against the conflicting claims of the central characters. It expresses communal hopes and fears, joys and tribulations. The chorus, seldom seen on the modern Western stage, may well be reactivated for the Caribbean theatre.

The most recent experiment in audience involvement was undertaken in February 1991 by Rawle Gibbons, director of the University's Creative Arts Centre in Trinidad. He created a show at the Queen's Hall in Port-of-Spain called *Sing De Chorus* and based on well-known and renowned calypsoes of the 1930s and 1940s. Each calypso was introduced by a group of performers who, by changing roles, acted out the event that inspired its composition. When the calypso was eventually sung, members of the audience, many of whom recalled the lyrics, spontaneously joined in singing the chorus, as they might have done in a calypso tent years ago or on the streets at carnival time. Although the format made for an episodic script, the underlying theme of the calypsonians' personal and professional lives and their defiance of official censorship gave the performance a unity of its own.

Two final components of a theatre rooted in the Caribbean experience are the salutation and closure. Traditional societies are aware of the importance of greeting and of showing hospitality. In West Africa when traveling players approach a town, they sing praises to the townspeople and to the town itself in expectation of a warm welcome. The traditional storyteller invariably prefaces his tale by greeting his audience. What form shall the salutation take in Caribbean theatre? Since the play about to be acted is for the audience, should not the performers begin by recognizing its presence? Perhaps the production might be dedicated to some worthy representative of the community. If there is an overture of words or music, the piece might be chosen as much for audience recognition as for relevance to the play being presented.

Applause at the final curtain is a conventional way of bringing a performance to a close. But a joyous ending could be marked by a festive dance on stage to which audience members could be conducted by the actors. This used to be standard practice in dance performances at the Little Carib Theatre in Trinidad, and it never failed to have an electrifying and bonding effect on the assembly. It has also proved effective, where appropriate, to end a play with a celebrative dance, the audience being invited to participate. The reverse is possible; the audience might join in a choral chant of sorrow when the play ends in tragedy.

As we have seen, Caribbean society at its base consists mainly of people of African descent who have come through slavery, colonialism, European and Euro-American imperialism, but have yet found ways to preserve their spirit and sustain their lives. Those ways represent the root sources of an indigenous culture. Cultures of other dispersed peoples who have made their home in the Caribbean have influenced the basic culture, which is not static. It is constantly undergoing change, particularly so in recent times when it has felt the full impact of imported mass media productions. Reinforced by the electronic age, these imports reach into the remotest areas of society and pummel the traditional forms relentlessly, sinking into the consciousness of Caribbean peoples an alien life-style through continuous exposure to foreign films, television, radio, music, plays, and dance. Having survived physical serfdom, political repression, and economic dictation, the region must not now fall victim to cultural domination.

Nor can Caribbean theatre artists become cultural chauvinists and isolate themselves from the rest of world theatre. They need to be versatile, not only in technical skills but also in their ability to understand and appreciate other cultures. World literature contains great works of theatre that need to be regularly rediscovered and reinterpreted in the Caribbean as elsewhere, and theatre artists must be accomplished in their craft in order to stage such works with intelligence and sensitivity. In any event, the Western stage tradition remains strong in the region, for it too, as we have shown, is part of Caribbean history.

Yet the words of the late Norman Manley, Jamaican statesman and national hero, written in 1939 and still cautionary today, apply not only to British but also to all foreign influences: "We can take everything that English education has to offer us, but ultimately we must reject the domination of her influence because we are not English nor should we ever want to be. Instead we must dig deep into our own consciousness and accept and reject only those things of which we, from our superior knowledge of our own cultural needs, must be the best judge."[21]

The Caribbean theatre needs the assurance of its own idioms; it needs to speak with its own authentic voices, to move to its own rhythms, to shape its own images, to captivate its own audiences. To reach these goals it must be grounded in its own traditions. That is the challenge facing contemporary Caribbean dramatists, choreographers, composers, and theatre practitioners as they look toward the twenty-first century.

Appendix A

Record of Productions by the American Company or Its Members in Jamaica in 1783

Saturday, January 18

Stevens's Sentimental, Satyrical and Comic *The Lecture on Heads* by Mr. Moore:

Part I: Alexander the Great, Cherokee Chief, Quack Doctor, Cuckold, Lawyer, with a case in point humourously described, Macaronies, Horse Jockies, Nobody, Somebody, Anybody and Everybody's Coats of Arms, Sciences, Probability, Statue of Flattery.

Part II: Riding Hood, Ranelagh Hood, Billingsgate Moll, Laughing and Crying Philosophers with a striking Dialogue, Venus's Girdle, French Nightcap, Old Maid, Young Married Lady, Old Batchelor, Lass of the Spirit, Male Quaker, French Head and Hat, English Head and Hat.

Part III: Blood, Woman of the Town, Tea Table Critic, Politician, with imitations, Gambler, Gambler's Funeral and Monument, Head of a Wit, Methodist Preacher, Tabernacle Harangue. Before the Lecture a *Prologue* addressed to the Inhabitants of Jamaica, with a Theatrical Piece called *The Court of Momus*, in which will be presented the following Dramatic Characters, viz.: Falstaff, Pistol, Fribble, Miser, Lord Foppington, John Moody, Lord Ogleby, Maw-worm, Scrub, and Mungo.

Boxes 13s.4d. Pit 7s.6d. To begin at Seven O'Clock precisely. Places for the Boxes to be had at the Theatre, and Tickets at the Royal Gazette Printing Office.

Monday, February 3

An historical play called *King Henry IV with the Humours of Sir John Falstaff*.

Sir John Falstaff, Mr. GIFFARD (Being his first appearance here these 15 Years.) Before the Play an occasional *Prologue* by Mr. Giffard. To which will be added the Farce of *The Citizen*.

Tuesday, February 4

Above bill "will positively be performed."

291

Wednesday, February 5

For the Benefit of Miss Wainwright & Mr. Woolls, At Dallas's Assembly Room in Church Street will be performed *A Concert of Vocal and Instrumental Music*, after which *A Ball*.

Tickets a Pistole each, to be had at His Majesty's Printing Office and of Mr. Woolls, in Upper King Street.

Thursday, February 6

By particular desire will positively be performed an historical play called *Henry IV with the Humours of Sir John Falstaff*. Sir John Falstaff, Mr. GIFFARD (Being his second appearance in that Character here these 15 Years.) King, Mr. MORRIS; Prince of Wales, Mr. WIGNELL; Sir Richard Vernon, Mr. HALLAM; Sir Walter Blunt, Mr. SALMON; Douglas, Mr. WOOLLS; Westmoreland, Mr. MORALES; Hotspur, Mr. MOORE. Hostess, Miss WAINWRIGHT; Lady Percy, Miss KIRK.

Before the Play, an occasional *Prologue* by Mr. Giffard.

To which will be added the Farce of *The Mock Doctor, or, The Dumb Lady Cured*.

Saturday, February 15

The Devil Upon Two Sticks, a comedy.

Asmodeus (the Devil), Mr. HALLAM; Sir Thomas Maxwell, Mr. GIFFARD; Sligo, Mr. MOORE; Apozem, Mr. MORRIS; Julep, Mr. SALMON; Invoice, Mr. WOOLLS; Habakkirk, Mr. MORALES; Doctor Last, Mr. WIGNELL. Mrs. Maxwell, Miss WAINWRIGHT; Harriet, Miss KIRK.

To which will be added the Farce of *The Reprisal, or, The Tars of Old England*.

Saturday, February 22

A Bold Stroke for a Wife, a comedy.

Anne Lovely, Mrs. GIFFARD (Being her first appearance in that Character here these 15 Years.)

To which will be added the Farce of *The Virgin Unmasked*. Lucy, by Mrs. GIFFARD.

Saturday, March 1

King Richard the Third, an historical tragedy.

King Richard, Mr. GIFFARD; King Henry, Mr. HALLAM; Tressel, Mr. MOORE; Buckingham, Mr. MORRIS; Stanley, Mr. SALMON; Lieutenant of the Tower, Mr. WIGNELL; Ratcliff, Mr. WOOLLS; Norfolk, Mr. MORALES; Prince Edward, Master WOOLLS; Duke of York, By a Little Master; Catesby, Mr. MOORE; Richmond, Mr. WIGNELL. Lady Anne, Miss KIRK; Duchess of York, Miss WAINWRIGHT; Queen Elizabeth, Mrs. GIFFARD.

To which will be added the Farce of *The Ghost*. Sir Jeffery Constant,

Mr. WIGNELL; Capt. Constant, Mr. MOORE; Trusty, Mr. SALMON; Clinch, Mr. MORRIS; Roger, Mr. HALLAM. Dolly, Miss WAINWRIGHT; Belinda, Miss KIRK.

Saturday, March 8

By very particular desire, A few Gentlemen of the Army, encouraged by the polite attention of the Public, shewn to them on former occasions, intend performing in the Comedy of *The Recruiting Officer*. The Principal Characters by Gentlemen of the Army. An occasional Prologue, *Silvia* (with an Epilogue in Character) by an Officer.
To which will be added the Farce of *Lethe*.

Saturday, March 15

School for Scandal, a comedy.
Sir Peter Teazle, Mr. GOODMAN; Sir Oliver Surface, Mr. MORRIS; Joseph Surface, Mr. WIGNELL; Sir Benjamin Backbite, Mr. GIFFARD; Crabtree, Mr. SALMON; Snake, Mr. MOORE; Rowley, Mr. WOOLLS; Moses, Mr. MORALES; Charles (with the Song), Mr. HALLAM. Maria, Miss KIRK; Mrs. Candour, Miss WAINWRIGHT; Lady Sneerwell, Mrs. GIFFARD; Lady Teazle, Mrs. MORRIS.
To which will be added the Farce of the *Contrivances, or, The Captain in Petticoats*. Rovewell, Mr. WOOLLS; Argus, Mr. MORRIS; Robin, Mr. WIGNELL. Betty, Mrs. GIFFARD; Arethusa, Miss WAINWRIGHT.

Tuesday, March 18

Concert of Vocal and Instrumental Music after which a *Ball* for the Benefit of Miss WAINWRIGHT & Mr. WOOLLS, at Dallas's Assembly Room in Church Street. Tickets to be had at His Majesty's Printing Office, and of Mr. Woolls in Upper King Street.

Saturday, March 22

Hamlet, Prince of Denmark, a tragedy.
Hamlet, Mr. HALLAM; King, Mr. SALMON; Horatio, Mr. GIFFARD; Laertes, Mr. WIGNELL; Polonius, Mr. MORRIS; Ostrick, Mr. MOORE; Marcellus, Mr. WOOLLS; Bernardo, Mr. MORALES; Player King, Mr. MOORE; Ghost, Mr. GOODMAN, Queen, Mrs. GIFFARD; Player Queen, Miss WAINWRIGHT; Ophelia (first time), Mrs. MORRIS.
To which will be added the Farce of *The Old Man Taught Wisdom, or, The Virgin Unmasked*. Goodwill, Mr. MORRIS; Coupee, Mr. WIGNELL; Quaver, Mr. WOOLLS; Thomas, Mr. MOORE; Blister, Mr. SALMON, Miss Lucy, Mrs. GIFFARD.

Monday, March 31

The Fair Penitent, a tragedy.
Sciolto, Mr. GOODMAN; Lothario, Mr. HALLAM; Altamont, Mr. WIG-

NELL; Rossano, Mr. WOOLLS; Horatio, Mr. MOORE. Lavinia, Miss KIRK; Calista, Mrs. MORRIS.

To which will be added the Farce of *High Life Below Stairs*.

Saturday, April 12

The Constant Couple, or, A Trip to the Jubilee, a comedy. Sir Harry Wildair, Mr. HALLAM; Beau Clincher, Mr. GIFFARD; Col. Standard, Mr. WIGNELL; Alderman Smuggler, Mr. MORRIS; Vizard, Mr. MOORE; Tom Errand, Mr. SALMON; Jubilee Dickey, Mr. WOOLLS; Young Clincher, Mr. ROBERTS. Lady Darling, Mrs. GIFFARD; Angelica, Miss KIRK; Parly, Miss WAINWRIGHT; Lady Lurewell, Mrs. MORRIS.

To which will be added a Musical Medley called *The British Heroes, or, French Perfidy, and Spanish Pride Rewarded*. Being a compilation from the best productions in honour of those glorious events, the signal Victory of the Twelfth of April, and the gallant Defence maintained at Gibraltar. Lieutenant Vigilant, Mr. WIGNELL; Mr. Import, Mr. MORRIS; Boatswain, Mr. MOORE; Kit Keel, Mr. GIFFARD; Tom Bowling, Mr. WOOLLS; Lame Soldier, Mr. MORALES; Captain Bombproof, Mr. MOORE; Duc de Crillon, Mr. WIGNELL; Serjeant O'Bradley, Mr. GIFFARD; Boatswain O'Thunder, Mr. GOODMAN. Goddesses, Mrs. GIFFARD, Miss KIRK, and Miss WAINWRIGHT; Britannia, Mrs. MORRIS.

To conclude with an Illumination Scene, and a new Song and Chorus adapted to the occasion.

Saturday, April 19

Chances, or, The Two Constantias, a comedy. Don John, Mr. HALLAM; Don Frederick, Mr. WIGNELL; Petruchio, Mr. MOORE; Duke, Mr. GIFFARD; Peter, Mr. MORRIS; Perez, Mr. WOOLLS; Surgeon, Mr. MORALES; Antonio, Mr. GOODMAN. 2nd Constantia, Miss KIRK; Mother-in-law, Mrs. GIFFARD; Landlady, Miss WAINWRIGHT; 1st Constantia, Mrs. MORRIS.

To which will be added a Musical Medley called the *British Heroes* [Cast as above.]

Saturday, April 26

For the Benefit of Mr. Hallam. By the American Company. *Much Ado About Nothing*, a comedy.

Benedick, Mr. HALLAM; Leonato, Mr. MORRIS; Claudio, Mr. WIGNELL; Don Pedro, Mr. MOORE; Borachio, Mr. GIFFARD; Conrade, Mr. WOOLLS; Verges, Mr. ROBERTS; Town Clerk, Mr. MORALES; Dogberry, Mr. GOODMAN. Hero, Miss KIRK; Margaret, Miss WAINWRIGHT; Ursula, Mrs. GIFFARD; Beatrice, Mrs. MORRIS.

In Act the 2nd will be introduced a *Malcharaata al Freico* with an elegant display of new Scenery, Illumination &c. To conclude with a Dance by the Characters.

To which will be added *The Spanish Friar.* Lorenzo, Mr. HALLAM; Gomez, Mr. MORRIS; Friar, Mr. WIGNELL. Elvira, Miss KIRK.

Saturday, May 3

For the Benefit of Mr. Moore. By the American Company. *Alexander the Great,* a tragedy.

Alexander, Mr. HALLAM; Lysimachus, Mr. WIGNELL; Hephestion, Mr. MOORE; Cassander, Mr. GIFFARD; Polypercon, Mr. MORRIS; Thessalus, Mr. WOOLLS; Clytus, Mr. GOODMAN. Roxana, Mrs. GIFFARD; Parisatis, Miss KIRK; Sysigambis, Miss WAINWRIGHT; Statira, Mrs. MORRIS.

In Act Second Alexander's Procession to the City of Babylon. Between the Play and Entertainment a *Hornpipe* by a Private Gentleman in character of a Sailor.

To which will be added an Entertainment called *The Mayor of Garrat.* Major Sturgeon, Mr. GIFFARD; Sir Jacob Jallop, Mr. MOORE; Roger & Sim. Snuffle, Mr. ROBERTS; Bruin, Mr. WOOLLS; Heeltap, Mr. MORRIS; Jerry Sneak, Mr. WIGNELL. Mrs. Sneak, Mrs. GIFFARD.

Saturday, May 10

For the Benefit of Mr. Wignell. By the American Company (for the last time this season). *The Constant Couple, or, A Trip to the Jubilee.* [See cast for April 12, except for Tom Errand omitted in this notice.]

To which will be added (never performed out of England) the celebrated speaking Pantomime in three acts called *Harlequin's Invasion of the Realms of Shakespear.* (Written on the Model of the Italian Comedy, by the late David Garrick, Esq. as it was acted upwards of Ninety Nights at the Theatre Royal, Drury Lane, with universal applause.) Harlequin, Mr. HALLAM; Snip, Mr. MORRIS; Simon Clodley, Mr. MOORE; Corporal Bounce, Mr. GIFFARD; Forge, Mr. GOODMAN; Mercury, and Old Woman (with songs), Mr. WOOLLS; Abraham, Mr. ROBERTS; Mons. Gasconade, Mr. WIGNELL. Mrs. Snip, Miss WAINWRIGHT; Sukey Chitterline, Mrs. GIFFARD; Dolley Snip, Mrs. MORRIS.

To conclude with the *Triumph of Shakespear & Defeat of Harlequin, A Grand Pageant,* and the Roundelay from the Jubilee, with new Scenes, Machinery, and other Decorations.

Saturday, May 17

For the Benefit of Mrs. Morris. By the American Company. Will be presented a Tragedy (never acted here) called *The Count of Narbonne,* as it is now performing at the Theatre Royal, Covent Garden with the greatest applause. Raymond (Count of Narbonne), Mr. HALLAM; Austin, Mr. GIFFARD; Fabian, Mr. MOORE; Renchild, Mr. GOODMAN; Thybalt, Mr. WOOLLS; Theodore, Mr. WIGNELL. Adelaide, Miss KIRK; Jacqueline, Mrs. GIFFARD; Hortensia (Countess of Narbonne), Mrs. MORRIS.

With new Scenery adapted to the piece. To which will be added (for the second time) the celebrated speaking Pantomime, in three acts, called *Harlequin's Invasion of the Realms of Shakespear*. [See cast for May 10.]

Saturday, May 24

For the Benefit of Miss Kirk. By the American Company. *Chances, or, The Two Constantias*, a comedy. [See cast for April 19.] To which will be added (for that night only) the new speaking Pantomime, in one act, called *The Touchstone, or, Harlequin Traveller*. Harlequin, Mr. HALLAM; Frenchman & Mezetin, Mr. WIGNELL; Ted Barney, with the favourite Song of Vauxhall Watch, Mr. GOODMAN; Beridon, Mr. WOOLLS; Pantaloon, Mr. MOORE; Custom-house Officer, Mr. GIFFARD; Pierrot, Mr. MORRIS. Columbine, Miss KIRK.

With new Scenes, Machinery, and other Decorations. To conclude with an elegant view of Vauxhall Illuminated, and a Dance by the Characters.

N.B. No Person can, on any account, be admitted behind the Scenes.

Saturday, May 31

For the Benefit of Mr. Woolls. By the American Company. *The Shipwreck, or, The Brothers*, a comedy. (Written by the Author of the West Indian.) Captain Ironsides, Mr. GOODMAN; Sir Benjamin Dove, Mr. MORRIS; Belfield, Mr. WIGNELL; Paterson, Mr. WOOLLS; Philip, Mr. MOORE; Skiff, Mr. ROBERTS; Old Godwin, Mr. MORALES; Belfield Junior, Mr. HALLAM. Violetta, Miss STORER; Sophia, Miss KIRK; Fanny, Miss WAINWRIGHT; Lucy Waters, Mrs. GIFFARD; Lady Dove, Mrs. MORRIS.

End of the Play (by particular desire) "The Wandering Sailor" by Mr. Woolls, after which, "Bucks Have At Ye All" by Master Woolls.

To which will be added (never performed here) a Comedy in two Acts, called *The Deaf Lover* (written by Mr. Pilon, Author of "The Invasion".) As it is now performing at the Theatre Royal, Covent Garden, with the greatest applause.

The Deaf Lover, Mr. HALLAM; Old Wrongward, Mr. MOORE; Young Wrongward, Mr. WOOLLS; John, Mr. MORRIS; Sternhold, Mr. ROBERTS; Cook, Mr. MORALES; Canteen, Mr. WIGNELL. Sophia, Miss STORER; Lady, Mrs. GIFFARD; Betsey Blossom, Miss WAINWRIGHT.

Saturday, June 14

For the Benefit of Miss Wainwright. By the American Company. A Tragedy (not acted these four years) called *Tamerlane the Great, or The Fall of Bajazet, Emperor of the Turks*. Tamerlane, Mr. GIFFARD; Monoses, Mr. WIGNELL; Axalla, Mr. MOORE; Omar, Mr. GOODMAN; Mirvan, Mr. WOOLLS; Stratocles, Mr. LARK; Haly, Mr. MORALES; Zama, Mr. ROBERTS; Dervise, Mr. MORRIS; Bajazet, Mr. HALLAM. Selima, Miss KIRK; Arpasia, Mrs. MORRIS.

To which will be added a Burletta called *Midas*.

Mortals—Midas, Mr. GOODMAN; Damactae, Mr. WIGNELL; Sileno, Mr.

MOORE; Pan, Mr. ROBERTS; Daphne, Mrs. MORRIS; Mysis, Miss WAIN-WRIGHT; Nysa, Miss STORER. Fabulous Deities—Jupiter, Mr. MORRIS; Mercury, Mr. MORALES; Juno, Mrs. GIFFARD; Venus, Miss KIRK.

Saturday, June 21

For the Benefit of Mrs. Giffard. By the American Company. *The Beggar's Opera.*

Captain Macheath, Mr. HALLAM; Filch, Mr. WIGNELL; Lockit, Mr. MORRIS; Mat o' the Mint, Mr. GOODMAN; Ben Budge, Mr. MOORE; Crook Finger'd Jack, Mr. MORALES; Peachum, Mr. GIFFARD. Lucy, Mrs. GIFFARD; Mrs. Peachum, Mrs. MORRIS; Jenny Diver and Diana Trapes, Miss WAINWRIGHT; Mrs. Coaxer, Miss KIRK; Molly Brazen, Mr. MOORE; Polly Peachum, Miss STORER.

To which will be added *The Upholsterer, or "What News?"* Quidnunc, Mr. MOORE; Pamphlet, Mr. GIFFARD; Rovewell, Mr. WOOLLS; Feeble, Mr. MORALES; Belmour, Mr. WIGNELL; Razor, Mr. MORRIS. Harriot, Miss STORER; Termagant, Miss WAINWRIGHT.

The Songs in the Opera will be accompanied by some Gentleman of this Town. Mr. Goodman having kindly undertaken the charge of letting the Boxes, such Ladies and Gentlemen who intend favouring Mrs. Giffard with their company, will apply to him at the Theatre.

Saturday, June 28

For the Benefit of Mr. Goodwin. By the American Company. The admired Tragedy of *King Lear.*

King Lear, Mr. HALLAM; Bastard, Mr. MORRIS; Gloster, Mr. MORRIS; Kent, Mr. GOODMAN; Albany, Mr. WOOLLS; Cornwall, Mr. GIFFARD; Burgundy, Mr. LARK; Gentleman Usher, Mr. MORALES; Edgar, Mr. WIGNELL. Goneril, Mrs. GIFFARD; Regan, Miss KIRK; Arante, Miss STORER; Cordelia (first time), Mrs. MORRIS.

To which will be added (for that night only) the celebrated Musical Entertainment (never performed here) called *The Camp, or A Trip to Coxheath.* O'Daube, Mr. GOODMAN; Sir Harry Boquet, Mr. WIGNELL; William, Mr. WOOLLS; Gauge, Mr. MORRIS; Old Man, Mr. GIFFARD; Monsieur Bluard, Mr. WIGNELL; Robin, Mr. MORALES; Recruits, Mr. LARK, &c.; Serjeant, Mr. MOORE. Nell, Miss WAINWRIGHT; Lady Plume, Miss KIRK; Lady Sarah Sash, Miss STORER; Margery, Mrs. GIFFARD; Nancy, the female Recruit, Mrs. MORRIS.

In Act Second a Grand View of the Camp at Coxheath, painted from a Drawing taken on the spot.

Saturday, July 12

By the American Company. *The Orphan, or The Unhappy Marriage*, a tragedy. Chamont, by HARPER (Being his first appearance on this stage.) Polydore, Mr. MOORE; Acasto, Mr. MORRIS; Ernesto, Mr. WOOLLS; Chap-

lain, Mr. GIFFARD; Page, Master WOOLLS; Castalio, Mr. WIGNELL. Serina, Miss STORER; Florella, Miss WAINWRIGHT; Monimia, Mrs. HARPER.
To which will be added, *The Devil to Pay, or Wives Metamorphosed.* Sir John Loverule (with "The Early Horn"), Mr. HARPER; Butler, Mr. MORRIS; Coachman, Mr. GOODMAN; Cook, Mr. MOORE; Footman, Mr. GIFFARD; Conjuror, Mr. MORALES; Jobson, Mr. WIGNELL. Lady Loverule, Mrs. GIFFARD; Lucy, Miss WAINWRIGHT; Nell, Miss STORER.

Saturday, July 19

By the American Company. *The Gamester,* a tragedy. Beverly, Mr. HENRY; Lewson, Mr. GOODMAN; Jarvis, Mr. MORRIS; Bates, Mr. HARPER; Dawson, Mr. WOOLLS; Stukely, Mr. WIGNELL. Charlotte, Miss STORER; Lucy, Miss WAINWRIGHT; Mrs. Beverly, Mrs. MORRIS.
To which will be added, *The Citizen.* The Citizen, Mr. WIGNELL; Old Philpot, Mr. MORRIS; Young Wilding, Mr. MOORE; Sir Jasper, Mr. GIFFARD. Corinna, Miss STORER; Maria, Miss WAINWRIGHT.

Saturday, July 26

By the American Company. For the Benefit of Mr. Goodman. The admired tragedy of *King Lear and his Three Daughters.* King Lear, Mr. GOODMAN; Bastard, Mr. HENRY; Gloster, Mr. MORRIS; Kent, Mr. MOORE; Albany, Mr. WOOLLS; Cornwall, Mr. GIFFARD; Burgundy, Mr. LARK; Gentleman Usher, Mr. MORALES; Edgar, Mr. WIGNELL. Goneril, Mrs. GIFFARD; Regan, Miss KIRK; Arante, Miss STORER; Cordelia (first time), Mrs. MORRIS.
To which will be added (for that night only) the celebrated Musical Entertainment, never performed here, called *The Camp, or A Trip to Coxheath.* [See cast for June 28, except Robin, by a Gentleman who never performed on this stage.]

Saturday, August 2

By the American Company. *The Gamester,* a tragedy. [See cast for July 19.] To which will be added, *High Life Below Stairs.* Lovel, Mr. HALLAM; Freeman, Mr. GOODMAN; Lord Duke's Servant, Mr. WIGNELL; Sir Harry's Servant, Mr. GIFFARD; Tom, Mr. MOORE; Coachman, Mr. WOOLLS; Kingston, Mr. MORALES; Philip, Mr. MORRIS. Lady Charlotte, Miss WAINWRIGHT; Lady Bab, Mrs. GIFFARD; Kitty (with a song), Mrs. MORRIS.

Saturday, August 9

By the American Company. *Jane Shore,* a tragedy. Lord Hastings, Mr. WIGNELL; Gloster, Mr. MORRIS; Belmour, Mr. GIFFARD; Ratcliff, Mr. WOOLLS; Catesby, Mr. HARPER; Derby, Mr. GOODMAN; Dumont, Mr. HENRY. Alicia, Mrs. HARPER; Jane Shore, Mrs. MORRIS.
To which will be added, *Love A-la-Mode.* Sir Callaghan O'Drallaghan (with songs), Mr. HENRY; Squire Groom, Mr. WIGNELL; Mordecai, Mr.

MORRIS; Sir Theodore, Mr. WOOLLS; Sir Archy M'Sarcasm (first time), Mr. GIFFARD. Charlotte, Miss STORER.

Saturday, August 16

By the American Company. For the Benefit of Mr. Morris. *The Provok'd Husband, or, A Journey to London,* a comedy. Lord Townly, Mr. HALLAM; Manly, Mr. WIGNELL; Count Busset, Mr. HARPER; John Moody, Mr. HENRY; Squire Richard, Mr. MOORE; Sir Fr. Wronghead, Mr. MORRIS. Lady Grace, Miss HARPER; Lady Wronghead, Miss WAINWRIGHT; Miss Jenny, Miss STORER; Myrtilla, Miss KIRK; Lady Townly, Mrs. MORRIS.

To which will be added *The Irish Widow.* Whittle, Mr. MORRIS; Kecksey, Mr. HARPER; Nephew, Mr. WIGNELL; Bates, Mr. MOORE; Thomas, Mr. WOOLLS; Sir Pat. O'Neale, Mr. GOODMAN. Widow Brady, with the Epilogue Song and (by particular desire) the Manual Exercise, Mrs. MORRIS.

Saturday, August 23

By the American Company, *The Clandestine Marriage,* a comedy. Lord Ogleby, Mr. HALLAM; Sir John Melville, Mr. HARPER; Sterling, Mr. MORRIS; Serjeant Flower, Mr. GIFFARD; Trueman, Mr. WOOLLS; Canton, Mr. ROBERTS; Brush, Mr. MOORE; Lovewell, Mr. WIGNELL. Fanny, Mrs. MORRIS; Mrs. Heidleburg, Mrs. GIFFARD; Chambermaid, Miss WAINWRIGHT; Betty, Miss STORER; Miss Sterling, Miss QUIN (Being her second appearance.)

To which will be added *The Devil to Pay; or, The Wives Metamorphosed.* [See cast for July 12 except character of Coachman omitted in this notice.]

Saturday, August 30

By the American Company. For the Benefit of Miss Storer. *The Mourning Bride,* a tragedy. Osmyn, Mr. HALLAM; Garcia, Mr. WIGNELL; Gonzalez, Mr. MORRIS; Perez, Mr. WOOLLS; Selim, Mr. HARPER. Heli, Mr. GIFFARD; Alonzo, Mr. LARK; The King, Mr. MOORE. Zara, Mrs. MORRIS; Leonora, Mrs. GIFFARD; Almeria, Mrs. HARPER.

To which will be added a Musical Farce called *The Virgin Unmasked.* Goodwill, Mr. MORRIS; Coupee, Mr. WIGNELL; Quaver, Mr. WOOLLS; Blister, Mr. HARPER; Tom, Mr. MOORE. Miss Lucy, Miss STORER.

Saturday, September 6

By the American Company. For the benefit of Mr. Henry. The Comic Opera of *Love in a Village.* Young Meadows, Mr. HENRY; Justice Woodcock, Mr. GIFFARD; Eustace, Mr. HARPER; Sir William Meadows, Mr. MORRIS; Hodge, Mr. WIGNELL; Hawthorn, Mr. WOOLLS. Lucinda (first time), Mrs. MORRIS; Deborah Woodcock, Mrs. HAMILTON; Margery, Mrs. HARPER; Rosetta, Miss MARIA STORER.

The original Overture by Abel. In Act II will be introduced a favourite Italian Song from Signior Rauzzini's new opera of "L'Eroe Cinese." The

Orchestra will be strengthened by the kind assistance of some musical friends.

To which will be added *Love A-la-Mode*. [See cast for August 9.]

Saturday, September 20

By the American Company. The Comic Opera of *The Maid of the Mill*. Lord Almworth, Mr. HENRY; Sir Harry Sycamore, Mr. MOORE; Fairfield, Mr. MORRIS; Marvin, Mr. HARPER; Ralph, Mr. WIGNELL; Giles, Mr. WOOLLS. Fanny, Miss WAINWRIGHT; Theodosia, Miss STORER; Lady Sycamore, Mrs. GIFFARD; Patty, Miss MARIA STORER.

To which will be added *The Mayor of Garrat*. Jerry Sneak, A GENTLEMAN (Being his first appearance on this Stage); Sir Jacob Jallop, Mr. MOORE; Lint, Mr. WIGNELL; Crispin Heeltap, Mr. MORRIS; Bruin, Mr. WOOLLS; Major Sturgeon, Mr. GIFFARD. Mrs. Bruin, Miss QUIN; Mrs. Sneak, Mrs. GIFFARD.

Royal Gazette, Supplement, September 20–27

A CARD.

MR. HENRY most respectfully informs the Public, that some reports having prevailed with regard to maltreatment of the Performers lately arrived:- Although he would not wish to intrude on them the petty disputes of a Theatre, yet, lest they might prejudice some feeling heart, amongst a community as eminent for humanity as impartiality, who is not acquainted with the circumstances—he has left at His Majesty's printing office, for the inspection of any person who chooses to apply, two letters that passed on the occasion, which he flatters himself will, by *stating facts*, do away every unfavourable idea that may have been conceived against him. *Theatre, Friday Noon.*

Saturday, September 27

By the American Company. The Comedy of *The Suspicious Husband*. Ranger, Mr. WIGNELL; Strictland, Mr. MORRIS; Bellamy, Mr. HARPER; Jack Megget, Mr. MOORE; Tester, Mr. WOOLLS; Buckle, Mr. GIFFARD; Frankly, Mr. HENRY. Mrs. Strictland, Miss WAINWRIGHT; Jacintha, Mrs. HARPER; Lucetta, Miss STORER; Landlady, Mrs. GIFFARD; Milliner, Miss KIRK; Clarinda (first time), Mrs. MORRIS.

To which will be added *The Virgin Unmasked*. Coupee, Mr. WIGNELL; Quaver, Mr. WOOLLS; Goodwill, Mr. MORRIS; Thomas, Mr. HARPER; Blister, Mr. MOORE. Miss Lucy, Mrs. GIFFARD.

Saturday, October 4

By the American Company. A Tragedy called *Edward & Eleonora*. Edward, Mr. WIGNELL; Gloster, Mr. MORRIS; Theald, Mr. WOOLLS; Assassin, Mr. MOORE; 1st Officer, Mr. GIFFARD; 2d Officer, Mr. HARPER; Selim, Mr. HENRY; Daraxa, Miss STORER; Eleonora, Mrs. MORRIS.

To which will be added a Pastoral, altered from the celebrated Allan Ramsay, by ——— Tickel, Esq. called *Patie and Roger, or, The Gentle Shepherd*. Patie, Mr. HENRY; Roger, Mr. HARPER; Sir William Worthy, Mr. MORRIS; Symon, Mr. GIFFARD; Glaud, Mr. MOORE; Bauldy, Mr. WIG-NELL. Jenny, Mrs. MORRIS; Madge, Miss WAINWRIGHT; Mause, Mrs. GIFFARD; Peggy, Miss MARIA STORER.

With the original Music, and new Accompanyments, as performed in London. By permission of Tho. Linley, Esq., the Composer.

Saturday, October 11

For the Benefit of Miss Maria Storer. By the American Company. The last new Tragedy (performed at Covent Garden forty-seven nights with uncommon applause) called *The Mysterious Husband*. The Principal Characters by Mr. HENRY, Mr. HARPER, Mr. MORRIS, Mr. GIFFARD, and Mr. WIGNELL. Mrs. HARPER, Mrs. GIFFARD, and Miss MARIA STORER.

After the play (by particular desire) Mr. HENRY will recite a Monody called *The Shadows of Shakespear, or, Shakespear's Characters Paying Homage to Garrick*.

To which will be added *The Padlock*. Don Diego, Mr. WOOLLS; Mungo, Mr. HENRY; Leander, Mr. HARPER. Ursula, Mrs. MORRIS; Leonora, Miss MARIA STORER.

Saturday, October 18

For the Benefit of Mr. & Mrs. Harper. By the American Company. *Cymbeline, King of Britain*, a tragedy. Leonatus Posthumus, Mr. HENRY; Cymbeline, Mr. MORRIS; Cloten, Mr. MOORE; Belarius (for this night only), Mr. GOODMAN; Arviragus, Mr. WOOLLS; Guiderius, Mr. LARK; Philario, Mr. MORALES; Caius Lucius, Mr. GIFFARD; Iachimo, Mr. WIGNELL. Queen, Miss KIRK; Helen, Mrs. GIFFARD; Imogen, Mrs. HARPER.

To which will be added a Ballad Farce called *Damon & Phillida*. Damon, Mr. HARPER; Lord Arcas, Mr. GIFFARD; Corydon, Mr. MORRIS; Mopsus, Mr. WIGNELL; Cimon, Mr. MOORE. Phillida, Mrs. HARPER.

Wednesday, October 29

By the American Company. A Comedy called *The Suspicious Husband*. [See cast for September 27. Play probably not presented on that date.] To which will be added *The Citizen*. [See cast for July 19.]

Saturday, November 8

By the American Company. A Tragedy called *The Mysterious Husband*. Lord Davenant, Mr. HENRY; Charles Davenant, Mr. HARPER; Sir Edmund Travers, Mr. MORRIS; Sir Harry Harlow, Mr. MOORE; Paget, Mr. GIFFARD; Capt. Dormer, Mr. WIGNELL. Marianne, Mrs. HARPER; Waiting Woman, Mrs. GIFFARD; Lady Davenant, Miss MARIA STORER. To which will be added a Pastoral, altered from the celebrated Allan Ramsay, called *Patie and Roger, or, The Gentle Shepherd.* The Band to be conducted by Mr. Hemmings from the Theatre Royal in Bath. [See Cast as for October 4, except Madge played by Miss STORER in this notice.] With a new Overture and accompanyments, as performed in London, by permission of Thos. Linley, Esq.

There will be a play on Tuesday and Thursday next when the Theatre will be closed until the American Company's return from Spanish Town and Montego Bay. This evening is the last night of Miss Maria Storer's agreement.

Saturday, December 6

King Richard III staged by Mr. Roberts at Spanish Town. Mr. ROBERTS performed Richard with universal applause in the year 1778 in Kingston.

302

Appendix B

Catalog of Original Jamaican Plays Listed Chronologically
by Date of First Performance or Publication

1. *Theatrical Candidates*, a farce by the American Company. Presented at the Kingston Theatre, February 16, 1780.
2. *School for Soldiers, or The Deserter*, a four-act drama by John Henry of the American Company. Presented at the Kingston Theatre, August 25, 1781.
3. *A West Indian Lady's Arrival in London*, a farce by Margaret Cheer Cameron of the American Company. Presented at the Kingston Theatre, October 6, 1781.
4. *The Kingston Privateer*, an adaptation by the American Company of *The Liverpool Prize* by Frederick Pilon. Presented at the Kingston Theatre, December 8, 1781.
5. *Scandal Club, or Virtue in Danger*, a comedy by "A West Indian Lady." Presented by the American Company, Kingston Theatre, February 7, 1782.
6. *Dialogue Between a Poet and a Doctor*. In *Daily Advertiser*, July 1, 1790.
7. *Rudolph: The Calabrian Banditti*, a melodrama by "A Gentleman of this City." Presented by Burnett's Company of Comedians, Kingston Theatre, February 23, 1822.
8. *The Exile*, a drama by "G." In *Jamaica Journal*, November 27, 1824.
9. *A West India Scene*, by "A Planter." In *Jamaica Journal*, December 4, 1824.
10. *Jamaica: A Comedy*, by "A Planter." In *Jamaica Journal*, December 11 and 18, 1824, and January 8, 1825.
11. *Pelham*, a drama in five acts by Anon. Taken from the novel by Bulwer-Lytton. Presented by the Kingston Amateur Theatrical Association at the Theatre Royal, April 3, 1847.
12. *The Mysteries of Vegetarianism*, a farce by Charles Shanahan. Presented by the Amateur Roscian Association at the Theatre Royal, September 20, 1853.
13. *The Spanish Warrior, or The Death of Vasco Núñez*, an historical

tragedy by Charles Shanahan. Presented by the Amateur Roscian Association at the Theatre Royal, December 14, 1853.

14. *The Two Governors: A Dialogue Between the Living and the Dead*, a dramatic duologue by "Asmodeus." In *Morning Journal*, October 14–15, 20, and November 1–2, 1853.

15. *Next of Kin, or Who Is the Heir?* a one-act farce by Philip Cohen Labatt. In *Selections from the Miscellaneous Posthumous Works of Philip Cohen Labatt in Prose and Verse*. Kingston, Jamaica: R.J. De Cordova, 1855.

16. *Edinburgh Castle, or The Last Days of Hutchinson, the Assassin*, an historical drama by "A Gentleman of this City." Presented by the Amateurs at the Theatre Royal, December 1, 1855.

17. *The Man of My Own Choice*, a farce by "A Kingston Gentleman." Presented by the Lanergan Company at the Theatre Royal, April 29, 1859.

18. *Did You Ever Send Your Wife to Spanish Town?* a farce by the Lanergan Company presented at the Theatre Royal, April 30, 1859.

19. *Political Roguery Unmasked, or, The Plotters Confounded*, a political drama by Anon. In *Jamaica Tribune*, July 9, 14, 30, and August 13, 1859.

20. *Dramatic*, a burlesque skit by Anon. In *Morning Journal*, May 14, 1868.

21. *The Modern William Tell*, a political skit by Anon. In *Morning Journal*, September 12, 1868.

22. *Women's Rights*, a comedy by Anon. Presented by the Athenian Dramatic Club in a Kingston drawing room, December 1870.

23. *Ye Opening of Ye Ten Seals*, a burlesque on religious controversy by the Reverend John Radcliffe. Published in Kingston, Jamaica, 1872.

24. *We Are All Honorable Men, or How They Play Their Parts in the Back Room of the Treasury*, a satiric sketch by "The Spirit of an old Receiver General." In *Colonial Standard*, April 5, 1872.

25. *The Almighty Dollar*, a political dialogue by Anon. In *Colonial Standard*, September 2, 1876.

26. *The Tropical Aquarius*, a political dialogue by Anon. In *Colonial Standard*, September 18, 1876.

27. *Scene on a Jamaican Sugar Estate*, a political dialogue by Anon. In *Colonial Standard*, September 29, 1876.

28. *Passing the Estimates*, a political dialogue by Anon. In *Colonial Standard*, October 24, 1876.

29. *The Old Year at the Gate*, a political burlesque by "Our Telephone." In *Gall's Newsletter*, December 25, 1879.

30. A Comedy arranged by Fr. Xavier Jaeckel. Presented by Mary Villa High School in Kingston, December 1879.

31. *Malcolm and Alonzo, or The Secret Murder of Leonard*, a revenge melodrama by John Duff Spraggs, 1880. Manuscript in Jamaica National Library.

32. *The Citizen Nobleman*, a comedy by Fr. Xavier Jaeckel. Adapted from *Le Bourgeois Gentilhomme* by Molière. Presented by Mary Villa High School at the Theatre Royal, June 22, 1881.
33. *The Smuggled Shawl: An Infernal Revenue Play*, a satiric sketch by Anon. In *Gall's Newsletter*, October 7, 1882.
34. *The Frolic of the Flowers*, an operetta by the Alpha Cottage Sisters. Presented by Alpha Cottage Orphanage at the Theatre Royal, April 16, 1892.
35. *Cupid's Delight*, a comedy by Anon. Presented by amateurs at the Lunatic Asylum auditorium, Kingston, June 13, 1892.
36. *In Stormy Days, or The Vow That Saved Jamaica*, an historical drama by the Alpha Cottage Sisters. Presented by Alpha Cottage High School at the Theatre Royal, June 29, 1897.
37. *The Demon Academy*, a comedy by J. S. Brown. Presented by amateurs at the Theatre Royal, January 20, 1898.
38. *A Las Armas*, a political pageant by Anon. Presented by Cuban amateurs at the Theatre Royal, February 17, 1898.

Notes

1. Prologue: Charting the Course

1. *Daily Gleaner*, Jamaica, January 12, 1911.
2. Richardson Wright, *Revels in Jamaica, 1682–1838* (New York: Dodd, Mead & Co., 1937). Anyone writing of the pre-Emancipation theatre in Jamaica is heavily indebted to this book. I acknowledge this debt although I have added to Wright's data and often reach conclusions different from his.
3. Henry Fowler, "A History of the Theatre in Jamaica," *Jamaica Journal* 2, no. 1 (March 1968): 53–59.
4. Wright, *Revels*, 228.
5. *Daily Advertiser*, Jamaica, February 11, 1802.
6. Gad J. Henman, "White Over Brown Over Black: The Free Coloured in Jamaican Society During Slavery and After Emancipation," *Journal of Caribbean History* 14 (1981): 46–68.
7. *Kingston Chronicle and City Advertiser*, May 6, 1813.
8. *Royal Gazette*, Jamaica, August 21–28, 1813; *St. Jago de la Vega Gazette* (additional postscript), April 1–8, 1815, and (postscript), May 13–20, 1815.
9. Ivy Baxter, *The Arts of an Island* (Metuchen, N.J.: Scarecrow Press, 1970), 78.
10. Edward Kamau Brathwaite, *Folk Culture of the Slaves in Jamaica*, rev. ed. (London: New Beacon Books, 1981).

2. Theatres of the Slave Era

1. Exceptions to this general principle of festival-inspired theatre for centuries were the small itinerant troupes of professional mimes, minstrels, and jugglers who performed for pay. In medieval Europe these entertainers played at manor houses whenever their services were needed for the private amusement of the lord and his guests, or at occasional public fairs and marketplaces when they might hope to attract and hold the attention of a fickle-minded audience.
2. Francis Hanson, Preface to *The Laws of Jamaica Passed by the Assembly and Confirmed by His Majesty in Council, 23 February, 1683* (London, 1683).
3. H. P. Jacobs, historian of Jamaica, suggests the possibility of theatres both in Port Royal and Spanish Town with actors leaving the former because of uncontrollable buccaneers in the audience and settling for the sedate

spectators in the capital town, "which then became ancestress to the American stage." See "They Took Their Pleasures Gladly," *Jamaica Annual 1951–52*. But Colonel A. B. Ellis argues that by 1682 the notorious buccaneers had left Port Royal for Hispaniola, having been expelled from Jamaica in 1677. See "The Great Earthquake of Port Royal," *Popular Science Monthly*, April 1892, 774.

4. [Charles Leslie], *A New History of Jamaica, From the Earliest Accounts to the Taking of Porto Bello by Vice Admiral Vernon* (London, 1740), 27. Wright mistakenly calls Vice Admiral Edward Vernon the author of this book.

5. John Oldmixon, *The British Empire in America*, 2d ed. (London, 1741), 416. The theatre is not mentioned in the first edition of 1708.

6. Percy Fitzgerald, *The Book of Theatrical Anecdotes* (London, [1874]), 124.

7. Frank Cundall, *Historic Jamaica* (London, 1915), 116.

8. Wright, *Revels*, 71.

9. Ibid., 41, note 14. The term *messuage* is defined as "a dwelling house with its belongings, outhouses, garden, etc." This obviously is not the same building as the King's Store or warehouse.

10. *Jamaica Courant*, June 22–29, 1754.

11. See Wright, *Revels*, 22ff., for a summary of her colorful career.

12. Edward Long, *History of Jamaica* (London, 1774), 2:117. Wright cites this extract as partial evidence for a theatre on the Parade, which he contends "was probably built in the middle of the Eighteenth Century" (67–68). However, in vol. 2, p. 106, Long describes the Parade and mentions only the barracks and church but no theatre. Further, on p. 116 in the same volume, he advocates erection of public buildings on "the East side of the parade, or square, in a line with the barracks." As this location will be the site of the next Kingston theatre and the first to be built on the Parade, it is fairly certain that no theatre stood on this site when Long wrote. He lived in Jamaica from 1757 to 1769 when he left for England, but his Jamaican connections went back a hundred years and he undoubtedly maintained contact after he left. Had a new theatre been built in Kingston before his book appeared in 1774, he would assuredly have mentioned it.

13. Eola Willis, *The Charleston Stage in the XVIII Century* (Columbia, S.C: The State Company, 1924), 87. About this reference Wright is content to say: "This mention of a theatre on Harbour Street adds to our mysteries" (224).

14. *Memoirs of William Hickey*, ed. Alfred Spencer, 4 vols. (London, 1913–25), vol. 2, *1775–1782*, 32–33. Cited by Wright, *Revels*, 65–66.

15. Wright, *Revels*, 63–64.

16. Peter Marsden, *An Account of the Island of Jamaica* (Newcastle, 1788), 6.

17. Wright, *Revels*, 261–63.

18. J. B. Moreton, *Manners and Customs in the West India Islands* (London, 1790), 34.

19. Langston Robertson, "The Kingston Theatre—A Brief History," memorandum submitted to the Deputy Keeper of the Records, Spanish Town, August 9, 1943, p. 11.

20. Wright, *Revels*, 288–89, 300.

21. *St. Jago de la Vega Gazette* (postscript), August 6–13, 1814.

22. Minutes of the Kingston Court of Common Council, November 21, 1814.

23. Wright, *Revels*, 253, quoting from the Supplement to the *Cornwall Chronicle*, July 15, 1786.

24. Ibid., 184.

25. *Cornwall Chronicle*, January 15, 1785, and Wright, *Revels*, 210. The report is of a performance in Kingston.

26. Supplement to the *Jamaica Mercury*, January 29, 1780.

27. Robertson, "Kingston Theatre," 5.

28. Wright, *Revels*, 284.

29. Ibid., 73.

30. *Cornwall Chronicle*, March 22, 1777.

31. See Wright, *Revels*, 200, and Fowler, "History of the Theatre," 55.

32. Wright, *Revels*, 322.

33. *St. Jago de la Vega Gazette*, March 5–12, 1814.

34. Ibid., October 1–8, 1814.

35. Matthew Gregory "Monk" Lewis, *Journal of a West Indian Proprietor* (London: John Murray, 1834), 166. Lewis was usually known as "Monk" from the title of his most famous novel *Ambrosio, or the Monk* (1795).

36. Wright, *Revels*, 143. In 1833 the theatre critic who called himself "An Old Stager" reported a conversation he had with an "important personage" who viewed the theatre as "a Jew concern—a Jew monopoly, and ought to be abolished." See *Kingston Chronicle*, September 9, 1833.

37. Wright, *Revels*, 333, incorrectly says this event took place in 1803.

38. Robertson cites this action as part of his evidence for Council control of the theatre. But the Council may have owned the land and not the building on it.

39. Robertson, "Kingston Theatre," 4ff. This was the first Kingston Theatre Committee on record. Its members were Aldermen Kinkead, Caldwell, and Fowles, and Common Councilmen Murray and Hardy, or any three of them.

40. The structural changes included a new flight of steps in a side lane that led to the segregated upper boxes for people of color. Hitherto access to these boxes was by a separate stairway at the front of the building.

41. James Hakewill, *A Picturesque Tour of the Island of Jamaica* (London, 1825), n.p.

42. *Daily Gleaner*, September 4, 1893, July 25, 1893.

43. The Maroons were runaway slaves of Spanish settlers who escaped to the mountains at the time of the English invasion in 1655. They considered themselves free people and were a constant threat to the stability of the island until brought under control. See Carey Robinson, *The Fighting Maroons of Jamaica* (Jamaica: William Collins & Sangster (Jamaica) Ltd., 1969).

44. [John Stewart], *An Account of Jamaica and Its Inhabitants by a Gentleman Long Resident in the West Indies* (London, 1808), 176.

45. *Daily Advertiser*, February 11, 1802. A year later Tessier found himself in trouble with the authorities and was secured to await deportation. He escaped and the council offered a reward of three hundred dollars for his apprehension. He must have been caught eventually for Wright records (*Revels*, 309) that in June 1809 Tessier was released from the county jail and deported with orders never to return to Jamaica. He had been imprisoned for smuggling French passengers into the city.

46. See Wright, *Revels*, 308.
47. *Jamaica Courant*, July 2, 1813.
48. *St. Jago de la Vega Gazette*, November 19–26, 1814.
49. *The Buckatoro Journal*, May 17, 1823.
50. *Jamaica Courant*, December 6, 1813.
51. *Royal Gazette*, Jamaica, (postscript), May 29–June 5, June 12–19, and August 21–28, 1813.
52. *St. Jago de la Vega Gazette*, April 1–8, May 13–20, and September 30–October 7, 1815.
53. [Michael Scott], *The Cruise of the Midge* (Edinburgh, 1836), 2:274–75.
54. F. W. N. Bayley, *Four Years' Residence in the West Indies* (London, 1830), 481–82.
55. *Jamaica Magazine*, October 1812, 290–93.
56. Wright, *Revels*, 355.
57. *Royal Gazette*, Jamaica, December 19–26, 1812.
58. *Daily Gleaner*, July 25, 1893. This article was part of a series under the title "Kingston's Disgrace" that took a retrospective look at the Kingston theatre.

3. Post-Emancipation Theatres

1. *Daily Gleaner*, July 25, 1893.
2. Ibid. Undated extract in files of Jamaican National Library. It was part of the *Gleaner*'s series of articles on the Kingston theatre and was probably published in August 1893.
3. Opening night playbill reproduced in *Daily Gleaner*, July 25, 1893.
4. Wright, (*Revels*, 333) is vague about this date. He refers to the Kingston theatre in 1812, then later adds, "By this time" the old theatre on the parade had disappeared, "probably having been destroyed by fire" and the new Theatre Royal built in its place. Vaz and Fowler are likewise in error, the former giving the date as 1828 and the latter as 1838. See also Horace D. Vaz, "The Drama in Jamaica; *The West Indian Review*, n.s., 4, no. 2 (Summer 1947): 30–35, 47.
5. *Morning Journal*, October 20, 1840.
6. *Colonial Standard*, April 1, 1868.
7. *Morning Journal*, January 6 and 12, 1841.
8. Ibid., March 24, 1841.
9. Robertson, "Kingston Theatre," 10.
10. *Colonial Standard*, January 29, 1864.
11. *Morning Journal*, January 12, 1875.
12. Robertson, "Kingston Theatre," 10.
13. In 1833 the Kingston Coloured Amateur Theatrical Society—the first nonwhite amateur group of record—had called its members to a meeting at the Kingston theatre but no record exists of a production by this society.
14. *Jamaica Despatch*, September 13, 1839, and December 3, 1839.
15. *Morning Journal*, April 27, 1841, and October 31, 1849.
16. *Colonial Standard*, January 16, 1873, March 10, 1875.
17. *Daily Gleaner*, September 19, 1879.
18. *Morning Journal*, September 19, 1849.
19. Ibid., August 4, 1840.
20. Ibid., October 8, 1842.

21. Ibid., October 22, 1842.
22. *Morning Journal*, May 30, 1874.
23. *Jamaica Despatch*, February 26, 1838.
24. *Colonial Standard*, January 24, 1868.
25. *Morning Journal*, August 2, 1847.
26. *Gall's Newsletter*, February 24, 1879.
27. Ever since the heyday of Puritanism in England, the nonconformist religions have been opposed to the stage. Oliver Cromwell closed down public theatres from 1642 to 1660, and in 1698 the clergyman Jeremy Collier issued his famous pamphlet attacking what he called *The Immoralities and Profanities of the English Stage*. There have been many earlier and later pronouncements against the theatre from religious bodies.
28. *Daily Gleaner*, September 26, 1879.
29. Ibid., November 7, 1879, December 4, 1879, January 26, 1880.
30. Ibid., January 14, 1880.
31. Ibid., April 29, 1880.
32. Ibid., June 3, 1880.
33. Ibid., November 17, 1880.
34. *Gall's Newsletter*, February 28, 1878.
35. Ibid., February 21, 1880.
36. *Daily Gleaner*, February 23, 1880.
37. Ibid., April 14, 1881.
38. Ibid., November 23, 1893, November 27, 1895.
39. Ibid., December 14 and 20, 1880.
40. *Colonial Standard*, September 28, October 6, and 16, 1882.
41. Ibid., February 11, 1889, September 18, 1888.
42. Ibid., April 13, 1890. See also issues of January 9, and April 14, 1890.
43. Ibid., May 10, 1890.
44. *Daily Gleaner*, January 28, 1891.
45. Ibid., January 28, 1893, and August 2, 1893. See also issues of July 15, 17, 25, 29, and August 1.
46. Ibid., July 10, 1895.
47. For a detailed description of the theatre see Sollas's Theatrical Souvenir, 1897, in files of the Jamaican National Library.
48. Ibid.
49. Fowler, "History of the Theatre," 53–59.

4. Plays and Players, 1682–1850

1. Hugh Clapperton, *Journal of a Second Expedition into the Interior of Africa* (London, 1829), 53–56; and Richard Lander, *Records of Clapperton's Last Expedition to Africa* (London, 1830), 1:115–21.
2. J. A. Adedeji, " 'Alarinjo': The Traditional Yoruba Travelling Theatre," in *Drama and Theatre in Nigeria: A Critical Source Book*, ed. Yemi Ogunbiyi (Bath, England: The Pitman Press for Nigeria Magazine, 1981), 221–47.
3. Hanson, *Laws of Jamaica*, 10.
4. Richardson Wright cites the case of one such actor, Anthony Ashton, who arrived in Jamaica in 1701 and became a law clerk and military cadet but apparently did no theatre during the year he spent on the island. See Wright, *Revels*, 8–11.

5. See Arthur Hornblow, *A History of the Theatre in America* (Philadelphia, Pa.: J.B. Lippincott Co., 1919), 1:50–51.

6. Fitzgerald, *Theatrical Anecdotes*, 124. Extract reprinted in *Gleaner*, September 4, 1893.

7. Frank Wesley Pitman, *The Development of the British West Indies, 1700–1763* (New Haven: Yale University Press, 1917), 376, app. 1.

8. [Charles Leslie], *New History of Jamaica*, 27.

9. Cundall, *Historic Jamaica*, 86, 159.

10. According to Wright (*Revels*, 39) members of Moody's troupe probably included David Douglass, Mr. and Mrs. Owen Morris, William Daniell and his wife Mary, Miss Hamilton, the leading lady, Mr. and Mrs. Smith, and Mrs. Kenshaw. Of their productions, the only bill that is advertised in surviving newspapers comes from the *Jamaica Courant* of June 22–29, 1754 (printed by William Daniell), which announces a performance on July 1, for the benefit of Master Marsh, of *The Orphan* and *Tom Thumb the Great*.

11. There is considerable speculation over Moody's travels at this time. Wright (*Revels*, 27) says that Moody went to England a second time to recruit players and that he finally left Jamaica in 1759. Wright's evidence for this date is Tate Williamson's *Memoirs*, which have been shown to be inaccurate (see *Dictionary of National Biography* [New York, 1894], 37:331). Besides, Moody has been placed in England with a touring company at Yarmouth, Norwich, and Bury in 1754–55, and at Norwich and Bury in 1757–58 (see Sybil Rosenfeld, *Strolling Players & Drama in the Provinces, 1660–1765* [Cambridge University Press, 1939], 85–92). Odell, citing Bernard, says Moody returned to England in 1749, was engaged by Garrick and remained in London, and that a group of players he had already recruited, including David Douglass, went to Jamaica on their own, arriving in 1751. (See George C. D. Odell, *Annals of the New York Stage* [New York, 1927], 1:68–69.) But, according to *DNB*, Garrick first employed Moody in 1759, that is, after Moody had played on the English provincial circuit. Even so, there is an unaccountable gap of four to five years between Moody's 1749 departure from Jamaica and his 1754 appearance at Yarmouth. Tate Williamson's anecdote of Moody's arrival in England escorting the suspiciously full-waisted Mrs. Osborne, as recounted by Wright (*Revels*, 341–42), is too vivid an image to be overlooked, however. We are reminded that the widow Osborne was a member of Murray & Kean's troupe in New York in 1750 and also of Robert Upton's company in New York the following year (see Charles P. Daly, *First Theatre in America* [New York, 1896], 9–10; and Thomas Clark Pollock, *The Philadelphia Theatre in the Eighteenth Century* [Philadelphia: University of Pennsylvania Press, 1933], 7). It is tempting to conjecture that Moody left Jamaica for America as others before him had done and spent a few years there, eventually linking up with Mrs. Osborne for their joint return to England. Hornblow even entertains the possibility that the Murray & Kean Company, whose origins are unknown, might have been part of the company recruited by Moody in England for Jamaica (see Hornblow, *Theatre in America*, 1:5). If so, Moody would have known Widow Osborne from an earlier date. But then why has his name not surfaced in records of American mainland theatricals?

12. William Dunlap, *A History of the American Theatre* (New York: J. & J. Harper, 1832), 21–22.
13. *Jamaica Magazine and Monthly Chronicler*, July 1781, 16–17.
14. See Wylie Sypher, *Guinea's Captive Kings* (New York: Octagon Books, 1969), 237.
15. George Colman the Younger, *Dramatic Works* (Paris, 1823), 1:xi; cited in Sypher, *Guinea's Captive Kings*, 133.
16. *Jamaica Magazine*, February–June 1812, 290–93.
17. *Royal Gazette*, Jamaica, July 24, 1813.
18. Lewis, *Journal*, 363.
19. *St. Jago de la Vega Gazette*, June 10–17, 1815.
20. Ibid., August 5–12, 1815.
21. *Kingston Chronicle*, October 5, 1819, May 2 and 4, 1821.
22. Joseph N. Ireland, *Records of the New York Stage from 1750 to 1860* (New York, 1866), 1:415.
23. *Sheridan's Jamaica Monthly Magazine*, October 1833, 302.
24. *Autobiographical Sketch of Mrs. John Drew* (New York: Scribner's Sons, 1899), 33–41.
25. *Jamaica Despatch*, September 13 and October 1, 1839.
26. *Morning Journal*, October 13, 1840.
27. Ibid., January 8, February 4, 19, and March 8, 1841.
28. Ibid., June 29, 1841.
29. Ibid., March 12, October 5, and November 4, 1842.
30. See Robertson, "Kingston Theatre," 8–9.
31. *Morning Journal*, May 13, June 15, and July 1, 1847.
32. Ibid., September 2, 1847, January 26, 1848.
33. Ibid., February 5, 1848.
34. Ibid., April 17, 24, May 2, August 4, October 13, 1849, and July 30, 1850.
35. Ibid., August 20, 1847. In a belated response several years later, the *Daily Advertiser* of October 29, 1857, pointed to the economic benefits accruing from a flourishing theatre enterprise. It argued that each amateur production cost at least £40, which went to storekeepers and others. The audience was well attired bringing further benefit in the purchase of blond laces, gloves, headdresses, and similar adornments. Since these items were dutiable they produced revenue to the country's purse. Fiddlers who comprised the orchestra received small sums, and even the cake sellers and pindar vendors reaped some good, "to say nothing of Rae, the Tavern Keeper." For many years the Shakespeare tavern stood next door to the theatre.
36. Philip Curtin estimates the loss to be between twenty-five thousand and thirty thousand of the working class. See *Two Jamaicas: The Role of Ideas in a Tropical Colony, 1830–1865* (New York: Atheneum, 1970), 160.

5. *Travail and Triumph, 1850–1900*

1. *Morning Journal*, July 13–14, 1882. The Kingston Philharmonic Society was first formed early in 1850 "to regale subscribers once a month with a concert of vocal and instrumental music." Its president was Dr. James MacFayden. In November of that year it lost both its president and conductor, Señor Jose Meana, to the cholera epidemic. See *Morning Journal*, December 22, 1849, and November 30, 1850.

2. Ibid., December 2–3, 1853.
3. Ibid., September 14, 1850.
4. *Daily Gleaner*, February 10, 1900.
5. *Colonial Standard*, April 8 and 16, 1873.
6. *Daily Advertiser*, October 20, 1855, and November 12, 1855.
7. See Mary Elizabeth Smith, "The Lanergans in Performance," *Theatre Survey* (November 1984): 211–23.
8. *Jamaica Tribune*, April 23, 25, and 30, 1859.
9. Ibid., February 18 and 23, 1860.
10. *Morning Journal*, December 10, 1861. The company on this, their third visit, comprised fourteen players and two scenic artists.
11. Ibid., January 21, 1862.
12. See L. Alan Eyre, "Jack Mansong: Bloodshed or Brotherhood," *Jamaica Journal* 7, no. 4 (December 1973): 9–14.
13. *Obi; or, Three Fingered Jack*, New British Theatre, no. 469 (London: T.H. Lacy, n.d.), 22–23.
14. *Colonial Standard*, April 29, 1864.
15. Ibid., December 9, 1864.
16. Ibid., July 7, 1866.
17. Ibid., March 23, 1866.
18. Ibid., November 5, 1866.
19. Ibid., September 5, 1868.
20. Ibid., March 19, 1868.
21. Ibid., June 29, 1872.
22. *Morning Journal*, July 1, 1872.
23. *Colonial Standard*, December 5, 1872.
24. Ibid., January 24, 1868.
25. It was Holland who in 1875 tried to get the Kingston City Council to rent him the theatre at £6 a week for two months with the proviso that he could sublet the building to other companies at the regular fee of £3 a night.
26. *Colonial Standard*, March 25 and 28, 1873.
27. Ibid., April 14 and 21, 1873.
28. *Gall's Newsletter*, May 11 and 24, 1873, and July 25, 1874.
29. Ibid., September 10, 1874.
30. Ibid., October 25, 1874.
31. *Colonial Standard*, January 26, 1876. See also performances by the Nomads on December 22, 1875, and January 26, 1876. Holland apparently did not have a base in America or England but kept his company on tour constantly in the Caribbean, beginning in 1872 when he went to Georgetown (Demerara) from New York. In Georgetown one of his leading actors, Wallace Britton, who played Othello, died of a heart attack on May 14. In Barbados, on April 8, 1874, another company member, the low comedy actor John L. Barrett, also died. See *Royal Gazette*, Demerara, May 16, 1872, and *The Era*, London, May 17, 1874.
32. *Colonial Standard*, November 27, 1875.
33. *Falmouth Post*, May 26, 1876.
34. *New York World* article reprinted in *Gall's Newsletter*, February 28, 1878.
35. Ibid.
36. See Odell, *New York Stage* (1938), 10:549, and (1939), 11:179.

37. *Daily Gleaner,* December 20 and 30, 1880.
38. The plays were Gilbert's *Engaged, My Uncle's Will, Pygmalion and Galatea, Old Love Letters,* and *H.M.S. Pinafore;* Boucicault's *Arrah na Pogue, Led Astray, The Shaughraun, The Colleen Bawn,* and *Kerry Road;* Robertson's *Caste, Ours,* and *School;* and Daly's *Alixe, Divorce,* and *Pique.*
39. *Daily Gleaner,* February 22, 1881, and March 20, 1893.
40. *Colonial Standard,* October 25 and 30, 1882.
41. "Theatricals," *Colonial Standard,* April 17, 1889.
42. *Daily Gleaner,* May 20, 1891.
43. *Colonial Standard,* March 23, 1893.
44. *Jamaica Post,* February 6, 1897.
45. Ibid., February 20 and March 12, 1897.
46. *Colonial Standard,* October 8, 1887.
47. *Jamaica Despatch,* December 11 and 31, 1839, January 4 and 14, 1840.
48. *Colonial Standard,* November 19, 1877.
49. *Daily Gleaner,* December 23, 1899. Performances of the pantomime and other plays produced at the end of the century were in aid of British forces engaged in the Boer War.

6. Jamaican Professional Actors

1. Wright, *Revels,* 1, 51, and 54.
2. Ibid., 43–44.
3. See the report of this tragedy in the *Newport Mercury,* August 24–31, 1767. Quoted by Wright, *Revels,* 345–47.
4. George Colman the Elder, *Prose on Several Occasions* (London, 1787), 3:254.
5. *London Magazine,* July 1784, 75.
6. *Walker's Hibernian Magazine,* Dublin, January 1786, 40. Wright affirms that Miss Woollery played at least four other roles during her month-long stay in Dublin. I have been able to verify only the two mentioned.
7. Ibid.
8. For more details on Master Betty see Dr. John Doran, *Annals of the English Stage* (London, 1897), chap. 47; and Giles Playfair, *The Prodigy: A Study of the Strange Life of Master Betty* (London: Secker & Warburg, 1967).
9. *St. Jago de la Vega Gazette,* October 12–19, 1816.
10. Ibid.
11. Lewis, *Journal,* 164.
12. *New York Evening Post,* July 26, 1819.
13. *Kingston Chronicle,* June 1, 1829.
14. *Daily Advertiser,* May 11, 1857. The letter was signed "Bardolph and Peto."
15. *Jamaica Tribune,* August 23, 1860.
16. *Colonial Standard,* March 19, 1864.
17. Ibid., August 14, 1874.
18. Ibid., August 24, 1874.
19. Isidore Singer, ed., *The Jewish Encyclopedia* (New York: Funk and Wagnalls, 1907), 9:30.
20. Odell, *New York Stage* (1940), 12:409.

21. *New York Times*, November 10, 1880:5.
22. Odell, *New York Stage* (1945), 4:249.
23. *Colonial Standard*, September 5, 1877.
24. Ibid.
25. *Daily Gleaner*, May 1, 1873.
26. *The Era*, London, May 30, 1885.
27. Ibid., September 26, 1885.
28. *New York Times*, October 30, 1892.
29. *Moving Picture World*, November 4, 1916.
30. *Daily Advertiser*, January 15, 1857.
31. *Colonial Standard*, March 19 and April 2, 1864.
32. HMS *Captain* was a newly built experimental frigate of the Royal Navy, which had been commissioned in July 1870. The ship was poorly designed, for less than two months later she capsized at sea off Cape Finisterre (northwestern Spain) owing to "pressure of sail, assisted by a heave of the sea." All but 18 of its crew of 475 lost their lives. A court-martial determined that "the ship lacked a proper amount of stability." See editorial in *The Times*, London, October 11, 1870, and Frank C. Owen, *The Sea: Its History and Romance* (London: Halton & Smith, 1925–26), 4:39.
33. For a summary of his career, see an address by Alfred Cork entitled "Reminiscences of Morton Tavares" that was published serially in the *Jamaica Times* on January 9, March 13 and 20, 1915.
34. *New York Dramatic Mirror*, July 7, 1900.
35. *Daily Advertiser*, August 8, 1857.
36. Ibid., September 14, 1857.
37. Ibid., February 9, 1858.
38. Ibid., August 28, 1858.
39. Ibid., November 4, 1858.
40. *Jamaica Tribune*, February 18, 1860.
41. Cork, "Reminiscences," *Jamaica Times*, January 9, 1915.
42. *Times*, London, December 29, 1869.
43. *The Era*, London, May 19, 1872.
44. Cork reports: "At this time occurred a crushing domestic bereavement, greatly his own fault, which led Tavares to see 'with what measure ye mete, it shall be measured to you again.'" *Jamaica Times*, January 9, 1915.
45. *Natal Mercantile Advertiser*, March 14, 17, and 21, 1882.
46. *Natal Witness*, April 3, 1882.
47. *Jamaica Times*, January 9, 1915.
48. *Natal Mercantile Advertiser*, March 14, 1882.
49. *Jamaica Times*, March 20, 1915.
50. Ibid., January 9, 1915.
51. *Daily Gleaner*, February 5, 1897.
52. Ibid., March 18, 1897.
53. *Jamaica Post*, March 20, 1897.
54. *Daily Gleaner*, April 30 and May 4, 1897.
55. Ibid., March 18 and April 1, 1897.
56. *Jamaica Post*, March 27 and April 3, 1897.
57. *Daily Gleaner*, May 1, 1873.

7. *The First Playwrights*

1. Wright, *Revels*, 105–6.
2. H. W. Pedicord and F. L. Begman, *The Plays of David Garrick* (Carbondale: Southern Illinois University Press, 1980), 2:308–15.
3. Wright, *Revels*, 152.
4. Ibid., 155.
5. *Port-of-Spain Gazette*, April 1, 1955.
6. Wright, *Revels*, 168.
7. *Daily Advertiser*, July 1, 1790.
8. The plays were published in the *Jamaica Journal* as follows: *The Exile* on November 27, 1824; *A West India Scene* on December 4, 1824; and *Jamaica: A Comedy* on December 11 and 18, 1824, and January 8, 1825.
9. *Kingston Chronicle*, February 23, 1822.
10. *Morning Journal*, September 29, 1853.
11. Ibid.
12. Ibid., December 16–17, 1853.
13. Ibid. Each part was published in a different issue of the newspaper on October 14–15, October 20, and November 1–2, 1853.
14. Ibid., October 14–15, 1853.
15. Ibid., October 20, 1853.
16. Ibid., November 1–2, 1853.
17. Ibid.
18. *Selections from the Miscellaneous Posthumous Works of Philip Cohen Labatt in Prose and Verse* (Kingston, Jamaica: R.J. De Cordova, 1855).
19. *Daily Advertiser*, November 27, 1855.
20. *Jamaica Tribune*, April 29, May 2, July 9, 14, 30, and August 13, 1859.
21. Ibid., August 13, 1859.
22. *Morning Journal*, May 14, 1868.
23. Ibid., September 12, 1868.
24. Ibid.
25. *Colonial Standard*, December 31, 1870.
26. Ibid., March 21 and 28, 1872.
27. Ibid., April 5, 1872.
28. Ibid., September 2, 18, 29, and October 24, 1876.
29. *Gall's Newsletter*, December 25, 1879.
30. Ibid., October 7, 1882.
31. *Daily Gleaner*, April 21, 1892.
32. The author of the script of *In Stormy Days* is believed to be Sister Veronica Doorly.
33. *Daily Gleaner*, July 1, 1897, and *Jamaica Post*, July 1, 1897. A summary of reviews appeared in *Catholic Opinion*, August 1897.
34. *Jamaica Post*, July 1, 1897.
35. *Colonial Standard*, June 15, 1892.
36. *Jamaica Post*, February 26, 1898.
37. *Daily Gleaner*, July 1, 1897.

8. Readers, Reciters, Storytellers

1. Gerald Kahan, *George Alexander Stevens and "The Lecture on Heads"* (Athens: University of Georgia Press, 1984), 29.
2. *Kingston Chronicle*, July 22, 1818.
3. *Morning Journal*, December 22, 1849.
4. *Daily Advertiser*, May 6, 12, and 15, 1858.
5. *New York Daily Tribune*, October 25, 1858.
6. Ibid., January 29, February 10 and 19, 1859.
7. J. de Cordova, *The Prince's Visit* (New York, 1861), 5–6, 9, 46–47.
8. *New York Tribune*, July 25 and 29, 1861.
9. *Colonial Standard*, March 23, 1877.
10. *Daily Gleaner*, August 8, 1939.
11. *Morning Journal*, January 28, 1863.
12. *Jamaica Tribune*, March 3, 1865.
13. *Colonial Standard*, March 6, 1865.
14. Ibid., December 18, 1865.
15. Ibid., January 4, 1876.
16. Ibid., May 10, 1867.
17. Ibid., May 18, 1867.
18. *Gall's Newsletter*, May 11, 1873.
19. *Colonial Standard*, November 12, 1883.
20. *Gall's Newsletter*, October 16, 1880.
21. *Pall Mall Gazette*, London, May 29, 1885.
22. *Colonial Standard*, Supplement, October 6, 1886.
23. *New York Times*, November 4, 1886.
24. *Saturday Review*, London, June 18, 1887, 872.
25. Obituary notice in the *Gleaner*, January 30, 1877.
26. *Colonial Standard*, January 11 and April 26, 1869.
27. Ibid.
28. Ibid., May 26 and October 25, 1869, November 2, 1871.
29. *Daily Gleaner*, May 17, 1880.
30. W. C. Murray, *A Day with Joe Lennan, the Rosewell Duppy Doctor* . . . (Kingston, Jamaica: Vendryes & Co., 1891), 15.
31. Ibid., Preface.
32. *Jamaica Advocate*, August 13, 1898.
33. Ibid., February 12, 1898.
34. Rev. John Radcliffe, *Lectures on Negro Proverbs* (Kingston, Jamaica: M. De Cordova, McDougall & Co., 1869), vii.
35. Ibid., xi.
36. *Colonial Standard*, November 19, 1866.
37. *Morning Journal*, November 2, 1868.
38. For a full listing of these sources see Izett Anderson and Frank Cundall, *Jamaica Negro Proverbs and Sayings*, 2d ed. (Institute of Jamaica, 1927); and *Daily Gleaner*, February 4, 1899.
39. W. G. Ogilvie, "Many Faces, Different Streams" (unpublished MS about author's family history), 20.
40. *Daily Gleaner*, July 19, 1988. A video drama on "The Adventures of Annancy" by the Jamaican Phyllis Galloway was nominated for a 1988 Emmy Award on American television. See *Sunday Gleaner*, July 3, 1988.

9. Slave Performances

1. H. T. De La Beche, *Notes on the Present Condition of the Negroes in Jamaica* (London, 1825), 2.
2. *Equiano's Travels: His Autobiography*, abr. and ed. by Paul Edwards (London: Heineman Educational Books Ltd., 1967), 3–4.
3. Bakary Traore, *The Black African Theatre and Its Social Functions*, trans. Dapo Adelugba (Nigeria: Ibadan University Press, 1972), 25, 23.
4. Adedeji, "'Alarinjo,'" 221–47.
5. Robert Dirks, *The Black Saturnalia: Conflict and Its Ritual Expression on British West Indian Slave Plantations* (Gainesville: University of Florida Press, 1987), 12.
6. Hans Sloane, *A Voyage to the Islands Madera, Barbados, Nieves, S. Christophers, and Jamaica . . .* (London, 1707–1725), 1:xlviii–xlix.
7. [Charles Leslie], *New History of Jamaica*, 310.
8. Long, *History of Jamaica*, 2:423–24.
9. See *A Short Journey in the West Indies* (London, 1790), 90; and Bryan Edwards, *The History, Civil and Commercial, of the British Colonies in the West Indies* (London, 1793), 2:84.
10. Lewis, *Journal*, 74.
11. John Stewart, *A View of the Past and Present State of the Island of Jamaica . . .* (Edinburgh, 1823), 272.
12. Michael Scott, *Tom Cringle's Log*, 1829 (London, 1895), 262–63.
13. Astley Clerk, *The Music and Musical Instruments of Jamaica* (Kingston, Jamaica [1913]), 20.
14. Long, *History of Jamaica*, 2:423.
15. Edwards, *British Colonies*, 2:85.
16. Lewis, *Journal*, 74–75.
17. Laz. E. N. Ekwueme, "African Sources in New World Black Music," *Black Images* 1, nos. 3 & 4 (Autumn and Winter, 1972): 7.
18. William Beckford, *A Descriptive Account of the Island of Jamaica* (London, 1790), 1:392.
19. Long, *History of Jamaica*, 2:424.
20. *A Short Journey*, 88–89.
21. Lewis, *Journal*, 74.
22. Alexander Barclay, *A Practical View of the Present State of Slavery in the West Indies . . .* (London, 1826), 10.
23. George Marly, *Marly; or, The Life of a Planter in Jamaica*, 2d ed. (Glasgow, 1828), 46–48.
24. Francis Egan, *West Indian Pot Pourri* (London, c.1823).
25. Postscript to *Royal Gazette*, Jamaica, December 12–19, 1835.
26. *Jamaica Watchman*, January 2, 1833.
27. *A Short Journey*, 69.
28. Louise Bennett, "Me and Annancy," in *Jamaica Song and Story*, ed. Walter Jekyll, 1907 (New York: Dover Publications, Inc., 1966), ix.
29. *Colonial Standard*, February 15, 1873.
30. Lewis, *Journal*, 211–13. The six Anansi stories commence on pp. 206, 207, 213, 246, 254, and 258.
31. Leonard E. Barrett, *The Sun and the Drum: African Roots in Jamaica Folk Tradition* (London: Heineman, 1976), 31.

32. Ibid.
33. Lewis, *Journal*, 295.
34. Quoted in Edwards, *British Colonies*, 2:90.
35. Stewart, *Island of Jamaica*, 277.
36. Edwards, *British Colonies*, 2:85.
37. Stewart, *Island of Jamaica*, 274–75.
38. The various names given to the masquerade include: John Canoe, John Connu, Johnny Canoeing, John Kuner, Joncanoe, Jancoonoo, Jonkanoo, and Jonkonnu. Most modern writers use the last one.
39. Sloane, *Voyage*, 1:xlviii–xlix.
40. Long, *History of Jamaica*, 2:424–25.
41. Scott, *Tom Cringle's Log*, 261–62.
42. Ibid., 262–63.
43. Ibid., 264–65.
44. Lewis, *Journal*, 56, 53.
45. Cynric R. Williams, *A Tour Through the Island of Jamaica from the Western to the Eastern End in the Year 1823* (London, 1826), 25–26.
46. Marly, *Marly*, i, 293–94.
47. Stewart, *Island of Jamaica*, 270.
48. Williams, *Tour*, 29.
49. Frank Cundall, ed., *Lady Nugent's Journal* (London, 1939), 66.
50. Lewis, *Journal*, 56–57.
51. Barclay, *Slavery*, 24.
52. De La Beche, *Negroes*, 42.
53. Lewis, *Journal*, 54.
54. Beckford, *Descriptive Account*, 1:389–90.
55. They are Lewis, *Journal*, 54–58; Williams, *Tour*, 62–64; Stewart, *Island of Jamaica*, 273–74; De La Beche, *Negroes*, 41; Barclay, *Slavery*, 11–12; Marly, *Marly*, 289–93; and Scott, *Tom Cringle's Log*, 265–66.
56. Barclay, *Slavery*, 11–12.
57. Marly, *Marly*, 289–90, 292–93.
58. I. M. Belisario, *Sketches of Character, in Illustration of the Habits, Occupation and Costume of the Negro Population in the Island of Jamaica* (Kingston, Jamaica, 1837).
59. See Curtin, *Two Jamaicas*, 82–89.

10. *Performance Modes after Slavery*

1. Robert Young, *An Essay on Dancing Addressed in the Form of a Letter to the Wesleyan Societies in the Island of Jamaica*, Wesleyan Mission House, Stoney Hill, Jamaica, July 4, 1825.
2. *Falmouth Post*, January 11, 1837. See also James Phillipo, *Jamaica: Its Past and Present State* (London, 1843), chap. 14.
3. *Jamaica Despatch*, January 6, 1840.
4. *Morning Journal*, December 30, 1840.
5. Colonial Office 137, item 261 (January 1842).
6. Ibid., item 273 (January 1843), encl. 6, 1.
7. *Falmouth Post*, March 16, 1847.
8. *Daily Advertiser*, January 4, 1854.
9. *Morning Journal*, January 5 and 16, 1854; *Falmouth Post*, January 10, 1854.
10. *Daily Advertiser*, December 30, 1858.

11. *Jamaica Tribune*, January 18, 1860.
12. Ibid.
13. *Morning Journal*, January 3, 1872.
14. *Jamaica Post*, December 21, 1897.
15. *Falmouth Post*, August 6, 1847.
16. B. W. Higman, "Slavery Remembered: The Celebration of Emancipation in Jamaica," *Journal of Caribbean History* 12 (1979): 55–74, 62.
17. Ibid., 71; *Falmouth Post*, March 3, 1857.
18. *Gall's Newsletter*, August 10, 1874.
19. Ibid.
20. *San Francisco Elevator*, August 1, 1874.
21. *Daily Advertiser*, July 5, 1854.
22. See Elizabeth Petras, "Black Labor and White Capital: The Formation of Jamaica as a Global Labor Reserve, 1830–1930" (Ph.D. diss., State University of New York at Binghamton, 1981), 143; and Velma Newton, *The Silver Men: West Indian Labour Migration to Panama, 1850–1914* (Kingston, Jamaica: University of the West Indies, 1984), 50–51.
23. *San Francisco Elevator*, August 1, 1874.
24. Olive Lewin, "Emancipation Songs and Festivities," *Jamaica Journal* 17, no. 3 (August–October 1984): 18–23.
25. See *Colonial Standard*, January 8, 1854; *Morning Journal*, August 22, 1864; *Daily Gleaner*, February 5 and April 14, 1880.
26. *Daily Advertiser*, April 16, 1855.
27. *Daily Gleaner*, March 8, 1892.
28. Ibid.
29. See Martha Beckwith, *Black Roadways: A Study of Jamaican Folk Life*, 1929 (New York: Negro Universities Press, 1969), 204; Claude McKay, *Banana Bottom*, 1933 (New York: Harcourt Brace Jovanovich, 1961), 74–80; and tea meeting videotapes aired by Jamaica Broadcasting Company in 1982 and 1986.
30. *Jamaica Standard*, October 31, 1842.
31. Ibid., November 8, 1842.
32. Reprinted in the *Falmouth Post*, July 26, 1859.
33. Edward Seaga, "Revival Cults in Jamaica: Notes Towards a Sociology of Religion," *Jamaica Journal* 3, no. 2 (June 1969): 3–15.
34. *Gall's Daily Newsletter*, June 9, 1883.
35. See *Daily Gleaner*, September 19 and 28, 1893; *Colonial Standard*, January 23 and May 2, 1895; and Beckwith, *Black Roadways*, 167ff.
36. J. H. Reid, "The People of Jamaica," chap. 4 of *Jamaica's Jubilee, or What We Are and What We Hope To Be*, by Five of Themselves (London, 1888), 102.
37. See Beckwith, *Black Roadways*; Joseph Graessle Moore, "Religion of Jamaica Negroes: A Study of Afro-Jamaican Acculturation" (Ph.D. diss., Northwestern University, 1953); George Eaton Simpson, *Religious Cults of the Caribbean: Trinidad, Jamaica and Haiti* (Rio Piedras: University of Puerto Rico, 1980); Barrett, *The Sun and the Drum*.
38. Joseph Graessle Moore, "Music and Dance as Expressions of Religious Worship in Jamaica," in *African Religious Groups and Beliefs*, ed. Simon Ottenberg (California: Folklore Institute, 1982), 266–67.
39. Rex Nettleford, "Pocomania in Dance-Theatre," *Jamaica Journal* 3, no. 2 (June 1969): 21–34.

40. *Morning Journal*, December 28, 1868.
41. Robert C. Toll, *Blacking Up: The Minstrel Show in Nineteenth Century America* (New York: Oxford University Press, 1974), 30, 54.
42. *Colonial Standard*, July 4, 1865.
43. Ibid., January 10, February 8, 9, 13, and 15, 1872.
44. See chap. 6, note 28, for details of this tragedy.
45. *Colonial Standard*, August 15, 1888.
46. *Daily Gleaner*, February 16, 1897.

11. Epilogue: A Caribbean Perspective

1. Growling Tiger [Neville Marcano], "Workers' Appeal" calypso. Recorded in New York on Decca No.17288-A (1936).
2. Rex Nettleford, *Caribbean Cultural Identity: The Case of Jamaica* (Los Angeles: University of California, 1978), 72.
3. Astley Clerk, "The Music and Musical Instruments of Jamaica," *Jamaica Journal* 9, no. 243 (1975): 59.
4. Edward Kamau Brathwaite, "The African Presence in Caribbean Literature," *Bim* 17, no. 65 (June 1979): 34.
5. Personal communication, November 7, 1978.
6. See editorial comment in *Port-of-Spain Gazette*, March 2, 1838, February 25, 1857, February 21, 1863, February 21, 1874, March 1, 1884, and Andrew Pearse, "Carnival in Nineteenth Century Trinidad," *Caribbean Quarterly* 4, nos. 3 & 4 (1956): 185.
7. Errol Hill, *The Ping Pong*, in *Caribbean Plays* (Jamaica: University College of the West Indies, 1958), 1:53–75.
8. The titles of Garvey's pageants were: "The Coronation of an African King," "Roaming Jamaicans," and "Slavery—From Hut to Mansion." They were presented in Kingston on August 18, 19, and 20, 1930. No scripts have yet been found for these pageants.
9. Typescript in author's files. The play was subsequently rewritten under the title "The Black Jacobins" and staged at the Arts Theatre, University of Ibadan, Nigeria, on December 14–16, 1967. The director was Dexter Lyndersay.
10. Archie Lindo, "The White Witch of Rosehall," Typescript in author's files.
11. Derek Walcott, *The Joker of Seville & O Babylon!: Two Plays* (New York: Farrar, Straus, and Giroux, 1978), 155–56.
12. Derek Walcott, *Dream on Monkey Mountain and Other Plays* (New York: Farrar, Straus, and Giroux, 1970).
13. Sylvia Wynter, "Maskarade." Typescript in author's files.
14. See Errol Hill, *The Trinidad Carnival* (Austin: University of Texas Press, 1972). In chap. 11, "Toward a National Theatre," I draw conclusions similar to those discussed here.
15. Rawle Gibbons, "Traditional Enactments of Trinidad: Towards a Third Theatre" (M. Phil. thesis, University of the West Indies, Trinidad, 1979).
16. Euton Jarvis and Ronald Amoroso, *The Master of Carnival*, in *Three Caribbean Plays*, ed. Errol Hill (London: Longman Caribbean, 1979), 65–100.
17. Marina Maxwell, "Play Mas'." Typescript in author's files.

18. Mustapha Matura, "Play Mas'." Typescript in author's files.
19. Lennox Brown, "Devil Mas'." Typescript in author's files.
20. Dennis Scott, *An Echo in the Bone,* in *Plays for Today,* ed. Errol Hill (London: Longman, 1985), 73–137.
21. Cited in Nettleford, *Caribbean Cultural Identity,* 67–68.

Selected Bibliography

Adedeji, J. A. "'Alarinjo': The Traditional Yoruba Travelling Theatre." In *Drama and Theatre in Nigeria: A Critical Source Book*, ed. Yemi Ogunbiyi. Bath, England: The Pitman Press for Nigeria Magazine, 1981.

Adelugba, Dapo. See Traore, Bakary.

Amoroso, Ronald. See Jarvis, Euton.

Anderson, Izett, and Frank Cundall. *Jamaica Negro Proverbs and Sayings.* 2d ed. Institute of Jamaica, 1927.

Andrade, Jacob A. P. M. *A Record of the Jews in Jamaica.* Kingston, Jamaica, 1941.

Autobiographical Sketch of Mrs. John Drew. New York: Scribner's Sons, 1899.

Barclay, Alexander. *A Practical View of the Present State of Slavery in the West Indies. . . .* London, 1826.

Barrett, Leonard E. *The Sun and the Drum: African Roots in Jamaica Folk Tradition.* London: Heineman, 1976.

Baxter, Ivy. *The Arts of an Island.* Metuchen, N.J.: Scarecrow Press, 1970.

Bayley, F. W. N. *Four Years' Residence in the West Indies.* London, 1830.

Beckford, William. *A Descriptive Account of the Island of Jamaica.* 2 vols. London, 1790.

Beckwith, Martha. *Black Roadways: A Study of Jamaican Folk Life.* 1929. New York: Negro Universities Press, 1969.

Begman, F. L. See Pedicord, H. W.

Belisario, I. M. *Sketches of Character, in Illustration of the Habits, Occupation and Costume of the Negro Population in the Island of Jamaica.* Kingston, Jamaica, 1837.

Bennett, Louise. "Me and Annancy." In *Jamaica Song and Story,* ed. Walter Jekyll. New York: Dover Publications, Inc., 1966.

Bigelow, John. *Jamaica in 1850; or, The Effects of Sixteen Years of Freedom on a Slave Colony.* New York: George Putnam, 1851.

Brathwaite, Edward Kamau. "The African Presence in Caribbean Literature." *Bim* 17, no. 65 (June 1979): 33–44.

———. *The Development of Creole Society in Jamaica, 1770–1820.* Oxford: Clarendon Press, 1971.

———. *Folk Culture of the Slaves in Jamaica.* Rev. ed. London: New Beacon Books, 1981.

Bridgens, Richard. *West India Scenery, with Illustrations of Negro Character. . . .* London: Robert Jennings and Co., [c.1836].

Clapperton, Hugh. *Journal of a Second Expedition into the Interior of Africa.* London, 1829.

Clerk, Astley. *The Music and Musical Instruments of Jamaica.* Kingston, Jamaica, [1913].

Colman the Elder, George. *Prose on Several Occasions.* London, 1787.

Colman the Younger, George. *Dramatic Works.* Paris, 1823.

Cork, Alfred. "Reminiscences of Morton Tavares." *Jamaica Times,* January 9, March 13 and 20, 1915.

Cundall, Frank. *Historic Jamaica.* London, 1915.

————. See Anderson, Izett.

————, ed. *Lady Nugent's Journal.* London, 1939.

Curtin, Philip. *Two Jamaicas: The Role of Ideas in a Tropical Colony, 1830–1865.* New York: Atheneum, 1970.

Daly, Charles P. *First Theatre in America.* New York, 1896.

De Cordova, J. *The Prince's Visit.* New York, 1861.

De La Beche, H. T. *Notes on the Present Condition of the Negroes in Jamaica.* London, 1825.

Dictionary of National Biography. Vol. 7. New York, 1894.

Dirks, Robert. *The Black Saturnalia: Conflict and Its Ritual Expression on British West Indian Slave Plantations.* Gainesville: University of Florida Press, 1987.

Doran, Dr. John. *Annals of the English Stage.* London, 1897.

Dunlap, William. *A History of the American Theatre.* New York: J. & J. Harper, 1832.

Edwards, Bryan. *The History, Civil and Commercial, of the British Colonies in the West Indies.* 2 vols. London, 1793.

Edwards, Paul. See *Equiano's Travels.*

Egan, Francis. *West Indian Pot Pourri.* London, c.1823.

Ekwueme, Laz. E. N. "African Sources in New World Black Music." *Black Images* 1, nos. 3 & 4 (Autumn & Winter 1972): 3–12.

Equiano's Travels: His Autobiography. Abridged and edited by Paul Edwards. London: Heineman Educational Books, Ltd., 1967.

Eyre, L. Alan. "Jack Mansong: Bloodshed or Brotherhood." *Jamaica Journal* 7, no. 4 (December 1973): 9–14.

Fitzgerald, Percy. *The Book of Theatrical Anecdotes.* London, [1874].

Fowler, Henry. "A History of the Theatre in Jamaica." *Jamaica Journal* 2, no. 1 (March 1968): 53–59.

Gibbons, Rawle. "Traditional Enactments of Trinidad: Towards a Third Theatre." M. Phil. thesis, University of the West Indies, Trinidad, 1979.

Hakewill, James. *A Picturesque Tour of the Island of Jamaica.* London, 1825.

Hall, Douglas. *Free Jamaica 1838–1865: An Economic History.* New Haven: Yale University Press, 1959.

Hanson, Francis. Preface. *The Laws of Jamaica Passed by the Assembly and Confirmed by His Majesty in Council, 23 February, 1683.* London, 1683.

Henman, Gad J. "White Over Brown Over Black: The Free Coloured in Jamaican Society During Slavery and After Emancipation." *Journal of Caribbean History* 14 (1981): 46–68.

Higman, B. W. "Slavery Remembered: The Celebration of Emancipation in Jamaica." *Journal of Caribbean History* 12 (1979): 55–74.

————, ed. *The Jamaican Censuses of 1844 and 1861.* Mona, Jamaica: University of the West Indies, 1980.

Hill, Errol. *The Ping Pong.* In *Caribbean Plays.* Vol. 1. Jamaica: University College of the West Indies, 1958.

————. *The Trinidad Carnival: Mandate for a National Theatre.* Austin: University of Texas Press, 1972.

————, ed. *Caribbean Plays.* Vol. 1. Jamaica: University College of the West Indies, 1958.

————, ed. *Plays for Today.* London: Longman, 1985.

————, ed. *Three Caribbean Plays.* London: Longman Caribbean, 1979.

Hornblow, Arthur. *A History of the Theatre in America.* Philadelphia, Pa.: J.B. Lippincott Co., 1919.

Ireland, Joseph N. *Records of the New York Stage from 1750 to 1860.* New York, 1866.

Jarvis, Euton, and Ronald Amoroso. *The Master of Carnival.* In *Three Caribbean Plays,* ed. Errol Hill. London: Longman Caribbean, 1979.

Jekyll, Walter, ed. *Jamaica Song and Story.* 1907. New York: Dover Publications Inc., 1966.

Kahan, Gerald. *George Alexander Stevens and "The Lecture on Heads."* Athens: University of Georgia Press, 1984.

Kendall, John S. *The Golden Age of New Orleans Theater.* Baton Rouge: Louisiana State University Press, 1953.

Korn, Bertram W. "The Haham De Cordova of Jamaica." *American Jewish Archives* 18, no. 2 (November 1966): 141–54.

Labatt, Philip Cohen. See *Selections from the Miscellaneous Posthumous Works.*

Lander, Richard. *Records of Clapperton's Last Expedition to Africa.* London, 1830.

[Leslie, Charles]. *A New History of Jamaica, From the Earliest Accounts to the Taking of Porto Bello by Vice Admiral Vernon.* London, 1740.

Lewin, Olive. "Emancipation Songs and Festivities." *Jamaica Journal* 17, no. 3 (August–October 1984): 18–23.

Lewis, Matthew Gregory. *Journal of a West Indian Proprietor.* 1834. London: G. Routledge & Sons, 1929.

Long, Edward. *History of Jamaica.* 3 vols. London, 1774.

McKay, Claude. *Banana Bottom.* 1933. New York: Harcourt Brace Jovanovich, 1961.

Marly, George. *Marly; or, The Life of a Planter in Jamaica.* 2d ed. Glasgow, 1828.

Marsden, Peter. *An Account of the Island of Jamaica.* Newcastle, 1788.

Memoirs of William Hickey, 1775–1782. 4 vols. London, 1918.

Moore, Joseph Graessle. "Music and Dance as Expressions of Religious Worship in Jamaica." In *African Religious Groups and Beliefs,* ed. Simon Ottenberg. California: Folklore Institute, 1982.

————. "Religion of Jamaica Negroes: A Study of Afro-Jamaican Acculturation." Ph.D. diss., Northwestern University, 1953.

Moreton, J. B. *Manners and Customs in the West India Islands.* London, 1790.

Murray, W. C. *A Day with Joe Lennan, the Rosewell Duppy Doctor. . . .* Kingston, Jamaica: Vendryes & Co., 1891.

Nettleford, Rex. *Caribbean Cultural Identity: The Case of Jamaica.* Los Angeles: Center for Afro-American Studies, University of California, 1978.

———. "Pocomania in Dance-Theatre." *Jamaica Journal* 3, no. 2 (June 1969): 21–34.

Newton, Velma. *The Silver Men: West Indian Labour Migration to Panama, 1850–1914.* Kingston, Jamaica: University of the West Indies, 1984.

Obi; or Three Fingered Jack. New British Theatre, no. 469. London: T.H. Lacy, n.d.

Odell, George C. *Annals of the New York Stage.* 15 vols. New York, 1927–1939.

Ogunbiyi, Yemi. *Drama and Theatre in Nigeria: A Critical Source Book.* Bath, England: The Pitman Press for Nigeria Magazine, 1981.

Oldmixon, John. *The British Empire in America.* 2d ed. London, 1741.

Ottenberg, Simon, ed. *African Religious Groups and Beliefs.* California: Folklore Institute, 1982.

Owen, Frank C. *The Sea: Its History and Romance.* Vol. 4. London: Halton & Smith, 1925–26.

Pearse, Andrew. "Carnival in Nineteenth Century Trinidad." *Caribbean Quarterly* 4, nos. 3 & 4 (1956): 175–93.

Pedicord, H. W., and F. L. Begman. *The Plays of David Garrick.* Vol. 2. Carbondale: Southern Illinois University Press, 1980.

Petras, Elizabeth. "Black Labor and White Capital: The Formation of Jamaica as a Global Labor Reserve, 1830–1930." Ph.D. diss., State University of New York at Binghamton, 1981.

Phillipo, James. *Jamaica: Its Past and Present State.* London, 1843.

Pitman, Frank Wesley. *The Development of the British West Indies, 1700–1763.* New Haven: Conn.: Yale University Press, 1917.

Playfair, Giles. *The Prodigy: A Study of the Strange Life of Master Betty.* London: Secker & Warburg, 1967.

Pollock, Thomas Clark. *The Philadelphia Theatre in the Eighteenth Century.* Philadelphia: University of Pennsylvania Press, 1933.

Radcliffe, Rev. John. *Lectures on Negro Proverbs.* Kingston, Jamaica: M. De Cordova, McDougall & Co., 1869.

Reid, J. H. "The People of Jamaica." In *Jamaica's Jubilee, or, What We Are and What We Hope To Be,* by Five of Themselves. London, 1888.

Roberts, George W. *The Population of Jamaica.* Cambridge: Cambridge University Press, 1957.

Robertson, Langston. "The Kingston Theatre—A Brief History." Memorandum submitted to the Deputy Keeper of the Records. Spanish Town, Jamaica, August 9, 1943.

Robinson, Carey. *The Fighting Maroons of Jamaica.* Jamaica: William Collins & Sangster (Jamaica) Ltd., 1969.

Rosenfeld, Sybil. *Strolling Players and Drama in the Provinces, 1660–1765.* Cambridge: Cambridge University Press, 1939.

Scott, Dennis. *An Echo in the Bone.* In *Plays for Today,* ed. Errol Hill. London: Longman, 1985.

[Scott, Michael]. *The Cruise of the Midge.* 2 vols. Edinburgh, 1836.

Scott, Michael. *Tom Cringle's Log.* 1829. London, 1895.

Seaga, Edward. "Revival Cults in Jamaica: Notes Towards a Sociology of Religion." *Jamaica Journal* 3, no. 2 (June 1969): 3–15.

Selections from the Miscellaneous Posthumous Works of Philip Cohen Labatt in Prose and Verse. Kingston, Jamaica: R.J. De Cordova, 1855.

A Short Journey in the West Indies. London, 1790.

Simpson, George Eaton. *Religious Cults of the Caribbean: Trinidad, Jamaica and Haiti.* Rio Piedras: University of Puerto Rico, 1980.

Singer, Isidore, ed. *The Jewish Encyclopedia.* 12 vols. New York: Funk and Wagnalls, 1907.

Sloane, Hans. *A Voyage to the Islands Madera, Barbados, Nieves, S. Christophers, and Jamaica. . . .* 2 vols. London, 1707–1725.

Smith, Mary Elizabeth. "The Lanergans in Performance." *Theatre Survey* (November 1984): 211–23.

[Stewart, John]. *An Account of Jamaica and Its Inhabitants by a Gentleman Long Resident in the West Indies.* London, 1808.

Stewart, John. *A View of the Past and Present State of the Island of Jamaica. . . .* Edinburgh, 1823.

Sypher, Wylie. *Guinea's Captive Kings.* New York: Octagon Books, 1969.

Toll, Robert C. *Blacking Up: The Minstrel Show in Nineteenth Century America.* New York: Oxford University Press, 1974.

Traore, Bakary. *The Black African Theatre and Its Social Functions.* Translated by Dapo Adelugba. Nigeria: Ibadan University Press, 1972.

Vaz, Horace D. "The Drama in Jamaica." *The West Indian Review,* n.s. 4, no. 2 (Summer 1947): 30–35, 47.

Walcott, Derek. *Dream on Monkey Mountain and Other Plays.* New York: Farrar, Straus and Giroux, 1970.

———. *The Joker of Seville & O Babylon!: Two Plays.* New York: Farrar, Straus and Giroux, 1978.

Williams, Cynric R. *A Tour Through the Island of Jamaica from the Western to the Eastern End in the Year 1823.* London, 1826.

Willis, Eola. *The Charleston Stage in the XVIII Century.* Columbia, S.C.: The State Company, 1924.

Wright, Richardson. *Revels in Jamaica, 1682–1838.* New York: Dodd, Mead & Co., 1937. Rev. ed. Jamaica: Bolivar Press, 1986.

Young, Robert. *An Essay on Dancing Addressed in the Form of a Letter to the Wesleyan Societies in the Island of Jamaica.* Wesleyan Mission House, Stoney Hill, Jamaica, July 4, 1825.

Index